JERUSALEM'S
TEMPLE MOUNT:
THE HOAX OF THE MILLENNIUM!

JERUSALEM'S
TEMPLE MOUNT:
THE HOAX OF THE MILLENNIUM!

Mike M Joseph

authorHOUSE®

AuthorHouse™
1663 Liberty Drive
Bloomington, IN 47403
www.authorhouse.com
Phone: 1-800-839-8640

First published by AuthorHouse   10/14/2011

ISBN: 978-1-4670-2840-0 (sc)
ISBN: 978-1-4670-2839-4 (hc)
ISBN: 978-1-4670-2838-7 (ebk)

Library of Congress Control Number: 2011916225

Printed in the United States of America

Any people depicted in stock imagery provided by Thinkstock are models, and such images are being used for illustrative purposes only.
Certain stock imagery © Thinkstock.

This book is printed on acid-free paper.

ORDER OF CHAPTERS

Books and lecture series by this author:

Middle East: Blueprint for the Final Solution.
Subtitle: *The Coming Fall and Rise of Western Democracy.* (710 Pages)
Http://www.authorhouse.com/bookstore/ItemDetail.aspx?bookid=16130
Hotline orders: 1-888-280-7715

Conspiracy Against Divine Sexuality.
Subtitle: *It all Started in Eden.*
Published under the pen name Moran M Judson
Http://www.authorhouse.com/bookstore/ItemDetail.aspx?bookid=19260
Hotline orders: 1-888-280-7715

Sorry . . . ! There is no afterlife!
Subtitle: *None Goes to Heaven or Hell!*
Http://www.authorhouse.com/bookstore/ItemDetail.aspx?bookid=49812
Hotline orders: 1-888-280-7715

Jerusalem's Temple Mount: The Hoax of the Millennium!
Http://www.authorhouse.com/bookstore/ItemDetail.aspx?bookid=344682
Hotline orders: 1-888-280-7715

Teaching The Law Series (OT & NT)
Website: www.teachingthelaw.org
Almost 800 lessons—free to download.

Albert Einstein once said: *"If at first the idea is not absurd, then there is no hope for it."*

DEDICATION

The author dedicates this work to all the children of Abraham: Jews, Christians, and Muslims. All were led to believe, mainly in the past Millennium, that the actual location of the "Temple Mount," where Solomon's Temple once stood, is situated where the two mosques—the Golden Dome and el-Aqsa—are presently located. All three religions consider this hotly contested area to be most sacred to them. Indeed, many of them are even willing to sacrifice their very lives for the sake of what they consider to be the most "holy ground" to their respective faiths. The naked reality or tragedy and the historic irony is that this erroneous notion—on the part of the rival religions—of the supposed "holiness" of the "Temple Mount" is baseless and without any shred of credible backing—as we shall amply prove in the following pages. In reality, this 'belief,' regarding the 'holiness' of the "Temple Mount" or "Harem esh-Sheriff" to Islam, is contrary to the plain teachings of the very Holy Books they claim to follow—the Bible or the Qur'an—as well as those recorded accounts of their respective historians about the original locations of both the ancient Temples and "Temple Mount." Nevertheless, members of the three religions have shed much needless rivers of blood, and still do and yet will, in their feverish attempts to maintain or wrestle control over the area they have erroneously come to believe is the original "Temple Mount." After the conquest of the "Temple Mount" by Caliph Omar, in the early part of the sixth century, its name became known as "Haram-esh-Sheriff" or the "Noble Enclosure" and the city was named "el-Quds" or "Holy City." Is this deeply entrenched belief in the hearts of the sincerely devout members of the three religions a mere fable concocted in the minds of those not valiant for the truth—as clearly recorded in the pages of their holy Books and their respective accounts of history? Is the mindless shedding of blood because of twisted, though not maliciously intentional, accounts of history about the supposed "Holy Site" to haunt all members of a common father—Abraham—forever? This power-keg of emotional explosives, which harbors destructive results for all concerned, will never be resolved until all parties are willing to acknowledge that the absolute and ultimate sovereignty over this contested area belongs solely to "The Great King." May all the children of father Abraham learn their lessons before it is too late for them—and may they all believe the following words in the pages of this work today—and if not today, then in the near future when all things shall come to pass.

In memory of my mother Hannah—shot and later bled to death in an Arab hospital at age 29; my older brother Shalom—shot and killed at the age of 8 by Arab policemen; my older brother Moshe—poisoned to death by a Muslim pharmacist before reaching his first birthday; my younger brother Hertzel—also poisoned to death by the same Muslim pharmacist before reaching his first birthday. All lost their lives by the hands of other children of Abraham in the city of Aden . . . because they happened to be of the Jewish faith. These events took place before this author had reached the tender age of 4 years old. May they all inherit the coming peace to all the children of Abraham, and sit together reconciled with their former destroyers and "Children of the Sword."

FOREWORD

Recently, on April 19, 2010, at even, a day before flying back to the States, seated in my sister's living room in Jerusalem—across the street from an Arab village and a little distance from the Western Wall—we were watching the somber yearly ceremony of the Memorial Day for the fallen dead soldiers and citizens of Israel's wars and those who died in the Holocaust. The distinguished speakers: The President, Prime-Minister, the Chief of Staff and Israel's Chief Rabbis were delivering emotionally-packed fiery and moving speeches. The Chief Israeli Army Cantor deeply moved the hearts of many with his chanted and soulful and mournful eulogy for the dead. Many were in tears. Staring intently at the background, behind the honorable leaders of Israel, the Western Wall or Wall of Tears stirred my disturbed thoughts which swept me back, through my mind's eye, to that very location—two thousand years ago—to the Jewish citizens of the second Temple era of Jerusalem. I felt that I knew what the down-trodden inhabitants of the beloved city would have felt and thought had they been present at that somber place and moment with the people of Israel and Jerusalem at that Memorial Day of April, 19, 2010. I knew they would have been in total shock and disbelief—not at what was taking place, but at the location where it was happening. Later on we shall elaborate.

Earlier that very day, few hours before boarding a plane that would take me back home to California I took the bus to the Western Wall. Once reaching that hub that for centuries has evoked and stirred passionate Jewish yearnings and feelings, I deliberately turned my back to it, crossed over to the other side of the street, and walked down a bit towards the ancient ruins of the City of David. I entered the busy compound, which was crowded with hundreds of school children, citizens, tourists and soldiers, and felt as if 'I have arrived.' Why? We'll find that out later.

I just 'happened' to read from a letter, written more than a century ago, which was E-Mailed to me, as well as to many others, by a Palestinian scientist from the West Bank. The writer of this letter, namely, Sigmund Freud—the father of psychoanalysis—was responding to a Zionist friend

xiii

who was attempting to recruit him for the Zionist cause of establishing a homeland in the ancient country. Freud was not too inclined and favorable to this idea, though he was sympathetic to the Jewish need for a homeland. What caught my eye was this statement by Freud: " . . . I concede with sorrow that the baseless fanaticism of our people is in part to be blamed for the awakening of Arab distrust. I can raise no sympathy at all for the misdirected piety which ***transforms a piece of a Herodian wall into a national relic***; thereby offending the feelings of the natives . . ." (emphases mine).

What did Freud mean by making this most unusual comment about "a Herodian wall becoming a national relic"? Did Freud, and one can presume many others, know something about "the Herodian wall" others have ignored for many centuries, and to our days? We shall elaborate more on that later.

Early morning on June 6, 1967, I was awakened by the familiar buzz of my faithful radio alarm. The news was on; it was very startling news. It was another war—a major war being waged by the perpetual enemies against the homeland I left behind on one June summer, four years earlier. Strangely, all the disheartening gloomy reports were forthcoming only from one side—that of the warring enemies of Israel. "We downed 67 Israeli jets," the excited Arab announcer was loudly blaring. "No, no, it was 76," and a bit later it was more. "The enemy is being defeated, Allah U-Akbar," the announcer was joyfully screaming. "We are destroying Tel Aviv, bombing Haifa, victory is at hand! Allah U-Akbar!" Still, nothing from the Israeli side! Dead silence. The Egyptian Ambassador was informing, almost apologetically, his counterparts of the great destruction his nation was inflicting on her hated enemy Israel. And still complete silence from the Israeli side! It seemed like an eternal nerve wracking silence that began to take its toll on many Jews, Israeli compatriots, and their many sympathizers at large.

Then, slowly, the news began to trickle in from the "defeated side," Israel. And what a dumb-founding shock it was to many ears! In the first few hours of the war, the Israeli Air Force had managed to completely destroy the entire air force squadrons of her enemies while still on the ground. The skies were free from any danger to Israel's armed divisions. That cleared the path for the ensuing land invasion.

Jordan was warned not to interfere, if it wanted her army to remain intact. King Hussein was highly pressured by his Arab 'friendly' fellow leaders and started to shell Jerusalem's Israeli side. Israel's Air Force sprang into action, and few days later, Jordan lost her Air Force, the West Bank, and East Jerusalem.

The fierce Israeli Para-troopers were dispatched into East Jerusalem. Their task was to wage a hand-to-hand combat against the well armed fierce Jordanian Legionnaires. They were instructed to minimize any civilian casualties in East Jerusalem. In the process, they lost several brave soldiers. Still the main goal was: capturing "The Temple Mount." And they did just that! It would have been easier and less costly, in Israeli casualties, to enter the city and capture it through the Dung Gate, which was closest to the "Western Wall." However, the decision was to be otherwise. They were instructed, instead, to enter the city—like warriors—through the distant "Lion's Gate." They did, and shortly after fierce hand-to-hand combat and several casualties on their side, the triumphant message was sent to their commanding General Moti Gur: "The Temple Mount is in our hands."

The Media was there when teary-eyed tough Israeli soldiers were facing "The Wall," the Millennia yearned-for and dreamt about "Wall of Tears." Not all of the soldiers were religious or devout in their Judaism, but all were in awe and with many tears streaming down their tired thorny faces. Their eyes were mesmerized as they stared at the "Western Wall" of the "Temple Mount." Who cannot remember the world famous historic picture of that young Israeli soldier, who in a moment of enraptured awe, simply took off his helmet and intently, with tears in his eyes, just stood there fastening his dreamy gaze on "The Wall," the holiest shrine of Judaism.

When the Roman legions, under the command of the young and a most determined General Titus, were about to capture the fiercely defended walls of Jerusalem, a band of Jewish Zealots fought their way into the heavily fortified Roman citadel where the tenth Roman legion was stationed. They broke in through its western wall and held the Roman legion at bay for a considerable period. Their attitude and feelings toward "that monument," as it was regarded then by the Zealots and defenders of Jerusalem, was quite unlike that of the Israeli soldiers who stormed into that very area about nineteen centuries later. What was the link between these two "Western Walls?" Later we shall find out.

Every year, at "Easter" time, devout Catholic, Protestant, and Orthodox believers from around the world enact the last journey a cross bearing Jesus had taken on his way to be crucified. That road is named the "Via Dolorosa" and final journey, with several stations along its path. At one station he "stopped to rest," at another "he was given some water," the story is told. And this "Passion" scenario is enacted every year in the ancient windy streets of Jerusalem. Yearly, many tourists from the four corners of the "Christian world" make their pilgrimage to the City "Jesus wept" for to "walk in his footsteps" and see other "holy sites" associated with him.

I have been there! I have seen, like many others, the street sign on the wall, the "Via Dolorosa." The question is: Was this street, "the Via Dolorosa," still in existence after the destruction of Jerusalem? Were all the sites associated with Jesus still standing after the Roman legions trampled over the streets of the Holy City? Was the room where Jesus took "the last supper" with his disciples, which the Vatican so eagerly desires to have and requests from the Israeli government, still intact after the fall of Jerusalem? This and many other questions will be answered later, after the true story of the city is unveiled from the pages of the Bible and recorded Jewish, Christian, and Muslim history.

Now back to the period of the "Six Day War."

The war was short! Many Israeli compatriots, Jews, and sympathizers from around the world yearned badly to go and help, do something for the tiny State of Israel in her hour of great distress. But alas, the airports were shut down to civilian traffic. But finally, about a month later, a whole plan load of young American Jews and non-Jews, including yours truly—the only young Israeli aboard—all 167 of us arrived at Tel Aviv airport. We were all filled with that old pioneering spirit of the first Israeli natives and immigrants, ready, willing and able to help in any capacity. The greatest need was in the fields of the agrarian communities whose civilian workers were still on the battleground. Some of us were sent to the border Kibbutz of *Misgav Am*. It was situated on the Lebanese border, on the opposite side of the *Golan Heights*. At one point, I straddled over the border fence and experienced the feeling of standing simultaneously on the soil of two different countries. Thankfully, the border town on the Lebanese side, *Taiba*, was a peaceful one.

I felt the urge to see Jerusalem, the Old City and the "Western Wall." This was a long time dream and yearning on my part to see, to touch the stones of the most holy religious relic to all Jews. Here was the mystical location where a devout Jew could touch, smell, see and breath the ancient reality of twenty centuries ago Jerusalem—the heartbeat of the Jewish nationhood. Here was the long dreamed of closure achieved for every Jew! But I was in for a great surprise—a most disappointing one in nature!

I made my way up the hills to Jerusalem. Once in the heart of the city, I took the bus to the Old City. Arriving near the Lions' Gate, I started walking towards the Western Wall via the indoor Arab market and winding narrow streets that lead to the "Temple Mount" and Wall. This was just one month after Israel captured the Old City from Jordan. The various foods and spices, along with the unsanitary conditions in the indoor market, produced unbearable stench and odors. Still, I speeded my pace and few moments later I reached the last turn that led directly to the Wall standing in front of my gazing eyes. I was not awestruck! The ancient Wall did not look impressive or inviting, and worse of all, I felt nothing inside! I could not understand why. For the next forty years I still could not understand why that void resided in my heart when staring at the Wall for the first time ever. I turned my back to the Wall and walked away, greatly disappointed and stupefied, into the stench-filled Arab market's narrow streets. My greatest desire at that point was to escape away from the disappointing sights and bad odors of the market. I almost fainted for lack of fresh air and barely made it into the open space outside of the market. Yes, it took me forty years to find out why I was gripped with such void that hot July in 1967 when standing before the "Wall of Tears."

I was invited, just about forty years after that disheartening experience with the Wall in the Temple Mount, to a lecture given by the editor of a book about "The Temple Mount." The actual title of the book discussed on that fateful day was, "The Temples Jerusalem had Forgotten." Strangely enough, the author of that most revealing subject was a former fellow faculty member and friend, who recently passed away, with whom I have spent in 1971-1972 two most enjoyable summers in Israel on the archaeological excavations on the Temple Mount. We were both then teaching at the same college in Pasadena, California. During those summers, since he was the director of that digging expedition from our colleges in Pasadena, California, Big Sandy, Texas, and Bricket Wood near London, England, Dr. Ernest L. Martin taught archaeology, while I taught Hebrew to our students on the "Big Dig." When the most fascinating lecture was over, I fully understood the source and reason for the void and empty feelings I had experienced when standing on that fateful first day in the summer of 1967, while staring with an empty heart at the Western Wall.

The man in charge of the Jerusalem Dig at that time, and until his passing away, was one of the greatest archaeologists and historians of Israel and former President of the Hebrew university in Jerusalem, Dr. Benjamin Mazar. I had the privilege of knowing him, though briefly, as well as his granddaughter, Eilat Mazar, who is now also the chief archaeologist in charge of the "Temple Mount" dig. Her older sister, Tally Mazar, had joined us in the summer of 1971 on a two weeks trip throughout Europe and then attended for the next two years at our sister college near London. She was quiet a charming and delightful person to have known.

Based on his expert knowledge and history of the "Temple Mount" and Jerusalem, Dr. Mazar, a descendant of the House of King David, had come to the conclusion at the end of his career on the "Temple Mount" site that the real location of the Temples of Solomon, Zerubabel and Herod, were actually in a different location. Based on his knowledge of the area and its history, Dr Mazar was leaning toward the conclusion that the Temples were located on the Ophel mount, just to the north of the original Mount Zion on the southeast ridge. He then asked his son, Ory, also an archaeologist, to look more deeply into the matter and ascertain the real location of the Temples by thoroughly examining all related historic documents and writings. Ory, Dr. Mazar's son, had then asked Dr. Earnest Martin to do a thorough research on the true location of the Temples, since Ory had other more pressing matters to tackle at the time. Dr Martin was more than glad and honored to do just that, since he was avidly searching for the true history of Temple time Jerusalem since 1961.

Dr. Martin was quietly shocked at the results of his historic research for the true location of the three Temples of Jerusalem. He was greatly amazed at the rich historic evidence about the true location of the Temples, still in existence up to the sixteenth century, which Jewish, Christian, and Islamic historians have left behind for all to read. Those historic records do contradict the erroneous assertions of both religious and secular sources regarding the true location of Jerusalem's Temples and "Temple Mount."

Since the destruction of Herod's Temple, Jews throughout the Diaspora have been reciting Psalm 137:5-6, which was first uttered by the Jewish captives taken into exile by King Nebuchadnezzar of Babylon:

"If I forget Thee, O Jerusalem, let my right hand forget her cunning. If I do not remember thee, let my tongue cleave to the roof of my mouth, if I prefer not Jerusalem above my chief joys."

When the Jewish captives, while sitting by "The Rivers of Babylon," had recited these mournful words, their main focus and intent was on the destroyed Temple of their beloved city of Jerusalem. The destruction and burning of the Temple of the God of Israel was a painful reminder and a stinging testimony to the fact that their God had abandoned them in their hour of darkness and greatest calamity. They knew the reasons for it and had acknowledged their responsibility in bringing upon themselves their great hour of darkness. Their solemn vow not to "forget" Jerusalem was an admission on their part of their failure to do so in the past.

Has the Jewish Diaspora kept this most solemn promise?

In the following pages of this book we shall find out the naked answer to this forgotten promise, and the reasons for this unintentional failure. It was not a question of willful forgetfulness, but as a result of historic 'dust' cast over the air of Jerusalem that gradually led to the blinding of the wise and devout children of the beloved city. It is this dust that produced "The Hoax of the Millennium!"

Still, there was another major factor that contributed to the creation of this "Hoax of the Millennium," especially in the world of Islam. This major factor stems from another intimately related hoax, which is most prevalent in all religions, and in specific has directly affected early Islamic 'religious' attitudes toward the "Temple Mount" and its supposed "holiness" to Islam. This global in nature hoax is based on the doctrine of the afterlife and the immortality of the soul, which is commonly believed by all religions, yet, shockingly enough, it is totally contradicted by the teachings of both the Bible and the Qur'an. To do this matter full justice, we shall first expose this unbiblical fallacy from the pages of the Old Testament or the "Hebrew Bible," and then from the pages of the New Testament or the "Christian Bible." Then, finally, we shall delve into the pages of the "infallible" Qur'an, as it is regarded by the Muslim community, and read what the "infallible" prophet of Islam—Muhammad—had to say about the doctrine of the afterlife and the doctrine of the immortality of the soul. It is the total rejection, on the part of the followers of the prophet of Islam—Muhammad—of his clear and emphatic teachings concerning the afterlife that largely was responsible for the invention of the notion regarding the "holiness" of the "Temple Mount" or Haram esh-Sheriff to Islam.

It is a fact of history: Israel came first, about 3500 years ago, since Mount Sinai's giving of the Law or Torah. The "Church" and the "New

Testament" era came later. About six centuries later, the religion of Islam became a reality. It is also a fact: All members of these three religions, with some exceptions, have strayed away from the original teachings of their "Holy Books" concerning the afterlife and the immortality of the soul. It is this rejection of the original teachings, mainly in the Muslim community, which led to the erroneous notion concerning the supposed ascension of Muhammad to Heaven via Jerusalem—therefore, the "holiness" of Jerusalem's "Temple Mount" to Islam. Only after we thoroughly uncover the true teachings about the doctrine of the afterlife and the immortality of the soul—as recorded in the pages of the "Holy Books" of the three involved religions—we shall be able to see clearly how the Jewish, Christian, and Islamic genesis of the "Hoax of the Millennium" concerning the "Temple Mount" originated in its naked reality.

CHAPTER 1

AFTERLIFE AND IMMORTALITY OF
THE SOUL IN RELIGION

Strange! There is one major teaching common to all three main religions that claim to have a physical or spiritual link to Father Abraham. Jews, Christians, and Muslims speak of Abraham and his faith as the source of their beliefs. These three religions profess to believe in the doctrine of the *afterlife*. With some variations, they teach their followers that immediately after death all good believers go to Heaven, while all the bad ones go to Hell. All followers of these three religions hold as true the doctrine of the *immortality of the soul*. All claim these beliefs are in accordance with the writings of their "Holy Books." We all heard this statement: "Sometimes truth is more fascinating than fiction." What's really strange is this amazing fact: A careful reading of the "Holy Books" of all the three major religions reveal diametrically opposite teachings about the doctrine of the *afterlife*, about 'the destiny' to Heaven or Hell immediately after death. Understanding the true teachings about these doctrines will determine whether or not Jerusalem or "el-Quds" and its "Temple Mount" or "Haram-esh-Sheriff" is truly holy to Islam.

Many of us read or heard the fictional story about the two scoundrels who came to the royal court of an Emperor of a certain imaginary land—who was not wise at all, but very vain and most gullible. They decided to play a trick on him by presenting themselves as merchants from a far away land in whose possession was the most remarkable fabric anyone has ever seen. "Only a very wise man could see it"—they assuredly declared. The price was very high, but anyone wearing cloths made from this fantastic fabric could know for certain which one around him was truly wise, and which one was not. The Emperor was most excited to find out whether those in his royal court were wise or fools. He paid the merchants very handsomely in gold coins and pleaded with them to speedily make his new cloths before the coming great event in his kingdom. Word has rapidly spread around: The Emperor is soon to display his most amazing new cloths, but only the wise could see it. On the due date, the Emperor 'put on' his new royal garments, made from the 'special' fabric, and strode into his royal ballroom hall. He walked very slowly to let everyone see his magnificent 'invisible' garments, which could be seen only by those who possess the gift of wisdom—like the wise Emperor, of course. Not wanting to be considered fools, each distinguished guest in the royal court uttered sounds of "Oooos" and "Ahaaas" when the proud and glowing-faced Emperor passed by them. Convinced that all in the royal court are 'wise,' the Emperor marched out of the royal court to greet his loyal, admiring subjects who were also anxious to prove to their beloved Emperor they too were 'wise' and could also 'see' the invisible magic garments their Emperor was attired with. At the end the long line of 'admirers' and 'well wishers' stood a little child with his mouth wide open—not understanding the purpose for all the seemingly excited royal court and cheering crowds. Finally, he exclaimed loudly: "Look . . . ! The Emperor is naked!" Before long, others started echoing the words of the little child, "The Emperor is naked; the Emperor is naked!"

This story about the child who alone, of all the 'wise and mighty' of the land, had 'eyes' to see and therefore able to proclaim, "The Emperor is naked," is a testimony to the commission of Isaiah the prophet about the state of affairs in the world of religion. He was told by the God of Israel: **" . . . Go, and tell this people, hear you indeed, but understand not; and see you indeed, but perceive not. Make the heart of this people fat, and make their ears heavy, and shut their eyes; lest they see with their eyes, and hear with their ears, and understand with their heart, and convert and be healed."**

Isaiah the prophet could not understand, like anyone of us, why and how long would this state of "partial blindness" would last, as the apostle Paul called it in his discourse to the Romans. And so he asked: **"Lord, how long?** [How long wouldn't people recognize that "the Emperor is naked?"] **And He [God] answered, until the cities are wasted without inhabitant, and the houses without man, and the land is utterly desolate, and the Lord has removed men far away, and there be a great forsaking in the midst of the land. But in it shall be a tenth** [only 10% would remain alive at the end-time], **and it shall return, and shall be eaten as a teil tree, and as an oak, whose substance is in them, when** they cast their leaves: so the holy seed [Israel] shall be the substance thereof" (Isaiah 6:9-13, KJV throughout).

This Biblical account describes not only the state of affairs among the *"People of the Book,"* and primarily among their 'spiritual leaders,' but also among all men of religion! Often time those at the top are the least able to 'see,' being steeped in the confusion of their own man-made teachings. It's the proverbial *"babes"* who, oftentimes, are able to see and proclaim, "The Emperor is naked." Why? Because their minds and hearts are still pure—they are still void of confusion. In the next chapters we'll find out who are 'the scoundrels' and who is 'the Emperor'; who are the 'wise' in the royal court and who is 'the child.'

As for the 'spiritual teachers' who are daily placing 'spiritual food' before their gullible followers, Isaiah the prophet wrote: **"All tables are full of vomit and filthiness, so that there is no place clean."** Then he asks: **"Whom shall He [God] teach knowledge? And whom shall He make to understand doctrine** [of the afterlife or others]**?"** His reply: **"Them that are weaned from the milk, and drawn from the breast"** (Isaiah 28:8-9). In His day, Jesus spoke of the 'spiritual teachers' of *"The people of the Book,"* who like most teachers in any religion had eyes but could not see, by stating: **" . . . I thank you O Father, Lord of Heaven and earth, because You have hid these things from the wise and the prudent** [in their own sight]**, and has revealed them unto babes"** (Matthew 11:25).

Blindness, be it spiritual or in every human endeavor, is a global malady! Men of religion or thinkers in any field of secular realm should not point the finger at each other—all are suspect to deception! Why? *"The Good Book"* tells us: **"And the great dragon** [Satan, at the end of the age] **was cast out, that old serpent, called the Devil, and Satan, WHICH DECEIVES THE WHOLE WORLD; he was cast out onto the earth, and his angels** [or demons] **were cast out with him"** (Revelation 12:9). When this future event takes place, then, a bit later, this final act would usher an end to man's darkened eyes, as John wrote: **"And I saw an angel come down from heaven, having the key of the bottomless pit and a great chain in his hand. And he laid hold on the Dragon, that old Serpent, which is called the Devil, and Satan, and bound him a thousand years, and cast him into the bottomless pit, and shut him up, and set a seal upon him, that he should deceive the nations no more, till the thousand years should be fulfilled . . ."** (Revelation 20:1-3).

As a result of these acts to shut down the source of blindness and confusion in all religions and nations, we read: **"And He [God] will destroy in this Mountain [of Zion] the face of the covering cast over ALL PEOPLE, and the veil [of deception and darkness] that is spread over ALL NATIONS. He will swallow up death in victory, and the Lord God shall wipe away all tears from off all faces; and the rebuke of His people shall He take away from off all the earth; for the Lord has spoken it"** (Isaiah 25:7-8).

Until this hopeful future arrives, only the "babes" shall continue to proclaim, *"The king is naked"*. Until that daylight awakens all the 'sleepers' on the earth—be they religious or secular—the agreed upon self-deception about the *afterlife* will be clung to, as an old rugged 'security blanket' by most of us. After all, since time immemorial, Truth and Facts never mattered to most! How one feels about it is what really counts! This being said, let's now see how the three major religions, with a link to the father of faithful—Abraham—perceive the universal doctrine of the **afterlife**, immediately after death, and the teaching about Heaven and Hell. How does their belief square with that of their own "Holy Books," be it the Bible or the Qur'an? The dilemma is very simple for the spiritual leaders: If they are right, the "Holy Books" are wrong; if the "Holy Books" are right, they are wrong, since both cannot be right when they contradict each other!

It is important to recognize this reality: the 'spiritual leaders' of all religions are the ones who taught the doctrine of the *afterlife*—the humanly contrived teachings of going to Heaven or Hell. We all know that Men in Education or medical professions, scientists, or politicians do not deal with religious dogma. It's the' spiritual leaders' who claim to derive their teachings from their "Holy Books." Yet, it's a fact: none of them had ever experienced the process of death and its immediate *afterlife* in either Heaven or Hell. Travelers go to far away countries and they come back to tell us about their experiences. They bring us credible evidence we can all accept, and so we believe them. 'Spiritual leaders,' however, can't claim to have traveled on a journey to the *afterlife*; they can't bring any credible evidence—yet we gullibly believe them! Why? They are unable to produce any shred of evidence, yet we put our trust in them and in their teachings—without checking on them—even though they gave us no proof.

We are commanded, **"To prove all things"** and not take things for granted. When the apostle Paul came to Berea, he " **. . . Went into** the Synagogue of the Jews. **These were more noble than those in Thessalonica, in that they received the Word with all readiness of mind,** [and most importantly] **searched the Scriptures daily,** [to prove] **whether those things were so"** (Acts 17:10-11).

Are you as "noble" as the Bereans? Why Not? Do Muslims attempt to prove all things before accepting the fallible words of their religious teachers? Because most people are not, deception is the consequence. Because most people do not have the love of the Truth, shrewd "scoundrels" can easily lead them astray. You have nobody to blame but your laziness that caused you 'to check your brains at the door.' Did you ever check the true source of the *immortality of the soul?* Have you ever read a clear statement in the Bible or in the Qur'an that plainly says you have an immortal soul? Did you ever read a statement in the Bible or in the Qur'an that plainly says, "When we die, we'll go to Heaven immediately after death?" Isn't it odd that neither the Bible nor the Qur'an is full with such statements?

In the book of Genesis we read this plain command: **"And the Lord God commanded the man, saying, 'of every tree of the garden you may freely eat; but of the tree of the knowledge of good and evil** [the true source of all humanly contrived religions], **you shall not eat of it; but in the day that you eat of it, you shall surly die'"** (Genesis 2:16-17). The statement was plain: you eat of it—you die! If you have an immortal soul, you don't die! The 'spiritual leaders' said: that's true! Your body dies, but you go to Hell. Is it clever? Not really, because it's a lie, and both "Holy Books," the Bible and the Qur'an, would testify to it, as we shall see later on.

First, let's consider these points! When God stated, "in the day that you eat, you shall surly die," He was speaking metaphorically and spiritually, but Adam didn't get it. He and Eve thought it was literal. When we sin, we are told in the Scriptures, we are "dead in our sins," though we are physically alive. Secondly, Biblically speaking, a day can be a year or a thousand years, as we read in several Biblical statements. Satan knew that, but Adam and Eve did not at that point, and so Satan took advantage of this ignorance on their part. And so he approached Eve, as the smooth salesman in the absence of the husband, and plainly lied to her by contradicting God—Whose intention he very well knew—saying: **"you shall not surely die"** (Genesis 3:4). When Adam and Eve ate of the forbidden fruit and did not die, the false doctrine of the immortal soul began to take root in their gullible minds, and in the minds of their

5

offspring. They saw them live years and hundreds of years beyond that point. And so this false doctrine is still with us today.

The Bible states emphatically these most ignored statements: **"The Soul that sins, it shall die"** (Ezekiel 18:4, 20). God repeated this statement twice for emphasis sake, but many still don't get it! Jesus stated: **"And fear not them which kill the body, but are not able to kill the soul; but rather fear Him which is able to destroy both soul and body in Gehenna fire** [a literal fire, as we shall see later]" (Matthew 10:28). How many of those who claim to be Christians believe His plain words! If the soul was truly immortal, it could not be destroyed. In Roman 6:23, the apostle Paul declares: **"For the wages of sin is death** [not immortal life in factitious 'hell fire'], **but the gift of God is eternal life through Jesus Christ our Lord."** Paul is contrasting death with eternal life, not eternal life in Heaven or Hell! The **"gift of God is eternal life"** for the believers, and he did not say where! In contrast, **"the wages of sin is death,"** not life, and he did not say where! Many have missed this important point. In the Resurrection Chapter, Paul states: **" . . . this mortal must put on immortality"** (I Corinthians 15:53, 54). If one has already an immortal soul, what need is there to put on immortality? In I Timothy 6:16, the apostle Paul states, speaking of God: **" . . . who only has immortality dwelling in the light . . ."** Only God has immortality, an immortal soul—man must put on immortality in the resurrection. The timing of this resurrection, we shall see later. It is certainly not immediately after death, as the "Holy Books" of the three religions clearly and emphatically affirm. And finally, the apostle Paul, speaking of the time God chose to offer us immortality, states: **"But is now made manifest by the appearing of our Savior Jesus Christ, who has abolished death, and has brought** [consequently] **life and immortality** [which no one had before] **to light through the Gospel"** (II Timothy 1:10). Only those who have eyes and ears; only those who are like the "more noble Bereans" can believe the plain statements of the Book they claim to base their faith on. Are you one of them?

Sadly, most of us are not propelled forward in our short journey on earth by the pure fuel of the Truth. Since the dawn of history, humanity was enamored with fables, superstitions, and mysteries. These sought-after tantalizing 'spices' of life have a tremendous allure for most of us who do not have a direct link and relationship with the Creator of us all. On one hand, we want security and truth, on the other, we like to 'be scared' and lied to. That's why Hollywood and the movie industry worldwide are ever churning horror movies, science fiction movies, and fables—like Harry Potter and the like. Politicians often lie to us and yet we keep voting for them. We believe the convincing yet deceitful ads and often avidly buy worthless products. As W.C. Field said, *"Every day a sucker is born."* Yet by far, religion—not God's pure religion, which is a 'way' of life—is the greatest source of deceptions, fables, superstitions, and mysteries. Of one such 'great' and very rich global religion, which is still with us to this day, the apostle Paul states: **"For the *Mystery of iniquity does already work . . ."* (II Thessalonians 2:7).

Later, the apostle John reveals more details of this religion. He wrote: **"And there came one of the seven angels which had the seven vials, and talked with me, saying unto me, come here; I will show you the judgment of THE GREAT WHORE that sits [or rules] upon many waters [or many nations]; with whom the kings of the earth have committed fornication [by absorbing and enforcing her teachings], and the inhabitants of the earth have been made drunk [spiritually] with the wine of her fornication [or teachings]. So he carried me away in the spirit into the wilderness; and I saw a woman [or a church, in Biblical lingo] sit upon scarlet colored beast, full of names of blasphemy, having seven heads and ten horns. And the woman was arrayed in purple and scarlet color, and decked with gold and precious stones and pearls, having a golden cap in her hand full of abominations and filthiness of her fornication; and upon her forehead a name was written, MYSTERY BABYLON THE GREAT, THE MOTHER OF HARLOTS [OR DAUGHTER CHURCHES] AND ABOMINATIONS OF THE EARTH. And I saw the woman drunk with the blood of the saints and with the blood of the martyrs of Jesus . . ."** (Revelation 17:1-6).

Since most students of the Bible know the identity of this *"woman"*, we shall not elaborate more at this point. The apostle Paul gives us some more clues by stating: **"Now the Spirit speaks expressly, that in the latter times some shall depart from the [pure] faith [which was taught by the apostles], giving heed to seducing spirits [and false teachers] and doctrines of Devils [or Demons]; speaking lies in hypocrisy [since they know better]; having their conscience seared with a hot iron; FORBIDDING TO MARRY [do you know of such religion which teaches celibacy?], and *COMMANDING TO ABSTAIN FROM***

MEATS..." [On certain days of the week—up to five months during the Middle Ages] (I Timothy 4:1-3).

But alas! Most people don't bother to check out, like the "more noble Bereans," the true background of their religion. Most of us go once or more times per week to our houses of worship so we can constantly be fed the steady diet of some truth and mostly, from God's point of view, vomit—as He said of His people's spiritual diet: **"All tables are full of vomit."** Most of us do not like to hear such blunt accusations—it hurts our ego and self esteem. As the apostle Paul said to the Galatian church in his letter to them (Galatians 4:16): **"Am I become an enemy by telling you the truth"?** Many, in time past, were considered to be enemies—and were burned at the stake for telling the truth. Do you know by whom?

Most of us, sadly, prefer to hear smooth words like "I am O.K., you are O.K.," not 'annoying' truths! And why do we like fables, superstitions, or mysteries instead of the 'naked truth'? All these are products of insecurities, and that's why we have idols! Idols are our security blanket. They give us confidence, hope, and measure of certainty. They fulfill our immediate needs in a world that does not operate by an invisible faith. Children want to see their parents, they want to touch and feel them; they want to be comforted, heard, and assured by them that everything will be alright. When we don't have in front of us, before our eyes, these basic needs, we invent them. The doctrine of the *afterlife* or of 'going to Heaven', immediately after death, is a product of man's quest for assurance in the world of the unknown and uncertainty. These illusive and non-Biblically substantiated wishful quests, nevertheless, give humanity hope and comfort—the ability to overcome grief even though it's not provable, it's false, a superstition. For many, it's a comfortable 'security blanket'—and that makes it right. When a person does not have an invisible means of support—the perfect definition for an atheist—his ever persistent quest for a religious experience leads him to invent those invisible means of support through a visible reproduction of idols, ideas, and philosophies, fables, superstitions, and mysteries. It's a scary reality if your Creator does not reveal Himself to you; if He does not impart knowledge and truth to you; if He does not reveal to your mind the facts of life. And if He 'fails' to do so, sure enough, man will invent it to satisfy his quest for the unknown.

The truth is: God has revealed Himself to His creation, yet His creation has shoved Him aside! Why? They did not like His rules! They were 'too restrictive' for them! Through His Prophet Hosea, our Creator has bemoaned this sorry reality: **"My people are destroyed for lack of knowledge."** Was it because they did not know it? His reply: **"Because you have rejected knowledge** [as most of you would, after reading this book], **I will also reject you, that you that you shall be no priest to me** [which was the roll of Israel]; seeing **you have forgotten** [because you rejected God's knowledge] **the Law of your God, I will also forget your children** [and that's "why God let Johnny die]" (Hosea 4:6).

Through His prophet Jeremiah, God stated: **"For My people have committed two evils; they have forsaken Me [though I did not] the fountain of living waters [or Truth], and hewed them out cisterns [sources of fables, mysteries, false doctrines], broken cisterns, that can hold no water** [as those fabricated doctrines of the **afterlife** and of going to Heaven or Hell, immediately after death]" (Jeremiah 2:13).

Likewise, the apostle Paul has stated in his letter to the Romans, addressing humanity as a whole: **"For the wrath of God is revealed from heaven against all ungodliness and unrighteousness of men, who hold back the truth in unrighteousness** [preferring fables]; because **that which may be known of God** [as plainly recorded in His 'manuscript for life'] **is manifest in them; for God has shown it unto them. For the invisible things** [and teachings] **of Him from the creation of the world are clearly seen** [to those who have eyes to see], **being understood by the things that are made, even His eternal power and Godhead, so they are without excuse; because that, when they knew God, they glorified Him not as God, neither were thankful, but became vain in their imaginations, and their foolish heart was darkened. Professing themselves to be wise, they became fools, and changed the glory of the incorruptible God into an image made like to corruptible man [or idols], and to birds, and four-footed beasts, and creeping things. Wherefore God also gave them to uncleanness through the lust of their own hearts, to dishonor their own bodies between themselves; who changed the Truth** [including the teachings about the afterlife] **of God into a lie, and worshiped and served the creation more than the Creator . . . For this cause God gave them up unto vile affections; for even their women did change the natural use into that which is against** [wholesome and intended] **nature; and likewise also the men, leaving the natural use of the woman, burned in their lust one toward another; men with men, working that which**

is unseemly [and no, God did not create homosexuals, as many would have you believe], **and received in themselves that recompense of their error** [as AIDS and the like] **which was meet** [or fit]. **And even as they did not like to retain God in their knowledge, God gave them over to a reprobate mind, to do those things which are not proper"** (Romans 1:18-28).

These are the people who have originally invented the fables and false doctrines about the immortal soul. They concocted the fables about the afterlife, immediately after death, about going Heaven, Hell, and Limbo—'the land of the dead! Not having 'the invisible means of support,' since they have rejected them, they went about inventing, with a healthy dose of inspiration from the wrong source—the Master Deceiver—"doctrines of Demons," as Paul labeled them. And alas, things have not changed much ever since!

Our Creator has revealed Himself to us in many ways, yet since the Garden of Eden most of us have rejected Him and His revelations. We have repeatedly scorned Him and chose, instead, the vain desire to be wise like the Emperor who sought to be attired with invisible cloths. This was the downfall of Mother Eve. She sought to be wise, through the manipulations of the wrong spirit, and the eating of the symbolic *"forbidden fruit"* from the "tree of the knowledge of **GOOD AND EVIL**." And so do many of us—be it in the sphere of religion or the secular world—to this very moment. We think we are wise, intelligent, advanced, enlightened—yet we go about, with greater intensity, making this formerly glorious, God-given planet, into a hell-hole. Aren't we so smart?

Speaking to His own followers in future generations, who should have known better, Jesus declared to them and to their shame: **"I know your works, that you are neither cold nor hot; I wish you were either cold or hot. So then because you are lukewarm** [never bothering to prove anything, like the "more noble Bereans"], **and are neither cold nor hot, I will spue you out of My mouth. Because you say: I am rich, and increased in goods** [of Biblical teachings], **and have need of nothing; and know not that you are wretched, and miserable, and poor, and blind, and naked"** (Revelation 3:15-17).

Had people checked, without ever taking anything for granted, on their 'religious' leaders, as God commanded us **"to prove all things and hold fast to that which is good,"** none would have been duped by them and their twisted teachings since time immemorial! But we don't! We prefer 'to check our brains at the door' and let others do the thinking for us. Can we blame anyone but ourselves? Because we fail to be on guard, as commanded, **"All tables are full of vomit and filthiness, so that there is no clean place"** (Isaiah 28:8). Hence, as God proclaimed: **"These people draw near Me with their mouth, and with their lips do honor Me, but have removed their heart far from Me, and their fear toward Me is taught by the precepts** [or traditions and fables] **of man. Therefore, behold, I will proceed to do a marvelous work among these people, even a marvelous work and a wonder; FOR THE WISDOM OF THEIR WISE MEN SHALL PERISH, AND THE UNDERSTANDING OF THEIR PRUDENT MEN SHALL BE HID** [and yet we place our trust and destiny in their hands]" (Isaiah 29:13-14).

When He appeared to His people, in the flesh, this is what He told them: **"You hypocrites, well did Isaiah prophesy of you, saying: This people draw near unto Me with their mouth, and honor Me with their lips; but their heart is far from Me. But in vain do they worship Me, teaching for doctrine** [or Torah in Hebrew] **the commandments of men"** (Matthew 15:8-9). This is applicable to every one of us to this day—whether we are Jews, Christians, or Muslims! All of us went astray! All of us, at least to a degree, worship God in vain, trusting in the words of our 'spiritual leaders'—without bothering to examine the original writings—at least in this area of the afterlife. In later chapters, we shall see this blindness of our leaders and ours more clearly!

The apostle Paul had to deal, like all true servants of God before him, with the scourge of the would-be 'spiritual leaders' of his day. He knew very well of the warnings of Jesus about the coming deception, who warned His future followers, saying: **" . . . Take heed that no man deceive you. For many [the majority in Biblical lingo] shall come in My name, saying, I am Christ** [by pointing people to Him as the Savior] **and** [still] **shall deceive many"** (Matthew 24:4-5). Are you sure you are not one of them? Before his last trip to Jerusalem, Paul gathered all the elders of Ephesus and delivered this stern warning: **"For I know this that after my departing** [or death] **shall grievous wolves enter among you, not sparing the flock. Also of your own selves shall men arise, speaking perverse things, to draw away disciples after them. Therefore, and remember, that by the space of three years I ceased not to warn everyone night and day with tears"** (Acts 20:29-31). Tragically, few took him seriously—and the results are still with us to this very moment.

11

Warning the Corinthian Church, and all believers, of such deceivers, he wrote: **"For such are false apostles, deceitful workers, transforming themselves into the apostles** [or servants] **of Christ. And no marvel; for Satan himself is transformed into an angel of light, therefore it is no great thing if HIS ministers** [the 'scoundrels' whose identity most are unaware of] **also be transformed into ministers of righteousness; whose end shall be according to their works"** (II Corinthians 11:13-15).

It's important to recognize this reality: Most of Satan's "ministers" are often decent people, God fearing, honest and kind, often with great charisma and sincerity—yet are deceived, nevertheless, and do not even know it! Their "love of the truth" is 'not all there,' and this is exactly why they are 'chosen' by the Master Deceiver to do his nefarious and deceitful work on those who are equally not "too hot" for the "love of the truth." These deceivers do not wake up one day and say to themselves: "'Self, I want to be a minister of the Devil and appear like those 'ministers of righteousness!'" Or "I want to deceive people." They do not enter into houses of worship and announce to everyone: "I am here to deceive you all, would you please follow me!" They just don't know any better! There are no schools advertising: "for false prophets only." On the other side of the coin, true servants of God do not have their own agenda; they do not have their own opinions—but do seek the purity of the truth even when it contradicts their own feelings, or the teachings of their religious background, or that of their revered spiritual leaders. They seek the "narrow path" and find it—and they are the only "few that find it."

Tragically, for most of us, truth and facts do not matter, but how we feel about it! This is applicable to every aspect of life—and we all know it—assuming we are honest about it. For most, it's the attitude of, "don't confuse us with the facts, since how we feel about it is most important to us." Therefore, ignorance is bliss to most 'believers,' and is the rule for most of us. Yet either ignorance or knowledge is a choice we all have to make, and most choose ignorance! And this is the choice and road most 'spiritual leaders' have chosen for themselves. And so, as mentioned earlier and is worth repeating, God bemoaned the state of His people: **"My people are destroyed for lack of knowledge [but why?]; because you have rejected knowledge, I will also reject you, that you shall be no priest to Me; seeing you have forgotten the Law [or Torah] of Your God, I will also forget your children** [and that's why 'God let Johnny die']" (Hosea 4:6). The apostle Peter, realizing this state of affairs among his people, stated: **"And now, brethren** [not you 'Christ killers', as many so called 'Christians' have branded God's people, and still do to this day], **I know that through ignorance you did it, as did also your rulers"** (acts 3:17).

Aaron the High Priest, chosen by God Himself, a prophet to whom God had spoken—he knew better! Still, out of fear for his life, he made the golden calf and proclaimed to all of Israel: **"This is your God** [or Elohim] **which brought you out of the land of Egypt."** In contrast, most of those who come in the name of God or Christ do not know God, though they think they do, and yet claim to be His true servants. That's why God constantly admonishes His people **"to prove all things"** and to **"test the spirits and see whether they be of God."** Still most of us, like dumb sheep, 'blessed' with the 'sheep instinct,' follow blindly the false shepherds who are equally blind and all "fall into the ditch."

If you don't take seriously the warnings of the true servants of God, and, above all, that of Christ himself, for those who call themselves Christians; if you don't follow the example of the "noble Bereans, who examined, daily, the words they heard from the apostle Paul with the Scriptures, how would you ever know when God or Satan speak? Yes, how would you know when God or Christ's true servants speak and when Satan's "ministers" speak? This is not just a Christian problem! The Devil, as we read earlier in Revelation 12:9, **"deceives the whole world."** He is not choosy! All are welcome into his camp! The deception is accomplished, cleverly, by giving the many who walk "in the broad way" much Biblical knowledge or truth, with few twists to go along with it. Those who do not "prove all things," get hooked on the seemingly valid information. Advertisers have learned to use the same gimmicks, and very successfully. 95% or 98% pure water with 2% to 5% poison would still kill you! Don't treat your life this cheaply!

God warned Adam and Eve in the Garden of Eden **" . . . Of every tree in the garden you may surely eat** [which included the tree of life], **but of the tree of THE KNOWLEDGE OF GOOD AND EVIL** [or poisonous source of information], **you shall not eat of it; for in the day that you eat thereof you shall surly die** [or be good as dead]" (Genesis 2:16-17). Tragically, neither Adam and Eve, nor their descendants have ever listened to the voice of the Master—and to our own detriment. Christ warned the Jews of His day, many of whom followed Him, to beware of the coming great deception. When His disciples inquired of Christ about the future of Jerusalem, the Temple, and the time of His return, He did not respond to any of their questions immediately, but first warned them of the most pressing need, saying: **"Take heed that no man deceive you. For many shall come in My name** [appearing as "ministers of righteousness"], **saying, I am Christ** ["Jesus is Lord," "would you give your heart to the Lord," "honor and praise the King," "Jesus died for you," "Jesus is the way," "Jesus saves" and so on], **and shall deceive many** [by teaching a mixture of truth and error—from the "tree of the knowledge of good and evil," along with disobedience to His Law or Torah]" (Matthew 24:4-5).

These "ministers of righteousness" are still doing the same to this very day! They are leading their blind and gullible followers into a way that leads to destruction. Christ warned His Jewish nation and disciples, saying: **"Therefore all things whatsoever you would that men should do to you, do you even so to them: for THIS IS THE LAW [OR TORAH] AND THE PROPHETS."** He added, **"Enter you in the strait gate [of the Torah]: for wide is gate, and broad is the way, that leads to destruction, and many shall be that go therein. Because strait is the gate, and narrow is the way, which leads unto life [eternal], AND FEW THERE BE THAT FIND IT** [not the many who prefer the "main stream" or the "broad way"]. **Beware of false prophets** [who appear as "ministers of righteousness" or 'ministers of the gospel'], **which come to you in sheep's clothing, but inwardly they are ravening wolves. You shall know them by their fruits . . ."** (Matthew 7:12-16).

As the Devil used his beguiling devices to try to lure Jesus Christ to worship him, so do his "ministers of righteousness" harvest the many foolish and blind sheep and causes them to bow down to him—while they think all along they are serving the true God. They are knowledgeable of the Scriptures and use them, often in ignorance, to deceive the many who do not check up on them like the "noble Bereans" did with Paul. Satan used the Scriptures to try to lead Jesus astray. At one point, as we read: **"Again, the Devil took Him up on an exceeding high mountain, and showed Him all the kingdoms [in a vision, obviously] of the world, and the glory of them; and said to Him: All these things will I give you IF YOU WILL FALL DOWN AND WORSHIP ME"** (Matthew 4:8-9). This is the mode of operation of many 'spiritual leaders' in their efforts, often in ignorance, to lead many to the wrong camp, to the "broad way." They assure their gullible followers with this false promise: "Follow our teachings and you'll go to Heaven, and if not, you'll go to Hell."

The true servants and followers of God are not that foolish; they do not follow anyone without a prior examination of all the facts, as presented in the Scriptures—just like the "noble Bereans" have done. **"My sheep know My voice,"** said Jesus, **"they will not follow others, but flee from them."** But why is it so? As Paul wrote: **"Lest Satan should get an advantage of us; for WE ARE NOT IGNORANT OF HIS DEVICES"** (II Corinthians 2:11). But what happens when "the many that walk in the broad way" do not do their 'homework' as commanded? They live the entirety of their lives believing they are traveling on "the narrow path" without ever even attempting to "prove all things," or as Paul admonished: **"Examine yourselves to see whether you are in the faith; prove your own selves. Know you not your own selves, how that Jesus Christ is in you, except you be reprobates?"** (II Corinthians 13:5).

What would happen to the many who do not heed this, and many other warnings! We read of the final results in these sober words of The Master: **"Not everyone that says unto Me, Lord, Lord, shall enter the kingdom of Heaven; but he that does the will of My Father** [the true Head and Source of the religion of "the narrow gate"] **who is in Heaven. Many** [or the majority in Biblical lingo] **shall say unto Me in that day, Lord, Lord, have we not prophesied** [or preached] **in Your name? And in Your name have cast out Demons? And in Your name have done many wonderful works?"** But Christ or God are not impressed with any of these 'accomplishments' if **THEIR TRUTH AND TORAH** are rejected and despised! And so we read: **"And then will I profess unto them, I NEVER KNEW YOU** [why?]**; depart from Me, you that work iniquity** [or are lawless and without Torah]**"** (Matthew 7:21-23).

The message is plain: God does not accept your faith in Him, your worship of Him, or your good deeds on His behalf—if the purity of His Law or Torah is not the motivating force in your life! And this is where the false prophets were remise in and led His children, in every given religion, astray. The Master said to the Samaritan woman: **"You worship you know not what; we** [the true followers] **know what we worship** [why?]**; FOR SALVATION IS OF THE JEWS. But the hour comes, and now is, when the true worshipers shall worship the Father in spirit and in truth; for the Father seeks such to worship Him in spirit and in truth. God is spirit; and they that worship Him, must worship Him in truth and in spirit"** (John 4:22-24).

15

Before entering the land of Canaan, this is what God revealed to Moses about the future conduct of Israel. And so we read: **"And the Lord said unto Moses, Behold, you shall sleep with your fathers** [in the grave, not go to Heaven]**; and this people will rise up, and go into adultery after the gods of the strangers of the land, where they go to be among them, and will forsake Me, and break My covenant which I made with them. Then My anger shall be kindled against them in that day, and I will forsake them** [and the nightmarish Holocaust is but one gruesome reminder of what happens when we are forsaken] **and I will hide My face from them** [and then many often bemoan, accusingly, "why did God let Johnny die"]**, and they shall be devoured, and many evils and troubles shall befall them; so that they will say** [finally] **in that day, 'Are not these evils come upon us, because our God is not among us?' And I will surely hide My face in that day for all the evils which they have committed, in that they turned unto other gods"** (Deuteronomy 31:16-18). That's why Paul had warned the elders and brethren daily, for three years, with tears. He knew of the sure tragic outcome!

Many Jews would claim, 'well, that may be true for the old days, but not now!' They should read the words of God to the prophet Ezekiel, in Chapter 20, which describes the history of Israel from their time of slavery in Egypt to the coming days of deliverance, in the near future! Let's read some passages in this chapter, which reveal God's opinion of His people from the days of old to the coming redemption—at the end-time—which certainly does not match their opinion of themselves and their beliefs in their God and His Word.

Ezekiel and a part of the captives of Judah, who were taken by the king of Babylon prior to the fall of Jerusalem, were fully settled in their land of captivity and living at peace. The elders of the initial captives wanted to know their future and that of their land. And so we read: **" . . . Certain of the elders of Judah came to enquire of the Lord, and sat before me. Then came the word of the Lord, saying, 'Son of man, speak to the elders of Israel, and say unto them, thus says the Lord God** [not man]**: Are you come to enquire of me? As I live, says the Lord God, I will not be enquired of by you** [or in plain words: I don't want to talk to you]**."** But why is it so? Why doesn't God want to talk to His people who are seeking Him? Why doesn't God listen to most of us when we pray to Him or plead for help? Let's find out.

And so He said to Ezekiel: **"Will you judge them, son of man, will you judge them? Cause them to know the abominations of their fathers** [and obviously their own failings too]**."** Through the prophet, God tells His people that while they were still in Egypt, He assured them of the coming deliverance, and placed this request before them: **" . . . Cast you away every man the abominations of his eyes, and defile not yourselves with the idols of Egypt** [which they did], **I am the Lord your God** [not they]. **But they rebelled against Me, and would not listen to Me** [as most still don't]**: They did not every man cast the abomination of their eyes, neither did they forsake the idols of Egypt: Then I said, I will pour out My fury upon them, to accomplish My anger against them in the midst of the land of Egypt."** This reality was conveniently omitted in the famous movie "The Ten Commandments." Why? For the same reasons God refuses to hear His people—because of their unwillingness to look at the mirror of His Word and acknowledge what they see. This is a human trait all of us are 'blessed' with!

To uphold the honor of His name in the sight of the nations, God did not destroy His people in Egypt. He, nevertheless, brought them out of Egypt; gave them His Laws, and still they chose their own ways. In Verse 14 we read: **"But the house of Israel rebelled against Me in the wilderness; they walked not in My statutes, and they despised My judgments, which if a man do** [any man on earth], **he shall even live in them** [yet to this day, most Jews, 'Christians,' and Muslims despise God's laws—to their own hurt]**; and My Sabbaths** [not Jewish, 'Christian,' or Muslim, but "My Sabbaths"] **they greatly polluted: Then I said, I would pour out My fury upon them in the wilderness, to consume them."** But again, God had to uphold His honor in the sight of the nations, and so, He spared them again. He warned their children, the second generation, not to walk in the destructive paths of their parents, but follow Him and obey His laws which were for their own good, **"But,"** we read, **"notwithstanding, the children rebelled against Me; they walked not in My statutes, neither kept My judgments to do them . . ."** Again, God wanted to destroy them and scatter them among the nations [Verse 23], but, again, He restrained Himself for the sake of His own honor, not because they deserved it. All of us, all of humanity is in the same 'boat,' and yet we still deceive ourselves to believe otherwise!

It is because of their rebellious heart, God told His people, He is not willing to listen to their pleas. **"Therefore, son of man** [He told

Ezekiel], **speak unto the house of Israel** [and everyone who has an ear to hear], **and say unto them, 'thus says the Lord God; yet in this your fathers have blasphemed Me, in that they have committed a trespass against Me . . . As I live, says the Lord God, surely with a mighty hand, and with a stretched out arm, AND WITH FURY POURED OUT, WILL I RULE OVER YOU"** (Verse 33). But this is not the end of the story! God now switches to the future, saying: **"And I will bring you out from the people, and will gather you out from the countries wherein you are scattered, with a mighty hand, and with a stretched out arm** [and fellow Muslims, children of our common father Abraham, it's not of the Zionists' doing, but of Allah, the God of Abraham. He will do it], **and with a fury poured out. And I will bring you into the wilderness of the people** [east of the Jordan], **and there will I plead with you face to face. Like as I pleaded with your fathers in the wilderness of the land of Egypt, so will I plead with you, says the Lord your God. And I will cause you to pass under the rod, and I will bring you into the bond of the covenant** [which the whole house of Israel has rejected since the days of Egypt]; **AND I WILL PURGE OUT FROM AMONG YOU THE REBELS** [who are alive today], **and them that transgress against Me: I will bring them out of the country where they sojourn, AND THEY SHALL NOT ENTER INTO THE LAND OF ISRAEL** [not Palestine]; **AND YOU SHALL KNOW THAT I AM THE LORD"** [since now you still don't, and many among you even claim "God does not exist"].

And so, God's message to His people at that time is: Do your own thing, worship your idols, and believe in your fables and superstitions, until I am ready to deal with you, at the end-time! When that time comes, God says: **"For in My Mountain** [not Jewish, Christian, or Muslim], **in the Mountain of the height of Israel** [not Palestine], **says the Lord God, there shall all the house of Israel** [not all Christians, Palestinians, Arabs, or Muslims], **all of them in the land, serve Me; there will I accept them . . . And you shall know that I am the Lord, when I** [and not man] **shall bring you into the land of Israel, into the country for which I lifted My hand to give it to your fathers. And there you shall remember your ways, and all your doings, wherein you have been defiled** [to this very day]; **and YOU SHALL LOATH YOURSELVES IN YOUR OWN SIGHT FOR ALL YOUR EVILS THAT YOU HAVE COMMITTED"**

(Ezekiel 20:34-43). These are plain words for all those who have ears to hear! Are you one of them?

What is not known to most of us is the identity of all the tribes of Israel—and their whereabouts in the past many centuries. The Jews, those who are still known as Jews, are but a small fraction of the whole house of Israel. It is not the intent of this author to reveal their identity or present location in this work, in detail. Suffice it to say, and believe it or not, most of those calling themselves Christians in the English speaking Anglo-Saxon world; most of those in NW Europe, in North America—and many white 'Muslims' in the "STAN" countries, like AfghaniaSTAN, PakiSTAN—and many countries around that region and Northern India, are descendants of the house of Israel! For more revealing and shocking details, please check out this author's monumental work (710 pages) in the real roots, and 4,000 years history of the Middle East conflict—and the true identity of all its players—both in the Middle East and the Western world. The Title of this work is mentioned on one of the first pages of this book. It is: ***Middle East: Blueprint For the Final Solution,*** subtitled: ***"The Coming fall and Rise of Western Democracy."*** By "Final Solution," we are not referring to Hitler's concept of destruction and death, but to God's ultimate solution, which is "Paradise" on earth. It can be obtained faster and for the best price directly from any major book—store or at Amazon.com or the publisher of this work's website at: http://www.authorhouse.com/bookstore/ItemDetail.aspx?bookid=16130

Yes, Truth can be more fascinating than fiction! The whole house of Israel is composed of hundreds of millions of Christians, Muslims, and few millions of known Jews. Unfortunately, most of them are confused about the true faith of their fathers due to millennia of misguided and mostly blind 'spiritual' teachers and instructions. This condition is a sad reality that prevails to this very day, yet not for long.

Through the prophet Zechariah, God recorded these words about the spiritual state of His people at the time of the soon coming days of deliverance: **"In that day there shall be a fountain opened to the house of David and to the inhabitants of Jerusalem FOR SIN AND FOR UNCLEANNESS. And it shall come to pass in that day, says the Lord of Hosts** [not man], **that I will cut off the names of the [modern day] idols out of the land [of Israel], and they shall no more be remembered. And ALSO, I WILL CAUSE THE PROPHETS [or 'spiritual' teachers]**

AND THE UNCLEAN SPIRIT TO PASS OUT OF THE LAND. And it shall come to pass in that day, that the prophet [who now thinks he is serving God and is teaching His Words] **SHALL BE ASHAMED EVERYONE OF HIS VISION** [or 'spiritual' concoctions, supposing it is for 'Heaven's name'], **WHEN HE HAS PROPHESIED** [not God]; **NEITHER SHALL THEY WEAR A ROUGH GARMENT TO DECEIVE"** (Zechariah 13:1-4).

These are plain words for those who have ears to hear and eyes to see! Whom are the 'spiritual teachers' kidding with their religious garments? Those who do not have "the love of the truth" are the ones easily taken in their snare. All these words are a bit of a background as to how the doctrines of *"The Afterlife"* or of Heaven and Hell, as well as many other fables, have crept into the minds of unsuspecting, gullible followers of the "Angel of Light" and his "Ministers of Righteousness." Tragically, many are paying bundles of treasures for fake 'Life insurance policies,' and don't even care to know about it! You don't have to be one of them!

God warned us: **"Woe unto them that call evil good and good evil; that put darkness for light, and light for darkness; that put bitter for sweet, and sweet for bitter! Woe unto them who are wise IN THEIR OWN EYES, and prudent in their own sight!"** (Isaiah 5:20-21). Why do we do that? We do it because to "walk in the light" we must reject darkness **AND OBEY THE TRUTH.** And that is just 'too much to ask!' We do not want to "walk in the narrow path," we prefer the "broad way." We don't like to be restricted—as even children, from a young age, hate it. Paul put it this way: **"The carnal** [or physical] **mind has animosity toward God; it is not subject to the Law** [Torah or instructions] **of God, neither indeed can be"** (Romans 8:7). But why is it so? Because as the comedian Flip Wilson used to say, "The Devil made me do it," and indeed he does, and to all of us! That's why most of humanity had fallen for the fables of the afterlife, of Heaven and Hell—and other such fiction of the confused human spirit. Hollywood, and the movie industry worldwide, exploit this weakness of the hopelessly superstitious masses and laugh all the way to the bank. Religion has exploited this weak-minded tendency of its followers—using it to control and exploit them. But it doesn't have to be so! We can scrutinize 'the fine lines' throughout the pages of "The Holy Books" of the three religions that claim to follow in the footsteps of the "father of the faith"—Abraham—and see, hopefully, the light!

And so now we shall begin with the religion of Judaism to unveil the differences between their concepts, in the past two millenniums, about the doctrines of the *afterlife* and Heaven and Hell, in contrast to the plain statements in their "Holy Book." They came first, and so to the Jew we shall go first!

CHAPTER 2

JEWISH CONCEPTS ABOUT
THE AFTERLIFE, HEAVEN & HELL

In order to properly cover this subject, we must first clarify many centuries' old misconceptions—both in the Jewish and Gentile world—about the origins of the Jews and their ancient link to many in the Christian and Muslim world. We shall present here a brief history of this critical issue, for sake of space, and due to the fact it is not the subject of this work. Those who want the whole story are encouraged to read this author's monumental work (710 pp.), titled, *"Middle East: Blueprint for the Final [Rosy] Solution,"* as mentioned earlier in this work. It contains an exhaustive Biblical and secular ancient historic writings about the 4,000 years saga of all the descendants of Abraham from his multiple wives.

It is most common to hear within the Jewish community and among non-Jews the following statements, among many others: "Abraham was the first Jew; the Jews were delivered out of Egypt; the Jews were given the Torah or Law in Sinai, and thus all their holidays, like Sabbath, Passover, Rosh Hashanah, and others are Jewish. The Jews are the chosen people and the rightful inheritors of the land of Canaan. All the covenants and promises were given to the Jews. To them, the Jewish Prophets came—from Moses to Malachi." What is missing in these statements? Let's put it this way: All Californians are Americans, but all Americans are not Californians! And this is what we need to clarify about the identity of the Jews before we can explore their concepts about the **afterlife**, about Heaven and Hell.

Let's get it strait! Abraham was not a Jew, or a Muslim, according to Islam! Father Abraham was the first Hebrew and progenitor of all the Hebrews. He was named, *"Abraham the Hebrew"* because he came from *"Over the River"* Euphrates. Abraham and all of his descendants were, initially, named *"the Hebrews."* Later, when Moses appeared before Pharaoh, he introduced God as *"the God of the Hebrews"* (Exodus

5:3). The first son of Abraham was Ishmael. His Mother, Hagar, was an Egyptian woman and Sarah's maid. Nevertheless, his father was Abraham the Hebrew—hence Ishmael was a Hebrew. In Biblical times, unlike in post-second-Temple rabbinic era, a child's status was determined by his father, not his mother. As time went by, Ishmael's descendants were no longer referred to as "Hebrews," even though, being sons of Abraham, technically, they are still Hebrews. Their future territory extended into much of the present Middle East lands. They also lived in proximity to other children of Abraham.

Isaac was the son of two Hebrews—Abraham and Sarah. His two sons, Esau or Edom and Jacob, later to be also named Israel, were twin sons of two Hebrews, namely, Isaac and Rebecca. As time went by, many of Esau's descendants gradually ceased to be called "Hebrews." They were scattered in later years into many areas and did not consider themselves any longer "Hebrews." Yet there was an exception with a large part of the Edomites, Jacob's brothers, who first settled immediately north of the land of Israel—present day Lebanon—anciently known as Phoenicia. Why was it called Phoenicia and by whom? Historians tell us that The war-like people of Phoenicia, displaced the original natives, subjugated the rest of them, and gave the land their own name, Phoenicia or 'Red,' which in Hebrew, the language of their ancestors Abraham, Sarah, Isaac and Rebecca, meant also red or Edom. The fascinating details and historic accounts can be further explored in this author's work, "Middle East..," which was mentioned earlier. The sea-exploring Phoenicians have established many colonies in different parts of the globe. Along with the navy crews of King Solomon, as we read in I Kings, they circumnavigated the whole world every three years. They established ancient colonies in the Americas, Europe, North Africa, and elsewhere. When their demise came in the land of the Red people (Edom) or Phoenicia, many of them migrated into their main colony in Europe—Spain or Biblical Tarshish. They named the whole peninsula *"Iberia"* or the *"Land of the Hebrews."* Yes, these are the Spanish people! Their main lands in the Middle East are: Iraq, the Gulf States, along the cost of The Red Sea (or Sea of Edom) in the western part of present day Saudi-Arabia, and in Yemen. Many of them are still living in and around the State of Israel, and they are known today as Palestinians. Yes, at times, truth is more fascinating than fiction! But there is much more to the story!

After the death of Sarah, Abraham married his third wife, Keturah. He also had many concubines. According to second Temple era, the Jewish historian Josephus Flavius, who initially fought the Romans and then joined them before the destruction of the second Temple, Abraham had thirty-two sons from his wife Keturah and the concubines. Before his death, Abraham sent them away eastward in order to avoid inheritance problems after his death. Imagine what would have happened in today's Middle East conflict had he not done that in his lifetime. All these sons were also known as Hebrews, until gradually they too lost that identity. What they had left in their collective historic accounts was the knowledge of being descendants of father Abraham the Hebrew. The descendants of these people were also later to be scattered into many areas. Many of them went into North Africa. Abraham's grandson Ephron's descendants migrated into present day Libya, and later named the whole continent after their father's name—Africa. Josephus called all of Abraham's sons, "colonialists." Wherever they went, they established colonies and gave them their own names. This was one major clue many savvy historians employed in tracking down the location of Abraham's offspring—throughout history and to this day.

Another grandson of Abraham, namely, Ashurim, settled an area adjacent to ancient Assyria. These were among the fiercest and most cruel destroyers of the ancient world. Yes, these are the very ancestors of the Germans who already, in ancient times, have established colonies in modern day Germany. The first colony, established by the ancient 'Germans' is the oldest city of Trier. The people of Ashurim, however, though very much admired by the Assyrians, were of a different nature. Josephus, again, tells us that the land of Assyria was named after these children of Abraham. In other words, there were two different peoples of Assyria, though living in adjacent lands. These people later migrated with the neighboring Assyrians into Western Europe, after their defeat by the Medes, with the help of the Israelite tribes that were taken one hundred years earlier captives by the Assyrians. The final destination of the fierce, though defeated Assyrians, was their ancient colonies in present day Germany. The People of Ashurim, the other Assyrian nation, joined their neighboring Assyrian migration and settled next to them . . . in present day Austria. According to some historians, in the chronology of the kings or dukes of Austria, the first one topping the list is no other than the Patriarch Abraham. Obviously, as time went by, these formerly known

24

Hebrews, descendants of the **"father of many nations,"** also gradually lost their identity as the children of 'the first Hebrew' Abraham. But this is not the end of the story—it gets more fascinating with the history of Israel!

When the tribes of Israel had entered into the land of Canaan, under the leadership of Joshua, they were all united and continued to be so until after the death of the elders who outlived Joshua. Shortly after the death of the elders of Israel, most of Israel went back to their old way—idolatry. God raised enemies against them to drive them back to Himself. Often He would raise them a deliverer who would lead them back to worship their true God, but soon after, they, again, would relapse into idol worship. These accounts are recorded in the book of Judges. The tribes at that low point in their history became divided and no longer cohesive as a nation. Their relapse into idolatry was influenced by the state of mind of their tribal and spiritual leadership. Their departure away from their God was sporadic. The tribes followed the customs and idols of those living in close proximity to their borders.

When the prophet Samuel came on the scene, he united again all the tribes of Israel under his leadership—leading them back to their God. Yet their loyalty to their Creator and Deliverer from Egypt was not complete or wholehearted. Later, King Saul, who was anointed by Samuel king over all Israel, according to the instructions of God, led all the tribes of Israel for a period of forty years. Toward the end of his reign, because of his unfaithfulness to his Heavenly King—God—he was rejected in favor of the future King David, **"the man according to God's own heart."** When King David took over the reign over Israel, it was a bitterly divided nation and at war from within. It was the first war between two rival and bitterly opposing factions—the South, led by Judah, against the North, led by Benjamin. David was a Southerner from Judah, while Saul's Royal House retained the loyalty of the North, the first 'Yankees' of history. Finally, the old 'Yankees' of Northern Israel's tribes agreed to come under the rule of the new King David—who in the early days of Saul's reign was the most loved champion of Israel—after killing the archenemy Goliath.

During his reign, his own son Absalom mounted a coup against his own father, David. Again, Judah remained loyal to King David, while much of Israel followed the short lived rebellion by his son. Again, David restored all of the tribes of Israel to a union under God and king. He conquered all of his enemies and built an empire that stretched from the

River Euphrates to the borders of Egypt. This was the "Promised Land." Forty years later, after having Solomon his son anointed king over all united Israel, David died. It was during the absolute and glorious reign of King Solomon that Israel prospered beyond imagination and was known as the 'Shangri-La' or dreamed of utopia of the ancient world. At no other time in Israel's history had "the chosen people" enjoyed the fabulous bounty and height of peace, riches, and security as it did in the days of the absolutely United Monarchy under the wisest king of Israel, Solomon, and God's beloved.

Tragically, this euphoric utopia did not last for long. Wise old King Solomon was not that wise after all at the end of his glorious reign. He allowed his many beautiful women, one thousand of them (perish the thought) to lead him astray into idolatry. His women came from many nations and religions. Many were given to him, as was then the custom, by the many foreign dignitaries who traveled the length and breadth of the earth to take a glimpse at the famous 'Shangri-La' of their days. When King Solomon died, his son Rehobam ascended to the Ivory Throne of his most famous and richest father. Shortly after, the whole country was thrown into the throes of a tax-based (what's new) fomented rebellion against the House of David. Again, it was to be a straight line division between North and South. The 'Yankees' and the South were at it again!

Jeroboam, a very talented leader from the tribe of Ephraim, who was previously chosen for his exceptional abilities by King Solomon, was appointed as the head of the building task force over his tribe. Toward the end of Solomon's reign, divisions arose between him and the king over the issue of heavy taxation and other matters. That conflict aroused the ire of King Solomon against Jeroboam who, in turn, was forced to flee into Egypt. Earlier, the Pharaoh of Egypt struck an alliance with King Solomon and gave him his daughter to wife. Later, however, perhaps during the reign of the next Pharaoh, King Solomon's relations with him became chilly. After the death of Solomon, Jeroboam had returned to assume the reign over his tribe Ephraim. Together, with the rest of the greatly disgruntled tribal leaders of Israel, because of the heavy burden of taxation and hard labor required for the grandiose building projects of the king, Jeroboam confronted the new and young king with most reasonable demands: Reduce the heavy burden of taxation and hard labor and we shall all serve you, but if you refuse to accept our demands, all of us will reject your reign over us! Initially, King Rehobam acted wisely.

He asked them to give him three days for consultations, to which they agreed, before giving them his final answer. He then proceeded, first, to ask the wise councilors of his father Solomon for an advice. Their reply was simple: "Be nice to them, they'll be nice to you." Then he proceeded to ask his own young, haughty, and inexperienced advisers for their counsel. Their reply was the height of arrogance and stupidity, which led to the downfall of the empire and the permanent division between North and South. It brought not only a political division, but worse, an almost total alienation in religion, culture, and brotherly relations between North and South. Their advice was: " . . . **Thus shall you speak unto this people that spoke to you, saying, 'Your father made our yoke heavy, but make you it lighter unto us;' thus shall you say unto them, 'My little finger shall be thicker than my father's loins** [a statement the king, wisely, did not convey]. **And now as my father did lay on you a heavy yoke, I will add to your yoke; my father had chastised you with whips, but I will chastise you with scorpions"** (I Kings 12:9-11). Upon considering these harsh words, one might say, after all, King George wasn't that bad. Now we are paying a far heavier burden of taxes than he required in his day.

Thus, North and South became perpetual avowed enemies, shedding much blood of their own brothers during the numerous wars between them. Had King Rehobam acted wisely, the history of the world would have been greatly different! By the same token, had King George acted differently, all American colonies would have been still subjects of the British Royal House. In both cases, such was not the will of the God of Israel, as we shall see later.

The United Monarchy of Kings David and Solomon was torn between the two rival camps. The southern part of the nation, headed by the tribe of Judah was joined by half of the tribe of Benjamin, most of Levi, and those Israelites who remained loyal to the royal house of David. Their capital was, of course, Jerusalem, and the Temple remained under the control of the smaller kingdom of Judah. When King Rehoboam attempted to reunite the nation by force, he was told by a Prophet of God to avoid doing it since such was the will of God (I Kings 12:22-24). Jeroboam, by God's design, became the king of the ten northern tribes of Israel. He soon moved to bring about a total separation, politically, culturally, and religiously from the southern kingdom. Fearing that at festival times, when all Israel came to keep God's Holy Days in the Temple at Jerusalem, his people will gravitate back towards the House of David. Jeroboam, the newly installed king of Israel, built two religious centers of worship to accommodate his people's desire to worship God. Unfortunately for him and the future of the new nation, Israel, he introduced again idol worship in the nation of God. He built two golden calves and placed them, one in Bethel—the place where Jacob first met God—and the other calf he placed in Dan, in the northern part of the country. Thus Jeroboam succeeded in fostering a total separation between the two newly divided kingdoms of Israel.

The two new nations, the North and South, coexisted side by side—at times at war against each other, at other times under mutual alliances. The first war between the two brother nations took place under the reign of Rehoboam's son, King Abijah. During his three short years reign, King Abijah was forced into waging war against King Jeroboam. The king of Israel was now attempting to subdue the kingdom of Judah in an effort to unify the land under his rule. But such attempt was not pleasing to God. King Abijah warned the king of Israel of the consequences and reminded him that the Temple and priesthood were still in Jerusalem. Judah, he reminded the warring king, was still faithful to her God—while Israel, under the instigation of the disobedient king, was led into rank idolatry. The response from the king and his armies was complete scorn and disdain for the king of Judah, his armies, and religion. The battle began with the king of Judah calling on God for help. The 'fierce lions' of Judah and 'devouring wolves of Benjamin' went into action. When after a one day battle the war was over, a macabre and gruesome scene was left behind on the ground. **HALF A MILLION SOLDIERS OF THE ARMIES OF ISRAEL HAD FALLEN DEAD**, drenching the ground of the "Promised Land" with their flowing brotherly blood. How many were killed on the side of the southern kingdom, how many wounded on both sides, we don't know. Yet certainly, this first war, after the division of the United Monarchy—a war between brothers—had left very deep and painful marks on the psyche of the northern nation for many years to come. It reminds one of the Anglo-American bitter wars between two brother nations, as well as the later civil war between the Northern and Southern Armies of the bitterly divided American brothers.

That first avoidable war between children of common ancestry, and those fought after, had sown the seeds of eternal hatred and animosities between the sons of Jacob—and its sour impact is still with us to this very day. Though the two nations of common ancestry and destiny were later to be separated from each other by consecutive captivities—the inbred animosities and ill feelings for each other followed them for many generations to come. At the end-time God promised to heal the breach between the "two sticks" of Judah and Joseph, as was recorded in a prophecy by Ezekiel the prophet.

The first time the term *Jews* appeared in the Bible is recorded in II Kings. It's one of the books that chronicles the history of **"both houses of Israel,"** as Isaiah the prophet referred to them (Isaiah 8:14). This event took place few years prior to the captivity of the northern kingdom of Israel by the armies of Assyria—the ancestors of the modern Germans. Here we read: **"Then Rezin king of Syria** [the Assad of that day] **and Pekah son of Remaliah king of Israel came up to Jerusalem to war; and they besieged Ahaz** [king of Judah]**, but could not overcome him. At that time Rezin king of Syria recovered Eilat** [today's southern port of Israel] **to Syria, AND DROVE THE JEWS FROM EILAT; and the Syrians came to Eilat, and dwelt there unto this day"** (II Kings 16:5-6). Imagine that! Syria in those days laid a claim, not to the Golan Heights, but to the southern port of Eilat at the tip of the Negev Desert. The Middle East conflict is an old story!

This strange event, which found Israel in an alliance with Syria against brother Judah, took place in the days of Isaiah the prophet. Speaking of this very event and treacherous conduct by Israel against brother Judah or the Jews, Isaiah was told to deliver the famous words—known by all in the Christian community—and many of them, though ignorant of it, are the very descendants of the people Isaiah is prophesying against in this prophecy. He wrote: **"For the head of Syria is Damascus and the head of Damascus is Rezin; and within three score and five years** [or 65 years] **shall Ephraim** [the northern kingdom of Israel] **be broken** [taken into captivity]**, that it be not a people. And the head of Ephraim is Samaria** [today the West Bank]**, and the head of Samaria is Remaliah's son . . . Moreover the Lord spoke unto Ahaz, saying, ask for a sign of the Lord your God . . . but Ahaz said, I will not ask for a sign, neither will I tempt the Lord . . . Therefore the Lord Himself shall give you a sign: 'BEHOLD A VIRGIN** [Alma, or maiden in Hebrew] **SHALL CONCEIVE AND BEAR A SON, AND SHALL CALL HIS NAME EMMANUEL [NOT JESUS]. BUTTER AND HONEY SHALL HE EAT, THAT HE MAY KNOW TO REFUSE THE EVIL, AND CHOOSE THE GOOD.** [Now notice what the Christian community has deliberately ignored in their arguments with the Jews, for the past many centuries, concerning this passage!] **FOR BEFORE THE CHILD SHALL KNOW TO REFUSE THE EVIL, AND CHOOSE THE GOOD, THE LAND THAT YOU [Ahaz] ABHOR SHALL BE FORSAKEN OF BOTH HER KINGS** [speaking of the lands of Israel and Syria]. **The Lord shall bring upon you, and upon your people, and upon your father's house, days that have not come** [or occurred], **from the day that Ephraim departed from Judah; even the king of Assyria"** (Isaiah 7:8-17).

What many do not consider, on both sided of the argument, is the background to these words of the Prophet. Isaiah had sons whose names symbolized future events in the history of his people. The first one was *"Shear-Jashub"* (Heb. Yashub). It means: *"The remnant (of Israel) shall return"* (Isaiah 7:3). The second son of Isaiah was named *"Maher-Shalal-Hash-Baz"* (Isaiah 8:1-3). This name refers to the coming invasion of the king of Assyria against Israel, the northern kingdom, and Syria. It describes the manner and actions of the Assyrians: *"Maher"* means **very quickly**; *"Shalal"* means **the spoil**; *"Hash-Baz"* means **swiftly be spoiled**.

Of his sons, Isaiah declared: **"And I will wait upon the Lord that hides His face from the house of Jacob, and I will look for Him. Behold, I AND THE CHILDREN THE LORD HAS GIVEN ME ARE FOR SIGNS AND FOR WONDERS IN ISRAEL FROM THE LORD OF HOSTS which dwells in Mount Zion"** (Isaiah 8:17-18). Then, shortly after describing the reasons for the names of his sons, Isaiah writes about another son. This son is not his, but Israel's son. He writes: **"For unto us** [not to me] **a child is born, unto us a son is given; and the government shall be upon His shoulders; and His name shall be called wonderful, counselor, the everlasting father, the Prince of peace. Of the increase of His government and peace there shall be no end, upon the throne of David, and upon His kingdom, to order it, and to establish it with judgment and with justice from henceforth even forever. The zeal of the Lord of Hosts will perform it"** (Isaiah 9:6-7).

This is the forth son mentioned by Isaiah, but who is the third son, born of **"the maiden"** or **"Alma"** in Hebrew, and translated into **"virgin"** in other languages? The account is very plain! Though in the New Testament this account is attributed to the engaged **"Alma"** Mary or Miriam who was also a virgin, Isaiah speaks of this child as a testimony of events in his days. As he plainly explains: **"For BEFORE [NOT EIGHT CENTURIES LATER] the child shall know to refuse the evil, and choose the good, the land that you [Ahaz] abhor shall be forsaken of both her kings** [Pekah king of Israel and Rezin king of Syria].**"** Let's remember that Isaiah was still present when the kingdom of Israel was taken into captivity! Could this third son be his from a second wife? Could he be from someone else's new wife? We are not told either way. What we know is this: Isaiah stated that his children were given to him as signs, from the Lord, for the house of Israel. **Linking the Virgin Mary to this maiden is a matter of metaphor, not literal!** Thus in reality, the argument is mute. This is an example of how 'spiritual leaders,' who lean to their own understanding, confuse the minds of many—because they are confused themselves. And this is the reason why we are bringing this issue, as well as others, as a background that would explain the formation of false doctrines among the children of Abraham.

The political division among the people of Jacob gave rise to a much more destructive element in the breakaway nation of the northern kingdom—Israel. It was the formation of a new religion—a mixture composed of the religion of God and foreign idol worship borrowed from the nations around. The golden calves erected by Jeroboam were a product of their idolatrous life in Egypt. Other elements were added from the religions of the nations around Israel. Most of the faithful Priests and Levites relocated into the nation of Judah so they could attend to the Temple services. The remaining Levites and Priests either kept the true faith in a hostile environment, or gradually faded away into the mixed religion of Israel. Jeroboam opened the door to the priesthood to anyone willing to buy the office. Most of them were ignorant of the Laws of God and His ways. The age of the false prophets was in full swing. Gradually, this new brand of priesthood was infiltrating the southern kingdom of Judah. From that time on, few and far in between were the true Prophets of God. Most of them lived under constant fear and threat in both kingdoms. A thorough reading of that period would quickly reveal how far down the spiritual drain both nations sunk into, and rapidly. The books of Kings, Chronicles, and the Prophets revealed and recorded for posterity, in detail, this spiritual demise of the once enlightened nation of Israel—the kingdom of God on earth.

Because of their rank apostasy, God caused their enemies to invade, destroy, and take the rest into captivity. The first nation to be conquered by what God labeled, "the worst of the nations," was Israel, the northern kingdom. They were taken by Assyria into the areas beyond the Euphrates, the lands of the Medes, and the Caucasus mountains. Since the day they had rejected the true religion of their God, in the days of their first king, Jeroboam, as a whole, they never returned to Him, His religion, and His Temple worship. As they went into captivity, they carried with them a mixed religion made of God's and many foreign religious teachings. After the fall of Assyria, which was defeated by the Medes and Persians, with help from the Israelites, many Assyrians began a long migration into their final destination and former colonies in present day Germany. Being pushed forward by the hordes of the Assyrians, many Israelites also began migrating, through different routes, towards the borders of the Roman Empire. Later, they began migrating in successive land journeys into Northwest Europe and the British Isles—where many Israelites were already settled, some since the days of Egypt as we can read in the old Chronicles of Ire or later Ireland. The 'Levites' and apostate Priests who joined these successive Israelite migrations into the new lands, brought with them what became later known as the religion of "the Druids." The doctrines of the "**afterlife**," of Heaven and Hell, of the Immortality of the soul, were already entrenched in this religion of the "Druids" since their days in the land of Israel. It is not the purpose of this work to cover this subject in detail. Those interested in the Biblical and historic background and details of the migrating Israelites are advised to consult this author's exhaustive and monumental work (over 700 pp.) titled, ***"Middle East: Blueprint for the Final . . ."***

Other Israelites, as was mentioned earlier, either remained in nearby lands or migrated into other Eastern countries. They are there to this very day, and many of them still retain the knowledge of their very tribal ancestry. Many joined the religion of Islam; some joined other eastern religions, while still practicing a mixture of their 'old' religion. All of them believed, and still do, in various concepts about the **afterlife**, immortality of the soul, and Heaven-Hell teachings.

When we consider the concepts of the Jews, all children of Israel, and their doctrines about the "**afterlife**," Heaven and Hell, or immortality of the soul, we should take into account the history of the northern kingdom of Israel. Without this critical information taken into consideration, it is impossible to understand and fully appreciate the Biblical teachings about all the tribes of Israel and their religious beliefs.

All the tribes of Israel were profoundly affected by the cultures and religions around them. Jacob's wife—Rachel—stole her father's gods when the whole family fled from Haran. Before going down to Egypt, Jacob commanded all members of his family to hand over all the foreign gods and pagan artifacts in their possessions. Though he buried them in the ground, under a big tree, many in his very family had already hidden them deep in their heart. Shortly after the death of Joseph and his brothers in Egypt, Pharaoh has forcibly enslaved Israel. But why is it so? As was mentioned earlier, the prophet Ezekiel, in Chapter 20, revealed the real causes for Israel's enslavement—rank idolatry with all the gods of Egypt. The 'golden calf' was worshiped by the Israelites at Mount Sinai, immediately after God spoke to them directly and gave them His commandments. He warned them not to worship any other false gods but Him alone! Why didn't they listen? God took them out of Egypt, but they refused to cast Egypt out of their hearts! The 'golden calf' was a natural consequence.

In his last words to the second generation, shortly before they were to enter into the "Land of Promise," Moses wrote: **"For I know that after my death you will utterly corrupt yourselves, and turn aside from the way which I have commanded you; and evil will befall you in the LATER DAYS; because you will do evil in the sight of the Lord, to provoke Him to anger through the work of your hands"** (Deuteronomy 31:29). In a song of testimony against His people, God told Moses to write the following words: **"THEY SACRIFICED UNTO DEMONS** [while wandering in the wilderness and later in the land], **not to God; to gods whom they knew not** [before entering into the land of Canaan], **to new gods that came newly up, whom your fathers feared not. Of the Rock that begat you, you are unmindful, and has forgotten God that formed you"** (Deuteronomy 32:17:18).

After Joshua and all the generation that conquered the land had died, we read: **" . . . And there arose another generation after them, which knew not the Lord, nor yet the works which He had done for Israel. And the children of Israel did evil in the sight of the Lord and served Baalim** [or Canaanite gods]**; and they forsook the Lord God of their fathers, which brought them out of Egypt, and followed other gods, of the gods of the people that were round about them, and bowed themselves unto them, and provoked the Lord to anger. And they forsook the Lord, and served Baal and Ashtarot** {a Canaanite goddess of fertility, later renamed Easter]. **And the anger of the Lord was hot against Israel, and He delivered them into the hands of spoilers** [the Arabs and Palestinians of their day] **that spoiled them, and He sold them into the hands of their enemies round about** [but to this day they never learn], **so that they could not any longer stand before their enemies. Wherever they went out, the hand of the Lord was against them for evil** [and they still don't get it], **as the Lord had said and as the Lord had sworn unto them . . .**" (Judges 2:10-15).

When the Northern nation of Israel was taken into captivity, this is what their King and Lord of Hosts, against whom they have rebelled at every turn of the way, had inspired to be recorded: **"The children of Israel had sinned against the Lord their God . . . and walked in the statutes of the heathen . . . they set images and groves in every high hill and under every green tree . . . and did wicked things to provoke the Lord to anger . . . and the Lord testified against Israel, and against Judah, by all the Prophets . . . notwithstanding they would not hear, but hardened their necks . . . and they rejected His statutes, and His covenant . . . and they left all the commandments of the Lord their God and made molten images, even two calves . . . and worshiped all the host of Heaven, and served Baal. And they caused their sons and their daughters to pass through the fire, and used divination and enchantments** [which many still do on every corner, on the internet, in newspapers' astrology sections, and on talk shows—since it's so popular to this day] **. . . and sold themselves to do evil in the sight of the Lord, to provoke Him to anger. Therefore the Lord was very angry with Israel, and removed them out of His sight; there was none left but the tribe of Judah only. Also Judah kept not the commandments of the Lord their God, but walked in the statutes of Israel, which they made. And the Lord rejected all the seed of Israel, and afflicted them** [as He continued to do whenever they would reject Him, and to this very day, though most are not aware of it], **and delivered them into the hands of the spoilers, until He has cast them out of His sight"** (II Kings Chapter 17).

All these statements should be taken into account when we consider the issues at hand! In the old days, as well as in our days, those who claim to serve God fail to look into the mirror of His Law—the Royal Law or Torah—to look at themselves the way God sees them. Therefore they believe all their teachings and actions are acceptable to Him and are pleasing in His sight. They fail to examine their own man-made teachings with those recorded in

His "Holy Books." These concepts include the ones on **'the afterlife'** and many others. In the pages of this book we shall do so!

When a small part of the Jews were allowed to return back to their ravaged homeland, this is what their most honest and genuine spiritual leaders confessed before their God, after recounting the whole history of their people. They declared: **"But they and our fathers dealt proudly, and hardened their necks, and harkened not to Your commandments, and REFUSED TO OBEY, neither were mindful of Your wonders that You did among them; but hardened their necks ... but You are a God ready to pardon, gracious and merciful, slow to anger, and of great kindness** [even though many are quick to portray Him, when things go wrong, as a harsh God], **and forsook them not."** After recounting more of the history of their people, they added: **"Nevertheless they were disobedient, and rebelled against You, and cast Your Law [or Torah] behind their back** [which most of them still do to this very day], **and SLEW YOUR PROPHETS which testified against them to turn them to You, and they committed great provocations. Therefore You delivered them into the hands of their enemies, who vexed them; and in the time of their trouble, when they cried unto You, You heard them from Heaven, and according to Your manifold mercies You gave them saviors, who saved them out of the hands of their enemies. But after they had rest, they did evil again ..."** (Nehemiah 9). Things are not different today, nor are they any better! They are not better among the people of Israel or the nations of the earth. None is guiltless!

All the nations around the land of Israel had practiced religions that taught fables, from God's point of view, as we shall see later, about the **afterlife,** immortality of the soul and Heaven and hell. Contrary to the wide beliefs among all the children of Abraham about these fables, superstitious, and notions about **'the world beyond,'** the Words inspired by God and were preserved by faithful men, tell us a different story. As long as the people of Israel followed the pure teachings of their God, their understanding of **'the world to come'** was far different than the concepts taught to them by their 'spiritual leaders' in the past two millenniums. You, the reader, will be given ample proof from the very pages of your "Holy Books" so you can know the difference between "the holy and the profane."

There is no need to believe any man's interpretation! Prove it for yourself! God warned us about putting our faith and trust in man, when

He told His Prophet Jeremiah to record these words for all those who have ears to hear. He declared, **"Thus says the Lord: Cursed be the man that trusts in man, and makes flesh his arm, and whose heart departs from the Lord"** (Jeremiah 17:5). Why do people believe in what they believe? Because they put their trust in man, they 'check their brains at the door' when they enter a house of worship—and that's how they "depart from the Lord"! That's how they end up believing fables and superstitions, while being convinced all along those ideas are found in their "Holy Books." They don't "prove all things." From the beginning, God warned our first parents not to eat from "the tree of the knowledge of good and evil." Yet Adam and Eve rejected this loving admonition—and so do almost all of their descendants to this very day. They eat of the "tree of the knowledge of good and evil" and then complain about the results. When calamities come, they immediately complain, like Gideon: **"Oh my Lord, if the Lord be with us, why then is all this befallen us** [why did God let Johnny die, or where was God in the Holocaust]? **And where are all His miracles which our fathers told us of, saying, did not the Lord bring us out of Egypt? But now the Lord has forsaken us** [it's all His fault, not ours] **and delivered us into the hands of the Midianites"** (Judges 6:13). What a copout? How convenient it is to place the blame on God when things go wrong! Man rejects the instructions of His maker, he eats of the wrong tree, he rejects God's Law or Torah, and he invents fables and superstitions and follows them, and then has the audacity to complain when things go wrong!

In contrast to this bigoted attitude on the part of many, David, "a man according to God's heart," wrote: **"The law [or Torah] of the Lord is perfect** [and there is no need to 'supplement' it with the poisonous fruit of the wrong tree. Therefore this Law is] **converting the soul; the testimony of the Lord is sure, making wise the simple** [so he can 'see' if the "Emperor is naked"]. **The statutes of the Lord are right** [not wrong], **rejoicing the heart; the commandment of the Lord is pure, enlightening the eyes. The fear [or reverence] of the Lord is clean, enduring forever; the judgments of the Lord are true and righteous altogether. More to be desired are they than gold; sweeter also than honey and the honeycomb. Moreover by them is your servant warned** [to keep out of the 'mine fields of life']; **and in keeping of them there is great rewards** [not miseries and calamities]. **Who can understand his errors** [and be honest enough to acknowledge them]? **Cleanse You me** from secrets faults. **Keep back Your servant from presumptuous sins; let them not have dominion over me. Then shall I be upright, and I shall be innocent from the great transgression. Let the words of my mouth, and the meditation of my heart, be acceptable in Your sight my Lord, and my Redeemer"** (Psalm 19:7-14).

David had 'eyes to see'—most of us are blind, do not know it, and are unwilling to acknowledge it. That's why we believe fables, and that's why we eat, ignorantly, from the wrong tree, believing we are eating of the "tree of life" of which God had commanded our first parents and all of us to eat from it freely. If we don't, it's because we lack true wisdom. Wise King Solomon wrote of such wisdom: **"Happy is the man that finds such wisdom and the man that gets understanding"** (Proverbs 3:13). David his father told us how one acquires such wisdom: **"The fear of the Lord is the beginning of wisdom; a good understanding have all they that do [not despise] His commandments . . ."** (Psalm 111:10). Many can't tell whether the "Emperor is naked" or not because they neither fear nor keep God's commandments. Solomon had more to say about "Wisdom," and declared: **"For the merchandise of it [of wisdom] is better than the merchandise of silver and the gain thereof than fine gold. She is more precious than rubies; and all the things you can desire are not worthy to be compared unto her. Length of days is in her right hand; and in her left hand riches and honor. Her ways are the ways of pleasantness, and all her paths are peace** [which is not to be found in illusive and wishful thinking of "peace negotiations"]. **She is a tree of life [only] to them that lay hold upon her, and happy is EVERY ONE that retains her"** (Proverbs 3:14-18).

How many are eating of this freely offered "tree of life?" For those seriously interested, this author has a series of over 700 free lectures describing, in detail, the nature of this "tree of life" or the Torah—from Genesis to the book of Revelation. Check out our free website at: www. teachingthelaw.org. It can be downloaded for free. In it you'll find out the answers even to the questions you did not know to ask.

A Jew, and yours truly is one of them, is taught from his youth to believe what his parents, the 'wise' and 'learned' Rabbis, or his teachers tell him about God. He is taught from his youth about the **afterlife**, about Heaven and Hell. What else does he know! They must be right, he figures. He does good deeds so he can 'go to Heaven,' and avoids bad deeds for fear of 'going to Hell.' If he is angry with someone, he 'sends him to hell.'

If he loves him, he just 'knows' this person is going to Heaven. He knows about angels—they are all in Heaven. "Good people," he is told, "shall be become like angels." As for demons, they are certainly somewhere down under—in a fiery Hell. And O, how many stories he knows about those loved ones in Heaven. He prays to them, he goes to their graves to talk to them and ask for help or forgiveness—depending on the circumstances. At funerals, he hears the 'spiritual leaders' speak about the blessed departed whose souls are carried up by "the white angels," and they are now in Heaven, with their Maker. They are at peace, they are watching over him or her—and so he is comforted.

Every good Jew 'knows' that Elijah went up to Heaven. Does not the Bible say that plainly? Enoch was taken up to Heaven—it says so, " . . . God took him." The Bible says Elijah is coming back "before the coming great and dreadful day of the Lord." Did not Malachi the prophet say that? And how many stories did we hear about Elijah, only God knows! Elijah comes to visit every Jewish home at Passover night—that's why we must leave the door open, we must pour a glass of wine for him in a cup we call "Elijah's cup." And if Elijah does not show up, well, at times, I was allowed to drink his cup of wine. Elijah also comes to visit us every time a child gets circumcised. Some have a special chair for him—they call it, "Elijah's Chair." We pray to the saints, we pray to revered Rabbis. They intercede for us. Miracles occur when they do speak well of us before the Throne of Mercy. We are sure of that, and no one can change our minds. We have faith—solid faith!

Rachel, our mother, prays for us—it says so in the Bible! Jeremiah wrote of that—he knows what he is saying, he is a true Prophet of God, and no one among us doubts that—so it must be true! We built a synagogue near her grave, and we pray at her grave for many things we have need of in this earthly life. She, being in Heaven, cares for us, she hears our cries and sees our tears, and so she intercedes for us. Many women pray to her, and ask for her help. Many believe that miracles happen as a result of bringing our petitions to her—just like Catholics believe when they bring their petitions to Mary. We go to the graves of the Patriarchs, the graves of revered rabbis in holy places in the Galilee, and even to the graves of revered rabbis buried in the old countries we left behind. We build Synagogues in those holy places and we make pilgrimages to their burial sites and bow down by their graves. We pray, we dance, we eat and celebrate there—and we, above all, pray to them for help. Some even pray for a victory in political elections! Why not?

And what about the Prophet Samuel, some may ask? Didn't he have a chat with King Saul—after he was already dead and gone? The Bible says so! The account, truly, is very strange—he came out of the ground, not from above! In our last chapter, we shall deal with many "what about questions" and we shall have by then, hopefully, a clearer view of the matter.

What about reincarnation? It's a big thing in Judaism, not only in other religions. We are born, many tell us, and if we are good, 'we get an upgrade' in the next round or life—but if not, we must come back as a lower form, maybe even a rock, and rectify our deeds so we can, after all, 'get an upgrade.' There are many variations, of course, to this teaching, but the idea is more or less the same. Where did this notion come from? Did anyone ever read it in the Books of Isaiah, Genesis, or maybe in the Psalms? It's very imaginative for sure, but is it the naked truth? We don't like to buy a 'cat in a sack!' Why not? Because we can't see it and we don't know for sure how it looks like! But we believe in reincarnation! If someone was there, let him come forth and tell us! I'm 'dying' to know for sure! This is one of the questions of "what about," but we shall have to leave it for the end of the journey.

Many in recent times, with "scientific proofs," tell us many stories about those who went 'up there' and came back to tell about it. They all went through a tunnel of light, they all saw a brilliant light at the end of it, and it felt so good, but they were told to come back, because 'there is still something to be finished on earth.' And many believe it! There are other stories like that, with some variations. We love these fascinating stories, we write books about them, and we even make movies—many movies—about these **afterlife** stories. They are very fascinating and we are never tired of seeing more of them.

More and more, in recent years, it is most common to see in our papers and magazines ads about lectures, or series of lectures, that deal with the reincarnation of the soul. Most of the teachers are Rabbis who studied extensively this realm of the **afterlife**, and therefore are 'able' to reveal to us many hidden aspects about this most fascinating and popular subject. Many of them, in their attempts to bring back many into the fold of Judaism, often expound, in detail, the mysteries of reincarnation. A very famous Rabbi in Israel has been striving very hard, through the teachings about reincarnation, about the **afterlife** and Heaven and Hell, to convince many to come back to the faith. Are these attempts, as sincere as they may be, in line with the teachings of the Torah and the prophets? Are they in vain? Do the following words, which were recorded by the prophet Isaiah, refer to these Rabbis and their teachings? Isaiah wrote, quoting God: **"For as much as this people draw near to Me with their mouth, and with their lips do they honor Me, but they have removed their heart far from Me, and their fear toward Me is taught BY THE TRADITIONS [or teachings] OF MEN. Therefore, behold, I [God] will proceed to do a marvelous work among this people, even a marvelous work and a wonder; for THE WISDOM OF THEIR WISE SHALL PERISH, AND THE UNDERSTANDING OF THEIR PRUDENT MEN SHALL BE HID"** (Isaiah 29:13-14).

Did that happen to 'our Sages' and revered Rabbis? Did the Torah ever teach about reincarnation, the **afterlife**, or Heaven and Hell? We need to know! And if not, what did it teach about these most important issues concerning the life to come! We have two choices: to listen to the explanations of men—none of whom ever claimed, "Thus says the Lord,"—or read, with our own eyes, the words of those men whose statements were recorded in the "Holy Books!" And this we shall do, so we can tell for sure whether "the Emperor is naked" or not.

Let's be fully aware of this reality: it is not just a Jewish 'thing!' Every nation, every religion has similar beliefs and convictions. Is it true or a cruel hoax? Is "the Emperor naked" or is the child just hallucinating? How can we find out for sure! Don't good people become angels when they go up there? Don't they walk, sing, and play on harps in Heaven? Don't they live in great mentions? Don't they enter through the "pearly gates" and walk on streets paved with pure gold? How can we tell? We've never been there? We don't know of any relative or friend who can tell us for sure—because he went up there and came back to tell us. Faith aside, can you know for sure, not possessing any hard facts? Did God ever tell you, "son, or daughter, when you die, you will definitely go up to Heaven and be with me for ever after?" If it's true, we should see Scriptures by the dozens in the "Holy Book" that tell us, and plainly so: "the righteous or good person shall surely go up to Heaven, while the wicked shall surely go down to Hell and burn forever in a Hellfire, and be tormented by demons." This curious Jew wants to know whether "the Emperor is naked" or not!

Long ago, in my childhood in Israel, I read a story about a very pious Hasidic Jew who greatly desired to know the identity of the Jewish person slated to share a room next to him in Heaven. He went to a very famous

Rabbi, somewhere in Eastern Europe, and asked him: "Rabbi, I would like to know the identity of the pious Jew destined to share a room next to me in Heaven for eternity." The 'wise' Rabbi gave him the name and address of that 'pious' Jew. Eager to know, the pious Jew immediately set his foot on the road to meet that wonderful pious Jew who is slated to share a room next to him in Heaven. That pious Jew did not live in a mention in the center of town. He lived in a little shack in the forest. The pious Jew approached the shack, wondering in his heart what kind of a pious Jew would live by himself—far away from the synagogue—in the middle of the forest. He knocked on the broken door, but no one responded. He heard clearly some noises coming from inside the shack and saw the flicker of a burning lamp through the cracks in the door. Pushing the door open, he saw a very big man dressed in most dirty clothes, seated by the table. In front of him was a large plate full of all kinds of food, mainly meat, chicken, and fish. He was eating voraciously, snorting in the process, and paying no attention to the uninvited guest. Full of disturbed emotions and feelings, the pious Jew wondered to himself, "How could this crude, big, and ill mannered person be the one to reside in the room next to me in the world to come?"

Momentarily, he lost his composure, but remembering the words of his revered rabbi, he summoned some courage and asked the ill clad man, "Why are you eating like a hungry bear?" The man continued to devour his food as if no one was in the room. Upon finishing every morsel of food on his large plate, he shoved it aside and stared straight into the eyes of his uninvited and inquisitive Jewish guest. "I'll tell you why, my friend," he snorted, "you see, my father was a very little and pious man. One day some Gentile rogues came to our house in the city, pulled my struggling little father outside of town and hanged him on a tree. They forced all of us to watch. Then they proceeded to set him on fire. Since my father was of little stature, he burned quickly like a little candle and soon was no more. At that point I swore to myself to eat all I can, so when they do that to me, I will burn like a proud Jew for a long time." The pious Jew was now fully content and honored to be the next-door roommate in the world to come to such a most pious and brave Jew.

It makes for a good story, and in my youth I was very impressed with this most wonderful 'reality' of the world to come—of the reward of the pious in Heaven. But what if it's just a fiction, a fable concocted in the brain of a hallucinating and active mind! Are there any validations to this, and many other similar wonderful stories in our "Holy Book"? Let's go to those who really are 'in the know!' If you don't have a Bible or Tanach, go get one so we can read it together and get this story strait once and for all. I'm 'itching to know'—how about you? In the next chapter we'll find out what the men and Prophets of God had to say about the subject at hand.

CHAPTER 3

OLD TEASTAMENT TEACHINGS ABOUT THE AFTERLIFE, HEAVEN & HELL

Most Jews, including rabbis, believe it or not, do not know how and when the doctrine of the immortal soul has been 'planted' in the heart and mind of the Jewish community. They do not know when the doctrines of Heaven and Hell or the **'afterlife'** were first taught in a Jewish Synagogue or school of learning. More shocking is the fact, as we shall amply prove in the next pages of this chapter: no Torah obedient Jew had ever believed—in the pre-second Temple era—in the doctrines of Heaven and Hell, in the teaching and belief about the **'afterlife'** immediately after death, in the Pagan concepts of India and other religions about the reincarnation of the soul. All these fables were first introduced into the psyche of the Jewish community around the middle of the first century—and mostly after the destruction of the second Temple by Rome. The man who first introduced it to the Jewish community was a philosopher, namely, Philo Judeus! Philo lived in Alexandria (20 B.C.E.-50 C.E.), a major site of a flourishing Jewish community. He was greatly influenced by the Greek culture, which dominated his world. He was an admirer of Plato, and hence embraced his concept of the immortality of the soul. Being a greatly admired philosopher in the Alexandrian Jewish community and elsewhere, he gradually began to introduce his 'understanding' of the 'immortality of the soul' into the circles of the more liberal Jewish community in Alexandria. Jerusalem and the rest of the Jewish community did not accept this teaching for many years to come. Yet, gradually, the whole Jewish community 'fell for it,' and to this day most believe these teachings to be Biblically oriented. During the rise of Islam, in the sixth century, many Jews throughout the Middle East still had not accepted such doctrines fully. The teachings of Muhammad in the Qur'an, as we shall see later, reflected this reality in the Middle Eastern Jewish Community.

The paramount question at hand is: What did all the men of God and the Jews believe and were taught from the Bible, prior to the teachings of Philo the Hellenist and Jewish philosopher? Let's find out, and please read it and check it out in your own Bible or Tanach. For the sake of the community at large, we shall be quoting, throughout, from the King James Version. However, it's advisable for all Jews to read it in their own favorite Jewish versions. We need to make sure no one is 'pulling the wool' over our heads! Fair enough? "Our God is Spirit and we must worship Him in truth and in spirit".

What did God reveal to us in the beginning about our state of being? What did He say to the first man—Adam? In Genesis 2:7, we read: **"And the Lord God formed Man of the dust of the ground, and He breathed into his nostrils the breath of life; AND MAN BECAME A LIVING SOUL."** Notice! He didn't say, 'and man had a living soul inside him,' but "man became a living soul." The Scripture tells us very plainly that **WE** are the living soul! Let's remember this very important Torah teaching as we continue on our Biblical journey into the truth of the matter. After Adam and Eve disobeyed the clear command of God concerning the prohibition against eating from the tree of the of the knowledge of "good and evil," we read: **" . . . In the sweat of your brow** [or face] **you shall eat bread, till YOU** [not your immortal soul] **return to the ground; for out of it YOU** [not your body] **was taken; for dust YOU are, and unto dust YOU shall return"** (Genesis 3:19). We shall elaborate on this point as we go along.

We Jews love to read the book of Psalms more than any other book—and so to Psalms we shall go now to be illuminated about the true fate of the dead!

King David was certainly a man of God. He was inspired by God, and spoke as the Spirit of God moved him—just like all the other men and Prophets of God. David was a prophet and king. He was chosen and anointed by God through the hands of the Prophet Samuel. It would be safe to say that King David, **"the man according to God's own heart,"** knew what he was talking about! He wrote: **"What profit is there in my blood, when I go to the pit** [or the grave]? **SHALL THE DUST** [or my dead body] **PRAISE YOU? Shall it declare Your truth?"** (Psalm 30:9). What is King David saying to us? When we, or our bodies (or souls), go to the grave, immediately after death we become non-existent or non-entity. We no longer have life in us—that is after death—hence we are totally unable to communicate with God or men. Do you believe that? Do you believe the words of the Prophet of God, David, or that of uninspired men?

In Psalm 88:9-12, we read the inspired words of one of the Temple musicians, namely, Ethan the Ezrahite. He wrote: **"My eyes mourn by reason of affliction; Lord, I have called daily upon You; I have stretched out my hands unto You. Will you show wonders to the dead? Shall the dead arise** [from the grave] **and praise You? Selah. Shall Your loving kindness be declared in the grave? Or Your faithfulness in destruction** [in the grave where the body disintegrates and corrupts]? **And Your righteousness in the land of forgetfulness** [where none can think anymore, where one's thoughts perish]?" Are these words different from those of King David's? Judge for yourself!

Let's go now to Psalm 146 to continue the thread of the story. What does this psalmist warn us against? He declares: **"Praise you the Lord O my soul. While I live I will praise the Lord** [since in death I can't]; **I will sing praises to my God while I have any being. Put not your trust in princes** [or religious leaders], **nor in the son of man,** [which most of us do gullibly, though they can't give us life, and in those] **in whom there is no help** [when death awaits us]. **His breath goes forth, HE returns to the earth; IN THAT VERY DAY HIS THOUGHTS PERISH** [along with his body or soul]" (Psalm 146:3-4). Do you believe the inspired words of this Temple of God Psalmist? Are his words different than those of the Prophet and King David—the "man according to God's own heart?"

What about the words of the wise King Solomon? Are they different than those of his father David? In the sunset of his life, King Solomon wrote: **"I said in my heart concerning the estate** [or fate] **of the sons of men, that God might manifest them, and that they might see that they themselves are beasts** [of the same composition and fate]. **That which befalls the sons of men befalls the beasts; even one thing** [death and corruption] **befalls them; as the one dies, so does the other** [since one dead body is just like the other], **yes, they all have one breath; so that man has no preeminence above a beast; for all is vanity** [or vapor]. **All go into one place** [the grave or dust]; **all are of the dust, and all turn to dust again** [unless God resurrects them from the grave—at the end time]. **Who knows the SPIRIT of man that goes upward** [not the soul, but "the spirit"], **and the SPIRIT of the beast that goes downward to the earth** [never to be resurrected]? **Wherefore I perceived that there is nothing better than that man should rejoice in his own works; for**

45

that is his portion; for who shall bring him [out of the grave] **to see what shall be after him** [if God does not resurrect him]?" (Ecclesiastes 3:18-22).

What is it that animates man? Is it the **'soul'** or, as the men of God tell us, the **'spirit?'** The Prophet Ezekiel quotes God: **"Behold, all souls are mine; as the soul of the father, so also the soul of the son is mine; THE SOUL THAT SINS IT SHALL DIE."** He repeated that statement again, for emphases' sake, in the same chapter: **"The soul that sins it shall die"** (Ezekiel 18:4, 20). In contrast, King Solomon tells us the 'spirit of man goes upward,' after death, it does not die! Is the **'spirit'** the same as an immortal soul'? Previous statements of King David and other men of God make it abundantly plain: when a man dies, his thoughts perish—he can't anymore praise God, unless he is resurrected back to life. Is there a conflict here between father and son's understanding of the words of God? We shall see later!

In another place, King Solomon bemoaned the fate of man and wrote: **"This is an evil among all things that are done under the sun, that there is one event unto all; Yes, also the heart of the sons of man is full of evil, and madness is in their heart while they live** [and walk in lies and fables], **and AFTER THAT THEY GO TO THE DEAD. FOR TO HIM THAT IS JOINED TO THE LIVING THERE IS HOPE** [as long as he is alive]; **FOR A LIVING DOG IS BETTER THAN A DEAD LION. FOR THE LIVING KNOW THAT THEY SHALL DIE** [being conscious]; **BUT THE DEAD KNOW NOT ANY THING** [since dead people don't think, feel, talk, or move], **NEITHER HAVE THEY ANY MORE REWARD; FOR THE MEMORY OF THEM IS FORGOTTEN. ALSO THEIR LOVE, AND THEIR HATRED, AND THEIR ENVY, IS NOW PERISHED; NEITHER HAVE THEY ANY MORE A PORTION FOREVER IN ANY THING THAT IS DONE UNDER THE SUN"** (Ecclesiastes 9:3-6). This is the state of the dead, according to wise King Solomon, in contrast to the fables taught by Biblically illiterate "Sages" and Rabbis in the Jewish community. You have a choice whom to believe!

In Chapter 12 of this book, King Solomon added: **"Remember now your Creator in the days of your youth, while the evil days come not, nor the years draw near, when you shall say; I have no pleasure in them."** Solomon goes on to describe the winding down of one's own life when his **"desire shall fail: because man goes to his LONG HOME**

[Heb., eternal home] . . . **THEN SHALL THE DUST RETURN TO THE EARTH** [the "long home"] **AS IT WAS** [in the beginning]; **AND THE SPIRIT SHALL RETURN UNTO GOD WHO GAVE IT. Vanity of vanities, says the preacher** [Solomon], **all is vanity"** (Ecclesiastes 12:1, 5, 7-8).

In the book of Proverbs, King Solomon states: **"The spirit of man is the candle of the Lord, searching all the inward parts of the belly** (Proverbs 20:27). If the spirit in man is a living entity, then after death a man should be able to communicate with others, he should be able to think, live on, move about, and do whatever he wishes to do. Yet the Scriptures, as spoken by the men of God, make it very plain: no man can do anything after death, unless God resurrects him back to life, unless God 'reactivates' him—at the last day! As we proceed, we shall find more details and see more of how God, through His Prophets, explains and reveals this life and death issues.

The Prophet Zechariah records the words of God: **"The burden of the words of the Lord for Israel, says the Lord, who stretches** [or expands] **the heavens; and lays the foundation of the earth, and FORMS THE SPIRIT OF MAN WITHIN HIM"** (Zechariah 12:1). What is the nature of the 'spirit in man?' What is this spirit, which after death does not have the ability to equip man with the powers of life? It does not allow, according to the men of God, the powers of life to be active, think, to communicate and feel, to see and so on. Again, the previous statements by the Prophets of God, whose plain words were stated in the Bible, make it very clear: only the living can think, praise, and communicate—the dead cannot!

So what the spirit in man can be compared like? We all know how the power of electricity functions. We tap into a power source, and from it we can, if need be, tap more power to a secondary power source. For example: if we want to have light or electricity in our homes, we must tap, via electric cables, power from an outside main power lines or source—which they themselves are linked to a central source or power grid. In our homes, we install sockets in the wall for electric power. If we want to activate or 'bring to life' any electrical gadget or instrument in our home—like a computer, a lamp, a video machine, or any such gadgets, we plug them in, via a cable or an electric cord, to the socket in the wall or any source of electrical power. If the power is on, everything hooked to the source of power will 'come alive'—if not, all will remain 'dead.' A battery without the 'juice' will go 'dead.' A car without electrical power, or an engine without fuel in the tank, will be 'dead.' And so is the soul, which is made of the dust of the earth—as every piece of machinery is made of—if it's not 'plugged' to the source of life—God—it will be 'dead.' It's as simple as that! As one famous 2nd Temple era Rabbi, namely, James or Yaakov in Hebrew, had stated: **"As the body without the spirit is dead, so faith without work is dead."**

This is what the men of God taught and believed! But this is not what 'spiritual leaders' in the past many centuries, who claim to be inspired by God, have taught and believed. Of such self appointed teachers and 'spiritual guides' it was stated: **" . . . Hear you indeed, but understand not; and see you indeed, but perceive not. Make the heart of these people fat, and make their ears heavy, and shut their eyes . . ."** (Isaiah 6:9-10). We also read of such self deluded 'blind teachers of the blind' in Isaiah's words: **"Wherefore the Lord said, 'for as much as these people draw near Me with their mouth, and with their lips do honor Me, but have removed their heart far from Me, and their fear toward Me is taught by the precepts of men** [not those of God]'" (Isaiah 29:13). Such was the case in the 'old days' and such is the case to this day! If you follow such 'religious leaders' and place your precious eternal destiny and trust in their hands, without ever checking up on them, as the wise should do, you have no one to blame but yourself!

Job the man was a very righteous servant in the sight of God! He said so! As we read in the book named after him: **"There was a man in the land of Uz, whose name was Job; and that man was perfect and upright, and one that feared God, and hated evil . . . Now there was a day when the sons** [or Angels] **of God came to present themselves before the Lord, and SATAN CAME ALSO AMONG THEM** [the one responsible for "deceiving the whole world"] **. . . And the Lord said unto Satan, have you considered My servant Job, that there is none like him in the earth, a perfect and upright man, and that fears God, and hates evil?"** (Job 1:1, 6-8). Would you say Job had a divinely sanctioned credibility and, therefore, his words could be trusted? This is what he wrote concerning life and death: **"O that You** [God] **would hide me IN THE GRAVE, that You would keep me in secret** [in the dust]**, until Your wrath is past, that You would appoint me a set time** [to be resurrected at the end time]**, and remember me! IF A MAN DIES, SHALL HE LIVE AGAIN? All the days of my appointed time will I wait** [in the grave]**, till my change comes** [in the resurrection—at the end time]**. You shall call and I will answer. You will have a desire to the work of Your hands" (Job 14:13-15).

The last time I quoted these very words, while officiating at a funeral of a friend's mother—which was attended by both Jews and Christian friends—all listened attentively, including the funeral director; all liked what was said, but none understood the meanings of the words! It simply went over their heads. Many centuries of deception have done their job well. How about you? Do you have eyes to see and ears to hear?

The Prophet Isaiah had much to say about the state and fate of the dead. Of the fate of the incorrigible sinners he wrote: **"O Lord our God, other lords beside You have had dominion over us; but You only will we make mention of Your name. They are dead, they shall not live** [because they have willfully rejected You]**; they are deceased, they shall mot rise** [from the grave, unless You resurrect them], **therefore have You visited and destroyed them, and made all their memory to perish"** (Isaiah 26:13-14). Then he spoke of the fate of the dead who were not willfully rebellious: **"Your dead shall live; together with my dead body shall they arise** [from the grave]. **Awake and sing, YOU THAT DWELL IN THE DUST; for your dew is as the dew of herbs, AND THE EARTH** [or the grave, not Heaven or Hell] **SHALL CAST OUT THE DEAD"** (Isaiah 26:19).

When righteous King Hezekiah, of the southern kingdom of Judah, was stricken with a grievous disease, Isaiah the prophet told that his days are numbered. Hezekiah pleaded with God to spare him from this untimely death, and God healed him by adding fifteen years to his life. Filled with gratitude, Hezekiah offered this prayer and thanks to God: **" . . . I said in the cutting off of my days I shall go to the gates of the grave . . . I said, I shall not see the Lord in the land of the living; I shall behold man no more with the inhabitants of the world . . . O Lord, by these things men live, and in all these things is the life of MY SPIRIT; so will You recover me and make me to live. Behold, for peace I had great bitterness; but You had in love to my soul delivered it from the pit of corruption** [or the grave] **. . . For THE GRAVE CANNOT PRAISE YOU, DEATH CANNOT CELEBRATE YOU; THEY THAT GO DOWN INTO THE PIT** [or grave] **CANNOT HOPE FOR YOUR TRUTH. THE LIVING, THE LIVING, he shall praise You, as I do this day . . ."** (Isaiah 38:1-22).

These are plain words for those who have ears to hear! Hope you are one of them. It does not take a rocket scientist to figure out, what some call, "The Plain Truth"! It is plainly evident: no true servant of God had ever believed or taught the doctrine of the **'afterlife'** or Heaven and Hell, immediately after death! Isaiah the Prophet recorded, one among many, this statement of fact: " **. . . He that puts his trust in Me shall possess the land, and shall inherit My Holy Mountain** [Jerusalem]" (Isaiah 57:13). Many other statements by the Prophets of God tell us, **"The meek** [or righteous] **SHALL INHERIT THE EARTH** [not Heaven].**"** Again, the Prophet Isaiah records the words of God about the time and future redemption of all of Israel: **"Your people also shall be all righteous; THEY SHALL INHERIT THE LAND** [not Heaven] **forever, the branch of My planting, the work of My hands, that I may be glorified"** (Isaiah 60:21). No one is given the promise to go to Heaven, and as we shall see shortly, even the most sinful people of Sodom are not presently in Hell. What many don't realize in our modern days is the fact that in old English the word **'hell'** meant the **'ground,'** and not the later connotation it took. English farmers would often place their potatoes in **'hell'** to preserve them. When the KJV (King James Version) of the English Bible was translated from other manuscripts, they used the word **'hell'** to mean, simply, the ground. What men of ignorance did with it later is another issue.

Speaking about the fate of the patriarchs of old, Isaiah wrote: **"Doubtless You are our father, though Abraham is ignorant of us** [being still in the grave—awaiting the resurrection at the last day], **and Israel acknowledges us not** [for the same reason]; You **O Lord are our Father** [and live forever], **our Redeemer, Your name from everlasting"** (Isaiah 63:16). This was common knowledge among the people of Israel until the doctrine of the **'afterlife'** and Heaven and Hell gained wide acceptance few centuries after the destruction of the 2nd Temple. Those who were later born into this fable took it for granted and believed it was a Biblical teaching. They did not possess copies of the "The Holy Book" in their homes and, therefore, were unable to check it out for themselves. Nowadays, everyone can own several copies of the "Holy Book," and many do, yet still we don't bother to find out for ourselves whether "the Emperor is naked" or not.

At the end of the book of Isaiah the Prophet, we learn of the glorious fate of those who fear and obey God's Law or Torah, in contrast to those who reject God's rule over them. We read: " **. . . It shall come, that I will gather all nations and tongues; and they shall come and see My glory** [in Zion or Jerusalem]. **And I will set a sign among them, and I will send those that have escaped of them** [from the armies annihilated at the Messiah's return to Jerusalem, see Zechariah 14] **unto the nations** [where the remnant of Israel have been scattered by their enemies] **. . . And they shall declare My glory among the nations. And they shall bring all your brethren for an offering unto the Lord out of all the nations . . . to My holy mountain Jerusalem** [which belongs **only** to God and His people], **says the Lord . . . For as the new heavens and the new earth** [which will be renewed as in the first days of creation], **which I will make, shall remain before Me, says the Lord, so shall your seed** [Israel, in spite of their enemies' desire to destroy them] **and your name remain. And it shall come to pass, that from one new moon to another, and from one Sabbath to another** [not Sunday or Friday], **shall all flesh come to worship before Me, says the Lord** [and those who would refuse to do so, as God said earlier, **"The nation or kingdom that will not serve you shall perish; yes, those nations shall utterly be destroyed"** (Isaiah 60:12)]. **And they shall go forth and look upon the carcasses of the men that have transgressed against Me; for their worm shall not die, neither shall their fire be quenched; and they shall be an abhorring unto all flesh"** (Isaiah 66:18-24).

To understand these words about the fate of the wicked, we must have a proper background of ancient Jerusalem. On the southeast outskirts of Jerusalem there is a valley into which the residents of Jerusalem used to dump their trash. Also, the remnants of the refuse from the Temple sacrifices were thrown into this valley. Also, the dead bodies of ritually unclean animals and executed criminals were dumped into that valley. By nature, it did breed worms continually and stunk. To avoid the spread of diseases, the authorities saw to it that certain men, placed in charge of the dumpsite, would set the trash on fire regularly. The little valley which was owned by the sons of a certain man called *Hinom*, was named, **"The valley of the sons of Hinom,"** or in short, in Hebrew, **"Gey Ben Hinom,"** and later, **"Geyhinom."** In later times, it was also referred to as **"Gehenna"** and **"Gehenna Fire."** It was a literal place one could see, walk through, and set trash on fire. Since it was a perpetual dumping ground for the city refuse; since its burning fire was ever present, and the worms feeding on the dead matter and carcasses of animals and criminals

51

were ever in sight, many in later ages, in complete ignorance of the reality of the time, allegorized this literal place and linked it with the imaginary fable of **"Hell Fire,"** the 'place for the wicked.' This is not a Biblical understanding, but pagan in origin! When God is speaking about the destruction of those who rebel against Him and His Law or Torah; when He talks about the ever-present fire and worms, He is speaking about a real place as that of **"Gey Hinom Fire."** When physical matter is thrown into it, like human waste or people, as we read in Malachi's prophecy, it will burn **"like stubble and leave behind neither branch nor root."** This is exactly what the last words of God to Isaiah are meant to convey! Those who know the entire story have no problems understanding it. But if they still reject it—they will be thrown into that **"Gey Hinom fire!"** As for "the blind who lead the blind," as wise King Solomon had stated: **"He that answers a matter before he hears it, it is folly and shame unto him"** (Proverbs 18:13). Most "spiritual leaders" do not consider the words of King David, who stated: **"The Fear of the Lord is the beginning of wisdom; a good** [not deficient] **understanding have all they that do** [or obey] **His commandments"** (Psalm 111:10). Had they truly feared God and obeyed His commandments and his teachings—not their own man-made—they would not have believed and taught the fables about the **afterlife**—contrary to the plain teachings of the "Holy Books."

Every devout Jew recites several times, daily, this prayer (from the Prayer Book) during "*the Amidah*" or 18 benedictions: **"He sustains the living with loving kindness, RESURRECTS THE DEAD** [from their graves—at the last day] **with great mercy, supports the falling, heals the sick, and fulfills His trust** [or faithful promise] **TO THOSE WHO SLEEP IN THE DUST. Who is like You, mighty One! And who can be compared to You, King who brings death and RESTORES LIFE, and causes deliverance to spring forth! YOU ARE TRUSTWORTHY TO REVIVE THE DEAD. Blessed are You Lord, WHO REVIVES THE DEAD."**

All Jews who recite this prayer—not considering the whole matter—do not compare it with the words of the true Prophets of God; they do not realize that the God—fearing men who wrote the prayers were of a different frame of mind then all those 'spiritual leaders' who came after them! The writer of this most revealing and moving prayer certainly feared God and obeyed His commandments! He made it very plain: The dead are not alive, the dead are sleeping (Biblical terminology for death) **IN THE**

DUST, the dead are awaiting the faithful promise of God to resurrect or bring them back to life! This God-fearing writer who was obedient to the Mitzvot or commandments of God, not man-made teachings, believed the words of the very righteous man, in the sight of God, Job, who stated: **"If a man dies, shall he live again? All the days of my appointed time** [in the dust or grave] **will I wait, till my change comes** [as it happens to any seed planted in the ground]. **You shall call, and I will answer You; You will have a desire to the work of Your hands"** (Job 14:14-15).

What happened to the self appointed 'spiritual leaders' of Israel? Why is it that there is no 'little child' among them who can see with his eyes and declare, "The Emperor is naked?"

Let's go now to the book of the Prophet Ezekiel, who was among the exile in Babylon. He was among those taken into captivity by the king of Babylon, prior to the final captivity and destruction of the 1st Temple and Jerusalem. In Chapter 16 of his book we read about the history of Israel, from God's point of view. In this chapter, God also mentions the fate of the people of Sodom and their present 'location' until the resurrection. Most are totally unaware of the content of this chapter, and therefore are ignorant of basic Biblical teachings!

Speaking of His people Judah's sins and conduct, this is what God had to say about them, about Israel, the northern kingdom, as well as about the people of Sodom: **"And your elder sister is Samaria** [Capital of Israel to the North]**, she and her daughters** [or tribes] **that dwell at your left hand; and your younger sister, that dwells at your right hand, is Sodom and her daughters** [or the cities around it]. **Yet have you not walked after their ways, nor done after their abominations; but, as if that were a very little thing, YOU WERE CORRUPTED MORE THAN THEY IN ALL YOUR WAYS** [and what a 'compliment']. **As I live, says the Lord God, SODOM YOUR SISTER HAS NOT DONE, SHE NOR HER DAUGHTERS, AS YOU HAVE DONE, YOU AND YOUR DAUGHTERS** [?]. **Behold, this was the iniquity of your sister Sodom** [and it's not what most have been led to believe]**, PRIDE, FULNESS OF BREAD** [and no care for others]**, AND ABUNDANCE OF IDLENESS** [the modern life-style of many] **was in her and in her daughters, NEITHER DID SHE STRENGTHEN THE HAND OF THE POOR AND NEEDY** [all are social injustices in nature]. **And they were HAUGHTY AND COMMITTED ABOMINATIONS** [and notice that sexual problems were listed last] **before Me; therefore I took** them away as I saw good." How many 'religious people' and 'spiritual leaders' do know the real main reasons for the utter destruction of the city of Sodom and her surroundings? How many are striving to rectify these social maladies before it's too late?

The account continues: **"Neither has Samaria committed half of your sins; but you have multiplied your abominations MORE THAN THEY, and has justified your sisters** [Samaria and Sodom] **in all your abominations which you have done. You also who have judged your sisters, bear your own shame for your sins that you have committed are more abominable they** [have committed]; **they are more righteous than you** [and that's how God felt about His people Judah, the southern kingdom]; **yes, be you condemned also, and bear your shame, in that you have justified your sisters."**

In our days we regard such accusations as 'anti-Semitism.' Now let's find out the ultimate fate of those who earn from God the 'highest compliments' for their shameful conduct! Most of us have been led to believe that for such vial behavior God sends such people strait into "Hell"! We have been told that all the people of Sodom, and all the wicked are still "Burning in Hell." The preachers of "Hell Fire" were often successful in 'scaring the Hell out of people in their attempts to 'lead them back to the right path.' So let's find out, from the mouth of God Himself, the fate of the wicked people of Sodom, her surrounding cities, and the wicked people among the people of Israel, or any wicked person on the planet.

We read: **"When I SHALL BRING AGAIN THEIR CAPTIVITY** [from the grave, not 'Hell'], **the captivity of Sodom and her daughters, and the captivity of Samaria** [the northern kingdom of Israel] **and her daughters, then I will bring again the captivity of your captives** [also from the grave] **in the midst of them; that you may bear your own shame** [which now many refuse to acknowledge], **and may be confounded in all that you have done, in that you are a comfort unto them** [when they realize they are not as bad in God's sight as you]. **When your sisters, Sodom and her daughters, shall return to their former estates** [after being resurrected], **and Samaria and her daughters shall return to their former estate, then you and your daughters shall return** [after being resurrected from the grave] **to your former estate"** (Ezekiel 16).

God and all of His true servants made it very clear for all who have ears to hear, eyes to see, and a heart to understand: **THERE IS NO AFTERLIFE** immediately after one's death, there is no such thing as 'going to Heaven or Hell' immediately after death—but all go to the "pit" or the grave to 'rest' and await there for the "sound of the Trumpet," at the last Day. Only then everyone will be brought back to life and to judgment. Every other teaching, which is contrary to this divinely inspired revelation, is of 'another spirit'—the one who has been deceiving humanity, directly or through his human servants on earth, and from the Garden of Eden. That's why few are those who can 'see' and proclaim, "The Emperor is naked."

The Prophet Ezekiel's prophecy about "the valley of the dry bones" is most famous in both Jewish and Christian circles—yet few are those who really understand it. As we reach the end of the journey in this book, all will understand it fully, assuming the 'lights upstairs are on.' Ezekiel was shown a vision of the future resurrection, from the grave, of the whole house of Israel. At the end of this Biblical journey into the truth, as recorded by the genuine servants of God, we shall understand the full scope of this vision and its timing. Yet at this point, we shall bring some important details that shall confirm the previous statements we have read so far. Ezekiel is asked by God to take part in the initiation of the resurrection of the whole house of Israel who lived since the days of the Patriarchs. And so he writes: **"So I prophesied as He commanded me, and the breath** [or "Neshama"] **came unto them, and they lived, and stood up upon their feet, an exceeding great army. Then He said unto me, son of man, these bones are the whole house of Israel; behold, they say, Our bones are dried** [since all were in the grave for a long time], **and our hope is lost** [not knowing whether they were going to come back to life or not]**; we are cut off** [from the living] **for our parts. Therefore prophesy and say unto them, Thus says the Lord God; Behold, O My people, I WILL OPEN YOUR GRAVES** [your 'resting place' since the day you died]**, AND CAUSE YOU TO COME OUT OF YOUR GRAVES, and bring you into the land of Israel** [in the far future, as we shall see later]**. And you shall know that I am the Lord** [because in your life time you didn't], **WHEN I HAVE OPENED YOUR GRAVES, O My people, AND BROUGHT YOU UP OUT OF YOUR GRAVES, and shall put My Spirit in you, and YOU SHALL LIVE** since until then you are both dead and buried]**, and I shall place you in your own land** [not Palestinian or Arab land]**; then you shall know** [since now you don't] **that I the Lord had spoken it, and performed it, says the Lord"** (Ezekiel 37).

Throughout the history of Israel, few were those who really 'knew the Lord.' Things have not changed much to this day! Those who were lead to believe in the fables about the **'afterlife'** or life immediately after death can never understand the prophecy of Ezekiel about "the valley of the dry bones." The dust of their man-made superstitions is blinding their eyes, but not for long, as God promised many times: **"When I bring you out of your graves** [both literal and spiritual] **then you shall know that I am the Lord."** We are all given the opportunity to know today, if we are willing to consider the words of the Psalmist—the Prophet and King David—who stated: **"Today if you will hear His voice, harden not your heart, as in the provocation, and as in the day of temptation in the wilderness; when your fathers tempted Me, proved Me, and saw My work. For forty years long I was grieved with this generation, and said, it is a people that do err in their heart, and they have not known My ways; unto whom I swore in My wrath that they should not enter into My rest** [or the Millennial Sabbath in the Land of Promise] (Psalm 95:7-11).

Let's go now the end of the period of the kingdom of Judah—prior to their first captivity and the destruction of the 1st Temple. How did the Jews of that time understand the teachings about the **'afterlife'** and Heaven and Hell? Did their state of rank idolatry affect their understanding of the **'afterlife?'** Let's see how Daniel the prophet, who was taken to Babylon in the earlier captivity, understood these crucial teachings of the former Prophets of God.

After receiving many visions from God, and revelations from His angel Gabriel, Daniel wanted to know the future and timing of those prophecies. He was told by the angel Gabriel: **"And at that time** [of 'the end of days'], **Michael shall stand up, the great prince which stands for the children of your people** [since he is ordained by God to be Israel's and **NO OTHER NATION'S** chief 'guardian angel']; **and there shall be a time of trouble, such as there never was since there was a nation even to that same time; and at that time your people shall be delivered** [from their enemies, false 'prophets' and their fables and sins], **everyone that shall be found written in the book [of life]. AND MANY OF THEM** [not all] **THAT SLEEP IN THE DUST OF THE EARTH** [since none went up to Heaven] **SHALL AWAKE** [or come alive when 'the electrical cord is plugged in again'], **SOME TO EVERLASTING LIFE** [or immortality], **AND SOME TO SHAME AND EVERLASTING CONTEMPT. And**

they that are wise [in the sight of God, not their own] **shall shine as the brightness of the firmament; and they that turn many to righteousness** [not to fables and superstitions] **as the stars forever and ever. But you Daniel shut up the words, and seal the book, even to the time of the end; many shall run to and fro, and knowledge shall be increased** [both spiritually and academically]." In Verse 6, an angel is asking the question: **"How long shall it be to the end of these wonders?"** Another angel responded by declaring: **" . . . a time, times, and an half a time; and when he** [the destroyer of Israel] **shall have accomplished to scatter the power of the holy people** [Israel], **all these things shall be finished. And I** [Daniel] **heard, but I understood not** [since truth has to be revealed from above]**; then said I, O my lord** [Gabriel], **what shall be the end of these things? And he said, go your way, Daniel; for the words are closed up** [by Heaven's decree] **and sealed till the time of the end. Many** [not all] **shall be purified, and made white** [or righteous], **and tried** [through persecutions by the unrighteous], **but the wicked shall do wickedly** [refusing to alter their life-style and behavior]**; and none of the wicked shall understand; but the wise shall understand."** (Daniel 12).

Students of prophecy who truly fear God, and obey His Law or Torah, do understand. Who are they? King David stated: **"The fear of the Lord is the beginning of wisdom; a good understanding have all they THAT DO HIS COMMANDMENT** [or Mitzvot]**"** (Psalm 111:10). It's as simple as that! No academic degree or any 'higher learning' can lead you to the purity of the truth! The more educated a person is, the more likely that person is afflicted with blindness. That person is less likely to have the child-like ability to see and proclaim: "the Emperor is naked!"

As The King of Israel had proclaimed: **" . . . The Heaven is My throne, and the earth is My footstool; where is the house that you** [mortals] **build unto Me? And where is the place of My rest?" For all those things have My hand made . . . says the Lord."** God is not impressed with any of our academic achievements, be they 'spiritual' or secular in nature. He is not impressed with any of our great works or technological abilities, **"but,"** as He stated, **"to this man** [or woman] **will I look** [and have respect for], **even to him that is poor** [or humble] **and of contrite spirit** [not arrogant and proud], **and trembles at My word"** (Isaiah 66:1-2).

The last Prophet of Israel, Malachi, who lived during the period of the Prophets Zechariah and Hagai—as well as the righteous servants of God,

Ezra and Nehemiah—does add more details to our Biblical understanding and genuine teachings about the **'afterlife'** and Heaven and Hell. The Prophet reveals to us how would God dispose of those who willfully reject His Law or Torah. These would be the few, in comparison to the majority, who would not accept the rule of God over their lives. These rebels would not submit despite the awesome promises the righteous will inherit. This small minority, among the countless who were born and died, will 'earn' an eternal destruction and punishment, **not punishing**, in a "lake of fire" that will consume them and leave no trace of their bodies or memory.

Malachi writes: **"Behold the day comes that shall burn like an oven; and all the proud, yes all that do wickedly, shall be STUBBLE; and the day that comes shall BURN THEM UP, says the Lord of Hosts, that IT SHALL LEAVE THEM NEITHER ROOT NOR BRANCH"** (Malachi 4:1). Think and consider! What happens to "stubble" when you "burn it up"? Does it leave a "root" or a "branch" to the "stubble"? Of course not! And that's exactly what God means by "burning in Hell"! Man is made of flesh not spirit, he does not possess an immortal soul—he is like "stubble" that when it burns, it leaves "neither root nor branch." This is the Biblical teaching throughout the entirety of the "Holy Book," yet this is not what confused men of religion have taught throughout history. This is what the God-fearing people of Israel have been taught and believed until long after Jerusalem was destroyed by Rome. Did the Jewish community, in the last decades of the 2nd Temple, in Jerusalem and Judea hold other teachings about the afterlife and Heaven and Hell than those held by the Prophets of God? We shall find out the answer in later chapters.

In Chapter 4, we shall illuminate the reader—Jew and Gentile—about the true teachings of the Jewish sect that followed Jesus of Nazareth. The writers of the New Testament were all Jews. They attended the Synagogue and prayed, when possible, in the Temple. They were considered by most in the Jewish community as just another Jewish sect. They obeyed the Torah and taught it even to the Gentile converts—contrary to later false assertions by men of ignorance. When considering the beliefs of the followers of Jesus from Nazareth—those who were converted from the Pagan mold—one of the leaders and "fathers" of the emerging religion, called "Christianity" in later times, namely, Origen, wrote in the 4th century, in his commentary on Isaiah the prophet, and I paraphrase: **"The Nazarenes are practicing their faith in like fashion and manner as the Jews, and they are no different from them, being fettered in keeping**

the Law (or Torah), **like circumcision, the Sabbath . . . except in their belief in Messiah . . . and therefore they are not Christians."** Epiphanies, another Church leader, wrote similar things about "The Nazarenes." For this reason and others, it should be of interest to the Jewish community to know, from a first-hand account, what did the Jewish community believe in—whether they followed Jesus or not—in the first century, before and after the destruction of the Temple. Was their belief in the **afterlife** the same as that of the Prophets of God, or has it changed to resemble that of later times in the Jewish and Christian communities! In the next chapter, we shall cover thoroughly the teachings and beliefs about the **afterlife** and Heaven and Hell, as believed in the Jewish and "Christian" community shortly before and after the destruction of the Temple.

CHAPTER 4

CHRISTIAN CONCEPTS ABOUT THE AFTERLIFE, HEAVEN & HELL

Every Christian, whether Catholic, Protestant, or Mormon—as well as all those in the other Orthodox churches—just 'knows' that good people go up to Heaven and bad people go down to Hell. There may be slight variations among the churches, but all basically adhere to the same teachings of their 'spiritual leaders and teachers' concerning the **afterlife** doctrine. Devout Christians have no doubt about that 'certain future fate' of the good and bad. Their faith in this crucial doctrine is very similar to that of Jews and Muslims. Like Jews and Muslims, they claim to follow the teachings of their "Holy Books" in this regard. The first Gentile Christians were those members who were later added to the Apostolic Church. In later times divisions arose between East and West in the Christian Roman Empire. After that, came "The Holy Roman Church," which was molded by Constantine to fit his personal agenda for the Roman Empire. In later times, in the twelfth century, the Catholic Church has emerged as the dominant one among all. Rome was declared to be the rightful inheritor to the "Seat of Peter." All those bishops of Rome who followed the first bishop, allegedly Peter, were regarded as the "Holy See." They were declared to be the Vicar of Christ" on earth and possessors of the "Keys to the Kingdom of Heaven." It was in 'their power' to grant the believer to either "go to Heaven or be sent to Hell." The Bishop of Rome later called "the Pope" or "Father," after consulting with the Cardinals and others, had the power to proclaim any one a "Saint." He had the authority to canonize any person, and permit the believers to pray to that newly Canonized 'Saint' as their "Saint Patron." Since 'all the Saints are in Heaven,' according to Catholic dogma, it's permitted to make statutes or icons of the saints who were Canonized and bow down and pray to them.

The apostles of Christ were certainly 'worthy' to be canonized by "the Church." Hence we see their statutes in every Catholic and Orthodox Church. We see them in many other religious institutions and even homes of the believers. Many bow down to them. They speak to them and ask for their help. "Mary the Mother of God" has been certainly canonized, being most 'worthy of all,' in the Catholic Church's sight, to be the chief Saint over all others. From her humble status as the young Jewish maiden who gave birth to The Savior of all mankind, she was elevated, in successive stages, to the highest position of "The Queen of Heaven." She is called upon, worshiped, prayed to, and adored by many as "The Virgin Mary." Catholics gave her a higher status in their sight and worship than those in the later Protestant churches. Mary is worshiped and revered as "The Madonna" of the catholic world. They built countless monuments for her all around the world. Every devout Catholic has at least one statue or picture of her in his or her home or business place. Prayers are offered to her, since she is "The Chief Intercessor in Heaven" for all those who seek help. She has countless followers, worshipers, and devout admirers and adherers—not only in the Catholic and Orthodox churches but also among many Muslims. Muhammad, the Prophet of Islam, spoke very highly of her.

The 'religion' of "Mariannism" or Mary worship, is global in scope. Throughout the many centuries, and even to our days, there have been 'sightings' of the "Mother of God," of "The Virgin Mary," of "The Madonna" in diverse places around the world. The "Holy Places" where an "appearance" of Mary was 'sighted' by mostly humble folks, as young maidens or children, were declared to be "Holy Shrines" worthy of being visited by millions of devout Mary-worshipers in the Church. These places became sites of pilgrimages for countless of millions of worshipers: the sick, the broken-hearted, and those just curious to see the sites where 'miracles' were and are being performed on behalf of the faithful.

Mary was first declared to be "The Virgin Mary." In later times, the Bishop of Rome had named, also, the "Virgin Mary" the new name, "The Immaculate Conception." The four Gospels tell us plainly that Mary and Joseph had children after Jesus was born. They were called "His Brothers." These brothers and their descendants were known to all in the Jewish community and elsewhere in the first century, as well as in later times. The Apostle John records these words about the family of Jesus: **"After this** [the marriage of Jesus' sister in Cana] **He** [Jesus] **went down to Capernaum,**

He, and His mother, and HIS BROTHERS, and His disciples . . ." (John 2:12). Matthew's Gospel records these words: **"Then Joseph being raised from sleep did as the angel of the Lord had commanded him, and took unto him his wife; AND KNEW HER NOT TILL SHE HAD BROUGHT FORTH HER FIRSTBORN** [not her **only** child], **AND HE CALLED HIS NAME JESUS"** (Matthew 1:25). Later, Matthew records these words of Jesus' city folks: **"And when He came into His own country, He taught them in their synagogue, insomuch that they were astonished, and said, from where has this man this wisdom, and these mighty works? IS NOT THIS THE CARPENTER'S SON? IS NOT HIS MOTHER CALLED MARY? AND HIS BROTHERS: JAMES, AND JOSES, AND SIMON, AND JUDAS? AND HIS SISTERS ARE THEY NOT ALL WITH US?"** (Matthew 13:54-56). The Apostle Paul wrote to the church in Corinth: **"Have we not power to lead** [or marry] **about a sister, a wife, as well as the other Apostles, AND AS THE BROTHERS OF THE LORD, and CEPHAS** [who was later considered to be "the first Pope of Rome," even though Catholic priests, certainly, have been forbidden to marry—contrary to the teachings of Christ and His Law]" (I Corinthians 9:5). But then, as ever, 'Truth and Facts don't matter—it's how we FEEL about it that really counts!' This is the naked truth in every area of life, and especially in religion! That's why many 'look,' but can't 'see' that "The Emperor is naked."

Let's bring up now a shocking reality to our attention, whether we are Jews or Gentiles. Let's discuss, in brief, the origin of the worship of the "Queen of Heaven!" Are "Christians" the first to worship the "Queen of Heaven?" Was Mary the first one to be worshiped as "The Queen of Heaven?" If not, let's find out who was the first one in the "Judeo-Christian" world to worship the "Queen of Heaven!" 'Sharpen' your eyes and read along!

The northern kingdom of Israel was taken into captivity, because of the many sins she committed against her God. One of those major sins was idol worship. Judah was also taken into captivity about two centuries later for the same reasons. Prior to the captivity, God and His Prophets had warned her, unless she repents, of her impending national calamity and captivity. God warned Judah either to turn away from idolatry or risk expulsion from her own land. Judah, like the northern kingdom before her, rejected God's warning and chose to continue the worship of many idols.

The Prophet Jeremiah revealed in his book the identity of one particular idol, one among many idols.

And so we read God's warning to Judah, and the identity of that particular idol which infuriated God greatly: **"Therefore will I do unto this House** [or Temple], **which is called by My name, wherein you trust, and unto the place which I gave to you and your fathers** [the land of Canaan], **as I have done to Shiloh** [where the Tabernacle was previously located]. **And I will cast you out of My sight, as I have cast all your brethren, even the whole house of Ephraim. Therefore** [God says to Jeremiah] **DO NOT PRAY FOR THIS PEOPLE, NEITHER LIFT UP YOUR CRY NOR PRAYER FOR THEM** [since when we go too far away from God, He will not listen to any of our prayers or of those very righteous men who pray for us], **NEITHER MAKE INTERCESSION TO ME; FOR I WILL NOT HEAR YOU** [and this is a sober warning for all]**."** Now notice the particular reason why God said that to Jeremiah! **"Do you not see what they do in the cities of Judah and in the streets of Jerusalem? The children gather wood, and the fathers kindle the fire, and the women knead their dough** [in a family effort], **TO MAKE CAKES TO THE QUEEN OF HEAVEN, and to pour out drink offerings unto other gods, that they may provoke Me to anger"** (Jeremiah 7:14-18).

Imagine that! Six centuries before Mary the mother of Jesus was born, her people were already worshiping **"THE QUEEN OF HEAVEN."** And because they did so, they had earned the great fury of their God and were cast away from their God-given land into Babylon. Let's be reminded of this sober reality: **"God does not change—He is the same yesterday, today, and forever!"** Also, let's remember, **"God is not a respecter of persons!"** He was furious with His own people when they worshiped **"THE QUEEN OF HEAVEN,"** and threw them out of His land. In like manner, He is furious with those who still do the same—and severe judgment is knocking at the door for those who are guilty of the same transgression. Many times, the Catholic Church has ordered the burning of the Bible in an attempt to hide the "damning evidence" against her Pagan oriented teachings—but who can really "burn the Truth" of the "God that does not change?" Whom are they kidding anyway?

The nation of Judah, tragically, did not heed God's warning to them through His Prophet Jeremiah. They were conquered; the land was destroyed; the Temple was burned to the ground, as well as all of

Jerusalem—and Judah went into captivity. The king of Babylon, however, allowed some of the poor folks to remain in the land and farm the ground. God promised them peace and prosperity if they would turn again to Him and remain in the land. Sadly, they and their leaders rejected the message of God to them through His Prophet Jeremiah. They chose, instead, to go down to Egypt—their former land of slavery. Jeremiah was forced to go down with them into Egypt. While in Egypt, God warned the remnant of the rebellious Jews that none of them would escape alive from the destruction He will bring on Egypt by the hand of the king of Babylon. He said to them: **"Therefore now thus says the Lord, the God of Hosts, the God of Israel; wherefore commit you this great evil against your souls, to cut off from you man and woman, child and suckling, out of Judah, to leave you none to remain; in that you provoke Me unto wrath with the works of your hands, burning incense unto other gods** [including **"THE QUEEN OF HEAVEN"**], **in the land of Egypt, where you went to dwell, that you might cut yourself off, and that you might be a curse and a reproach among all the nations of the earth? . . . For I will punish them that dwell in the land of Egypt, as I have punished Jerusalem, by the sword, by the famine, and by the pestilence. So that none of the remnant of Judah, which are gone into the land of Egypt to sojourn there, shall escape or remain . . ."**

Notice the reaction of the men and women of Judah to this ominous warning from God through His Prophet Jeremiah, and compare it to your own reaction—especially those of you who are still worshiping **"The Queen of Heaven,"**—to this sober warning by the God that "does not change."

The account continues: **"Then all the men which knew that their wives had burned incense unto other gods, and all the women that stood by, a great multitude, even all the people that dwelt in the land of Egypt, in Pathros, answered Jeremiah, saying: as for the word that you have spoken unto us in the name of the Lord, we will not listen to you, but we will certainly do whatsoever goes out of our own mouth, TO BURN INCENSE UNTO THE QUEEN OF HEAVEN, AND TO POUR OUT DRINK OFFERINGS UNTO HER, AS WE HAVE DONE, WE, AND OUR FATHERS, OUR KINGS, AND OUR PRINCES, AND IN THE STREETS OF JERUSALEM; FOR THEN WE HAD PLENTY OF PROVISIONS, AND WERE WELL, AND SAW NO EVIL. But since we left off to burn incense to THE**

QUEEN OF HEAVEN, and to pour out drink offerings unto her, we are lacking in all things, and have been consumed by the sword and by the famine." They forgot that God was the One punishing them for that very reason. The **"Queen of Heaven"** was greater in their sight then even God Himself. The account continues: **"And when we burned incense to THE QUEEN OF HEAVEN, and poured out drink offerings unto her, did we make her cakes** ["hot cross buns"] **to worship her, and pour out drink offerings unto her, without our men?"** (Jeremiah, Chapter 44).

Do those of you who worship "The Queen of Heaven" feel the same? Are you able to understand these plain words and draw personal conclusions? Who was this **"QUEEN OF HEAVEN?"** When did people begin to worship her as the **"Queen of Heaven?"** For those interested in the whole history and origin of this mysterious **"Queen of Heaven,"** the one also considered to be the first **"MOTHER AND CHILD MADONNA,"** any history book about the religions of Assyria, Babylon, or Egypt would provide abundance of information. In brief, the first woman assuming this roll was the ancient queen of Assyria, Semiramis. Some historians tell us she was the mother/wife of the great warrior Nimrod mentioned in Genesis 10:8-10. He was the first empire builder and dictator of the ancient world. After his death, he and Queen Semiramis were deified by the masses and were given different names in different countries. In Egypt, they were called, *Isis* and *Osiris*. In Canaan the "Queen" was known as *Isht*ar, later *Easter*. In ancient cultures, this "Queen" was considered to be **"the Consort of God"** and **"THE QUEEN OF HEAVEN."** She was also known as **"The goddess of fertility."** The Greeks called her **"Venus."**

When the Faith about Christ began to spread throughout the Pagan Greek and Roman world, the uneducated masses flocked to the "new Faith" with two agendas in mind: on one hand, they desired to follow the Savior who offered them hope and deliverance from their miserable conditions. On the other, they wanted to retain many of their pagan practices and beliefs, and mix them with the "new faith." They all believed in the concept of the **Trinity.** They had many statutes throughout the empire of the **"Mother and Child Madonna,"**—the ancient Queen Semiramis and her child. They worshiped their gods on Sunday and kept the feast of Saturnalia on December 25th at the dead of winter. The "liberal" church leaders were perplexed at first, and then finally came up with the "ingenious solution" to resolve the matter and allow the "Church" to grow rapidly. They invited the masses with the alluring message: 'come as you as you are, Jesus loves you!' The Pagan Emperor Constantine, who desired to unify the Eastern and Western Empire under his absolute rule, cleverly and politically embraced the new rapidly growing "Christian" religion by molding it to his own liking. As a result of this appropriation of the "new Faith" by the Pagan Emperor Constantine, many of the Pagan religious practices were "Christened" and renamed to please The Emperor and the masses, as well as the "liberal" church leaders. As a result, the Sabbath was changed to Sunday—the lucky day of the masses. The "Mother and Child statutes of the ancient Madonna" were renamed "Mary and Jesus. Mary, in later times, became "The Queen of Heaven." Saturnalia was renamed Christmas, and Passover was renamed Easter—after the ancient goddess *Ishtar*. They have conveniently forgotten the Biblical fact: "Christ is our Passover," not our 'Easter!' Thus the religion of **"CHRISTIANITY"** was born! Those who insisted on following the true religion of the Apostles and Prophets of God were labeled "heretics." In the first few centuries, the "heretics" were known as the "Nazarenes." All unbiased historians of that period recognize fully this most amazing "transformation" of the "Church" known to this day as "Christianity." If The Truth and Facts of the Bible and history do matter, instead of "feelings and emotions," than we have the responsibility to look and proclaim: "The Emperor is naked"! If not, then may God have mercy on us all, since He did not have mercy on His own people when they departed away from Him and preferred, instead, to follow the fables, superstitions, and man-made concepts of "the spiritual deceivers" of their day.

The teachings about the **afterlife** and about Heaven and Hell were part and parcel of the ancient Pagan world—with some variations in different cultures and nations. The Gentile Church of Rome had absorbed many of those ancient Pagan concepts, since all of her members were of Pagan origin. Biblical knowledge was not highly esteemed by the followers of this Gentile church—and to this day they are not, and for obvious reasons! More so, it was mostly despised and many attempts were made, often successfully, to burn copies of the Bible. Followers of this Gentile religion were forbidden, throughout most of its history, from reading the Bible. "It is a venial sin," they were told, to read the Bible. When the Protestant "Reformation" came about, and with it the desire to read the Bible in one's own language, many of the translators were branded as "heretics," and some were burned at the stake.

In the 13th Century, the Italian poet from Florence, **Dante** (or full name, **Durante**) **Alighieri** appeared on the Italian Catholic scene. He was born in Florence (1265-1321), and from 1308-1321 he wrote his *philosophico-political poem* and masterpiece of world Literature named originally, *"Commedia"* and later *"Divina Commedia."* His true intent was to poke fun at the religious dogma and superstitious faith of his day. Dante wrote his *"Divine Comedy"* in *"Terza Rima"* or rhymes, consisting of 100 Cantos. In this poem, **Dante** was recounting an imaginary journey of the author through Hell, Purgatory, and Paradise. In this journey, Dante was guided through Hell and Purgatory by **Virgil**, and through Paradise by beautiful **Beatrice**. At first, the Church leaders did not like it, perceiving its true intent. Yet, being politically astute, they quickly embraced it and used it to their own double-fold advantage. First, they exerted fear and control over the illiterate and gullible masses—from birth to beyond the grave. Secondly, for sake of monetary manipulation, they felt that if they are successful in convincing the ignorant followers of the "veracity" of the *"Divine Comedy,"* and in the Church's power to determine the fate of the believers' **afterlife** destiny, they could hold absolute sway over their bodies and riches.

The *"Divine Comedy"* was a "blessing" for the Church. It made it possible for the Bishop of Rome, and every church leader to sell **"indulgence"** notes—which were 'able' to rescue any loved one from Hell or Purgatory—and send them, instead, to Paradise. That meant Mammon, and lots of it. The masses were scared to death, and were willing to pay through the nose while their 'spiritual leaders' and the bishops of their souls were laughing all the way to their 'banks.' This was, in great measure, the reason for the "Reformation," which was initiated by Martin Luther. It was the abuse and robbery against the masses, through fear—not the concepts of the **doctrine of the afterlife** itself that led to the revolt by Luther, and later other church leaders! The Protestant churches that sprang out of the Roman Church still believe in the same teachings about the **hereafter** in Heaven or Hell, and to this day! The understanding of the Apostles and the early Apostolic Church of these matters, as we shall uncover in the next chapter, were diametrically opposite to those of later time religion of "Christianity."

What about the later churches of the "Reformation" or the so called, the "Protestant Churches?" How much different are they from the "Mother Church" in regard to the subject at hand? Is their concept about the

afterlife or Heaven and Hell different than that of the Universal Church? Did they 'reform' anything in this area? Do those Protestant Churches, who claim to believe and read the Bible, and accept it as the sole infallible authority to their beliefs and teachings, have a similar understanding as that of the Apostles of Christ?

For centuries to come, the Protestant churches were inundated with many "Hell-Fire and brimstone" preachers. In their "Revival Tent Meetings" they would often "scare to death" their gullible and Biblically ignorant listeners about the "Horrors of Hell." To this day, one can hear those same "Fiery Sermons" in many churches of Fundamental Christianity." Many are "being saved" and "give their heart to the Lord" as they sheepishly walk down the aisle for the "altar call," because of their mortal fear of the dreaded "Eternal Hell Fire." Is this a true religion, or mere "vain worship?"

At funerals, one can often hear the "comforting" words of the preacher: "He or she is now with the Lord, and they are no more suffering. They are smiling at you and you can now pray to them, since they are now your guardian angels. At night, when you look up, you can see their stars." And many are being "comforted" by such most assuring words! In countless movies and books, the theme of the **afterlife** is very much evident. The stories of **"Peter in the pearly gates"** are most common and known to many. The hope and yearning of the "believers" in entering through the "pearly gates," in meeting Peter or other angels, in walking on the "streets paved with pure gold," is very much a part and parcel of every "devout Christian." Even in the world of comedy there is a great repertoire and jokes about "Saint Peter at the Pearly Gates." Are these all Biblically oriented teachings or mere hallucinations in the minds of those 'blessed' with fertile imagination? We need to know if "the Emperor is truly naked or not!" Much more can be said about the matter in Protestant circles, but this is not our emphasis in this work. We all know much about it! What we need to know is the truth of the matter!

Another "great" religion within the world of "Christianity" is the rapidly spreading and influential "Faith" of Mormonism. This is the religion, according to their believers, of the **"Later Day Saints."** They claim to possess the **"Last Revelation of Jesus Christ."** Their "Bible" or **"The Book of Mormon"** is, according to their teachings, **"Another Testament of Jesus Christ."** Are their concepts about the **afterlife** different from those of any other "Christian Church?"

On the first page of their "Book of Mormon" one can see a picture of Jesus in a standing position. He is laying on hands on one of the disciples, ordaining him as His apostle. Jesus, in this picture, appears to be a tall man with Nordic look, with long blond hair cascading down to His shoulders. Now, first of all, no one besides those who saw Him knows how Jesus looked like! In "Christian art" we can see paintings of Jesus and in modern times also pictures of Jesus. In some, He appears with short dark hair or long dark hair. In others, He is portrayed to have long blonde or short hair. In yet some other paintings, the artist decided to give Him curly hair—sometimes reddish, other times dark or blonde. So which one of this paintings or pictures depicts the true Jesus? Is anyone bearing a true witness in their depiction of the face of Jesus? What about the long hair in this "Book of Mormon?" Did Jesus have long Hair? Who was allowed and commanded to have long hair in Israel? The answer is: the one with the Nazarite vow. They were commanded to have long hair as long as their vow is in force. After that period, assuming it was a short—term vow, the Law or Torah commands all Nazerites to shave off their hair and burn it in a ceremonial act in the Temple.

The plain fact is this: Jesus was no Nazarite. He drunk wine—unlike His cousin John the Baptist who was under the Nazarite vow from his birth. And what does the Scripture tell us about a man donning long hair when he is not under the Nazarite vow? The Apostle Paul addressed this question to the church of Corinth. He wrote: **"Does not even nature itself teach you, that IF A MAN HAS LONG HAIR, IT IS A SHAME UNTO HIM?"** (II Corinthians 11:14). The person who placed this "picture" of Jesus on the first page of "The Book of Mormon" needs some illumination! It's a bad start for a book that claims to be "the Last Revelation of God." Also, the Ten Commandments contain an injunction against making a picture or representation of God. Those who visit the "Mormon Tabernacle" In Salt Lake city can see on the wall, in the visitors' building, a large painting portraying the Father and Jesus in full color. Now let's see what else we can read about the origin of the faith of Mormonism!

In the introduction to the Book of Mormon we read: "The Book of Mormon is a volume of Holy Scripture comparable to the Bible. The Book was written by many ancient prophets by the spirit of prophecy and revelation . . . The crowning event in the Book of Mormon is the personal ministry of the Lord Jesus Christ among the Nephites soon after his resurrection . . . It puts forth the doctrines of the gospel, outlines the plan of salvation, and tells men what they must do to gain peace in this life and eternal salvation in the world to come . . . After Mormon completed his writings, he delivered the account to his son Moroni, who added a few words of his own and hid up the plates in the hill Cumorah. On September 21, 1823, **THE SAME MORONI, THEN A GLORIFIED, RESURRECTED BEING**, appeared to the prophet Joseph Smith and instructed him relative to the ancient record and its destined translation into the English language.

"In due course, the plates were delivered to Joseph Smith, who translated them by the gift and power of God. The record is now published in many languages as a **NEW AND ADDITIONAL WITNESS** that Jesus Christ is the Son of the living God and that all who will come unto him and obey the laws and ordinances of his gospel [to the Mormons?] may be saved. Concerning this record, the prophet Joseph Smith said: "I told the brethren that the Book of Mormon was the most correct book on earth, and the keystone of our religion [how many religions does God have?], and a man would get nearer to God by abiding by its precepts, **THAN BY ANY OTHER BOOK**." [Does that include the Bible?]

"We invite all men everywhere to read the Book of Mormon . . . and then to ask God, the Eternal Father, in the name of Christ if the book is true . . . Those who gain this divine witness from the Holy Spirit will also come to know that by the same power that Jesus Christ is the Savior of the world, that Joseph Smith is his revelator and prophet in these last days, and that the Church of Jesus Christ of Latter-Day Saints is the Lord's kingdom once again established on the earth, preparatory to the second coming of the Messiah."

If the Mormon Church is "the Lord's kingdom established on this earth," should anyone continue to pray, "Thy kingdom come?" Whom was Jesus talking about when He said to His disciples: **" . . . Take heed that NO MAN deceive you. For MANY** [majority, in Biblical terminology] **shall come IN MY NAME, saying I am the Christ; and shall deceive many"** (Matthew 24:4-5). Remember also the warning of the Apostle Paul to the Galatian church: **"I marvel that you are so soon removed from Him that called you into the grace of Christ unto another Gospel. Which is not** [really] **another Gospel; but there be some that trouble you and would pervert the Gospel of Christ. BUT THOUGH WE, OR AN ANGEL FROM HEAVEN** [Moroni?]**, PREACH ANY OTHER GOSPEL UNTO YOU THAN THAT WHICH WE HAVE**

PREACHED UNTO YOU LET HIM [the angel] **BE ACCURSED. As we said before, so I now say again, IF ANY MAN** [Joseph Smith?] **PREACH ANY OTHER GOSPEL UNTO YOU THAN THAT YOU HAVE RECEIVED, LET HIM BE ACCURSED"** (Galatians 1:8-9). These are strong words and we must know the truth!

Did that deception take place in the past many centuries? Is it still taking place in our times? How can we tell? Was Moroni, who according to Mormons' dogma is **"A GLORIFIED RESURRECTED BEING,"** truly a "man" of God? We are all admonished **"to try the spirits and see whether they are of God."** How can we tell if Moroni is speaking the truth? How can we know if what the Mormons call, "Another Testament," is truly from Christ? How can we "prove all things," as Scripture commands us? How can we really tell if the "Emperor is naked?" In the next chapter we shall present the answers from The Book and Words of God, His Christ, and His true servants!

So let's now compare the teachings of the "spiritual leaders," who claim to be the "Ministers of the Gospel of Jesus Christ," with those statements Jesus and His disciples spoke and recorded for all to read! One does not have to be a Christian, or even religious, to understand these plain statements or teachings of Jesus and His Apostles in the New Testament. It is also extremely important to bear in mind: all the Apostles and disciples (in the early church) of Jesus Christ were Jews; all were raised on the Torah and the Prophets of God; all grew up in the Synagogue and were obedient to the Law or Torah of Moses. They were not Catholics, Protestants, Greek or Russian Orthodox, nor Mormons! They were all Torah abiding and true servants of God and His anointed—The Redeemer of Israel!

CHAPTER 5

NEW TESTAMENT TEACHINGS ABOUT THE AFTERLIFE, HEAVEN & HELL

It was about two thousand years ago when the prophesied Messiah appeared "unto His own." He was born to a Jewish mother, and raised in a Jewish community. He attended the synagogue every Sabbath day, and made pilgrimages with his family to the Temple in Jerusalem on every Holy Day—as ordained by God and kept by the Jews. Jesus obeyed His Heavenly Father and kept all of His laws or Torah. In order to be the perfect Lamb—without spot or blemish—Jesus could not transgress one single Law of His Father—be it small or great! His religion was that of His Father, not of His own making—and He made that very clear to all! He told His people and disciples, **"Man shall live by every word that proceeds out of the mouth of God** [His Father]**."** He did not invent a new religion for His followers!

In His first words to His people, this is what we read: **"Now after John was put in prison, Jesus came into Galilee PREACHING THE GOSPEL OF THE KINGDOM OF GOD. And saying, the time is fulfilled, and the Kingdom of God is at hand; REPENT YOU, AND BELIEVE THE GOSPEL"** (Mark 1:14-15). Before we can have any relationship with God or Christ, we must remember the words of the Apostle Paul and the crux of his ministry. He stated: **"Testifying both to the Jews, and also to the Greeks, REPENTANCE TOWARD GOD, and FAITH toward our Lord Jesus Christ"** (Acts 20:21). This was the main emphasis of Jesus' ministry! He reminded all of His kinsmen, the people of Judah, of His loyalty to the Torah of His Father, stating: **"Think not that I am come to destroy the Law** [Torah]**, or the Prophets; I am not come to destroy** ["by nailing it to the cross"]**, but to fulfill. For verily I say unto you, till Heaven and earth pass, one jot or one title** [or one iota] **shall in wise pass from the Law** [or Torah]**, till all be fulfilled.**

Whosoever therefore shall break one of this least commandments, and shall teach men so, shall be called the least in the Kingdom of Heaven; but whosoever shall DO AND TEACH them, shall be called great in the Kingdom of Heaven. For I say unto you, that except your righteousness shall exceed the righteousness [not unrighteousness] **of the scribes and Pharisees, you shall in no wise enter into the Kingdom of Heaven"** (Matthew 5:17-20).

Do the "Christian churches" teach this "Gospel" of Jesus Christ? Does the Mormon Church abide by the Laws of the Torah of God and His Christ? Are all the teachings of the so called "Christians"—be they Catholics, Protestants, Orthodox, or Mormons in accordance with the Torah or Law of Christ, which He said He came to fulfill? His Torah, which is the same as that of His Father's Torah, or that of His people Israel, according to Him, will not pass away **"until all things are fulfilled."** Are "Heaven and earth" still with us today? When one of His followers asked Him, **" . . . Good Master, what shall I do to enter into life,"** did he tell him, 'forget all about the Law or Torah—I'm going to nail it to the cross?' No! He replied, **" . . . If you want to enter into life, KEEP THE COMMANDMENTS** [or Mitzvot in Hebrew]" (Matthew 19:16-17). Do all "Christians" keep God's and His Commandments or Torah? **"If you love Me,"** He admonished His followers, **"keep My Commandments."** He knew that most would not, therefore He asked: **"Why do you call Me Lord, Lord, and do not do what I say?"**

What did Christ say? What are Christ's Commandments anyway? When did He first give these Commandments, and to whom? Let the Apostle Paul, the one "sent to the Gentiles," respond! He stated: **"Moreover, brethren, I do not want you to be ignorant** [as many are to this day], **how that all OUR FATHERS** [not yours] **were under the cloud and all passed through the sea; and were all baptizes unto Moses in the cloud** [where God dwelt] **and in the sea; and did all eat the same SPIRITUAL** [not physical] **MEAT; and did all drink the same SPIRITUAL** [not physical] **DRINK: for they drank of that SPIRITUAL ROCK that followed them; AND THAT ROCK WAS CHRIST"** (I Corinthians 10:1-4). Have the "spiritual leaders" of "Christianity" taught their followers, in the past many centuries, this teaching of the Apostle to the Gentiles—Paul?

What did Christ feed His people Israel with in Sinai and for the next forty years in the wilderness through Moses? Is it a mystery? This Christ that came down on Mount Sinai and gave His people Israel, whom He married then, His Law or Torah—the same as that of His Father's—stated through His Prophet Malachi these words: **"Remember you the Law [or Torah] of Moses My servant, WHICH I [Jesus] COMMANDED UNTO HIM IN HOREB [or Sinai] FOR ALL ISRAEL, WITH THE STATUTES AND JUDGMENTS"** (Malachi 4:4). Which part of this clear statement we do not understand?

Christ made many statements about the importance of keeping the Law of His Father, yet few are those who pay attention to Him or to His teachings about the Law. Did His Apostles teach anything different? John, the beloved disciple of Christ stated: **"And hereby we do know that we know Him, IF WE KEEP HIS COMMANDMENTS. He that says, I know Him, and keeps not His Commandments, IS A LIAR, and the truth is not in him"** (I John 2:3-4). In Chapter 3:4, John declared: **"Whosoever commits sin transgresses the Law [or Torah], for SIN IS THE TRANSGRESSION OF THE LAW [or Torah].** In Chapter 5:3 John added: **"For this is the love of God that we keep His Commandments, and His Commandments are not grievous"** [as many "Christians" teach]. Are you being taught by your "spiritual teachers" to obey the Commandments of God and His Christ? Why not?

How about the Apostle to the Gentiles, Paul? Did he teach any other doctrine or Gospel? This is what he said to the church in Rome: **"For there is no respect of persons with God [the Father of Christ]. For as many as have sinned without [the knowledge of the] Law, shall also perish without Law; and as many as have sinned in the Law shall be judged by the Law; FOR NOT THE HEARERS OF THE LAW [or Torah] ARE JUST BEFORE GOD, BUT THE DOERS OF THE LAW SHALL BE JUSTIFIED"** (Romans 2:11-13). Do "Christian churches" teach, faithfully, these plain words of the Apostle to the Gentiles? Do the "spiritual leaders" of "Christianity" teach their followers that we are not **ONLY** saved by Grace, but must also be keepers of the Torah or Law of God if we are to be **JUSTIFIED?** That's why Paul taught **"Repentance toward God and faith in Jesus Christ."** Did your pastor ever give you a sermon about this most crucial doctrine of Christ and the Apostle Paul? Why not?

Of this Law of God, Paul declared: **"Wherefore the Law [or Torah] is Holy, and the Commandment Holy, and just, and good."** He added: **"For we know that the Law [or Torah] is spiritual, but**

I am carnal, sold under sin" (Romans 7:12, 14). Why is the Law or Torah so important to God? Why did David, **"the man according to God's own heart,"** declare: **"The fear of the Lord is the beginning of wisdom; a good understanding have all they who DO** [not reject] **His Commandments?"** (Psalm 110:111). The Apostle to the Gentiles, Paul, explained it this way: **"Love works no ill to his neighbor; therefore, love is the fulfilling of the Law** [or Torah]**"** (Roman 13:10). Those who do not understand the nature of God, which is Love, and obey the Royal Law or Torah of Love, in any given religion, are in darkness in many areas of the Truth and do not even know it. That's why many are confused about the doctrines of Heaven and Hell, about the **afterlife**, about many other teachings that proceeded out of the mouth of God. To that end, Jesus, who was fully obedient to the Law or Torah of His Father, stated: **"Man shall not live by bread alone, but by every word that proceeds out of the mouth of God"** (Matthew 4:4). He made that statement to **THE DEVIL** who was attempting to lead Him away from God. And this is the problem with most men of religion: they do not follow in the footsteps of the perfect example—Jesus the Christ—who was obedient to His father's Commandments unto death! And if **"Satan deceives the whole world"** (Revelation 12:9), it is because most of us do not have "the love of the truth" in our hearts and our minds. We love to be lied to through fables, superstitions, and fairy tale stories. We love to watch movies or read novels about demons, about the dead, or Ghosts and witchcraft. Is there any wonder why the movies and books about Harry Potter and the likes are the biggest hits among young and old worldwide? Who among these people care about the Truth?

As was mentioned earlier, it bears repeating again—the warning of the apostle Paul about the state of mind of People at the end time. He wrote to Timothy: **"Now the Spirit speaks expressly, that at the later times some shall depart from the faith, giving heed to seducing spirits, and doctrines of demons** [taught by the 'spiritual teachers' as the truth]**; speaking lies in hypocrisy; having their conscience seared with hot iron; forbidding to marry and commanding to abstain from meats . . ."** (I Timothy 4:1-4). What 'Church' teaches this "doctrine of demons" to her clergy? To the Corinthian church the Apostle Paul wrote, warning them about the deceivers: **"For such are false apostles, deceitful workers, transforming themselves into the apostles of Christ. And no marvel** [they are able to do it]**; for Satan himself is transformed into an**

angel of light. Therefore it is no great thing if HIS MINISTERS [whom their gullible followers are not able to discern] **also be transformed as the ministers of righteousness** [having, like their mentor the Devil, a perfect alibi, yet] **whose end shall be according to their works** [since nobody can deceive God]" (II Corinthians 11:13-15).

Christ had warned earlier all those willing to listen: " **. . . Take heed, that no man deceive you. For many shall come in My name** [and they do it in every "Christian" church], **saying, I am Christ** [not denying His name, and that's how the deception begins]**; and shall deceive many** [because few check up on them]" (Matthew 24:4-5).

So what did Jesus and His true servants tell us about man's destiny, immediately after death? What did they tell their fellow Jews, who were all raised on the Law or Torah and the Prophets, about the **hereafter**, about Heaven and Hell?

John the Baptist, a Jewish Priest and Nazarite, raised on the Torah and the Prophets wrote: **"NO MAN HAS SEEN GOD AT ANY TIME; THE ONLY BEGOTTEN SON** [who saw Him] **WHO IS IN THE BOSOM OF THE FATHER, HE DECLARED HIM**" (John 1:18). Jesus' task, among other things, was to reveal the Father to man, since no one has ever seen or heard Him before. Speaking to Nicodemus, a ruler of the Jews and a chief Rabbi, Jesus declared: **"AND NO MAN** [or woman] **HAS ASCENDED UP TO HEAVEN, BUT HE THAT CAME DOWN FROM HEAVEN, EVEN THE SON OF MAN WHO IS IN** [or from] **HEAVEN"** (John 3:13). Does one need to be a rocket scientist to understand this plain statement, or just a little faith?

Jesus continued: **"And as Moses lifted up the serpent in the wilderness, even so must the Son of man be lifted up; that whosoever believes in Him should not perish but have eternal life"** (John 3:14-15). What was this serpent all about? Did you ever ask yourself why was Jesus crucified and not stoned to death—as the manner of the Jews was in accordance with the Law—for the sin of blasphemy? Stephen was stoned to death for the supposed 'sin,' which the Jews called blasphemy. Why wasn't Jesus stoned likewise? Why were Jesus crucified by the hands of Roman soldiers? The Jews never crucified anyone, yet some of their chief Priests cried out: "Crucify Him, Crucify Him!" This is totally contrary to Jewish Law, so why did God allow it to be so?

Let's now cover the account of the serpent in the wilderness that Jesus referred to in His talk to Nicodemus (John 3:14). In the book of Numbers,

Chapter 29, we read this account: **"And the people spoke against God** [as many still do], **and against Moses, Why did you bring us up out of Egypt to die in the wilderness? For there is no bread, neither is there any water; and our soul loathes this light bread** [or manna]. **And the Lord sent FIERY SERPENTS among the people, and they bit the people; and much people of Israel died. Therefore the people came to Moses, and said, we have sinned, for we have spoken against the Lord, and against you; pray unto the Lord, that He take away the serpents from us. And Moses prayed for the people."** Still, this did not stop the plague. God wanted Israel to learn a lesson about faith—with future implications. The account continues: **"And the Lord said unto Moses, MAKE YOU A FIERY SERPENT AND SET IT UPON A POLE; AND IT SHALL COME TO PASS, THAT EVERYONE THAT IS BITTEN, WHEN HE LOOKS UPON IT, SHALL LIVE. And Moses made A SERPENT OF BRASS, and put it upon a pole, and it came to pass, that if a serpent had bitten any man, WHEN HE BEHELD THE SERPENT OF BRASS, HE LIVED"** (Numbers 21:5-9). That's why Jesus was crucified and not stoned, according to the Law!

Israel, at that time, did not fully understand the full implications of the true purpose for the brass serpent on the pole until its fulfillment on the stake by their Redeemer! Those who were willing to look up, with faith, at the serpent of brass—a symbol of both sin and the Devil, lived—those who did not, died. This was the ultimate lesson and purpose of the serpent of brass that was placed on the pole: look up with faith on the one hanging on it, Christ, and live! Those who would refuse to accept the sacrifice on their behalf, and look up, would not live. The Israelites remembered this lesson of faith well, and for many generations to come! But what happens when people are idol worshipers by nature? They make an idol or icon out of the Symbol of health and life, and begin to worship the creation more than the Creator—the One represented by the icon! Let's see what the people of Israel did with this symbol and icon of life in later generations. Let's find out how human nature works in such cases, and see if we can learn some lessons from it.

We are now in the days of righteous King Hezekiah of Judah, and about 700 years later. What were the people of God doing throughout this many years with the serpent of brass? Of the acts of King Hezekiah, we read: **"And he did that which was right in the sight of the Lord, according to** all **that his father David did. He removed the high places** [where

God's people worshiped idols], **and broke the images, and cut down the groves** [where people worshiped foreign gods], **AND BROKE IN PIECES THE BRASS SERPENT THAT MOSES HAD MADE; FOR UNTO THOSE DAYS THE CHILDREN OF ISRAEL DID BURN INCENSE TO IT; and he called it Nehushtan. He trusted in the Lord God of Israel; so that after him there was none like him among all the kings of Judah, nor any that were before him** [since David]. **For he did cleave to the Lord, and departed not from following Him, but kept His Commandments** [one of which was to eradicate idol worship from Israel], **which the Lord commanded Moses"** (II Kings 18:4-5).

God never commanded Israel to offer incense, or regard as an icon the brass serpent. Israel, led by their misguided "spiritual leaders" had done it on their own! Since human nature is always the same, it is most probable that many in Israel made themselves replicas of the brass serpent to place in their homes, places of worship or, perhaps, carry around their necks. How different are many, who call themselves "Christians" in their treatment and veneration of "The Cross?" Paul called it, **"The shame of the cross."** He stated: **"Cursed be he that hangs on the tree,"** quoting the Law or Torah. He said: **"Christ became a curse for us."** He took upon Himself the curse of the Law, which was death, in order to offer those who look up at Him—as Israel did on the serpent of brass—the gift of life. This is what the brass serpent was to symbolize. And the question for us is very simple: Who told "Christians" to treat the Cross as an object of worship and veneration, an icon to hang around their necks or carry in processions? Why do many bow down to it? Idol worshipers made replicas of their gods and other items of religious significance. They placed them in their homes, in their places of worship, on their ears and around their necks. As King Solomon had said, **"There is nothing new under the sun."**

In the Scripture many claim to be their favorite one, Jesus stated: **"For God so loved the world that He gave His only begotten Son, that whomsoever believes in Him should not perish, but have everlasting life"** (John 3:16). How many believe the fable about 'going to Heaven' in contrast to the Biblical teaching about eternal life versus perishing? Jesus told His people concerning those who died when the tower fell on them (like those who perished when the "Twin Towers" fell on them in 9/11): **" . . . Except you repent** [of breaking God's Law or Torah], **you shall all likewise perish"** (Luke 13:3). The unfortunate people in 9/11 were incinerated when the Twin Towers fell—and so did the Prophets of God, as we saw earlier, describe the fate of those who refuse to repent from either teaching or following false prophets and their teachings. God loves us, but He is not to be mocked—"whatever we sow, we shall reap." The children of Israel died in the wilderness and could not enter into "the land of promise," and such will be the fate of those who follow in their footsteps.

During the fall Feast Season, perhaps on the day of the Feast of Trumpets (John 5:1), Christ was teaching in the Temple. These were His words to His fellow Jews: **"Verily, verily, I say unto you, the hour is coming, and now is** [approaching], **WHEN THE DEAD** [not the living in Heaven] **SHALL HEAR THE VOICE OF THE SON OF GOD; AND THEY THAT HEAR SHALL LIVE . . . MARVEL NOT AT THIS; FOR THE HOUR IS COMING, WHEN ALL THOSE IN THE GRAVES SHALL HEAR HIS VOICE, AND SHALL COME FORTH** [out of the graves]**; THEY THAT HAVE DONE GOOD, UNTO THE RESURRECTION OF LIFE; AND THEY THAT HAVE DONE EVIL, UNTO THE RESURRECTION OF CONDEMNATION"** (John 5:24-28).

It's important to note! None of the Jews (except the Sadducees) had disputed the reality of the resurrection from the dead. None had questioned Jesus' statements about coming out of the grave. This was common knowledge among the Jews at that time. This total absence of any dispute between Jesus and His people, and later, between the Apostles and their Jewish kinsmen, is a resounding testimony to the prevailing understanding in the Jewish community about the teachings of the Prophets concerning the state of the dead and their future. No Jew in the first century and no Rabbi had believed or taught about an **afterlife**, immediately after death, or the doctrine of going to Heaven or Hell! These false teachings came later and gradually took roots in the Jewish community—yet **"in the beginning it was not so,"** as Christ stated about other matters.

Shortly before the Passover (John 6:4), Jesus spoke these words to His people: **"I came down from Heaven not to do My own will, but the will of Him that sent Me. And this is the Father's will who sent Me, that of all whom He has given Me I should lose no one, but SHOULD RAISE HIM UP** [from the grave] **AGAIN AT THE LAST DAY. And this is the will of Him who sent Me, that everyone who sees the Son, and believes on Him, MAY HAVE ETERNAL LIFE** [since no one has it now, and no one has an immortal soul]**; AND I WILL RAISE HIM UP**

AT THE LAST DAY . . . NO MAN CAN COME TO ME, EXCEPT THE FATHER WHO HAS SENT ME DRAWS HIM [since no one can "give his heart to the Lord," unless the Father first invited him to do so], and I WILL RAISE HIM UP IN THE LAST DAY . . . NOT THAT ANYONE HAS SEEN THE FATHER, SAVE HE [Jesus] WHO IS OF GOD, HE HAS SEEN THE FATHER [since all of the servants and Prophets of God are still in the grave awaiting the resurrection]. Whoso eats My flesh and drinks My blood [or My teachings] has [the promise of] eternal life; AND I WILL RAISE HIM UP AT THE LAST DAY . . . These things He said in the synagogue, as He taught in Capernaum" (John 6:39-59).

Notice how many times Jesus repeated the statement: "AND I SHALL RAISE HIM UP IN THE LAST DAY!" How many who call themselves "Christians" or followers of Christ believe His words? How many times does He have to repeat Himself before He is believed? Many claim, "I love the Lord," "Jesus is Lord," I gave my heart to the Lord," yet by their "faith" in the **afterlife**, and other fables, are denying Him! Are you one of them? Why?

During the "Last Supper," which was eaten **"before the feast of the Passover"** (John 13:1-2), Jesus told His disciples: **"Little children, yet a little while I am with you. You shall seek Me; and as I said unto the Jews, WHEREVER I GO** [back to Heaven, after the resurrection]**, YOU CANNOT COME** [since no one goes to Heaven except the One who descended from Heaven] **. . ."** (John 13:33). Should we believe and put our trust in the Master's words, or the words of our 'spiritual leaders' on this matter? What do you think?

Matthew tells us: **"Jesus, when He had cried again with a loud voice, yielded up the spirit. And behold, the veil of the Temple was torn in two from the top to the bottom; and the earth did quake, and the rocks shuttered; AND THE GRAVES WERE OPENED; AND MANY BODIES OF THE [Jewish] SAINTS WHICH SLEPT** [in the dust or graves] **AROSE** [or rose to life from the dead]**, AND CAME OUT OF THE GRAVES** [not from Heaven] **AFTER HIS RESURRECTION, AND WENT INTO THE HOLY CITY AND APPEARED UNTO MANY"** (Matthew 27:50-53). How much more plain can it be? Why is it that no "Christian" who believes in the fable of the **afterlife**, considers this account? The truthful answer is simple: In the absence of the love of the truth, facts and truth do not matter! That's why "the Emperor is naked" and almost no one can 'see' it!

Luke records this account: **"Now upon the first day of the week** [Sunday]**, very early in the morning, they came unto the sepulcher, bringing the spices which they had prepared . . . and they found the stone rolled away from the sepulcher.** **And they entered in and found not the body of the Lord Jesus.** **And it came to pass, as they were much perplexed thereabout, behold two men** [or angels] **stood by them in shining garments; and as they were afraid, and bowed down their faces to the earth, they said unto them, WHY SEEK YOU THE LIVING AMONG THE DEAD? HE IS NOT HERE BUT IS RISEN; remember how He spoke unto you when He was yet in Galilee, saying, The Son of man must be delivered into the hands of sinful men, and be crucified, and the third day rise again** [from the grave, not Heaven or a fictitious Limbo]" (Luke 24:1-7).

Christ was dead in the grave for three days. He did not go anywhere immediately after death! Still, those who call themselves "Christians" believe that one's "immortal soul" leaves the body immediately after death. If a person is righteous, they believe, he goes to Heaven through the "Pearly Gates." If so, how come Jesus had to rise from the dead, after three days, and then come out of the grave once the stone was rolled away by the angels and the earthquake? John's account tells us that when Mary saw Jesus near the sepulcher, she did not recognize Him at first. When she did, after he called her by name, she attempted to touch His garment. But, we read, **"Jesus said unto her, touch Me not FOR I AM NOT YET ASCENDED TO My Father . . ."** (John 20:11-17). Even after Jesus rose from the dead, He still had not ascended up to Heaven to meet the Father and be accepted as the perfect sacrifice for sin!

Let's go now to the book of Acts and see what the Apostles told their fellow Jews about the **afterlife**! Peter reminded his countrymen about their roll in delivering Jesus to the hands of the Romans so He can be crucified. Yet, he told them also that: **" . . . God had raised** [Jesus] **up, having loosed the pains of death** [without which Jesus would still be in the grave to this moment]**; because it was not possible that He should be held by it . . . For David spoke concerning Him . . . because You will not leave my soul** [David's] **in Hell** [or the grave]**, neither will You allow Your Holy One to see corruption** [in the grave] **. . . Men and brethren, let me freely speak unto you of the patriarch David, THAT HE IS BOTH DEAD** [not alive in Heaven] **AND BURIED, AND HIS SEPULCHER IS WITH US UNTO THIS DAY . . . HE SEEING THIS**

BEFORE SPOKE OF THE RESURRECTION OF CHRIST [from the dead in the grave], **THAT HIS SOUL WAS NOT LEFT IN HELL** [or the grave], **NEITHER HIS FLESH DID SEE CORRUPTION. THIS JESUS HAD GOD RAISED UP** [since He was dead in His grave for three days, not alive]." Then Peter made this very plain statement, in the Temple, to his Jewish audience about the fate of David: **"Men and brethren, let me freely speak unto you of the Patriarch David, THAT HE IS BOTH DEAD** [not alive] **AND BURIED and his sepulcher is with us unto this day . . . FOR DAVID HAS NOT ASCENDED INTO THE HEAVENS . . ."** (Acts 2:22-34).

None of the Jews or leaders in the Temple had disputed that fact about David's death to their day! Why? Because none of them believed, to that day, in the fable of the **afterlife**! As for the 'faith' of those in later times, well, it's a different story.

Christ confirmed earlier this reality, which most so-called "Christians" do not believe to this day: **"AND NO MAN HAS ASCENDED UP TO HEAVEN, BUT HE THAT CAME DOWN FROM HEAVEN . . ."** (John 3:13). No Jew at that time has contradicted the words of Peter concerning David, because they too believed the same teaching! In later times, this true Biblical teaching about the **afterlife** was gradually to be rejected by Jews and "Christians." Why? The answer is: Because the love of the Truth is lacking in both communities of "believers."

Many read the parable of Lazarus and the rich man without comprehending its true meaning. Jesus in this **PARABLE**, which was not a real account, was trying to make a point. In Middle East culture, stories or parables are told for the sake of making a point. In the Western culture many tend to get confused by ascribing truth to the parable itself, while forgetting the point it is intended to make. Most of those reading the parable of Lazarus and the rich man, assume the story is real and are misled to believe a false concept about Heaven and Hell. We shall cover this **PARABLE** in a later chapter dedicated to "what about questions." We must understand: God never contradicts Himself, and neither His true servants. If we do not understand, it's because we do not consider the whole matter, as King Solomon admonished all to do!

In Luke 23, we read about the two thieves crucified with Jesus. The two robbers were Jews, not Catholics or Protestants! They, like all Jews, were raised on the teachings of the Law and the Prophets. They knew the original Biblical teachings about the **afterlife**. One of them, in a spirit of repentance, turned and " . . . **said unto Jesus, Lord, remember me when You come into Your kingdom. And Jesus said unto him, verily I say unto you, today shall you be with Me in Paradise**" (Luke 23:39-43).

When we die, just like in our sleep, we no longer are aware of the passage of time. When God resurrects us, in the last day, it's still the same day and moment for us. When the repentant thief is resurrected and finds himself in the Kingdom of God, on earth, as all the Prophets and Christ Himself made very plain, it shall be a split second later for him after his death. This is what Jesus meant by "today" and not what men of ignorance have concocted in their darkened minds many years later! Many conveniently forget the fact that Jesus Himself did not ascend to Heaven until few days later. He was dead and buried in His grave until "the third day." His word "today," to the repentant robber, obviously did not mean "today!"

Jesus taught His disciples to pray: **"Our Father who is in Heaven, Holy is Your Name. Your kingdom come, Your will be done ON EARTH as it is done in Heaven . . ."** (Matthew 7:9-10). What need is there for this prayer, if after death all go to Heaven or Hell? If "the Church is the kingdom of God," as many teach; if Heaven is the destination and hence the "Kingdom of God," why does the Messiah need to return to earth to establish the "Kingdom of God," as all the Prophets of God have testified from the beginning in hundreds of prophecies?

Speaking of the time when He (Jesus) shall judge all men, Jesus spoke of the last day coming judgment on a group of sinners, which most 'religious' people believed, and still do, were all sent to "Hell." Jesus sent His disciples on a local missionary activity among the people of Judah, telling them: **"And whosoever shall not receive you, nor hear your words, when you depart out of that house or city, shake off the dust of your feet. Verily I say unto you, it shall be more tolerable for the land of Sodom and Gomorrah in the Day of Judgment** [in the last day], **than for that city**" (Matthew 10:14-15). Obviously, this statement makes it very clear: the people of Sodom and Gomorrah are not in Hell, but are dead. They, like everyone else—the good and the bad—are awaiting the resurrection and judgment in the last day.

As we mentioned earlier in Chapter 2, the people of Sodom and the like, as we read in Ezekiel Chapter 16, will be brought back to life, will be judged and then restored to their former estates—according to God. What ignorant and blind men of religion said, and still do, about the supposed fate of sinners—who are slated "to burn forever in Hell"—is certainly a figment of their own hateful imagination. It exposes them for what they really are made of, and what spirit is really in them. These blind self-made "spiritual" leaders forget that God does not want the **"wicked to perish, but that he should turn away from his deeds,"** as the true Prophets and Apostles of God have often stated. The people of Sodom and the like, will be given their first chance to know God and repent in the coming final judgment day—after God first resurrects them from the grave. And when they do, they shall enter into God's kingdom on earth and experience Paradise instead of Hell. To that end, God **"so loved the world and gave His son so that none who is willing to believe** [either in this lifetime or in the judgment] **should not perish"** (John 3:16).

Isaiah the prophet writes: **"Listen to me you that follow after righteousness** [not fables and deceptions], **you that seek the Lord** [and not the false teachings of confused men]**; look to the Rock from whom you were hewn, and to the hole of the pit** [or grave] **from where you are dug. Look unto Abraham your father** [in the resurrection, as Lazarus would], **and unto Sarah that bare you; for I** [God] **called him alone, and blessed him, and increased him. For the Lord** [the God of Israel and her Redeemer] **shall comfort Zion** [or the nation of Israel], **He will comfort all her waste places; and HE WILL MAKE HER WILDERNESS LIKE EDEN AND HER DESERT LIKE THE GARDEN OF THE LORD . . ."** (Isaiah 51:1-3). This is the "Kingdom" or "Paradise" the thief and Jesus were thinking of, not the later fable men of ignorance have invented and deceived many to believe in!

The Apostle Peter was commissioned by Christ, as were all the other 11 disciples, to **"go to the lost sheep of the house of Israel."** They were forbidden to go the Samaritans or the way of the Gentiles (Matthew 10:5-6), unlike Paul whose commission was to both Jew and Gentile—with emphases on the Gentiles (Acts 9:15). Of this commission, Paul wrote to the Galatians: **" . . . When they** [the Church leaders in Jerusalem] **saw that the GOSPEL** [or good tidings] **OF THE UNCIRCUMCISION** [or Gentiles] **WAS COMMITTED UNTO ME, AS THE GOSPEL OF THE CIRCUMCISION** [or Israelites] **WAS UNTO PETER . . . And when James, Cephas, and John, who seemed to be pillars, perceived the Grace that was given unto me, they gave me and Barnabas the right hand of fellowship; THAT WE SHOULD GO UNTO THE HEATHEN** [Gentiles], **AND THEY UNTO THE CIRCUMCISION"**

(Galatians 2:7-9). The Church of Rome, many years later, in order to gain the preeminence over both halves of the Roman Empire, begun to claim that Peter was "the first bishop of Rome or Holy See," and thus giving the Bishop of Rome the 'right' to establish a line of succession, which is still in place to this day. The Apostles, including Paul and Peter, had a different opinion of this frivolous claim!

Peter, who was then located in the center of the Jewish community in Babylon, wrote to his fellow Israelites in Asia Minor, present day Turkey: **"But there were false prophets** [in Israel] **among the people, even as there shall be false teachers among you** [Israelites]**, who privately** [or in secret first would] **bring damnable heresies, even denying the Lord** [through false teachings] **that bought them, and bring upon themselves swift destruction. AND MANY** [or the majority] **SHALL FOLLOW THEIR PERNICIOUS** [or lascivious] **WAYS; BY REASON OF WHOM THE WAY OF THE TRUTH SHALL BE EVIL SPOKEN OF. And through covetousness shall they with feigned words make merchandise of you; whose judgment now of a long time lingers not, and their damnation slumbers not"** (II Peter 2:1-3). And that's why **"The Emperor is naked!"** Foolishness is, after all, a consequence of choices we make! If a mortal man can give us salvation, let's follow him! But if not, then what are we doing in the cesspool of spiritual vomit, as God calls it? He said of man's concoctions: **"All tables are full of** [spiritual] **vomit and filthiness, so that there is no place clean"** (Isaiah 28:8). Does God know what He is talking about?

Of the dominant religious organization in the Western world, this is what Jesus told His disciple John through His angel: **"And there came one of the seven angels which had the seven vials, and talked with me, saying unto me, 'come here; I will show unto you the judgment of the great whore** [or fallen away church, since the Bible refers to churches as 'women'] **that sits upon many waters** [or nations]**; with whom the kings of the earth have committed** [spiritual] **fornication, and the inhabitants of the earth have been made** [spiritually] **drunk with the wine** [or teachings] **of her fornications** [or adulterated doctrines]**. So he carried me in the spirit into the wilderness; and I saw a woman** [or church] **sit upon a scarlet colored beast** [or civil and military power]**, full of names of blasphemy, having seven heads and ten horns. And the woman was arrayed in purple and scarlet color** [as can be seen in the attire of the church Cardinals]**, and decked with gold and precious**

stones and pearls [being a very rich church], **having a golden cup in her hand FULL OF ABOMINATION AND FILTHINESS OF HER** [spiritual] **FORNICATION; and upon her forehead a name written, MYSTERY BABYLON THE GREAT, THE MOTHER OF HARLOTS** [or offshoots and smaller churches] **AND ABOMINATIONS OF THE EARTH. And I saw the woman drunk with the blood of the Saints** [who remained faithful to the pure teachings of God and His true servants], **and with the blood of the martyrs of Jesus . . ."** (Revelation 17:1-6).

The "great church" in Rome was fully aware of the intent of these words and its damming indictment against her. It is for this specific reason that she often ordered the burning of the Bible on many occasions. Those who attempted, in time past, to expose the identity of the "whore" to the masses, were often burned at the stake. Reading the Bible became a "venial sin" in this church, and those who asked too many questions of the priest, were, at best, excommunicated. It is this church that has spread and taught the non-Biblical fables about the **afterlife**, about Heaven and Hell, about Ghosts and other superstitions. When unbiased historians looked at the turbulent and dusty period in the Roman Empire, after the death of the original Apostles of Christ, they all noticed that the newly emerging church on the scene—once the curtains of history were raised again—was a brand new church which had little resemblance to the Apostolic Church established by Christ and His disciples. It is during that turbulent period and age of upheaval that all historians noticed the different doctrines about the immortality of the soul, about the **afterlife,** about Heaven and Hell, and many others begin to emerge. These previously unknown teachings, in the Apostolic Church, did rapidly take deep roots in the minds of the Biblically illiterate "former" Pagans that inundated the "church" by the millions. They brought with them their old fables and superstitions and mixed them with "the new faith," taught by the genuine Disciples of Christ and their faithful followers.

Since it is not the main purpose of this work to deal with the adulteration of the Biblical record by many, we shall concentrate on the subject at hand. Those interested in deeper information and details, can listen to the free online series on the "Law" at: www.teachingthelaw.org. More detailed information can be found in other works mentioned at the beginning of this book. They can be purchased from the publisher at: Http://www.authorhouse.com. Their hotline for phone orders is: 1-888-280-7715.

Let's go now to the writings of the Apostle Paul who had much to say about this subject. In his book to the Romans, in Chapter 9, Paul explained the difference between life and death, and the relationship between these two opposites to sin and righteousness. We sinned, but Jesus did not! Still, according to the will of God, Christ paid the penalty for our sins by being scourged, crucified, speared to death, and finally buried in the grave for three days. If God did not resurrect Him after three days from the grave, Jesus would have still been dead to this day—and humanity would not have a savior to resurrect us all from the grave and death! This is the simple and sober teaching Paul gave everyone he met. He said: **"Now if we be dead with Christ** [first, dead to sin while alive, then dead in the grave while awaiting for our resurrection by Christ from the grave], **we believe that we shall also live with Him** [after our resurrection, at the end time] **. . . For the wages of sin** [or transgression of the Law/Torah] **is death; but** [in contrast] **the gift of God is eternal life through Jesus Christ our Lord"** (Romans 9:8, 23).

Notice how Paul, a man raised on the teachings of the Torah and the Hebrew Prophets, contrasted **"the wages of sin"** that lead to death with **"the gift of God,"** which is eternal life. What comes in between is the grave and death—or captivity—in Biblical language! Unless we are to be resurrected at the end time by the Redeemer of Israel, there will be no "gift of Eternal life" for us. We must all die because of sin, as God warned Adam. We must all remain in the grave, if we died prior to the end time return of the Savior, at the last day, until the day of resurrection.

To His fellow Hebrews, Paul wrote: **"And it is appointed unto men once to die** [with no immediate life after, either in Heaven or Hell, until the resurrection], **but after this the judgment. So Christ was once offered to bear the sins OF MANY** [excluding the unrepentant]**; and unto them that look for Him** [during their life time] **shall He appear the second time without sin unto salvation"** (Hebrews 9:27-28). This was no new teaching to the Hebrews, but the same as that taught by all the Prophets of God! This was made plain and clear previously in Chapter 2 to those who have eyes to see and faith to believe! Sadly, many prefer to follow men and their lies and fables rather than God, or the "simplicity in Christ," as recorded in the Scriptures. Of such attitude in His people, God declared: **"Woe unto them that call evil good, and good evil; that put darkness for light, and light for darkness; that put bitter for sweet, and sweet for bitter"** (Isaiah 5:20). That's why we believe in the fables of the **afterlife,** as well as in many others! When will we all wake up and with open eyes declare: "The Emperor is naked?"

To the Corinthian church Paul wrote: **"Moreover, brethren, I declare unto you the Gospel** [or Good Tidings] **which I preached unto you, which also you have received, and wherein you stand; by which also you are saved if you keep in memory what I have preached to you, unless you have believed in vain** [which many do to this day]. **For I delivered unto you first of all that which I also received, how that Christ died for our sins** [as did the animals offered to God on behalf of the sins of His people] **according to the Scriptures; AND THAT HE WAS BURIED, AND THAT HE ROSE AGAIN** [from the dead—in a state of total cessation of life until] **THE THIRD DAY ACCORDING TO THE SCRIPTURES. And that He was seen of Cephas, then of the twelve; after that, He was seen of above five hundred brethren; of whom the greater part remain** [alive] **unto this present, BUT SOME ARE FALLEN ASLEEP** [awaiting the resurrection at the end of time]" (I Corinthians 15:1-6). To believe in the **afterlife**, immediately after death, makes a mockery of the all the clear teachings from Genesis to Revelation!

Paul continues: **"Now if Christ be preached that He rose from the dead, how say some among you** [who heard all things first-hand from Paul] **that there is no resurrection from the dead? But if there be no resurrection from the dead** [which many of the Temple priests taught and believed in Jesus' day], **then Christ was not raised; and if Christ was not raised, then our preaching is vain, and your faith is also vain** [just like that of those who believe in the **afterlife**, immediately after death]. **Yes, and we are found false witnesses of God** [as many are to his day]; because **we have testified of God that He raised up Christ; whom He raised not up, if so be that the dead rise not. For if the dead rise not, then Christ did not rise; and if Christ was not raised, your faith is vain; you are yet in your sins. Then they also which have fallen asleep** [and are still dead in their graves] **in Christ are perished . . . But now Christ was raised from the dead, and became the first fruit of them that slept** [the Biblical terminology of the state of the dead]. **For since by man** [Adam] **came death, by man** [Christ] **came also the resurrection of the dead. For as in Adam all die** [not go to Heaven or Hell], **even so in Christ shall all be made alive** [including the men of Sodom, as we saw earlier in Ezekiel 16]. **But every man in his own order: Christ the first**

fruits; AFTERWARD THEY THAT ARE CHRIST'S [when?] **AT HIS COMING** [not a moment earlier!]" (I Corinthians 15:12-23).

Paul touches on yet another point that many are confused about, inventing their own fables and confusing many thereby. Paul asks: **"Else what shall they do which are BAPTIZED FOR THE DEAD, if the dead rise not at all? Why are they then baptized for the dead?"** (I Corinthians 15:29). Paul was speaking about the death of Christ, since He was the only One who died and rose from the dead! By His death and resurrection, He made life possible for those who would follow in the footsteps of the "First Fruit." Those who did not believe that He really died and then rose again were making a mockery out of the act of baptism in the name of the "dead"—Christ! This is the point the Apostle Paul was trying to bring to their attention! For many years, the Catholic Church, being in the dark on this plain teaching of Paul, did teach that "believers" can actually be baptized for the sake of their dead loved ones—thus "springing them up" into Heaven from "limbo" or "Hell." Gullible and Biblically illiterate people believed it, paid handsomely for it, and the "spiritual Leaders" pocketed the money and 'laughed all the way to the bank.' Remember the words of W.C. Field, "Every day a sucker is born!" You don't have to be that person, if you are a "Noble Berean!"

To his beloved "son in the faith," Timothy, Paul wrote: **" . . . Keep this commandment without spot, without rebuke, UNTIL THE APPEARING OF OUR LORD JESUS CHRIST** [at the end time]**; who in His times He will show who is the Blessed and only Potentate, the King of kings, and Lord of lords; WHO** [is the] **ONLY** [One that] **HAS IMMORTALITY, dwelling in the light which no man can approach unto; WHOM NO MAN HAS SEEN, NOR CAN SEE** [since we are all mortal or dead in the grave]**, to Him be honor and power everlasting, Amen"** (I Timothy 6:13-16).

Paul makes it very clear: **Only God has immortality.** God was not seen by any immortal, nor can be seen by any one . . . until the resurrection! John, the "beloved disciple" of Christ, made it also very plain when he declared: **"Behold, what manner of love the Father has bestowed on us, that we should be called the sons of God; therefore the world knows us not, because it knew Him not. Beloved, now are we the sons of God, and it does yet appear what we shall be** [once we are resurrected]**; BUT WE KNOW THAT, WHEN HE** [Christ] **SHALL APPEAR** [at the end time]**, WE SHALL BE** [just] **LIKE HIM** [in spiritual composition, not like angels, according to human fables]; **FOR WE SHALL SEE HIM AS HE IS**" (I John 3:1-2). This is certainly not what most ignorant preachers of religion teach from their pulpits!

Certainly, the teachings of the Apostle Paul are not contradicting those of the Hebrew Prophets—and he certainly does not contradict the teachings of Christ and the Apostles before him! Those who believe in life immediately after we die, believe in vain and do contradict all the statements spoken by the Prophets, by Christ, and by His Apostles! We all have a choice as to whom we are going to believe and follow. So far, tragically, most Jews and "Christians" have chosen to follow in the footsteps of "the Piper." And as it was stated, "**When the blind follow the blind, all fall into the same ditch.**"

Speaking of what The Savior brought to man, Paul stated: "**. . . But is manifest by the appearing of our Savior Jesus Christ, WHO HAS ABOLISHED DEATH** [without which no man can be brought back to life from the grave], **AND HAS BROUGHT LIFE AND IMMORTALITY** [which no man had before] **TO LIGHT THROUGH THE GOSPEL** [or good tidings]" (II Timothy 1:9-10). Those who believe and teach that man has an immortal soul are in direct contradiction to the words of the Apostle Paul! Who is correct and who is "naked?" Christ warned His Church of this condition of blindness, stating: "**. . . I will spue you out of My mouth, because you say, I am rich, and increased with goods, and have need of nothing; and does not know that you are wretched, and miserable, and poor, and blind, and NAKED. I counsel you to buy of Me gold tried in the fire, that you may be rich; and white raiment, that you may be clothed, AND THAT THE SHAME OF YOUR NAKEDNESS DO NOT APPEAR, and anoint your eyes with eye salve, that you may see. As many as I love, I rebuke and chasten; be zealous, therefore, and repent. Behold, I stand at the door and knock; if any man hears My voice, and opens the door** [of his/her mind], **I will come in to him, and will sup with him, and he with Me**" (Revelation 3:16-20). These are plain words! What are you going to do about it—you who call yourself a "Christian?"

Paul wrote again to Timothy, admonishing him: "**Remember that Jesus Christ of the seed of David was RAISED FROM THE DEAD ACCORDING TO MY GOSPEL . . . If we died with Him, we shall also live with Him . . . if we deny Him, he shall also deny us**" (II Timothy 2:8-12). In Chapter 4, Paul added: "**I charge you before God,** and the Lord Jesus Christ, **WHO SHALL JUDGE THE LIVING AND THE DEAD** [after He resurrects them] **AT HIS APPEARING AND HIS KINGDOM** [in the last day, not immediately after they die]" (II Timothy 4:1). It is for this Kingdom that Christ's followers were commanded to pray **"Thy Kingdom come. Thy will be done on earth as it is in Heaven"** (Matthew 6:10).

Where is this kingdom going to be? The Apostles of Christ presented this last question to Him, before He ascended up to Heaven. We read in the book of Acts: **"To whom** [the Apostles] **He also showed Himself alive after His passion by many infallible proofs, being seen of them forty days, and SPEAKING OF THE THINGS PERTAINING TO THE KINGDOM OF GOD . . . When they therefore came together, they asked Him** [one last question], **saying, LORD, WILL YOU AT THIS TIME RESTORE THE KINGDOM TO ISRAEL** [as all the Prophets foretold Israel, as well as Christ Himself]? **And He said unto them, it is not for you to know the times or the seasons, which the Father has put in His own power"** (Acts 1:1-7).

In total disregard to this plain statement of Jesus Christ, misguided "spiritual leaders" began to invent, many years later, different doctrines about the Kingdom of God. The Catholic Church began to call it "The Kingdom of Christ," and referred to the Church itself as being the "Kingdom of Christ, or of God. Those churches that later emerged from her—the Protestant churches—followed in her example and terminology for the "Kingdom of Christ or God." The Mormon Church considers itself to be the true "Kingdom of God." The Jewish Apostles of Jesus Christ, The King of that coming Kingdom on earth, simply asked, knowing full well what God revealed through His Hebrew Prophets about His Kingdom: **"LORD, WILL YOU, AT THIS TIME, RESTORE AGAIN THE KINGDOM TO ISRAEL."** They did not ask, "Lord, will you, at this time, restore the Kingdom to the Church of Rome, to the Protestant Churches, or to the Mormon Church. To 'resolve this technical difficulty,' they invented the "Replacement Theology." "The Church," they said, "is now the true Israel." As we go along, we shall see what God and Christ think of this one more fable of "the blind that lead the blind."

Speaking of this coming future Kingdom to Israel and their part in it, Peter asked Jesus: " **. . . Behold, we have forsaken all, and followed You; what shall we have therefore? And Jesus said unto them, verily I say unto you, that you which have followed Me, in the regeneration [or** resurrection] when the Son of man shall sit in the Throne of His glory [at His second coming to earth], **YOU SHALL SIT UPON TWELVE THRONES, JUDGING THE TWELVE TRIBES OF ISRAEL**" (Matthew 19:27-28). Is the Gentile Church composed of the twelve tribes of Israel? Only the willfully 'blind' can miss the true meaning of this clear statement! The Kingdom is returning back to Israel! The King is returning back to His people Israel! The twelve Jewish Apostles, under the rule of David—the overall ruler of Israel, according to the Scriptures—will each rule over one tribe of Israel! Everything is going to be on earth, not in Heaven!

Knowing of the coming confusion among God's people, Paul admonished Timothy: **"Preach the Word, be instant in season, out of season, reprove, rebuke, exhort with all longsuffering and** [sound] **doctrine. For the time will come when they will not endure sound doctrine; but after their own lusts** [for power] **shall they heap to themselves teachers** [who are not of God, nor are led by His Spirit], **having itching ears, and they will turn away their ears from the truth, AND SHALL BE TURNED UNTO FABLES"** (II Timothy 4:2-4). And true to the prophecy of the Apostle Paul, all these things came to pass! That's why, in spite of the clear teachings of the men of God, most of God's people are wallowing in the mire of fables, superstitions, and lies in many areas of their "spiritual" life.

Let's consider one of those fables, which are believed in both Judaism and Christianity, in contrast to what Paul wrote to his Hebrew kinsmen. Speaking about what Jesus had to do to save humanity, he wrote: **"But we see Jesus, who was made a little lower than Elohim** [not "angels," as wrongly translated, but "Elohim" as David stated in Psalm 8, and correctly quoted by Paul] **for the suffering of death, crowned with glory and honor that by the grace of God He should taste death for every man"** (Hebrews 2:9). When Moses killed the sacrifice and used its blood to ratify the Old Covenant, that lamb was truly dead—and so was Christ! God did not resurrect the lamb, but had He not resurrected Jesus from the dead, three days later, He too would have still remained in the grave to this day—dead!

According to the teachings of Judaism and Christianity, as soon as a person dies, his soul goes up to Heaven, assuming that person was "good." If this is true, then Christ's soul ascended up to Heaven, immediately after His death. After all, if ordinary "good" people do go to Heaven immediately after death, how much more The Messiah! Paul told his Hebrew people, in plain words, that Jesus had to taste death for every person and, unlike those who supposedly go to Heaven immediately after death; Christ had to remain in the grave for three days awaiting the resurrection by His Father. The reality was simple for the Jews of Paul's day: Christ, indeed, had to taste death for three days before being resurrected by the Father. As for everyone else, they are still in the grave, dead, and are awaiting the resurrection at the last day. As for the Jews and "Christians" of later generations, their belief in the **afterlife** is in direct contradiction to the plain Biblical teachings—both in the Old and New Testaments.

In the days of Christ, the Sadducees who served in the Temple as the Priests of God did not believe in the resurrection. They did not accept the words of the Prophets about the resurrection. They 'believed' in Moses, but not in the teachings of the Prophets of God. Since Moses did not speak plainly about the resurrection of the dead, the Sadducees felt they were right in their contention that there is no resurrection. In their attempt to justify their erroneous belief about the resurrection, they approached Christ and asked Him, **"Master, Moses wrote unto us** [while disregarding the words of the Prophets on the matter], **if a man's brother die, and leaves his wife behind him, and leave no children, that his brother should take his wife, and raise up seed unto his brother. Now there were seven brothers; and the first took a wife, and dying left no seed. And the second took her, and died, neither left he any seed; and the third likewise. And the seven had her, and left no seed; after all, the woman died also. In the resurrection, therefore** [which they did not believe in], **when they shall rise** [in the last day], **whose wife shall she be of them? For the seven had her to wife."** Their question was a dishonest one in nature, since they did not believe in the resurrection. We also must remember that no Jew at that time, or before, believed in the superstitious 'doctrine' about going to Heaven or Hell immediately after death.

Let's see what did Christ reply to their tricky question. We read: **"And Jesus answering said unto them, do you not therefore err, because you know not the Scriptures** [on this matter], **neither the power of God? For when they shall rise from the dead** [since they are neither in Heaven, nor in Hell], **they neither marry, nor are given in marriage; but are as the angels that are in Heaven** [who are spirit beings, just as those who are to be resurrected]. **And as touching the dead** [not the living in Heaven or Hell], **that they rise** [from the dead]; **have you not read in the book** of Moses how in the bush God spoke unto him, saying, I am the God of Abraham, and the God of Isaac, and the God of Jacob? He is not the God of the dead [who remain dead], but the God of the living; you therefore greatly err" (Mark 12:18-27).

God considers those things that are not as though they are, because it is in His hand to bring it to pass! It is for this reason He considers all of His servants as though they are alive, even when they are still in their graves! The Sadducees did not understand this Divine reality.

One major basic doctrine the Apostles taught, as did the Prophets of old before them, was the doctrine "of resurrection of the dead" (Hebrews 6:2). One central teaching of the Apostles was the resurrection from the dead of Jesus and, at the end time, the resurrection of His followers. For "Christians" to claim, on one hand, that Christ died and rose from the dead three days later, and on the other, that His followers go immediately after death to Heaven, is an oxymoron doctrine. If the dead go to Heaven immediately after death, what need is there for them to be resurrected from the grave at Christ's second coming? As quoted before by the Apostle Paul and it is worth repeating: " . . . It is appointed unto [all] men once to die, but after this the judgment [at the end time]. So Christ was once offered to bear the sins of many, and unto them that look for Him shall He appear the second time [at the end of time] without sin unto salvation" (Hebrews 9:26-27).

All men must die! After that, "We must all appear before the judgment seat of Christ," as the apostle Paul stated in II Corinthians 5:10, and give account for our deeds. When will this judgment take place? Christ told His disciples: "When the Son of man shall come in His glory [at the end time], and all the holy angels with Him, then shall He sit upon the Throne of His glory; and before Him shall be gathered all nations . . ." (Matthew 25:31-32). In verse 41, we read of the fate of the wicked who willfully rejected God's way of life: "Then shall He say also unto them on the left hand, 'depart from Me, you cursed, into everlasting fire, prepared for the Devil and his angels [or demons]." In the last chapter, we shall cover the exact timing this judgment is to take place.

Paul wrote to the Hebrews of this final judgment: "For if we sin willfully after that we have received the knowledge of the truth, there remains no more sacrifice for sin, but a certain fearful looking for of judgment and fiery indignation, which shall devour the adversaries"

(Hebrews 10:26-27). And how will the adversaries be devoured? The Prophet Malachi Described the manner of this end time devouring of the **WILLFULLY UNREPENTANT ADVERSARIES.** He wrote: **"For behold the day comes, that shall burn as an oven, and all the proud, yes, all that do wickedly, shall be stubble; and the day that comes SHALL BURN THEM UP, SAYS THE LORD OF HOSTS, THAT IT SHALL LEAVE THEM NEITHER ROOT NOR BRANCH. But unto you that fear My name shall the sun of righteousness arise with healing in its wings . . . and YOU SHALL TREAD DOWN THE WICKED; FOR THEY SHALL BE ASHES UNDER THE SOLE OF YOUR FEET IN THE DAY THAT I SHALL DO THIS, SAYS THE LORD OF HOSTS"** (Malachi 4:3). This is the Biblical concept of "Hell" for the wicked, like stubble, they shall all be burned up and become ashes. Yet, neither Jews nor "Christians" have been taught these true teachings of God by their "spiritual leaders" and revered teachers! Truly, "the Emperor is naked," yet almost no one seems to notice!

Let's go now to the "Chapter of Faith" in the book of Hebrews! Paul mentions all those men of faith who died—serving God to the last day of their life. They included: Able, Enoch, Noah, Abraham, Sarah, Isaac, Jacob, Joseph, Moses, David, Samuel, and a host of other men and women of righteousness. Of all these faithful servants of God, who lived and died in the faith, Paul declares: **"THESE ALL DIED IN FAITH, NOT HAVING RECEIVED THE PROMISES** [of eternal life and blessings], **But having seen them afar off, and were persuaded of them, and embraced them, and confessed that they were strangers and pilgrims on earth . . . but now they desire a better country, that is a Heavenly** [from, not in Heaven]. **Wherefore God is not ashamed to be called their God; for HE HAS PREPARED FOR THEM A CITY"** (Hebrews 11:13-16). In Verse 10, Paul states about Abraham: **"For he looked for a city which has foundations, whose builder and maker is God."** Then Paul concludes: **"And these all, having obtained a good report through faith, RECEIVED NOT THE PROMISE. God had provided some better things for us, that they without us should not be made perfect** [or complete]" (Hebrews 11:39-40).

Paul makes it very plain: All the servants of God are dead. They never received the promises during their lifetime or immediately after death. All are awaiting the **"Better Resurrection"** (Hebrews 11:35) at the end of time, and for the perfection of all those to follow in their footsteps. All the men and women of faith have looked for **"the city whose builder and maker is God."** We shall discuss in the last chapter the location and future coming of that mysterious **"City of God."**

To the Thessalonians' brethren Paul wrote: **"But I would not have you ignorant, brethren, concerning those who are ASLEEP** [Biblical terminology for death], **that you sorrow not even as others which have no hope. For if we believe that Jesus DIED AND ROSE AGAIN, even so them also who SLEEP IN JESUS** [in their graves, until the resurrection] **WILL GOD BRING** [from the dead] **WITH HIM. For this we say unto you by the word of the Lord, THAT WE WHO ARE ALIVE** [in contrast to those who are dead] **AND REMAIN UNTIL THE COMING OF THE LORD** [at the end time] **SHALL NOT PRECEDE THEM WHO ARE ASLEEP** [and are still in the grave]. **For the Lord Himself shall descend from Heaven, with a shout, with the voice of the archangel, and with the trump of God, AND THE DEAD IN CHRIST SHALL RISE FIRST** [from the grave, not from Heaven]. **Then we who are alive and remain** [until the end] **SHALL BE CAUGHT UP TOGETHER WITH THEM IN THE CLOUDS** [not in Heaven], **TO MEET THE LORD IN THE AIR** [not in Heaven]; **and so shall we ever be with the Lord** [whose Throne shall be in His Temple on earth—in Jerusalem]" (I Thessalonians 4:13-17).

Paul's message to the Church is very clear: The dead in Christ shall still be in their graves awaiting the resurrection and the sound of the last trump. When they hear it, they shall be the first to rise from the grave and meet Christ in the clouds, as He descends to earth. The others, who are still alive, shall rise next to meet Christ in the air—and all together shall descend on the Mount of Olives near Jerusalem. The Prophet Zechariah described this very scene and wrote: **"Behold the day of the Lord comes, and your spoil** [Jerusalem] **shall be divided in the midst of you. For I will gather all nations against Jerusalem** [including Arab nations] **to battle; and the city shall be taken** [captive], **and the houses rifled, and the women ravished** [or raped]; **and half of the city shall go into captivity, and the residue of the people shall not be cut off from the city. Then shall the Lord go forth and fight against those nations, as when He fought in the day of battle** [to deliver His people]. **AND HIS FEET SHALL STAND IN THAT DAY UPON THE MOUNT OF OLIVES** [as He comes down with the resurrected saints and those still alive at His coming], **which is before Jerusalem on the east . . . And the**

Lord shall be King over all the earth; IN THAT DAY SHALL THERE BE ONE LORD AND HIS NAME ONE" (Zechariah 14:1-4, 9).

The Prophet Isaiah comforted his people with these words of God: **"Comfort you, comfort you My people, says your God. Speak you comfortably to Jerusalem, and cry unto her, that her warfare is accomplished, that her iniquity is pardoned** [while according to many "Christians" in time past, all Jews went to Hell, and most Muslims wish they were]**; for she has received of the Lord's hand double for all her sins. The voice of him that cries in the wilderness** [of spiritual confusion]**, prepare you the way of the Lord; make strait in the desert a highway for our God . . . Behold, the Lord will come with strong hand, and His arm shall rule for Him; behold, His reward** [of eternal life] **is with Him, and His work before Him"** (Isaiah 40:1-3, 10).

All the Apostles of Christ were fully versed in all these words of the Prophets. Everything they wrote was in accordance with the teachings of Moses, David, and the rest of the Hebrew Prophets. They never contradicted them, nor taught anything different. They admonished all the churches to wait for the promise of Christ's coming—at the end of the age.

Jesus told His disciples: **"For the Son of man shall come in the glory of His Father with His angels; and then** [not immediately after death] **He shall reward every man according to his works. Verily I say unto you, there are some standing here, who shall not taste death, till they see the Son of man coming in His kingdom** [speaking about the vision of the Kingdom He was going to show some of His disciples]**"** (Matthew 16:27-28). Yes, the reward of eternal life is coming at the end time, not immediately after death! This is exactly what the Apostle Paul had conveyed to the Hebrews about the Patriarchs and the men of faith, stating, **"All have died, not receiving the promises."** You who call yourself a "Gentile Christian" or a "Christian," do you believe the words of Jesus and the Apostle Paul in this matter?

Christ declared to all of His followers to this day: **"HE THAT SHALL ENDURE UNTIL THE END, THE SAME SHALL BE SAVED"** (Matthew 24:13). In every generation, the true followers of Christ, just like the men of faith before them, had to endure until the end of their life to be saved. They all knew the reward would come at the resurrection from the dead, not immediately after they die. Until that time, all knew their "long home," as King Solomon called it, would be the grave—in the dust, not Heaven!

The naked reality is plain, as Christ had declared to those who have a heart to understand, eyes to see, and ears to hear: **"NO MAN HAS** [ever] **ASCENDED UP TO HEAVEN, BUT HE THAT CAME DOWN FROM HEAVEN, EVEN THE SON OF MAN!"** So let's get it strait: The Patriarchs and Matriarchs are not in Heaven; the Prophets of God are not in Heaven; the Apostles of Christ are not in Heaven; all the saints and people of faith are not in Heaven; Mary, the mother of Jesus, adored, prayed to, worshiped by millions as the "Queen of Heaven," is not in Heaven: Moroni, the "Founder" of Mormonism, is neither an angel or a "glorified being," and he definitely is not in Heaven! All are dead, in the grave, awaiting the resurrection **AT THE LAST DAY!** If you don't believe that, your faith is in vain—and your worship of God is in vain. Jesus declared to His people Israel, citing the words He earlier spoke through Isaiah His Prophet, **"You hypocrites, well did Isaiah prophesy of you, saying, this people draw near unto Me with their mouth, and honor Me with their lips, but their heart is far from Me. But IN VAIN DO THEY WORSHIP ME, teaching for doctrines the commandments of men"** (Matthew 15:8-9). Will you continue do so until you stand before the judgment seat of Christ, or will you do something about it before it's too late? The choice is yours!

Any kind of worship and adoration of angels, by any one, is strictly prohibited by God and His servants throughout the Bible. The Apostle Paul had warned the church: **"Let no man beguile you of your reward in a voluntary** [false] **humility and WORSHIPING OF ANGELS, intruding into those things which he has not seen, vainly puffed up by his fleshly** [or carnal] **mind"** (Colossians 2:8). **"Worship God and Him alone,"** was always the admonition. Yet many religions, throughout history, have began by "angels" and gullibly followed by men. If the angels speak words in accordance with the Word of God, that's a different issue. Unfortunately, being often Biblically illiterate, many follow "teachings of "angels" without proving, from the Bible, whether they be of God or not. As mentioned before, **"Satan appears as an ANGEL of light"** and his ministers appear as **"ministers of righteousness."** Paul warned the Galatians: **"Though we, or an ANGEL from Heaven, preach any other Gospel to you than that which we have preached, let him be accursed"** (Gal. 1:6). How many people who call themselves "Christians" listen to this warning?

Most people don't even know how angels really look like! Even though God's angels have often appeared in the form of man, so they would not scare people when they see them, this is not how they look like in reality. The Bible gives us many descriptions of how do angels look like, yet few are those who pay attention to this Biblically revealed knowledge. God told Moses: **"For I will pass through the land of Egypt this night, and will smite all the firs born in the land of Egypt, BOTH MAN AND BEAST; AND AGAINST ALL THE GODS OF EGYPT I WILL EXECUTE JUDGMENT. I am the Lord,** [not they]**"** (Exodus 12:12). Who were the gods of Egypt? They were: the Pharaoh, the Nile, the snake, the bull, the falcon and all manner of creatures. Why would the Egyptians worship the beasts of the field and creatures of the earth as gods? Because that's how God's angels and demons, also angels, look like! God had created man after His kind, **"in His image and likeness,"** and the beasts and creatures of the earth after the angelic kind. God's angels appear to men, when God dispatches them to deliver a message, in the image of man. Demons, on the other hand, appear to men, if permitted by God, in their true form—unless they take possession of their bodies and speak through their mouth, which they do often. This is called, **"demon possession."**

Paul wrote of this practice of idol worship of demons by men, throughout history, when writing to the Romans: **"Because that, when they knew God, they glorified Him not as God, neither were thankful; but became vain in their imaginations, and their foolish heart was darkened; professing themselves to be wise, they became fools, and changed the glory of the incorruptible God into an image made like to corruptible man** [like Pharaoh]**, AND TO BIRDS, AND TO FOUR FOOTED BEASTS, AND CREEPING THINGS"** (Romans 1:21-23). The men of old knew how angels looked like, that's why they worshiped the creatures as gods.

The Prophet Ezekiel gives us a description of the Cherubim [plural form] or high rank angels of God, who carry the traveling Throne of God wherever He wishes to go. One can read this description in Chapter 1, where Ezekiel writes: **"And I looked, and, behold, a whirlwind came out of the north** [where God's Throne is located]**, a great cloud and a fire enfolding itself, and a brightness was about it, and out of the midst thereof as the color of amber, out of the midst of the fire. Also out of the midst thereof came the likeness of four living creatures. And this was their appearance; they had the likeness of a** man. And every one had four faces, and every one had four wings. And their feet were strait feet; and the sole of their feet was like the sole of a calf's foot, and they sparkle like the color of burnished brass. And they had the hands of a man under their wings on their four sides; and they four had their faces and their wings. Their wings were joined one to another; they turned not when they went; they went every one strait forward. As for the likeness of their faces, they four had the face of a MAN, and the face of a LION, on the right side; and they four had the face of an OX on the left side; they four also had the face of an EAGLE . . . Thus were their faces; and their wings were stretched upward; two wing of every one were joined one to another, and two covered their bodies. And they went every one strait forward; wherever the Spirit [God] was to go, they went and they turned not when they went. As for the likeness of the living creatures, their appearance was like burning coals of fire, and like the appearance of lamps; it went up and down among the living creatures; and the fire was bright, and out of the fire went forth lightening. And the living creatures [not men] ran and returned as the appearance of a flash of lightening" (Ezekiel 1:4-14). In the rest of this chapter, Ezekiel continues with the description of the other heavenly hosts, and that of God Himself who appears to him in the form of a MAN (Verse 26).

The prophet Isaiah had another encounter with the traveling Throne of God, and this time with His Seraphim—other kind of angels. Read Isaiah, Chapter 6, for the full description. In short, angels, Cherubim, or Seraphim, do not resemble man's ideas of angels. In Catholic literature and paintings one can see "cherubs" depicted as cute little babies with pink cheeks and little wings, which are the figment of imagination of ignorant men. The song *"you look like an angel,"* sung by Elvis, is a testimony to this form of ignorance that has infected the minds and hearts of those who walk in darkness.

In Genesis, Chapter three, the Devil had appeared to Mother Eve as a serpent. Speaking about the future end time, Isaiah wrote: **"In that day the Lord with His sore and great and strong sword shall punish Leviathan the piercing serpent; and He shall slay the dragon that is in the sea"** (Isaiah 27:1). Who is that serpent or dragon? Confronting Job at the end of his painful ordeal, brought on him by Satan with God's permission (Job 1; 2:1-8), God spoke to him about the Dragon or serpent in the sea: **"Can**

you draw out Leviathan with a hook?" God continues by describing this unknown and never seen by men strange creature. He declared: **"Out of his mouth go burning lamps, and sparks of fire leap out. Out of his nostrils comes out smoke, as out of seething pot or caldron. His breath kindles coals, and a flame goes out of his mouth . . . He makes the deep to boil like a pot; he makes the sea like a pot of [boiling] ointment. He makes a path to shine after him . . . upon the earth there is not the like of him, who is made without fear. He beholds all the high** [or mighty and proud] **things; HE IS KING OVER ALL THE CHILDREN OF PRIDE"** (Job 41). Who is this dreadful creature that no one had ever seen?

We read of his full description in the last book of the Apostle John—Revelation. Here we read: **"And there was a war in heaven** [not at the Throne of God, but in the sky above earth]**; Michael and his** [holy] **angels fought against the dragon; and the dragon fought and his angels** [or demons]**, and prevailed not; neither was their place found anymore in Heaven. AND THE GREAT DRAGON WAS CAST OUT, THAT OLD SERPENT, CALLED THE DEVIL, AND SATAN, WHICH DECEIVES THE WHOLE WORLD; he was cast out unto the earth, and his angels were cast out with him"** (Revelation 12:7-9).

The ancient world knew how the Devil and his angels or demons looked like. Many saw the two Cherubim God placed at the entrance to the Garden of Eden. They looked like fire-breathing dragons. The Chinese, to this day, have their dragon processions and mythology of those ancient pre-flood dragons. Certainly, no man looks like them—be they the angels of God or the demons and angels of Satan! Elvis, obviously, didn't know that when he sang his famous song, *"You look like an angel."*

At the end of the visions John was given, we read: **"And after this things I saw another angel come down from Heaven, having great power; and the earth was lit with his glory. And he cried mightily with a strong voice, saying, BABYLON THE GREAT IS FALLEN, AND IS BECOME THE HABITATIONS OF DEVILS** [or demons]**, AND THE HOLD** [or prison] **OF EVERY FOUL SPIRIT, AND A CAGE OF EVERY UNCLEAN AND HATED BIRD"** (Revelation 18:1-2). Thus, we can see that both God's holy angels and the fallen angels or demons look like the beasts and birds of the earth, and all other little creatures which were destroyed in the plagues God brought on Egypt. God called them, **"all the gods of Egypt,"** in Exodus 12:12.

In Chapter 11, in the book of Revelation, we read about the "two witnesses" who will soon be raised by God to deliver His end-time warnings to humanity from Jerusalem. After they finish their task, God would allow the "Beast" to "kill them" and leave their dead bodies exposed for three days in the streets of Jerusalem. They would not allow, by God's design, anyone to bury them. Then we read in Verse 11, **"And after three days and a half the spirit of life from God entered into them, and they stood upon their feet; and great fear fell upon them which saw them. And they heard a great voice from Heaven saying unto them, come up here. And they ascended up to Heaven** [or rather into the sky to join the descending Christ] **in a cloud; and their enemies beheld them** [as the Disciples of Christ did when He ascended up in a cloud]" (verses 1:12). Then we read about the next events which lead to the final fall of this world's kingdoms, **"And the seventh angel sounded: and there were great voices in Heaven, saying, the kingdoms of this world are to become the kingdoms of our Lord** [God], **and of His Christ; and He shall reign forever and ever** . . . **and the nations were angry, and Your wrath is come, and the time of the dead** [who are still in their graves to that moment] **that they should be judged, and that You should give reward unto Your servants the Prophets** [who are to be resurrected at that moment]**, and to the** [resurrected] **saints, and them that fear Your name, small and great; and should destroy them which destroy the earth"** (verses 15-18). Those responsible for the destruction and pollution of planet earth will soon have their day in court!

These words are very plain to those who have eyes "to see and ears to hear!" Until Christ returns again to earth, all of His servants would still be dead and buried. All will be awaiting the resurrection of the dead at the "last Trumpet" and final days of this Satan-influenced World.

When ignorant people think they are going to be "angels" when "they go to Heaven," they are doing so because they are Biblically illiterate in these matters. When the Mormon Church claims that the angel Moroni, once a man while in the flesh and now "a Glorified Being," is the head of their church and source of "truth," they do so because they are, like all the earth, in the same mist of darkness the Devil has ensnared humanity with. As we read in Revelation earlier: " . . . **Satan which deceives the WHOLE WORLD** [not just some, or many, but all] . . ." (Revelation 2:12). Whether we choose to believe this Biblical truth now, is of no relevance to God! In the near future, when God removes the veil from our eyes, all shall see, hear, and understand what God has been trying to tell us all along through His true servants since the days of Adam and Eve!

Through the prophet Isaiah, God had revealed this truth to anyone who has now eyes to see and ears to hear: **"And He WILL DESTROY in this** [Holy] **Mountain** [of Jerusalem] **THE FACE OF THE COVERING** [or deception] **CAST OVER ALL PEOPLE** [by the Devil], **and THE VEIL THAT IS SPREAD OVER ALL NATIONS** [barring none] . . ." (Isaiah 25:7). Until that time comes, few will be willing to acknowledge they 'have been had' by the Master Deceiver—the Devil. Most would rather continue to be **IDOL WORSHIPERS, since believing in fables and false doctrines makes one an idol worshiper in God's sight**!

Many of you, who call yourselves "Christians," prefer to worship dead men and women who are still in the grave to this moment? Why? Do you still want to keep praying, venerating, bring petitions to the dead, or adoring Mary and other saints? Have fun doing it! At the same time realizes, and if not now, then later—it is all in vain! Nobody is listening—except demons that love to play games with your willing minds and gullible emotions. Paul wrote to the Church: **" . . . Because they received not the love of the Truth** [though it is freely given to them] **that they might be saved. And for this cause, God shall send them strong delusion** [or demons]**, that they should believe a lie; that they all** [in any given religion] **might be condemned who believed not the Truth but had pleasures in unrighteousness"** (II Thessalonians 2:10-12). Yes, most would rather continue to believe in fables, superstitions, myths, mysteries, and plain foolish make-believe stories—like those about Santa Claus—than believe the clear and simple words of their Maker and His true servants from the days of old to this day. And why do we do it?

Earlier, in the days of Isaiah the Prophet, God spoke of His foolish people Judah and Israel. The northern kingdom, Israel, was soon after taken into captivity, and later became a part of the world of "Christianity." He said: **" . . . Yes, they have chosen their own ways, and their soul delights in their abominations. I also will choose their delusions** [or deceiving demons]**, and will bring their fears upon them; because when I called** [through My servants]**, none did answer; when I spoke** [through My Prophets]**, they did not hear; but they did evil before My eyes** [and to this day]**, and chose that in which I delighted not"** (Isaiah 66:3-4).

We are all stuck with this painful dilemma: If our "spiritual teachers," in any given religion, are correct in their understanding of the **afterlife,** of Heaven and Hell—or in other erroneous doctrines—then God, Christ, their Prophets and Apostles have been lying to us all along! But if, after checking up on all the Scriptures in this book, we are able to determine and prove them to be the unadulterated Truth, then somewhere, someplace, a child with open eyes should proclaim: "The Emperor is naked!"

In the next two chapters, we shall read what post-Muhammad religious leaders of Islam had taught about the **afterlife**—immediately after death—in contrast to what the Prophet Muhammad himself had recorded in the Qur'an. We shall delve into their own writings about the supposed **"ascension"** of Muhammad to the seventh Heaven—from Jerusalem—in contrast to what he himself said about his own death and the timing of his future resurrection. The present ever-boiling Middle East conflict is a direct result, as we shall fully demonstrate, of the fable of the **afterlife**—as taught by post-Muhammad misguided "spiritual" Muslim clerics and leaders. Are the "devout" Muslim clerics faithful to the teachings of their own revered Prophet and his words in their "Holy Book?" Are they responsible, by their misguided teachings, for the "Martyr Syndrome" the world is ravaged by these days? Let's find out!

CHAPTER 6

BIBLICAL ACCOUNTS OF JERUSALEM'S FATE AND TRUE LOCATION OF THE TEMPLE MOUNT

The story of Jerusalem and Holy Temple is actually far more 'ancient' than that of the City of David and Temple of Solomon. There are actually two cities of Jerusalem—the one above or Heavenly Jerusalem, and the earthly Jerusalem. Long before man and earth were created, we read of an account regarding the history and events that took place in Jerusalem above, the one also called, "Mount Zion." It is also called, "The City of God" by the Psalmist.

In the book of Isaiah we read of a fallen great angel whose great ambition was to topple the King of Zion or Heavenly Jerusalem. Isaiah wrote of him: **"How are you fallen from Heaven, O Lucifer, son of the morning! How are you cut down to the ground, you who weakened the nations! For you said in your heart; 'I will ascend into Heaven** [from earth, where he was assigned to with one third of God's angels, as we read in Jude's letter, Verse 6], **I will exalt my throne above the stars** [angels] **of God; I will also sit on the Mount of the Congregation** [Heb. Ohel Moed] **on the farthest sides of the north; I will ascend above the heights of the clouds, I will be like the Most High** [after toppling Him].' **Yet you shall be brought down to Sheol, to the lowest depths of the pit"** (Isaiah 14:12-15).

The prophet Ezekiel adds more details to this account of the first rank rebellion, in the universe, against the Supreme Ruler of Heavenly Jerusalem and Mount Zion. He wrote: **" . . . Thus says the Lord God** [of rebellious Lucifer]: **You were the seal of perfection, full of wisdom and perfect in beauty. You were in Eden** [before he was assigned to earth], **the Garden of God; every precious stone was your covering . . . The workmanship of your timbrels and pipes was prepared on the DAY YOU WERE CREATED. You were the anointed Cherub who covers** [the very Throne of God]; **I established you; you were on the Holy Mount of God** [Mount Zion]; **you walked back and forth in the midst of the fiery stones. YOU WERE PERFECT IN YOUR WAYS FROM THE DAY YOU WERE CREATED, TILL INIQUITY** [OR PRIDE] **WAS FOUND IN YOU . . .**" (Ezekiel 28:12-15).

We shall have more to say of this subject in the last chapter of this work!

What is important to remember, at this point, is the link between the ancient history of that first "Star Wars" incident and the very nature and history of Jerusalem and its "Temple Mount." What the fallen mighty angel, formerly Lucifer, could not achieve—taking over "Jerusalem above" and toppling her ruler, God—he is trying to achieve on earth below. His aim is conquering the City of The Great King of Zion or Jerusalem. Yet, as he was not successful in toppling the City of Jerusalem above, ultimately he would not prevail against earthly Jerusalem and her Great King of Israel.

Both cities have a King, a Temple, and a River—as well as righteous inhabitants. As Jerusalem above is called, "The City of The Great King," so does the City on earth. No invaders or unrighteous people shall ever inhabit the City of Zion forever! If many despise the name "Zion" or the people of "Zion," it is because of utter ignorance of the story and nature of Her Supreme Ruler—God!

Let's now unravel the history of Jerusalem, its lawful inhabitants, and their fate when in opposition to the Supreme Ruler of the City of The Great King."

In the book of Genesis, Chapter 22:1-2, we read of father Abraham's ultimate test—the willingness to sacrifice his greatest treasure, his son. And so we read: "Now it came to pass after these things that God tested Abraham, and said to him, **"Abraham!" And he said, "Here I am." Then He said, "Take now your son, your only son Isaac** [after Hagar and Ishmael were sent away]**, whom you love, and go to the land of MORIAH, and offer him there as a burnt offering on one of the mountains which I shall tell you."**

It was in that very mountain or hill that King David, according to later accounts, built his altar to the Lord—after the plague by God's angel was stopped. We read**: "So the Lord sent a plague upon Israel from the morning till the appointed time** [of three days]. **From Dan to Beersheba seventy thousand men of the people died. And the angel of the Lord stretched out his hand over Jerusalem to destroy it, the Lord relented** from the destruction, and said to the angel who was destroying the people, "It is enough; now restrain your hand. And the angel of the Lord was by the threshing floor of Araunah the Jebusite . . . And [the prophet] **Gad came that day to David and said to him, "go up, erect an altar to the Lord on the threshing** floor of Araunah the Jebusite." " . . . Then Araunah said, **"Why has my lord the king come to his servant?" And David said, "To buy the threshing floor from you, to build an altar to the Lord, that the plague may be withdrawn from the people . . . And David built there an altar to the Lord, and offered burnt offerings and peace offerings. So the Lord heeded the prayers for the land, and the plague was withdrawn from Israel"** (II Samuel, Chapter 24:15-25).

The very place where "Hell" was stopped, was near the life giving spring of the Gihon—the very place that later on was used as the water source for the Temple needs. In the following accounts, we shall read of the link between the Gihon Spring, which is located one third of a mile southeast of the present day "Temple Mount," and the actual area where Solomon's Temple was actually built.

Earlier, as we read in II Samuel 5:6-9, David conquered Jerusalem and took over "the stronghold of Zion (that is the City of David)." He told his servants, **"Whoever climbs up by the way of THE WATER SHAFT and defeats the Jebusites . . . he shall be chief and** captain." The "water shaft" was linked to the Gihon Spring. Later, David brought up the Ark of God and placed it near the Gihon Spring. We read: **"David built houses for himself in the City of David; and he prepared a place for the Ark of God, and pitched a tent for it"** (I Chronicles 15:1). Again, **"So they brought the Ark of God, and set it in the midst of the Tabernacle that David had erected for it . . ."** (I Chronicles 16:1).

After David heard of the death of his son from Bath Sheba, we read: **"He arose from the ground, washed and anointed himself . . . and he went into the house of the Lord [by the Gihon Spring] and worshipped"** (II Samuel 12:20).

Before his death, King David gave his servants orders to anoint his son Solomon king in his stead at the Gihon Spring. We read: **"And David said, 'Call to me Zadok the priest, Nathan the prophet, and Beniah the son of Jehoiadah,' so they came before the king. The king also said to them, 'Take with you the servants of your lord, and have Solomon my son ride on my own mule, AND TAKE HIM DOWN TO GIHON . . .**

So Zadok the priest, Nathan the prophet, and the Pelethites went down [to the Gihon Spring] and had Solomon ride on King David's mule, and took him to Gihon. Then Zadok the priest took a horn of oil from the Tabernacle [situated near or over the Gihon] and anointed Solomon. And they blew the horn, and all the people said, "Long live King Solomon!" Again we read: "So Zadok the priest and Nathan the prophet had anointed him king at Gihon; and they have GONE UP FROM there rejoicing, so that the city [of David, just south to the Gihon Spring] is in an uproar" (I Kings 1:33, 38-39, 45).

We read again of the Gihon Spring in the days of King Hezekiah. "This same Hezekiah also stopped the water outlet of upper Gihon, and brought the water by tunnel to the west side of THE CITY OF DAVID . . ." (II Chronicles 32:30). Of King Hezekiah's son, Mannaseh, we read: "After this he built a wall outside THE CITY OF DAVID on the WEST SIDE OF THE GIHON, in the valley, as far as the entrance of the Fish Gate; and it enclosed THE OPHEL, and he raised it to a very great height . . ."(II Chronicles 33:14).

The Psalmist spoke as well of the River or spring of the Gihon, which was located under the Temple ground, southeast to the present day alleged "Temple Mount." In Psalm 46:4 we read, "There is a River whose streams shall make glad THE CITY OF GOD [or Jerusalem and Zion], the Holy Place of the Tabernacle of the Most High." Of this city, another psalm states: "'His foundation is in the holy mountains, The Lord loves the gates of Zion [a name most Muslims despise nowadays] more than all the dwellings of Jacob. Glorious things are spoken of you, O City of God! Both the singers and the players on instruments say, 'All MY SPRINGS ARE IN YOU'" (Psalm 87). There are no "springs" on the alleged "Temple Mount" or "Haram esh-Sheriff" to Islam!

In the next chapter we shall have more to say of the historic accounts concerning the Gihon Spring and its location under the Temple Mount—southwest of the present "Temple Mount."

Let's consider now the recorded accounts that describe the fate of the Temples of God, first in Shiloh, then on the Temple Mount, next to the City of David.

The first location of God's Sanctuary was in Shiloh. Because of the rebellious attitudes on the part of God's priests—Eli's sons—God brought an utter destruction on that location by the hands of the enemies of Israel—the Philistines. They were the "Palestinians" of that day to Israel.

We read: **"So He [God] forsook the Tabernacle of Shiloh, the tent He placed among men, and delivered His strength into captivity, and His glory into the enemy's hands"** (Psalm 78:60). God was never a "respecter of persons." When His people forsook Him, He, in turn, would forsake His people and Sanctuary. So it was with Shiloh and with His other Temples.

God later told Jeremiah the prophet: **"But go now to My place which was in Shiloh, where I set My name at the first, and see what I did to it because of the wickedness of My people Israel. And now because you have done all these [evil] works, 'says the Lord,' and I spoke to you, rising up** early [through the prophets' voice] **and speaking, but you did not hear, and I called you, but you did not answer, therefore I will do to the House** [or Temple] **which is called by My name, in which you trust, and to this place** [Temple Mount] **which I gave to your fathers, as I have done to Shiloh"** (Jeremiah 7:12-14).

In the next passage, God explains to Jeremiah and His people why He plans to destroy His very Holy Place.

We read: **"'Therefore, thus says the Lord of hosts: 'Behold I will refine them and try them; for how shall I deal with the daughter of my people? There is an arrow shot out; it speaks deceit. One speaks peaceably to his neighbor with his mouth, but in his heart he lies in wait. Shall I not punish them for these things?' says the Lord. 'Shall I not avenge myself on such a nation as this? I will take up a weeping and wailing for the mountains, and for the dwelling places of the wilderness a lamentation, because they are burned up, so that no man can pass through; nor can men hear the voice of the cattle. Both the birds of the heavens and the beasts have fled; they are gone.**

"I WILL MAKE JERUSALEM A HEAP OF RUINS, A DEN OF JACKALS. I WILL MAKE THE CITIES OF JUDAH DESOLATE, WITHOUT AN INHABITANT'" (Jeremiah 9:9-11).

This was God's verdict against His people, City, and "Temple Mount" in the first and second captivity, and so it would be in the final one to come. Only complete and genuine repentance on the part of God's people would avert such sure-to-come fate.

Later, because of the heinous acts of the rulers and people of Judah, who did burn their own children in the valley of Hinom as a sacrifice to idols, God told Jeremiah, **"Say to them, 'thus says the Lord of hosts: Even so I will break this people and this city, as one breaks a potter's** vessel, which cannot be made whole again; and they shall bury them in Tophet [or Valley of Hinom] till there is no place to bury. Thus I will do to this place,' says the Lord, 'and to its inhabitants, and make this city like Tophet. And the houses of Jerusalem and the houses of the kings of Judah shall be defiled like the place of Tophet, because of all the houses on whose roofs they have burned incense to all the host of heaven, and poured out offerings to other gods'" (Jeremiah 19:11-13).

In Jeremiah 26:6-9 we read: "'**Then I** [God] **will make this House** [or Temple] **like Shiloh, and will make this city a curse to all the nations of the earth** [as it is to this day]**. So the priests and the** [false] **prophets and all the people heard Jeremiah speaking these words in the House of the Lord. Now it happened when Jeremiah had made an end of speaking all the words that the Lord had commanded him to speak to all the people that the** [rebellious] **priests and the** [false] **prophets and all the people seized him, saying, 'You shall surely die! Why have you prophesied in the name of the Lord** [imagine that!]**, saying, 'This House shall be like Shiloh, and the city shall be desolate, without an inhabitant?' And all the people were gathered against Jeremiah in the House of the Lord'"**

How different things are today?

Let's go now to other Scriptures that speak about the manner in which destruction to the city and Temple were to occur.

The rebellious priests, prophets and people of Jerusalem seized Jeremiah and they brought him before the rulers for judgment. We read: "'**When the princes of Judah heard these things, they came up from the king's house to the House of the Lord and sat down at the entry of the New Gate of the Lord's House. And the priests and the prophets spoke to the princes and all the people, saying, 'This man deserves to die! For he has prophesied against this city, as you have heard with your ears.' Then Jeremiah spoke to all the princes and all the people, saying: 'The Lord sent me to prophecy against this House and against this city with all the words that you have heard. Now therefore, amend your ways and your doings, and obey the voice of the Lord your God; then the Lord will relent concerning the doom that He has pronounced against you. As for me, here I am, in your hands; do with me as seems good and proper to you. But know for certain that if you put me to death, you will surely bring** innocent blood on yourselves, on this city, and on its inhabitants; for truly the Lord has sent me to you to speak all these words in your hearings.' So the princes and all the people said to the priests and the prophets, 'this man does not deserve to die. For he has spoken to us in the name of the Lord our God.' Then certain of the elders of the land rose up and spoke to all the assembly of the people, saying: 'Micah of Moresheth prophesied in the days of Hezekiah king of Judah [about two centuries earlier], and spoke to all the people of Judah, saying, 'Thus says the Lord of Hosts:

"ZION SHALL BE PLWOED LIKE A FIELD, JERUSALEM SHALL BECOME HEAPS OF RUINS, AND THE MOUNTAIN OF THE TEMPLE LIKE THE HIGH [OR BARE] HILLS OF THE FOREST.

'Did Hezekiah king of Judah and all Judah ever put him to death? Did not he fear the Lord and seek the Lord's favor? And the Lord relented concerning the doom, which He had pronounced against them. But we are doing great evil against ourselves" (Jeremiah 26: 10-19).

Let's backtrack to the days of the prophet Michah and read what he told the people of his day!

The prophet Micah prophesied against the Northern kingdom of Israel and its Capital Samaria, as well as against the Southern kingdom of Judah and its Capital Jerusalem. This is what he said of Samaria: **"Therefore I [God] will make Samaria a heap of ruins in the field, places for planting a vineyard** [or a farmland]; **I will pour down her stones** [by the hands of her enemies from Assyria] **into the valley, and I will uncover her** [rocky] **foundations . . ."** He added in verse 9, **"For her wounds are incurable. For it has come to Judah; it has come to the gate of My people—Jerusalem"** (Micah 1:1, 6-7, 9).

Of Jerusalem, he declared: **"Now hear this, you heads of the house of Jacob and rulers of the house of Israel, who abhor justice and twist all equity** [to this day], **who build up Zion with bloodshed and Jerusalem with iniquity; her heads judge for a bribe, her priests teach for pay, and her** [not God's] **prophets divine for money. Yet they lean on the Lord, and say, 'Is not the Lord among us? No harm can come upon us.' THEREFORE BECAUSE OF YOU ZION SHALL BE PLOWED LIKE A FIELD, JERUSALEM SHALL BECOME HEAPS OF RUINS, AND THE MOUNTAIN OF THE TEMPLE LIKE THE**

BARE HILLS OF THE FOREST" (Micah 3:9-12). In chapter 4, Micah describes the opposite and glorious future of Jerusalem.

The prophet Amos also describes the fate of his people in Northern Israel. He wrote: **"Then the Lord said: 'Behold, I am setting a plumb line in the midst of my people Israel; I will not pass by them anymore. THE HIGH PLACES OF ISAAC** [SAMARIA] **SHALL BE DESOLATE, AND THE SANCTUARIES OF ISRAEL SHALL BE LAID WASTE"** (Amos 7:7-9). As was the fate of Israel, so it became for Judah and Jerusalem!

Let's now see what was in store for Jerusalem, as God had foretold Jeremiah the prophet. In II Kings 21:10-15, we read: **"'And the Lord spoke by His servants the prophets, sayings, 'Because Manasseh king of Judah** [a son of righteous King Hezekiah] **has done these abominations (as he acted more wickedly than all the Amorites who were before him, and has made Judah sin with his idols), therefore thus says the Lord God of Israel: 'Behold, I am bringing such calamity upon Jerusalem and Judah, that whoever hears it, both his ears will tingle. And I will stretch over Jerusalem the measuring line of Samaria and the plummet of the house of Ahab; I WILL WIPE JERUSALEM AS ONE WIPES A DISH AND TURNING IT UPSIDE DOWN. So I will forsake the remnant of My inheritance and deliver them into the hand of their enemies; and they shall become victims of plunder to all their enemies. Because they have done evil in My sight, and have provoked Me to anger since the day their fathers came out Egypt, even to this day.'"**

When the armies of the king of Babylon came to destroy Jerusalem, soldiers from the people of Edom, brother of Jacob, came with them to war against Jerusalem. They were seeking revenge against the descendants of uncle Jacob. In this author's monumental work on the 4,000 years history of the children of Abraham, the reader can find all the details concerning the intense animosity and rivalry between the descendants of the two twins—Jacob and Esau. The title of this work, mentioned earlier, is "Middle East . . ."

And so we read in Psalm 137 a description of the unbridled hatred of the soldiers of Edom against Jerusalem and its Jewish inhabitants: **"By the rivers of Babylon, there we sat, yea, we wept when we remembered Zion. We hung our harps on the willows in the midst of it. For there those who carried us away captive asked of us a song, and those** who plundered us requested mirth, saying, 'sing us one of the songs of Zion!' How shall we sing the Lord's song in a foreign land? If I forget you, O Jerusalem, let my right hand forget its skill! If I do not remember you, let my tongue cling to the roof of my mouth—if I do not exalt Jerusalem above my chief joy [and thus how "Zionism" was born]."

At this point, the captives are shifting their attention to the Edomite soldiers' roll in the hateful destruction of their beloved city. They exclaimed: **"Remember, O Lord, against the sons of Edom [twin brother of Jacob] the day of Jerusalem, who said, "Raze it, raze it to its very foundation!" Then switching back to the main enemy, Babylon, they voice their desire for revenge: "O daughter of Babylon who is to be destroyed, happy is the one who repays you as you have served us! Happy is the one who takes and dashes your little ones** [as was done by them to Jerusalem's inhabitants] **against the rock!"**

The Temple Psalmist Asaph had earlier described the coming fate of Jerusalem in both captivities—in the first and second destructions of the Temple, and in the, yet, to come final destruction and captivity of Jerusalem. See the Prophet Zechariah's accounts in chapters 12 and 14 for details. Also the Prophet Joel, as well as other prophets, in his book, chapter 3, described this final fate of Jerusalem and the land.

In Psalm 74 Asaph bemoaned the future total destruction and fate of his beloved city, and Temple, crying: **"'O God, why have you cast us off forever? Why does your anger smoke against the sheep of Your pasture? Remember Your congregation, which You have purchased of old, the tribe of Your inheritance, which You have redeemed—this mount Zion where You have dwelt. Lift up Your feet to the perpetual desolations. The enemy has damaged everything in the sanctuary. Your enemies roar in the midst of Your meeting place; They set up banners for signs. They seem like men who lift up axes among the thick trees. And now they break down its carved work, all at once, with axes and hammers. They have set fire to your sanctuary; they have defiled the dwelling place of Your name to the ground. They said in their hearts, 'let us destroy them altogether.' They have burnt up all the meeting places of God in the land'"** (Psalm 74:1-8).

Asaph, again, bemoaned the fate of his city and people and wrote: "God, the nations have come into Your [not man's] **inheritance; Your Holy Temple they have defiled; THEY HAVE LAID JERUSALEM IN**

HEAPS, the dead bodies of Your servants [people of Judah] **they have given as food for the birds of the heavens, the flesh of Your saints to the beasts of the earth. Their blood they have shed like water all around Jerusalem, and there was no one to bury them. We have become a reproach to our neighbors** [today's Arab nations and Palestinians]**, a scorn and derision to those who are around"** (Psalm 79:1-4).

In Psalm 83, the Temple Psalmist Asaph prophetically wrote, again, concerning the future fate of his people and Jerusalem—anciently, and in our time. We read: **"'Do not keep silent, O God! Do not hold Your peace, and do not be still, O God! For behold, Your** [not just our] **enemies make a tumult; and those who HATE YOU** [yet proclaim, "Allah U' Ackbar] **have lifted up the head. They have taken counsel against Your people** [Israel—those "hated Zionists"]**, and consulted together against those sheltered ones** [from the ovens and death camps of Nazi Germany and pogroms in Arab countries]**. They have said, 'Come, and LET US CUT THEM OFF FROM BEING A NATIOM, THAT THE NAME ISRAEL MAY BE REMEMBERED NO MORE** [daily Arab and Muslim propaganda].' **For they have consulted together with one consent; they form a confederacy AGAITNT YOU** [God, not just against Israel or "hated Zionists"]**; The tents of** [brother] **Edom** [whose modern identity, and that of their confederates is described in this author's book, "Middle East . . ."] **and** [secondly, in order of animosity] **the Ishmaelites; Moab** [present day Jordan] **and the Hagarites; Gebal** [Lebanon or Hizboallah]**, Amon** [Jordan]**, and Amalek** [Palestinians]**; Philistia** [Gaza] **with the inhabitants of Tyre** [in Southern Lebanon—Hezbollah's terrain]**; Assyria** [modern Syria and Germany] **also has joined with them; they have helped the children of Lot** [present day Jordan] **. . . Who said, 'LET US TAKE FOR OURSELVES THE PASTURES OF GOD** [NOT MAN'S OR ISRAEL'S] **FOR A POSSESSION"** [Psalm 83:1-8, 12).

These ancient words still echo in our ears and are true to this very day!

When the Prophet from Nazareth, Jesus The Christ, spoke of the fate of His beloved city and people, He had all these words of the prophets in mind. After all, He was the very One who had inspired these very words, as recorded by the true prophets of Israel. See I Peter 1:11 for details.

Let's now read Jesus' very words about the fate of Jerusalem and Temple, as He related them to His people and disciples in the writings of the New Testament.

We read: "'Then Jesus went out and departed from the Temple, and His disciples came up to show Him the buildings of the Temple. And Jesus said to them, 'Do you not see all these things? Assuredly, I say to you, NOT ONE STONE shall be left here upon another, that shall not be thrown down'" (Matthew 24:1-2).

Mark recorded these same words in his book. Again we read: "'Then as He [Jesus] went out of the Temple, one of His disciples said to Him, 'Teacher, see what manner of stones and what buildings are here!' And Jesus answered and said to him, 'Do you see these great buildings? NOT ONE STONE SHALL BE LEFT UPON ANTHER THAT SHALL NOT BE THROWN DOWN'" (Mark 13:1-2)

Luke added more details, as Jesus was entering the city of Jerusalem. He wrote: "'Now as He drew near, He saw the city and WEPT OVER IT, saying, 'If you had known, even you, especially in this your day, the things that make for your peace! But now they are hidden from your eyes. For days will come upon you when your enemies will build embankment around you, surround you and close you in on every side, AND LEVEL YOU, AND YOUR CHILDREN WITHIN YOU, TO THE GROUND; AND THEY WILL NOT LEAVE IN YOU ONE STONE UPON ANOTHER, because you did not know the time of your visitation'" (Luke 19:37-44).

Luke adds: "'Then some spoke of the Temple, how it was adorned with beautiful stones and donations, He said, 'These things which you see—the days will come in which NOT ONE STONE SHALL BE LEFT UPON ANOTHER THAT SHALL NOT BE THROWN DOWN'" (Luke 21:4-5).

The "Christian Community" and its leaders knew and believed all these words of Jesus. As a matter of historical facts, until the end of the eleventh century, the three communities—the Jewish, Christian, and the Muslims did not believe that the Temple was located in its supposed present area of the "Temple Mount." In the next chapter, we shall discuss the historic accounts that affirm these facts—as recorded by Jewish, Christian, and Muslim historians, as well as other eyewitness travelers.

CHAPTER 7

ISLAMIC TEACHINGS ABOUT THE AFTERLIFE & HISTORIC LINKS TO JERUSALEM'S "TEMPLE MOUNT"

A most famous video about a young twelve years old Palestinian child, Muhammad al-Dura, was being circulated throughout the Middle East and other Muslim nations in recent times. Muhammad, according to the Palestinian version of the story, was caught in a cross fire between Israeli army soldiers and Palestinian combatants. His father was trying desperately to shield him from the flying bullets, yet without complete success. Muhammad was finally hit by Israeli bullets, and later died from his wounds. The live pictures of this dramatic gun battle, and Muhammad's final demise, were broadcast widely and seen in every Muslim home worldwide. It fostered a wave of rage and desire to avenge his blood through martyrdom. To exploit this volcanic stream of anger, the Palestinian Authority produced a video in which the child Muhammad al-Dura is seen frolicking on the beach while flying a kite. He was calling on many children to join the ranks of Martyrs or "**Shahids,**" and take vengeance by killing the hated "Zionists." Muhammad is in now Paradise, according to this famous video. Whether the Prophet Muhammad would agree with this assertion, we shall find out in the next chapter.

What many do not realize is this: Many of the underlying causes of the present turbulent conflict in the Middle East and the Persian Gulf area are based—purely and simply—on one belief—that of the pagan **doctrine of the afterlife**! Based on this pagan doctrine, which was condemned by Muhammad, all Muslims claim and believe that Muhammad had ascended up to Heaven from Jerusalem—from Haram esh-Sharif or the "Temple Mount." The Shiite Muslims, in like manner, believe that their Mahdi, the 12th Imam, who 'went up to Heaven' around 873 A.D. according to their belief, will return to earth and "bring peace and justice" throughout the world—under the rule of Islam, of course. And this is, according to the present president of Iran, is "the reason for the Iranian revolution" and nuclear Iran.

Long before the young Muhammad al-Dura was killed and allegedly went up to Paradise, another, later to be extremely famous, young boy, also named Muhammad, was "taken up by God to Paradise," according to Islamic Shiite belief. This young boy, age five, was the twelfth Imam of the Shiite sect in Islam. His full name was Imam Hujjat al-Mahdi. Born at 868 A.D., Muhammad al-Mahdi was the son of the eleventh Imam Hasan al-Askari. He is supposed to be of the lineage of the Prophet Muhammad, according to Shiite and Sufi belief. He is also the eleventh generation down from the Prophet of Islam. According to "*twelver*" Shiite Muslims (who believe in the twelve Imams), Imam Hujjat al-Mahdi is the ultimate savior of mankind. When Hasan al-Askari, the eleventh Imam died in 873 A.D., his five-year old son insisted on leading his father's funeral. Soon after, according to Shi'a belief, the five-year old Mahdi, after falling into the well, according to tradition, was taken up to Paradise by God. He is hidden from the world until he is to be sent back to earth, right before the judgment day, along with Jesus, to deliver mankind from the great calamities to come, and to establish Islam over all the earth. This period of being hidden from the world by the five years old twelfth Imam is called "*occultation*." It is divided into two stages: minor and major. The minor period began at 874-939 A.D., a period in which the Mahdi communicated with his followers through four intermediaries. The second stage is from 939 A.D. to the day God would send him back to earth to fulfill his mission.

According to Shiite and Sufi beliefs, as well as some Sunni Muslims, there are references in the Qur'an and the *Hadith* (or reports) that predict the reappearance of Muhammad al-Mahdi, who according to God's command, will bring justice and peace to the world by establishing Islam throughout the world. His coming will be during a period of world chaos and civil wars—globally raging and causing death and destruction for no reason. This period will be immediately before the resurrection day. At this point, Shiites believe, half of the true believers will ride from Yemen carrying white flags to *Mecca*, while the other half will Ride from *Karbala*, in Iraq, carrying black flags to Mecca.

It is interesting to note, in regards to those who come from Yemen, the Hebrew Prophet Habakkuk, in his prayer to God, spoke of a similar event. He wrote: **"O Lord, I have heard Your speech, and I was afraid; O Lord, revive Your work in the midst of the years, in the midst of the years make known; in wrath remember mercy. GOD CAME FROM TEMAN** [south in Hebrew. "Yemen" means south]**, and the Holy One from mount Paran** [in Sinai]. **Selah. His glory covers the heavens, and the earth was full of His praise. And His brightness was as the light** [of the sun]**; He had horns** [lightening] **coming out of His hand . . . before Him went the pestilence, and burning coals went forth at His feet. He stood and measured the earth; He beheld and drove asunder the nations; and the everlasting mountains were scattered, the perpetual hills did bow; His ways are everlasting"** (Habakkuk 3:2-6). Jews think of the coming Deliverer, Christians think of the coming Christ or Messiah, and many Muslims think of the coming Mahdi—and their understanding and descriptions of such events often coincide.

To the Shiites, as well as other Muslims, when the Mahdi returns after the two groups of true believers, from Yemen and Karbala, march towards Mecca, he will come wielding God's Sword, *"the blade of evil's bane Zulfiqar,"* the double-blade sword (or "double edge sword" of the book of Revelations). With this sword, many Muslims believe, the Mahdi will bring peace to earth and judge the nations.

We are alive today in the age of Messianic aspirations—be it religious or political and social in nature. Politicians and world leaders are pressing in this direction—willing to use their lethal store of weapons to advance their "messianic" aspirations—and one of them is the president of Iran. As mayor of Teheran, Mahmud Ahmadinejad is reported to have instructed the city council to build a boulevard to prepare for the coming of the looked-for twelfth Mahdi. A year later, as Iran's president, he budgeted $17 Million (some say $20) for a blue tiled Mosque in Jamkaran that is directly tied to the Mahdi. In 2006, the Washington Post reported: "The expansion [of the city of Qom] is driven by an apocalypse vision: that Shiite Islam's long hidden 12th Imam, or Mahdi, will soon emerge—possibly at the Mosque of Jamkaran—to **INAUGURATE THE END OF THE WORLD**. The man who provided $20 million to prepare the Shrine for that moment, Iranian President Mahmud Ahmadinejad, has reportedly told his cabinet that he expects the Mahdi to arrive within the next two years.

In a speech two years ago, Iran's President Ahmadinejad stated: "Our revolution's main goal is to pave the way for the reappearance of the twelfth

Imam, the Mahdi. Therefore Iran should become a powerful, developed, and a model Islamic society. Today, we should define our economic, cultural, and political policies based on the policy of Imam Mahdi's return. We should avoid copying the West's policies and systems."

Anton La Guardia, writing in London's daily telegraph, stated: "Iran's president actually relishes a clash with the West in the conviction that it would rekindle the spirit of the Islamic revolution and—who knows—speed up the arrival of the hidden Imam."

On the holy topic of suicide bombings (an act not sanctioned by the Qur'an), Ahmadinejad said last year: "Is there an art that is more beautiful, more divine, and more eternal than the art of martyrdom? A nation with martyrdom knows no captivity." It is often the case that those who speak and encourage martyrdom, do not offer themselves as the "divine sacrifice," but the lives of others. How brave!

President Ahamadinejad believes in a personal responsibility to expedite the return of the Mahdi, and is, therefore, preparing for the apocalypse. A world on the brink of a nuclear holocaust is offered to all of us by the president of Iran—and on what basis? In the next chapter we shall expose the naked reality of such grandiose suicidal "plans" and contentions about the soon coming of the Mahdi by the president of Iran. We shall do it by quoting the very words the Prophet of Islam brought to his "devout believers" in the Qur'an. Is the hidden Mahdi truly coming back soon? Are the suicidal nuclear ambitions of Iran, which are linked to the soon 'reappearance' of the Mahdi, justifiable by the teachings of the Prophet of Islam in the Qur'an?

Many young Muslims, both men and women, are encouraged by their mentors—who themselves avoid such fate—to die as martyrs by blowing themselves up among, mostly, civilian targets in Israel and elsewhere. The reward for the men is the promise of 72 virgins in Paradise. The belief in Islam is that every Muslim believer who dies, especially as a martyr, goes immediately to Paradise. The bad ones, of course, they believe, go to Hell, also immediately after death. Do the Prophet of Islam and the Qur'an support this belief?

According to Islamic clerics and historians, after his death, the Prophet of Islam, Muhammad, ascended up to Heaven from Jerusalem and was taken directly to the Throne of God. But how did that happen and why from Jerusalem? Why not from Mecca where he died and was buried? Much of the Middle East conflict in the last fourteen centuries, and especially in our days, revolves around the Islamic contention that Jerusalem is most holy to Islam. This contention is certainly on the mind of President Ahmadinejad. Their reasons, among others, are: because their revered Prophet, Muhammad, had ascended up to the seventh Heaven from Jerusalem, because the second caliph Omar or Umer had a vision from Muhammad about a certain location in Jerusalem, and the need to build there a Mosque, because the "footprints" of God and Muhammad were left on the "Rock," therefore the need to build the Mosque over it. This Mosque was later on known to all as "The Dome of the Rock." There are many other reasons about the 'holiness' of Jerusalem to Islam, which we will explore in this chapter. Most of these reasons are connected to the subject at hand: the **afterlife** or the ascension to Heaven, immediately after death, of the "true believers." In the next chapter we shall present the very teachings of the Prophet of Islam, Muhammad, concerning these matters. Let's find out in the following pages the fascinating story, from the records of history, concerning the reasons for the 'holiness' of Jerusalem to Islam!

At the beginning of his Islamic journey, Muhammad was full of hope that the Jews, "The people of the Book," as he referred to them, would gladly accept his message and embrace him the as end-time Prophet of God. To encourage the Jews to follow him and believe in his message, Muhammad decreed that since Jerusalem was the site of David's city and Solomon's Temple, all Muslims should pray with their faces directed towards Jerusalem. The first direction of Islam or *Kiblah* was to be Jerusalem, not Mecca. When Muhammad, later, had to flee from Medina, being rejected by the Jews there, he abruptly changed the *Kiblah* or direction of prayer towards Mecca. Jerusalem was no longer to be regarded as a holy place for Islam, and for that reason there is no one single mention of it in the Qur'an. But how was it that after Jerusalem was rejected by Muhammad as the *Kiblah* for Muslims, after his death, 'he chose' to ascend up to Heaven from Jerusalem after all! Why didn't he ascend to Heaven from the "holy city" of Mecca?

Few decades after the death and "ascension to Heaven," according to Islamic historians and clerics, of the revered Prophet of Islam, Muhammad, Jerusalem was declared to be, after all, a holy city to Islam and all Muslims. What brought about this change of heart in Islam? Much of the contention today about Jerusalem between Jews and Arabs, and especially the Palestinians, centers over the "holiness" of the City for both peoples. The Jews claim an absolute right for the City for historic and religious reasons. Arabs and Muslims, on the other hand, claim an absolute right for the City for reasons we shall cover now from the pages of their own history, as well as that of old accounts of Jewish and Christian sources. The main reason, of course, according to Islam, why Jerusalem is revered by Muslims has to do with "the ascension" of the Prophet of Islam, Muhammad, to Heaven from that very Holy City. So let's first read of this "historic account," as recorded in Islamic writings, after the death of the Prophet of Islam.

We are told in one Islamic account that in 682 C.E., about fifty years after the death of the Prophet Muhammad, Abd Allah ibn Zubayer rebelled against the Islamic rulers of Damascus, conquered Mecca and prevented pilgrims from reaching Mecca for the *hajj or pilgrimage*. Abd al Malik, the Umayyad Caliph and third in succession after Caliph Omar, the one who first conquered Jerusalem, needed an alternative site for the pilgrimage and settled on Jerusalem which was under his control. He was the one who built The Dome of the Rock mosque north of Al-Aqsa mosque. In order to justify this choice, a verse from the Qur'an was chosen (Surah 17, Verse 1) which states (as translated by Majid Fakhri) "Glory to Him who caused His servant to travel by night from the sacred Mosque to the farthest Mosque, whose precincts We have blessed, in order to show him [Muhammad] some of Our signs, He is indeed the All Hearing, the All seeing."

Muslim commentators are divided in their opinions as to the true meaning of this statement. Some take it literally—some feel it is a vision. The "Sacred Temple" or Mosque is regarded as the one in Mecca. The second Temple, however, or "the farthest one," was interpreted **years later** as being located in a certain site in Jerusalem. From there, later Muslim commentators claimed that Muhammad had ascended up to the Throne of God, accompanied by the angel Gabriel. The meaning of the verse quoted above by Muhammad about "the farthest Temple" was interpreted as referring to "al-masjid Al-Aqsa, the Mosque located south of the Dome of the Rock in Jerusalem. Later, it was claimed by Muslim commentators that Muhammad was conveyed there one night on the back of *al-Buraq*, his magical horse, with the head of a woman, wings of an eagle, tail of a peacock, and whose hoofs reach to the horizon. He led the horse through the southern wall of the Haram esh—Sharif, later to be considered also the "Temple Mount," and from the "Rock" he ascended to the seventh Heaven led by the angel Gabriel. On his way, he met the prophets of other religions who are the guardians of the second Heaven: Adam, Jesus, Saint John, Joseph, Seth, Aaron, Moses, and Abraham who accompanied him on his way to the seventh Heaven, to Allah, who accepted him as their Master (see commentary of *Al-Jalalayn* on this verse).

Since Caliph Omar, fifty years earlier (632 C.E.), had signed a divine treaty in the name of Allah with the Patriarch of Jerusalem, Sophronius, not to build more than one mosque in Jerusalem, Caliph Abd al-Malik had to renegotiate this contract with the Christian authorities. He was finally allowed to build a mosque over the holy Christian site, the "Rock," which formerly was the location of the "Church of the Holy Wisdom" that was destroyed in 612 C.E. by Persian and Jewish soldiers. He built the mosque in the form of a Christian church to please the local Christian authorities. That spot was still revered as a holy Christian site, because of the belief that the "footprints" of Jesus, when he stood before Pilate's judgment seat, were imbedded on the "Rock." Earlier, Omar refused to recognize the sanctity of the "Rock" and did not embrace it as a part of his building program in Jerusalem. He did not want to place the *qibla* (direction of prayer) over the "Rock," as his advisors had repeatedly suggested. Though he greatly honored Jesus as a great prophet, next to Muhammad, he did not want Muslims to regard this site as a holy place to Islam and hence revere Jesus more than they ought to or should. Consequently, he had always, and deliberately so, turned his back to the "Rock" when praying towards Mecca. Yet, fifty years later, Caliph Abd al-Malik was facing a dilemma that he had to deal with. The first one was the growing reverence of Muslims for the "Rock," because of the discovered "footprints" of Jesus. The second, and just as pressing, was the rebellion of the leaders in Mecca against the rulers of Damascus.

Once the Dome of the Rock Mosque was erected, to give it legitimacy, a rumor began to spread that "the footprint of Allah" was found on the "Rock," thus making "The Dome of the Rock" a most holy place to Islam. It is claimed that Abd al-Malik himself was behind this rumor. Soon after, a flood of rumors, inspired by Islamic theologians, about miraculous discoveries began to emerge. By the time of the Crusades, about 400 years later, The "Rock" was considered to be the very "Holy of Holies" and location of the Temple of Solomon. By that time, the events of the "night journey" and ascension of Muhammad to Heaven were transferred, among many other miracles, to the Dome of the "Rock" Mosque. As it was done in the Christian community, 300 years earlier, when many events associated with the Temple and Biblical personalities, whether true or mere fable, were transferred to the Church of the Holy Sepulcher to enhance its prestige, so now the Muslim community was doing the same. As the Muslims began to believe that the "Rock" was the very site of the Temples of God, so did, eventually, the Christians, and finally the Jews themselves were convinced the "Rock" was the site of the Holy Temple. And so, to this day, all refer to it as "The Temple Mount."

Let's go back now to the days of the first successor of the Prophet of Islam—the Caliph Omar—and see what he had done and said of this matter of the "holiness of Jerusalem" to Islam. The source of the following information is taken from the fascinating work of a former friend and colleague (now deceased), namely, Dr Ernest L. Martin. His great work, **"The Temples that Jerusalem Forgot,"** exposes the last one millennium confusion about the supposed location of "The Temple Mount." It also reveals the true identity of the so-called "Temple Mount," in contrast to the "true" location of the Temples of God in Jerusalem. This great work is a must read for the unbiased reader who is more interested in the love of the truth and facts than those fables and traditions of men. It can be obtained from **ASK** Publications' website at: www.askelm.com. For those interested in the fascinating lectures on this subject, and on the true location of the tomb of King David and Solomon, as well as on other related subjects, Email David Sielaff at: dsielaff@comcast.net or call his office at (503) 292-4352.

Dr Martin quotes, among many other sources, from the works of tenth and fourteenth century Christian Arabic history that recounts the first days of Islam in Jerusalem. These documents do contain information of the true locations of the Jewish Temples in Jerusalem, and they do cover a period from the fourth to the fourteenth century of our era. One such document is the tenth century history of *Said bin al Bitrik*, also called Euthychius, Archbishop of Alexandria. Another Muslim account, from the fourteenth century, titled **"Muthir al-Ghiram,"** summarizes early events at the beginnings of Islam. These historic accounts were in later times translated by Peters in his work **"Jerusalem,"** pp. 187-190. In this account we are told that Omar, the second Caliph and second successor to Muhammad, came to Jerusalem in 638 C.E., wishing to pray at the very location where King David did erect his altar—which in the days of his son, King Solomon, became the site of the first Temple. The account relates that Omar was given a divine revelation from God in which the

Prophet Muhammad showed him the very location from which he did ascend up to Heaven from "the farthest Mosque." In later times, Muslim commentators claimed that location to be in Jerusalem. The Man in charge of that area at the time of Omar's visit to Jerusalem was the Patriarch of the ***Church of the Holy Sepulcher***, Sophronius.

Omar requested an interview with the Patriarch, and being religiously inquisitive, he first asked Sophronius for the true location where David prayed. Omar was well aware that Christians and Jews had four locations competing for the real site of the Temple—all were outside of the Haram es-Sharif or present "Temple Mount" area. Though, according to him, Muhammad had "revealed to him" in his visionary encounter certain geographical aspects of the site of David's prayer, yet he did not reveal to Omar any specific location in Jerusalem. Sophronius responded immediately to Omar's quest by telling him that David prayed on the very site the Church of the Holy Sepulcher was built on, or in other words, where the Temple of Herod stood. The Patriarch was not trying to fool Omar! It was a Christian belief for the previous three centuries that the Church of the Holy Sepulcher was built on top of the Former site of the Temple of Herod. This church was built west of Haram esh-Sharif (the "noble enclosure") and outside of its walls and present day "Temple Mount."

For the last 800 years, Jewish, Christian, and Muslim authorities, be they religious or secular, dogmatically asserted, and still do, that the Temples of Solomon and those that were built later were located on "The Temple Mount" site or "Haram esh-Sahrif." Most claim it was built on top of the "Dome of the Rock" site. In reality, there are seven possible "locations" for the Temples' site, according to different competing contentions since the Crusaders' time. In all, there are eleven sites proposed for the true location of the Temples since the third century C.E. Only one of them, of course, is the true site—but which one? From the fourth to seventh century there were four well-known competing sites for the location of the Temple. All were outside of the "Temple Mount" present site. Omar, the Caliph and successor of Muhammad, did not agree with the location Sophronius had first suggested. It did not fit the description in the vision he 'received' through Muhammad. Omar did not want to pray at the site of the church. Instead, he stepped aside and knelt in prayer for the first time in Jerusalem. Since Omar was viewed by early Islamic adherents as having prophetic and inspirational powers directly from God, that very first spot where the Caliph Omar knelt in prayer was chosen, years later, as the first holy place for an Islamic Mosque. It was called "Mosque of Omar," not to be confused with the later Dome of the Rock Mosque built eastward. Some Muslims, who considered all of Omar's acts to be holy, began, in later years, to believe that the first Mosque location was the actual site of David's altar. That Mosque was later destroyed by the Crusaders and no one after accorded any holiness to it.

Omar commanded, again, Sophronius, according to various Islamic accounts then, not to fool him but reveal to him the true location of the altar of David. To comply, Sophronius suggested, "let's go to "Mount Zion." Since it was known that Mount Zion is synonymous with the Temple Mount, Omar initially agreed to this suggestion. At the time, be it Jews, Christians, or Muslims, all knew that many Scriptures have equated "Mount Zion" with the "Temple Mount." And so Omar followed Sophronius to that site. The Patriarch took Omar about a third of a mile south of the Holy Sepulcher church, which was located outside and west of Haram esh-Sharif, to the location known then as "Mount Zion." Omar knew then that "Mount Zion" was synonymous with the "Temple Mount." And, indeed, from 1150 C.E. until 1875 C.E., all scholars believed this was the true site of the original "Mount Zion" of King David. Between 1875-1885 C.E., the British Scholar professor Birch discovered the true location of the original "Mount Zion," along with the discovery of "Hezekiah's Tunnel" in 1880 C.E., and placed it on the southeastern ridge of Jerusalem—about a third of a mile south of present day Al-Aqsa Mosque and southern wall. In other words: The original "Mount Zion," which according to many Scriptures is synonymous with "The Temple Mount," is located a third of a mile southeast and away from the southern wall of Haram esh-Sharif or present day "Temple Mount." The irony is baffling, to say the least: while all modern scholars and religious authorities believe now in the true location of the original site of "Mount Zion" on one hand, they adamantly reject the equally true Biblical and historic evidence which was known by all until the Crusaders conquered Jerusalem. Go figure!

After considering the second spot Sophronius had suggested to Omar, the Caliph was still unconvinced of that location as being the place of David's altar and later site of the Temple of Solomon. This new spot did not fit the architectural looks shown to him by Muhammad's vision. Omar rejected this site also and demanded from Sophronius to quit deceiving him and show him the true site of the Temple. Omar also told Sophronius that he wanted pray where David erected his altar, and since Jerusalem was the first *quibla* (or direction of prayer) ordered first by Muhammad (for the first 18 months before his flight to Medina), he wanted to build there a mosque to honor David's altar and Solomon's Temple. Also, he wanted to make the City of Jerusalem the third holy site for Islam after Mecca and Medina. Sophronius quickly realized this new request by Caliph Omar would make Jerusalem a holy City to Islam—hence a competition and bone of contention between both communities, in addition to the Jewish community. However, since Omar did not accept the Holy Sepulcher church as the true site of David's altar and did not pray there, Sophronius was relieved. He knew that the Holy Sepulcher church, being the holiest site of Christianity at the time, would not be turned into a mosque since Omar did not pray at that site. This new information prompted Sophronius to suggest a new site—the one accepted by the Jews then as the original and true site of all the Temples of God.

The Patriarch Sophronius was well aware of the site the Jews claimed as their Temple location since Herod's time. He knew that Hadrian, the Roman emperor (135 C.E.), condemned the site out of hatred and contempt for the Jews he defeated in the early second century, and ordered it to be turned into a dump site for his "new Jerusalem," the city of Aelia. The Temple Mount and original City of Jerusalem became the **refuse site** for the Roman city Aelia, and later also for the Christian community nearby. Constantine, later, also reconfirmed this site as the official dump—site for both the Roman and Christian communities. To this sorry and condemned site, located in the lower City of Jerusalem, on the southeast hill just at the end of the Kidron valley, an area from which the Jews were forbidden, Sophronius had finally taken Caliph Omar. According to Peters, in his book, *"Jerusalem,"* page 191, taken from Jewish sources, we are told that an elderly Jewish man helped Omar discover a stone underneath the refuse that represented the area where the Holy of Holies once stood. This was the third location believed to be at the time as the original site of the Temple. Historic records did not show any major buildings that were built there by the Romans, and even by the Byzantines before Constantine. The area was vacant and only the Jews showed any interest in this site. After the edict of Milan by Constantine at 313 C.E., the Jews had interpreted his decree as a permission to rebuild their Temple again. For a period of 12 years they went on to build, energetically, the new Temple and many buildings and synagogues around it. Shortly before the Temple was almost fully built in 325 C.E., the bishops, who vehemently opposed the Temple's building, convinced Constantine to change his mind and forbid the Jews from completing it. In 361 C.E. Emperor Julian ("the apostate"), Constantine's nephew, permitted the Jews to erect their Temple again, but since he died two year later, the Jews again were forbidden to complete their Temple. It was destroyed soon after, and among the several ruins left behind was, notably, the Western Wall of the Holy of Holies of the last two Temples—those built in Constantine's and Julian's time. Of Herod's Temple, historic accounts clearly show, nothing was left after its destruction by Titus, as we shall see later.

To the Days of Sophronius, Christians avoided building anything on top of the former Temple and original site of Jerusalem to honor the words of Christ (Matthew 24:2) that "no stone should remain on top of each other." Yet Sophronius knew that the Jews, to his day, still held that site in honor and reverence being the site of their beloved Temple and City of Jerusalem. The Patriarch made a deal with Omar, after agreeing to take him to the very spot the Jews claimed to be their Temple site—and made only two requirements in his contract with Omar to which Omar had quickly agreed: one, that he can build only one structure in Jerusalem, and second, that he would forbid any Jews from living in Jerusalem. Shortly after, however, Omar convinced Sophronius to allow seventy Jewish families to establish residence in the Temple area near the dump site. He had one condition for them: the Jews must remove all refuse from that area and keep it clean to preserve its sanctity.

The first Christian Arab Historian, *Said bin al Bitrik,* whose Greek name was Eutychius, was the Archbishop of Alexandria. He had recorded some accounts about the meetings between Omar and Sophronius, the Patriarch of Jerusalem. These accounts of Euthichius were to later be translated by F.E. Peters in his work *"Jerusalem,"* pp. 189-190. We read: "'Then Omar said to him [Sophronius]: 'You owe me a rightful debt. Give me a place in which I might build a sanctuary [masjid].' The Patriarch said to him: 'I will give to the commander of the faithful a place to build a sanctuary where the kings of Rum [Byzantines] were unable to build [because of the dump site over the Temple area and to honor the words of Christ that "no stone shall be left on top of each other"]. It is the [small portable] rock where God spoke to Jacob [also called "Jacob's pillar" in Genesis 28:18] and which Jacob called the gate of Heaven, and the Israelites [called it] the Holy of Holies. It is in the center of the world and was a Temple for the Israelites who held it in great veneration [while Rome and Christians held it in contempt, turning it into a dump-site] and wherever they [Jews] were, they turned their faces towards it in prayer, but on this condition, that you promise in a written document that no other sanctuary will be built inside Jerusalem.

"Therefore, Omar ibn al-Khattab wrote him the document on this matter and handed it over to him. [Sophronius then remarked that this area was in ruins when] they were Romans [unlike Haram esh-Sharif or former Fort Antonia], when they embraced the Christian religion, and [when] Helena, the mother of Constantine, built the churches of Jerusalem. The place of the rock [that is Jacob's rock found under the site of the Holy of Holies] and the area around it were deserted ruins, and they [the Romans] poured dirt over the rock [which was under the Holy of Holies] so that great was the filth above it. The Byzantines [Rum], however, neglected it and did not hold it in veneration, nor did they build a church over it because Christ our Lord said in the Holy Gospel 'Not a stone will be left upon a stone which will not be ruined and devastated.' For this reason the Christians left it as a ruin and did not build a church over it.'"

In contrast, records show that Helena ordered a minor church to be built over the "Rock" where the Dome of the rock now stands. It was the main natural object over and around which Herod greatly enlarged the citadel, originally built by Simon Hashmonean to protect the Temple on its north side. Later, Herod renamed it Fort Antonia in honor of Mark Anthony. It was on that "Rock," according to Christians, as recorded in the Gospel of John (Chapters 18-19) that Pilate judged Jesus, and later "the footprints of Jesus" were "discovered" on it. It is for that specific reason that Helena ordered the minor church to be built. She named it "Saint Cyrus and Saint John Church." It was actually built about thirty years after her death. Later, this church was enlarged and renamed "The Church of Holy Wisdom." The Dome of the "Rock" was originally a Christian holy site—at the very time Muhammad had allegedly "ascended up to heaven from it—and hence was deliberately disregarded by Omar and the two Caliphs after him. Their reason was a teaching in the Qur'an that claimed that Jesus was not really crucified, but was taken up to Heaven while another imposter took his place on the cross. Since the "footprints" of Jesus were believed to be on that rock, which contradicted the Qur'an's teaching about Jesus and since it was then still regarded as a Christian holy site, Omar and the two Caliphs after him did not want to accord it any sanctity. They did not want Muslims to pay homage to that Christian site. In 612 C.E., that Church building of the Holy Wisdom was later destroyed by Persian and Jewish forces, yet still remained a venerated site by all Christians.

The account continues: "'So Sophronius took Omar ibn al-Khattab by the hand and stood him over the filth. Omar [being filled with sadness for the desecration of that Holy Place], taking hold of his cloak, filled it with dirt and threw it into the valley of Gehenna. When the Muslims [Omar's entourage] saw Omar ibn al-Khattab carrying dirt with his own hands, they all immediately began carrying dirt in their cloaks and shields and what have you until the whole place was cleansed and the rock [which was under the Holy of Holies] was revealed. Then they all said: 'Let us build a sanctuary and let us place this stone [which was small and portable] at its heart.' 'No,' Omar responded . . . 'We will build a sanctuary and place the stone at the end of the sanctuary.' Therefore Omar built a sanctuary and put the stone at the end of it'" (Peters, *"Jerusalem,"* pp. 189-190).

According to Theophanes who wrote about this account in 814 C.E., Omar built a "Temple" which was later called "Solomon's Temple." The main reason it was called "the new Solomon's Temple" was due to the many stones Omar used from the Temple site in building his mosque. Theophanes wrote: "In this year [643 C.E., five years after he came to Jerusalem], Omar began to build a Temple in Jerusalem." Since Omar transferred a part of the "Stone," which he may have "cut off" from the larger slab of stone under the Holy of Holies, and placed it at "the end of the new sanctuary," this act "sanctified" the "New Temple" through a ritual Muslims call *"Baraka."* This ritual transfers the spiritual powers or influence from one holy site or person to another. In later centuries, many began to confuse the portable "stone" Omar placed at the end of his mosque with the "Rock" under the Dome of the Rock. And so it is believed, erroneously, to this day. When the love of the truth is absent from the heart of man, this kind of confusion takes deep roots in our minds.

Omar, along with Sophronius and his Muslims aids, carried the stone or portable rock, and entering through the south gate of Haram, a third of a mile to the northwest, he placed the stone at the southern end of the future mosque, later to be called Al-Aqsa, which he built about five years later. Why did he do that? Around that time the legend of the "Night Journey" or *isra* of Muhammad, which took him through the south gate of the Haram into the inner area of the "Noble Enclosure," from which Muhammad, according to the legend, had ascended up to Heaven, was already firm in the minds of many. When Omar looked at the southern gate of the Haram's walls (the former Praetorium and Fort Antonia), he was convinced this was the place through which the Prophet had entered into the "Noble Enclosure" on his way to Heaven. In placing the dedicated "stone," which he carried from the larger pavement that was under the Holy of Holies, Omar was achieving two purposes: establishing the *qibla* or direction of prayer toward Mecca, and having the believers' prayers travel through the location of the Holy of Holies, a thousand feet to the south and ten degrees to the east—the exact direction toward Mecca. The Caliph then named the southern gate of the Haram, the **bab al-Nabi** (the gate of the Prophet), in honor of the *isra* or the Night Journey. In addition, Omar also took many other stones for the building of his "new Temple of Solomon" from the previous two Temples built by the Jews during Constantine and Julian "the apostate." Thus Omar had 'transferred' the holiness of the former Temples to his Temple. Earlier, the same 'transfer' of holiness through Temple stones was done to enhance the prestige of the Church of the Holy Sepulcher—and for this reason it came to be regarded, for the previous three centuries, as the 'true' site of the Temple.

Once Omar completed this "new Temple of Solomon" (as Muslims considered it), which was located on the southern part of the platform of the Haram esh-Sharif, other architectural features associated with the original Temple of Solomon, were transferred to the northern area. Among these newly transferred features were, in particular, the names of the gates of the former Temple. The Jews requested of Omar to allow them to live near the southern area where the ruined Temple stood. They needed to be living near the Spring of Gihon over which the Temple was built for their ritual purification. Omar did not object and granted their petition on condition they keep the area clean from generations of accumulated refuse. Omar, however, since he decided to build his mosque to the northwest and away from the original site of the Temple, saw no reason why he could not transfer the stones of the Temple and the names of the gates to the Haram area. With the passage of time, many, including Jews and Christians, began to believe the Haram esh-Sharif is the true location of the original Temple of Solomon.

Moshe Gil adds some information about the location Omar granted the Jews to occupy. He writes: "A section of the Jewish chronicle mentioned above [from the Geniza document], which was copied (or written) sometimes during the eleventh century, notes that, when they [the Jews of Tiberias] spoke with Umar [or Omar] about the possibility of a renewed Jewish community in Jerusalem, the Jews asked for permission to settle in the **southern** part of the city [northeast of Haram esh-Sharif or the former Fort Antonia], near the gates of the 'Holy site' (that is the Temple) and near the **pool of Siloam** [a must feature of the Temple]. On receiving Umar's consent, the Jews proceeded to build there, using construction materials that were readily available [from the old Temples and buildings around it] and that have previously been used in the old, now ruined structures. According to this source, the area in which the Jews took residence is the site of the Jewish marketplace 'to this very day'" (*"The Jewish Community* in the *History of Jerusalem,"* p. 171). Words in parentheses are Gil's.

Though the Jews were allowed by the Islamic authorities to reside near the Temple site and the Gihon Spring for a period of 460 years, from 638 C.E. to 1099 C.E., as the period of the friendly Umayyad's dynasty came to an end, life for the Jews became more difficult. The next dynasties of the Abbasids and Fatimids, being unsympathetic toward the Jews, imposed many restrictions on them. The Abbasids begun to rule in 750 C.E. and were followed by their equally unfriendly to the Jews Fatimids. **For the next 200 years, the Jews were not allowed into the Haram esh-Sharif area**, but were allowed to continue to reside in their Jewish quarter near the Temple, about a third of a mile southeast of the Haram esh-Sharif.

In a contemporary report written by an Italian Jew, Rabbi Ahima'as, during his visit to Jerusalem, we read the translation of his report: "At that time there was a Jew named Rabbi Ahima'as who went up to Jerusalem, the glorious city, three times with his vowed offerings. Each time he went on, he took with him 100 pieces of gold, as he had vowed to the Rock of his salvation, to aid those who were engaged in Torah study and for those who mourned for the **ruined House of His Glory** . . ." (*"Ahima'as,"* 1924:65, translated by Harari, in Peters, *"Jerusalem,"* p.224).

This eyewitness account (during the Fatimid rule) by Rabbi Ahima'as about the **ruined House or Temple** is similar to another eyewitness account by Rabbi Paltiel, Head of the Jewish community in Egypt, also under the Fatimid dynasty. Rabbi Paltiel was appealing for financial help from the Jewish community at large for those in Jerusalem. He was asking for *"oil for the inner altar of the Sanctuary* *at the Western Wall*; and for the synagogues and communities, far and near: and for those who *were mourning the loss of the Temple* [even though the Western Wall of the Temple built during Constantine was still standing], those who grieved and mourned for Zion; and for the teachers and their students in the Yeshiva [in southeast Jerusalem] . . ." (*Ibid.* 1924:95-97, p. 225).

Remember! These eyewitness accounts were written during the Fatimid dynasty when Jews were forbidden from setting foot on the Haram esh-Sharif grounds for a period of 200 years. Rabbi Paltiel was referring to the ruined Temple and the inner altar in use at the time on the Temple grounds southeast of the Haram area. The Jews were meeting in a "Sanctuary" or Synagogue located in a "cave" with an entrance very near "The Western Wall" of the "Holy of Holies." The Jewish worshipers who prayed in that underground cave (no relations to the cave under The "Rock" since it was forbidden to Jews) were referred to as" going down there" or "going down to the *Kanisa* [synagogue]. These references were preserved in the recently found documents of the *Geniza* in Egypt, which were translated by Gil Moshe in his work, *"A History of Palestine"* (638-1099), pp. 536, 607, 639, 647-653. They were also mentioned in *"The History of Jerusalem"* by Joshua Prawer and Haggai Ben Shammai's compilation of articles.

The famous Jewish Rabbi Maimonides wrote (around 1180 C.E.) that in the area of the "Holy of Holies" there were also underneath the still standing "Western Wall" some "deep and winding tunnels." These "tunnels" were located in the southeast ridge of the City (about a third of a mile south of the Haram area). To this day, one can visit these tunnels located on the original site of Mount Zion, south of the Haram area. There are no such winding tunnels or caves under the Dome of the Rock mosque! The Jews first could first enter an initial cave that was linked to other branches or tunnels. It led to a larger cave used as the main Sanctuary or synagogue with an inner Altar associated with it. It was for the needs of this synagogue and inner altar that Rabbi Paltiel, the head of the Jewish community in Egypt, was requesting financial assistance. At that very spot there was a gate named "*the Priest's Gate*," which was never mentioned in the Biblical record, but was mentioned in the final days of the Talmudic period (5th century C.E.). The Talmud mentions a "*Priest's Gate*" associated with the "Western Wall" of the Holy of Holies. This Priest's Gate was located over the Gihon Spring.

Moshe Gil writes: "'The Midrash mentions the Priest's Gate together with the Western Wall and the Hulda Gates; the latter were certainly situated **in the south**, according to the *Mishna* (*Middot* 1:3). On the Priest's Gate, it is said in *Shir Ha-shirim rabbah*: 'Behind the Western Wall of the Temple, why? For the Lord has sworn that it will never be destroyed.' In *Numbers Rabba* (xi:3) we read: it is 'the Western Wall of the Temple' that has never been destroyed; and also in *Lamentation Rabba*. The version of the Song of Solomon *Rabba* should therefore be viewed as an interpretation, as it intended to say: the Western Wall has never been destroyed, being that the Priest's Gate and the Hulda Gate were not destroyed'" (Gil, *"A History of Palestine,"* 634-1099, p.42).

Note that Gil states that this area is located "in the south," not in Haram esh—Sharif to the north. The Jews were forbidden for a period of about 200 years by the **Abassid** and **Fatimid** Muslim rulers to set foot on the Haram area of Muslim holy sites. Still, they continued to reside and pray on the real site of the Temple Mount, an area which the Muslim rulers did not forbid them to occupy. The writings of the **Geniza** make it very plain.

Moshe Gil quotes from another letter in the **Geniza** that has a reference to the synagogue in the "cave" inside the tunnels. He writes: "'In the same [**Geniza**] letter, Joseph ha-Kohen mentions along with the synagogue also the **cave**. Despite the letter's poor condition it easy to discern that 'the cave' is used as synonym for the synagogue. Indeed, 'the cave' is frequently mentioned in the sources as the place where the Jews of Jerusalem congregate [while forbidden to set foot on the Haram area to the north for 200 years], and it is clear that they are referring to the synagogue. Solomon ben Juda writes to Ephraim ben Shemaria that on the morrow after receiving his letter, they hastened to declare his rival excommunicated in Jerusalem: 'On Monday, we had a large public gathering **in the cave** and we took out the scrolls of the Torah and banned all those 'that cause unrighteous decrees' (Isaiah 10:1). After mentioning the collapse of a wall [the Western Wall] that caused damage to the synagogue, he writes, following the work of reconstruction, 'the **cave** [or synagogue] was restored.' As to the collapse, it occurred on the first day of Passover, when the synagogue was full of people, but no one was injured. It seems that he is referring to the collapse of a part of the Temple Mount Wall that is the Western Wall . . . This collapse is explicitly mentioned in Ibn al-Jawzi, who links it with the earthquake which occurred on 5 December, 1033 C.E.'" (*Ibid.* 648).

It is extremely important to note: all these events and accounts are taking place during the period the Jews were forbidden from residing or setting a foot on the Haram esh-Sharif Muslim area of Jerusalem—located north of the Temple Mount site and residence of the Jews.

During the late *Abassid* period, the *Karaite* Jews arrived in Jerusalem. These were the Jews who earlier had rejected all teachings of the Rabbis, and insisted on living only in accordance with the teachings of the Hebrew Scriptures. They too knew the true location of the Temple site, southeast of the Haram area, but since the rabbinic Jews had already occupied the Temple Mount site, the Karaites decided to live over and around the Temple Mount area near the Gihon Spring in the village of Silwan, east of the Kidron Valley and the former City of David. Several documents from the Geniza collection show the Karaites's desire to live only in the southeastern part of Jerusalem. They were concerned only with Biblical Jerusalem, not the traditional sites both Christians and Muslims considered to be holy. The Karaites made no attempt to reside in the northern part of Jerusalem or anywhere near the Haram area. The Karaites also avoided the Western area of Jerusalem where Christians considered some parts of southwestern Jerusalem to be holy. During their 200 years residence in the City of Jerusalem, they lived nearby the rabbinic Jews, southeast of the Haram esh-Sharif.

In the tenth century period, during the time Jews were forbidden to set foot on the Haram esh-Sharif Muslim holy sites, we read this illuminating letter of appeal: "Greetings to you from the faithful Lord, the eternal City [Jerusalem], and from the head of Sion's Yeshivas, from the City in which the seventy-one members of the *Sanhedrin* sat with their students before them . . . the City which is now widowed, orphaned, deserted, and impoverished with its few scholars [and certainly the Haram esh-Sharif area was not in that condition] . . . Many competitors and rebels have arisen [speaking of the Karaites], it yearns for the day the All-Merciful Lord will redeem it.

"We the Rabbinate community [in contrast to the Karaite], a pitiful assembly, **living in the vicinity of the Temple site** [southeast of Haram esh-Sharif], regret to inform you that we are constantly harassed by those foreigners **who overrun the Temple grounds**. We pray: 'How long, O Lord, shall the adversary reproach? Shall the adversary blaspheme Your name forever'? (Psalm 74:10). Our sole comfort shall be when we are again permitted to walk freely about its gates, to prostrate ourselves in prayer for Jerusalem's total liberation **with its Temple restored** . . . Yes, there is a synagogue on the Mount of Olives to which our Jewish confreres gather during the month of Tishri. There they weep upon its stone, roll in its dust, encircle its walls, and pray. It was God's will that we found favor with the Ishmaelite rulers. At the time of their invasion and conquest of Palestine from the Edomites [the Romans/Byzantines], the Arabs came to Jerusalem and **some Jews showed them the location of the Temple.** This group of Jews has lived among them ever since [on the southeast ridge around and over the Temple site and Gihon Spring]. The Jews agreed [even to the tenth century] to keep the site [of the Temple Mount] clear of refuse [and certainly he is not speaking of the Haram's Muslim holy sites], in return for which they [the Jews] were granted the privilege of praying at its gates. They [the Rabbinic Jews] then purchased the Mount of Olives [which was the location of their synagogue], where the *Shekinah* [or 'Presence' of God] is said to have rested, as we read in Ezekiel 11:23: 'The glory of God went up from the midst of the City and stood upon the mountain which is on the eastside of the City . . . Here [on the Mount of Olives] we worship on Holy Days facing the Lord's Temple, especially on *Hoshana Rabba* [last day of *Sukot or Feast of Tabernacles*]. We entreat the Lord's blessings for all of Israel wherever they might reside. All who remember Jerusalem [southeast of Haram esh-Sharif] will merit a share in its joy. Everyone can partake of it by supporting Jerusalem's residents. Life here is extremely hard, food is scarce, and opportunities for work very limited. Yet our wicked neighbors exact exorbitant taxes and other 'fees.' Where we not to pay them, we would be denied the right **to pray on Mount of Olivet** . . . These intolerable levies and the necessary frequent bribes compel us to borrow money at high rates of interest in order to avoid imprisonment or expulsion. Help us, save us; redeem us. It is for your benefit too, for we pray for your welfare'" (A. Holtz, *"The Holy City: Jews in Jerusalem"* (New York: W. W. Norton 1971, pp. 122-3).

The Jews were finally able to purchase the whole area of the southern part of the Mount of Olives—the area facing directly the original location of the Temple site—so they could worship while facing the Temple which was located southeast of Fort Antonia, later renamed Haram esh-Sharif.

The Jewish traveler who visited Jerusalem in 1334 C.E., Isaac ben Joseph, had more to say about Omar's Temple: "The king [Omar], who had made a vow to build up the ruins of the sacred edifice [or Temple], if God put the Holy City in his power, demanded of the Jews that they should make known the ruins to him. For the uncircumcised [first the Romans and later the Christians] in their hate against the people of God, have heaped rubbish and filth over the spot, so that no one knew exactly where the ruins stood. Now there was an old man then living who said, 'if the king will take an oath to preserve the wall [the Western Wall of the Holy of Holies rebuilt by Jews in Constantine's and Julian's days], I will discover unto him the place where the ruins of the Temple were.' So the king straightway placed his hand on the thigh of the old man [according to Middle Eastern tradition which father Abraham also observed] and swore an oath to do what he demanded. When he had shown him the ruins of the Temple under amount of defilements, the king had the ruins cleared and cleansed, taking part in the cleansing himself, until they were all fair and clean. After that he had them [the scattered stones] all set up again with the exception of the [Western] Wall [of the Holy of Holies], and made them a very beautiful Temple [later to be renamed Al-Aqsa], which he had consecrated to his God" (E. N. Adler, *"Jewish Travelers: A treasury of Travelogues from nine Centuries,"* NY: Dover Pub., pp.130-31).

In the book, *"Getting Jerusalem Together,"* Archeological Seminar Ltd., by Fran Alpert, p. 32, the author quotes an account from *"Sefer HaYshuv"*: "'When the Caliph Omar visited Jerusalem shortly after the conquest, he asked the Jews: 'Where would you wish to live in the city? And they answered, 'in the **SOUTHERN PART**; and that is the market place of the Jews.' Their intention was **TO BE CLOSE TO THE TEMPLE AND ITS GATES**, as well as **THE WATERS OF SILOAM** [or Gihon, in the southeast part of the city] for ritual bathing. The Emir of the believers granted this to them.'"

Reuven Hammer, in his work, *"Jerusalem Anthology,"* p. 148, adds: "'Omar decreed that the seventy households should come. They agreed to that [though earlier they requested that 120 families should come]. After that he asked: 'Where do you wish to live within the City?' They replied: 'In the southern section of the City, which is the market of the Jews' [before the Byzantine rulers forbade them to reside in the City of Jerusalem]. Their request was to enable them **TO BE NEAR THE SITE OF THE TEMPLE AND ITS GATES, AS WELL AS TO THE WATER OF SHILOAH THAT** could be used for immersion. The Emir of the believers granted them this. So seventy households, including women and children, moved from Tiberias and established settlements in buildings whose foundations had stood many generations.'" It was during the days of Emperors Constantine and his nephew Julian that Jews, still on the premise, had erected these buildings in the early 4th century, as we read earlier.

As Omar, the first Caliph, was kind and respectful toward the Jews of his day, unlike today's Arab leaders, so was his successor the second Caliph *Mu'awiya* (661-681 C.E.). The early Jewish sage, **Simon Bar Yohai** (whose tomb can still be seen near *Meron* in Galilee) prophesied about this benevolent second Caliph: "The second king who arises from Ishmael will be a lover of Israel [how different from today's Arabs and sons of Ishmael]; he restores their breaches of the Temple. He hews [cuts down and levels] Mount Moriah and makes it all straight and builds a meeting hall on the Temple rock [which was under the Holy of Holies southeast of the Haram]." The Caliph, with Jewish approval, built this "meeting place" outside and south of Haram esh-Sahrif. Not until the third Caliph, Abd al-Malik from 689-692 C.E., who built the Dome of the Rock, did any Caliph show the slightest interest in the "Rock" within the Haram enclosure.

A Christian account from the sixth century called *"Brevarius* (or short account) *of Jerusalem,"* relates that south of the Church of the Holy Wisdom (built on top of the Dome of the Rock to honor the discovery of "Jesus' footprints") "you come to the Temple built by Solomon, but there is nothing left there apart from a single cave." See Wilkinson's book, *"Jerusalem Pilgrims before the Crusades,"* p. 61. In 333 C.E., the pilgrim from Bordeaux (later France), visiting Jerusalem, wrote about a "pierced stone" (or cave) at the Temple site. This cave, according to many historic accounts, including those found in the *Gnizah* (in the synagogue's basement) in Egypt about a century ago, did become a main meeting place for the Jews after Omar (in 638 C.E.) allowed them back on the Temple Mount site, which was about a third of a mile southeast of the Al-Aqsa Mosque. To the time of the Crusades, the Jews have enjoyed this privilege accorded them by the noble Caliph Omar. The documents in the *Geniza* tell us that the Jews used that "Cave" in southeast of Jerusalem as a synagogue. They felt this was the precise place where David built his altar.

A modern scholar, Moshe Gil, in his monumental work, *"A History of Palestine 634-1099,"* writes: "According to Muslim tradition the

Byzantines turned the Temple Mount into Jerusalem's refuse dump from the time of Helena the mother of Constantine" [actually Emperor Hadrian, in 135 C.E., was the first to do so] (*ibid.* p.65). In later times, after the period of the Crusades in the 12th century, many Muslims, Christians, and later Jews as well, began to assume the place Helena had turned into a refuse dump for the area residents was the Dome of the Rock. This, obviously, is an absolute impossibility! Firstly, "The Rock" under the later to be built Dome of The Rock was a holy and sanctified Christian site at the time. Secondly, the "footprints of Jesus" many believed to be imprinted on that very "Rock." Thirdly, Helena herself had ordered a church to be built on top of that "Rock." Finally, the first minor church built over the Dome of the Rock was enlarged to resemble the Temple structure and renamed The Holy Church of Wisdom.

Furthermore, Emperor Hadrian, out of hatred and contempt for the Jews, consigned the Temple Mount and original City of Jerusalem as a dumpsite for his new city Aelia. He certainly would not have done it had the Temple Mount and Jerusalem were located over the present area of Haram esh-Sharif. Firstly, by all historic and eyewitness accounts, the present Haram esh-Sharif area was not touched, much less destroyed, by Titus's Roman army. Fort Antonia was used as a monument for ages to come of the glory of Imperial Rome. To this day, everyone can still see the untouched great stones (about 10,000) of its walls. Secondly, since 6 C.E., according to Josephus and other accounts, Rome had taken control of the fort built by Herod, which he renamed Fort Antonia. Thirdly, the tenth legion (5,000 soldiers according to Josephus) was stationed there until 289 C.E. before it was relocated to Eilat. That tenth legion, according to Josephus, was in charge of guarding the Temple site, the City of Jerusalem, and the palace and forts built by Herod in the upper city. Also, after Titus destroyed the Temple and the City to its foundation, and then heaped huge amounts of dirt on top, he left the tenth legion in the walled and defensible Fort Antonia to guard the interests of Rome throughout the region. Within the fort there were about forty cisterns of water that were later tapped to supply the water needs of Hadrian's new city. With all these in mind, why would Hadrian, the Byzantine rulers, and later Helena and Constantine, who considered the place of the "Rock" to be a holy site, ever contemptuously use the area of the "Rock" as a refuse site for their city?

In a sixth century work written by the ***Piacenza Pilgrim***, the writer described accurately the church structure named the "Holy Wisdom." It was built as a Byzantine Church around the fifth century, and was opened to the general Christian public to view. Its central attraction was "The Oblong Rock." This is what the Piacenza Pilgrim wrote: "We also prayed at the **Praetorium** [or Fort Antonia, the former site of the Tenth Roman Legion until the end of the third century and later the headquarters of Roman officials and visiting dignitaries since 6 C.E.], where the Lord's case was heard [before the Roman governor Pilate]: what is there is the basilica of Saint Sophia [the Holy Wisdom Church], which [is located] in front [or north] of the Temple of Solomon below the street [east and down slope] which runs down to the stream of Siloam [or Gihon] outside of Solomon's porch [the eastern wall of Solomon's Temple]. In this basilica is the seat where Pilate sat to hear the Lord's case, and there is also the **oblong stone** [the "Rock"] that used to be in the center of the **Praetorium** [since the praetorium tent was moveable]. The accused person whose case was being heard was made to mount this stone [the "Rock"] so that everyone could hear and see him. The Lord mounted it when he was heard by Pilate, and his footprints are still on it. He had a well shaped foot, small and delicate" (*ibid.* pp. 60, 84).

Certainly, no Christian would have turned this revered place into a refuse site! Yet as for the despised Jewish City and Temple site, which were about a third of a mile to the south of the Roman Praetorium, also later renamed Haram-esh-Sharif, well, that was regarded differently by Hadrian, the Byzantine rulers, by Constantine and his mother Helena. These are facts of history!

In later times, more legends were added to justify the sanctity of the "Rock" and other places in the Holy Land. Wilkinson quotes the Muslim historian **Ibn Taymiyya** (died 1328 C.E.), the great critic of relics and marvelous stories, about the legend of Muhammad's footprints on the "Rock," under the Dome of the Rock Mosque. Ibn Taymiyya said: "What some of the ignorant ones [or Muslims] have mentioned is that there is a footprint of the Prophet—God bless him and grant him salvation—or a trace of his turban or the like on it [the Rock]. All of this, however, is a lie. The greatest lie is from those who think that is the place of the footprint of the Lord {Allah], and likewise, that it is the place mentioned as the cradle [or footprint] of Jesus [in the "Rock"]—peace be upon him. It is nothing more than the baptismal font of the Christians" (Translation in E. F. Peters, **Jerusalem: "The Holy City in the eyes of the Chroniclers . . ."** p. 377)

In his book, *"The Shape of the Holy,"* p. 50, Professor Oleg Graber states: "In 661, the head of the *Umayyyad* clan, *Mu'awiya ibn abi Sufyan*, governor of Syria and of the truly brilliant Arab leaders of that century, was elected to the Caliphate and received in Jerusalem the homage of Arab Muslim leaders [and was also well admired by the Jews because of his benevolence toward them]. On that occasion, Mu'awiya is said to have visited the Church of the Holy Sepulcher, the Church of the Ascension on the Mount of Olives, and the tomb of the Virgin Mary in Gethsemane. No mention is made of a visit to the mosque on the Haram [because there was none at the time]." The Caliph simply showed no interest in the "Rock" because it was a Christian church, and because of the Christian belief that Jesus' footprints were indented on it—which is in contradiction to Muhammad's teaching about Jesus' fate. The third Caliph, Abed al-Malik, trying by any means to prevent a budding Muslims' veneration of the "Rock", had finally erected the Dome of the Rock Mosque over the "Rock" and claimed, as some later alleged, that the footprint of Allah Himself are indented on the "Rock." And as was mentioned earlier by the Muslim critic of relics, Ibn Taymiyya, " . . . The greatest lie is from those who think that is the place of the footprint of the Lord [Allah] . . ."

During the eleventh century, the city of Jerusalem was almost devastated by three earthquakes. It finally forced the Jewish community to relocate, first to Tyre, and finally to Damascus for a period of fifty years. Joshua Prawer tells us: "The City [of Jerusalem] suffered badly during the eleventh century from a series of earthquakes: in 1016, in 1033, and again in 1067. In the last one, it is reported, 25,000 people were killed and only two houses remained" (*"The History of the Jews in the Latin Kingdom of Jerusalem"*—Clarendon, Oxford, p. 15). As a consequence, the Jewish community that was permitted to live around their Temple by the Islamic rulers for over 450 years, on the southeast ridge of Jerusalem near the Gihon or Shiloah Spring, was forced to abandon Jerusalem. The earthquakes have ruptured the bedrock of the City, and caused the septic system of Jerusalem to mix with the pure and sweet ground water of the Gihon or Siloam spring and channels of water. The Jews, who could no longer drink of the defiled water, nor take their ritualistic bath in them, saw it as a divine retribution for their sins. They remembered that in the days of Jeremiah the same thing happened, where the sweet waters of the Spring of Shiloah had turned bitter. Beginning with the twelfth Century, after the Jews returned to Jerusalem—after an absence of fifty years—they too were swept by the wave of legends circulating by both Muslims and Christians. They eventually began to believe that the Dome of the Rock was the very site of the Temple. They began to believe that the "Rock" was to be considered holy to Jews too. When the Crusaders captured Jerusalem, in 1099 C.E., they too believed it was the true location of the Temple of God and Solomon.

It is important to note that when David brought back the Ark of God to Jerusalem, he placed it near the Gihon spring. It is in that very location that Solomon, in his fourth year, built the Temple. We find out this important information at the time Solomon was coroneted by the High Priest Zadok. We read: **"So Zadok, the priest . . . caused Solomon to ride upon King David's mule, AND BROUGHT HIM TO GIHON. And Zadok the priest took a horn of oil OUT OF THE TABERNACLE** [located near Gihon], **and anointed Solomon . . ."** (I Kings 1:38-39). When King David was told by Nathan the Prophet that his son, from his adulterous relationship with Bath Sheva, would die, **"David therefore besought the Lord for the child: and David fasted, and went in [into the Tabernacle's courtyard], and lay all night upon the earth."** After he found out that his son died, we read: **"Then David arose from the earth and washed** [in a ritualistic manner with the living water from the Gihon Spring], **and anointed himself, and changed his** [mourning] **apparel** [of the traditional sackcloth and ashes], **AND CAME INTO THE HOUSE OF THE LORD, AND WORSHIPED; then he came to his own house** [located south of the Tabernacle] . . ." (II Samuel 12:16,20).

From the days of King David, to the days the Jewish community was forced to abandon their Temple site (1077 C.E.)—after the earthquakes have caused the sweet waters of the Siloam to be polluted—everyone knew the true location of the Temple site was over and above the Gihon (Siloam or Shiloah) Spring of "living waters." Aristeas, a visitor from Egypt, recorded a detailed description of the Temple and Jerusalem, being an eyewitness, about fifty years after the time of Alexander the great. Professor Gifford from England had later translated Aristeas' eyewitness accounts in which he gives a rendition preserved by Eusebius. He states: **"There is an inexhaustible reservoir of water**, as would be expected from **an abundant spring gushing out naturally from within [the Temple];** there being moreover a wonderful and indescribable cistern underground of five furlongs [3000 feet away], according to their showing, all around the foundation of the Temple, and countless pipes from them, so that these **streams** on every side met together [at the Temple site]. And all these have been fastened with lead at the bottom and the side walls, and over these has been spread a great quantity of plaster, all have been carefully wrought" (Eusebius' recording of Aristeas, *"Preparation of the Gospel,"* ch.38).

Aristeas also describes the City of Jerusalem as a "crescent shaped" of one single mountain ridge (unlike the Haram-esh-Sharif). He says: "When we arrived in the land of the Jews, we saw the City [of Jerusalem] situated in the middle of the whole of Judea **on top of a mountain [one single mountain]** of considerable altitude. On the summit, the Temple had been built in its great splendor and was surrounded by three walls . . . The Temple faces the east and its back is toward the west" (Charles, *"Pseudepigrapha,"* Vol. II. p. 105, lines 83-4). Brackets and emphases mine.

The single mountain Aristeas saw had two summits. On the northern summit the Temple was located, while alongside it, on the southern summit, the Citadel that protected Jerusalem was built. Aristeas and his companions climbed up the "the neighboring Citadel and looked around us" to look down into the Temple to view all that went on within its outer visible courts. Since the Citadel and Temple were built on the same single mountain, on two different summits alongside each other, Aristeas and his companions were able, by ascending the Citadel, to look at the work of the Levites and Priests inside the open Temple outer courts. Had the Temple been located on the Haram-esh-Sharif plateau, a third of a mile to the north, they would not have been able to look inside the courtyard of the Temple. The Citadel was built as the special fortress for "guarding the Temple precincts" according to Aristeas (line 101). According to Charles, "The Citadel was the special protection of the Temple, and its founder had fortified it so strongly that it might efficiently protect it [the Temple from the south]" (*ibid.* line 104

In the book I Maccabees 1:33-33, we read: "He [Antiochus Epiphanaes] plundered the City [of Jerusalem] and set fire to it, demolishing its houses and its surrounding walls, took captive the women and children, and seized the cattle. Then **they built up the City of David** with its high, massive walls and strong towers, **and it became their Citadel** [or their Akra]." Antiochus placed a garrison of his soldiers in the Citadel to keep an eye on the work of the Levites and priests in the Temple down below. These soldiers would often harass the Temple workers with obscene gestures.

When the Macabees retook the City, after defeating the Syrians, the status of the Citadel and City of David was changed. Josephus records: "The Hasmoneans in the period of their reign, both filled up the flat-like ravine [between the Akra and the third hill where later Herod enlarged Fort Antonia], with the object of uniting the City [of David or Akra] with the Temple [located on the middle hill or Ophel], and also reduced the elevation of Akra by [initially] leveling its summit, in order that it would not block the view of the Temple [located north of the Akra]" (*"War,"* V. 4, 1, brackets are mine).

Josephus also tells us that Simon the Hasmonean had ultimately totally leveled the Akra or City of David to its foundation—thus creating a leveled area lower than the Temple, which he named "the Lower City." He writes: "He [Simon] thought it would be an excellent thing and to his advantage to level also the hill on which the Citadel [or City of David] stood, in order that the Temple might be higher than this. Accordingly, he called the people to an assembly and thought to persuade them to have this done, reminding them how they had suffered at the hands of the [Syrian] garrison and the Jewish renegades, and also warning them of what they would suffer if a foreign ruler should occupy their realm, and a garrison should be placed therein. With these words he persuaded the people since he was recommending what was to their advantage. And so they all set and began to level the hill, and without stopping work night or day, after three whole years brought it [the original Mount Zion and City of David] down to the ground and the surface of the plain. And thereafter the Temple stood high above everything else, once the Citadel and the hill on which it stood had been demolished. Such was the nature of things accomplished in the time of Simon [the Hasmonean]" (Josephus, *"Antiquities,"* XIII. 6, 7, pp. 215-218, Loeb translation, brackets mine).

This Akra or Citadel was the exact location of the City of David. It was situated alongside the Temple to protect it from foreign invaders. It was located about one third of a mile southeast from the *Baris*, built by Simon, to protect the Temple from the north. Later, it was enlarged by Herod and renamed Fort Antonia, and finally, after the conquest of Jerusalem by Omar, it was, again, renamed the "Haram esh-Sharif." This area was later also referred to as "the Temple Mount" by those Jews who returned to the City after the Crusaders' defeat in the early twelfth century. The great Geographer of Jerusalem, George Adam Smith, wrote: "By the author of first Maccabees **the Akra is identified with 'the City of David,'** that is the earlier Jebusite stronghold of Sion. **If we accept this identification, THE QUESTION IS AT ONCE SOLVED**, for, as we have seen, the stronghold of Sion lay on the East Hill, south of and below the Temple, or **IMMEDIATELY ABOVE GIHON**" (*"Jerusalem,"* Vol. I., p. 445, emphases mine).

The Roman historian Tacitus, describing the Temple, as it had existed before its destruction in 70 C.E., wrote: "The Temple resembled a citadel, and had its own walls, which were more laboriously constructed than the others. Even the colonnades with which it was surrounded formed an admirable artwork. **It [the Temple] contained an inexhaustible spring**; there were subterranean excavations in the hill, and tanks and cisterns for holding rainwater. The founders of the state had foreseen that frequent wars would result from the singularity of its customs, and so had made every provision against the most protracted siege" (Tacitus, *"History,"* Bk. 5, para.12).

We also read of another account about the Gihon spring as given by Polyhistor (writing in early first century B.C.E.), who cited accounts of earlier writers about Jerusalem. This quote of Polyhistor is cited by Eusebius in his work, *"Preparation of the Gospel,"* Bk. IX, ch. 36. He writes: "Timochares, in his *"Life of Antiochus,"* says that Jerusalem has a circuit of forty furlongs [including lands surrounding the city for 2,000 cubits], and is difficult to take being shut on all sides by abrupt ravines: and **the whole City is flooded with streams of water which flow from the City**. But the country from the City as far as forty furlongs [or five miles] **is without water**: but beyond the forty furlongs it is well watered." This description by Timochares describes the Jerusalem before Simon the Hasmonean. The next reference by Polyhistor quoted by Eusebius states: "The author of the *"Metrical Survey of Syria"* says in his first book that Jerusalem lies upon a lofty and rugged site; and that some parts of the wall are built of polished stone . . . and that **there is also within the place a SPRING which SPOUTS ABUNDANCE OF WATER**" (Eusebius, **"Preparation For the Gospel,"** Bk. IX, ch. 35).

Polyhistor further quoted Philo (who lived in the second century B.C.E. or earlier), saying: "'Philo too says, in his *"Account of Jerusalem,"* that there is a **fountain** [or a single spring], and that it is dried up in winter, but becomes full in summer'" (Eusibius, ibid., ch. 37). Philo adds that **this fountain produced a "joyous stream, flooded by rain and snow,** [which] rolls swiftly on beneath the neighboring towers." According to Eusebius, this account of Philo calls the single spring **"the High Priest's fountain."** Aristeas wrote fifty years after Alexander, and Tacitus 300 years later, stated dogmatically that **the natural spring was found within the precinct of the Temple** at Jerusalem.

In Psalm 87:1-3,7 we read: **"His** [God's] **fountain is in the holy mountains. The Lord loves the gates of Zion more than all the dwellings of Jacob. Glorious things are spoken of thee, O city of God. Selah . . . The singers as the players on instruments shall be there [in the Temple]: All my SPRINGS are in thee [Zion]."** Many other Psalms speak of the same feature of a natural spring within the Temple. Though this spring is a perennial spring, it spouts water like a geyser. As a Karst-type of spring, it thrusts out its water five times a day in the springtime, with time interval, but the Gihon gushes out intermittently.

In the *"Book of Legends,"* we read: "Rabbi Phinehas said in the name of Rabbi Huna of Sephoris: **The spring that issued from the Holy of Holies** resembled at its source the [tiny] antennae of locusts; when it reached the entrance to the Temple hall [further east], it became wider, as wide as a thread of warp; when it reached the entrance to the Porch [even further east], it grew as wide as the thread of weft; when it reached the entrance to the Temple court [further east], it became as wide as the mouth of a small narrow-necked jug. From there onward [in an underground channel], it grew wider and wider as it rose, until it reached the entrance of the House of David [at the lower end of Mount Zion]. After it reached the entrance of the House of David, it became a swiftly flowing brook in which those (who were ritually unclean) immersed themselves in order to become clean" (Bialik and Ravintzky, *"The book of Legends,"* NY: Schocken Books, 1992, p. 161).

Many Psalms speak of "The Fountain of Life" in the midst of the Temple. The present site of the alleged "Temple Mount" on Haram esh-Sahrif does not and never contained a spring or fountain of water. There is only one such spring or fountain of running or "living" waters in Jerusalem—the Gihon or Siloam Spring—a third of a mile southeast to Al-Aqsa. Many historic accounts make this abundantly clear. In the *"Temple Scroll"* which describes the future Temple, found at the Dead Sea area, we read: "You shall make a channel all around the laver within the building [Temple]. The channel runs [from the building] of the laver to a shaft, goes down and disappears in the middle of the earth so that the water flows and runs through it and is lost in the middle of the earth" (The *"Temple Scroll,"* Col. Xxxii, 12-13, Martinez' trans.).

It must be understood that God's Temple must have "living waters" or spring in its midst for the sake of ritualistic purification of the believers and animals—as well as for the Temple itself. All the Scriptures make that abundantly clear. We are told: "In the Temple courtyard there was a bath house for the High Priest. He used to immerse himself in water on the eve of the day of Atonement" (Vilnay, *"Legends of Jerusalem,"* p. 88). The Gihon was known, from an early period, as the "Spring of the High Priest." Philo had noted this point and called the Spring in Jerusalem "'the High priest's fountain and the canal that carries off the water, he [Philo, as Eusebius quotes him] proceeds as follows: 'A headlong stream [from the fountain] by channels underground, the pipes pour forth'" (Eusebius, *"Preparation of the Gospel."* Bk. IX, ch.36).

Both Tacitus and Aristeas stated that **the Gihon Spring was within the Temple precinct**, but there were also many Jewish accounts that confirmed this evidence. One Jewish writer, Zev Vilnay, wrote in his work, *"Legends of Jerusalem,"* the following: "To the Jews of Jerusalem, the **Fountain of Gihon** [or Siloam to Christians] **is known as the Bath of Ishmael the High Priest.** They relate that on the day of Atonement, before entering the Holy of Holies, the High Priest used to dip his body and purify himself in its waters" (Vilnay, *"Legends of Jerusalem,"* p. 277). He adds, "The ritual bath of the High Priest was in the Temple courtyard" (*"Legend,"* VIII: 2). In another quote, Vilnay states: "'It is said of the Fountain of Gihon: 'It was the ritual bath of Rabbi Ishmael the High Priest,' who was among the 'ten martyrs of Israel.' And a big fountain fills it with water every day before the break of dawn; and the waters were sweet and pure from the moment they gushed forth from the spring till sunrise. But after the sun shined and flashed its rays over the surface, they became so salty that no man could drink from them'" (*ibid*).

The main purpose for all this information brought to the attention of the reader is not, after all, just to prove to the unbiased reader the correct location of the Temple site. It is not the main purpose of this chapter either. The main reason is to demonstrate what happens when the love of the truth is lacking in anyone of us—be it in the doctrine of the **afterlife**, or the true location of the Temple, which is 'historically' linked to the dogmatic belief that Muhammad had "ascended to Heaven" from the "Temple site"—from the Haram-esh-Sharif.

"God is Spirit," we are told, and He demands to be worshiped "in truth and in spirit," or else all is in vain! This is a problem all of humanity is infested with, and therefore few are those who can see and are willing to admit: the "Emperor is naked." Where do you stand? If you truly have the love of the truth—though it may contradict your inherited beliefs and religious dogmatism—you too can "see" the light. You too can see how "naked" all of us are before God to one degree or the other.

Through His Prophets, God had foretold the fate and total destruction of His beloved City Jerusalem or Mount Zion—both in the first and second calamities that came upon it and His people. Let's now read some of those accounts and compare them with the present state of the alleged "Temple Mount" site.

As was mentioned in an earlier chapter, the Prophet Micah, living during the period of Isaiah, first revealed the fate of the northern kingdom of Israel. He wrote: **"Therefore I [God] will make Samaria as an heap of the field, and as plants of a vineyard; and I will pour down the stones** [of its palaces and houses] **thereof into the valley, and I will discover the foundations thereof"** (Micah 1:6). It is very important to notice the manner in which God was, through enemy human instruments, was going to destroy the northern Capital of His people Israel. Now let's compare the fate of Samaria with that of Jerusalem. In Chapter 3 we read about the fate of Jerusalem in her future two separate captivities. The Prophet declares: **"Therefore** [because of the sins of Judah] **shall Zion for your sake be plowed as a field, and Jerusalem shall become heaps** [or pile of stones]**, and the mountain of the House** [or Temple] **as the high places of the forest"** (Micah 3:12). Later historic accounts reveal, in both captivities and destructions, the tragic fulfillment of this prophecy, to the last detail.

We find another such description, as was mentioned earlier, which describes the impending destruction of both Temples and City of Jerusalem, in the words of Asaph—King Solomon's Temple musician and prophet. He writes prophetically: **"God, the heathen have come into Your inheritance; Your Holy Temple they have defiled; They have laid Jerusalem on heaps** [or a pile of rocks]**. The dead bodies of Your servants have they given to be meat unto the fowls of heaven, the flesh of your saints unto the beasts of the earth. Their blood have they shed like water round about Jerusalem; and there was none to bury them. We have become a reproach to our neighbors, a scorn and derision** to those who are about us [and today things are no different]. **How long, Lord? Will You be angry forever? Shall Your Jealousy burn like fire** [because of our sins]? **Pour out Your wrath upon the heathen that have not known You, and upon the kingdoms that have not called upon Your name** [and He did, and yet will, as promised]. **For they have devoured Jacob, and laid waste his dwelling place**" (Psalm 79:1-7). These tragic events did come to pass, and one last time it will happen again in the near future—and for the same reasons.

The Prophet Isaiah was commissioned by God to deliver the same message—yet to no avail—nobody was listening. He declared: **"Ah sinful nation, a people laden with iniquity, a seed of evil doers, children that are corrupters; they have forsaken the Lord, they have provoked the Holy One of Israel unto anger, and they are gone backward. Why would you be stricken anymore? You will revolt more and more; the whole head** [leadership] **is sick, and the whole heart faint** [or weak minded]. **From the sole of the foot even unto the head there is no soundness in it; but wounds, and bruises, and putrefying sores; they have not been closed, neither bound up, neither mollified with ointment. Your country is desolate** [as a consequence], **your cities are** [or will be] **burned with fire, your land, strangers are devouring it in your presence, and it is desolate, as overthrown by strangers. And the daughter of Zion is left as a cottage in a vineyard, as a lodge in a garden of cucumbers, as a besieged city. Except the Lord of Hosts had left unto us a very small remnant, we should have been as Sodom, and should have become like unto Gomorrah"** (Isaiah 1:4-9).

History tells us that all these predictions of Isaiah came to pass. Later, we shall read of some historic accounts that describe the fulfilled words of Isaiah and Micha, as recorded by eyewitness historians and travelers, beginning with Josephus. At the end of his book, Isaiah added these bemoaning pleas to God: **"Your Holy cities are a wilderness, Zion is a wilderness, Jerusalem a desolation** [and totally devastated]. **Our Holy and our beautiful House** [or Temple], **where our fathers praised You, is burned up with fire** [in both captivities]**; and all our pleasant things are laid waste"** (Isaiah 64:10-11).

During the reign of the most wicked king of Judah, King Manasseh, son of one of the most righteous kings of Judah, King Hezekiah, we read: **"And the Lord spoke by His servants the Prophets** [soon after the death of Isaiah the Prophet]**, saying, because Manasseh king of Judah has** done these abominations . . . Therefore thus says the Lord God of Israel, Behold, I am bringing such evil upon Jerusalem and Judah that whosoever hears it, both his ears shall tingle. And I will stretch over Jerusalem the line of Samaria [making it, likewise, a pile of rocks], and the plummet of the House of Ahab [the idolatrous king of the Israel to the north]; and I WILL WIPE JERUSALEM AS A MAN WIPES A DISH, WIPING IT AND TURNING IT UPSIDE DOWN," [and that's how Jerusalem looked like after both captivities and destruction by the King of Babylon and later by Titus]. And I will forsake the remnant of My inheritance [temporarily, until they learn their lessons the hard way], and deliver them into the hands of their enemies; And they shall become a prey and a spoil to all their enemies. Because they have done that which is evil in My sight, and have provoked Me to anger, since the day their fathers came forth out of Egypt, even unto this day" (II Kings 21:10-15). God does not hide the 'dirty laundry' of His people—and for that matter, no other nations' sins! And nobody can accuse God of being an anti-Semite!

The Prophet Jeremiah, who lived through the first destruction of Jerusalem and the Temple, recorded some relevant information about those events. He wrote: "And I [God] will make Jerusalem heaps [or piles of stones], and a den of dragons; and I will make the cities of Judah desolate, without an inhabitant" (Jeremiah 9:11). In Chapter 19:11-13, Jeremiah is told by God: "Then you shall break the bottle [of clay] in the sight of the men that go with you [to the valley of Hinnom, verses 1-2], and shall say unto them [the leaders and people of Jerusalem, verse 3], Thus says the Lord of Hosts; even so I will break this people and this City, as one breaks a potter's vessel, that cannot be made whole again . . ." Later, Jeremiah quotes the words of some of the leaders of Judah: "Then rose up certain of the elders of the land, and spoke to all the assembly of the people, saying, Micah the Morshthite prophesied in the days of Hezekiah king of Judah, and spoke to all the people of Judah, saying, 'Thus says the Lord of Hosts; Zion shall be plowed like a field [being turned into a farmland], and Jerusalem shall become heaps [or piles of stones], and the Mountain of the House [or Temple] as the high places of a forest" (Jeremiah 26:18).

After all these prophesied tragic calamities came to pass, and the remaining captives of Judah were taken into Babylon, we read these words of anguish of the defeated and broken captives: "By the rivers of

Babylon, there we sat down, yea, we wept [too little, too late], when we remembered Zion . . . If I forget you, O Jerusalem, let my right hand forget her cunning. If I do not remember you, let my tongue cleave to roof of my mouth; if I prefer not Jerusalem above my chief joy. Remember, O Lord, the children of Edom in the day of Jerusalem; who said, RASE IT, RASE IT, EVEN TO THE FOUNDATION THEREOF [which they did, according to God's will]. O daughter of Babylon who are to be destroyed; happy shall He be [God, through human instruments] that rewards you as you have served us. Happy shall he be that takes and dashes your little ones against the stones [as you have done to our children]" (Psalm 137). The above accounts, for sake of emphasis, are repeated again from a previous chapter.

To have a full understanding of this passage, and the true history and future of the Middle East conflicts since the days of Abraham—and to know the true identity of Edom, Babylon, and all the other players in our days, and their coming punishment—read the monumental work mentioned earlier at the beginning of this book. Its title is: "*Middle East: Blueprint For the Final Solution.*" You will not be the same after reading it—guaranteed!

Now why would the children of Edom say, "Raze it, raze it, to the foundation thereof?" Jerusalem was a very rich City. It had palaces and fancy houses—and beyond that, a very decorated and adorned Temple, covered heavily with gold, silver, and bronze. Many of Jerusalem's palaces and rich homes were, likewise, covered with precious metals. When the armies of Babylon, and the Edomite soldiers among them, conquered the City, they burned all of its gilded structures and surrounding walls, including the Temple, with fire. The intense heat caused all the precious metals to melt and sip down to their foundations. The only way to retrieve the precious metals was by turning every stone upside down—all the way to their rock bottom level and very foundation. When this mass looting of the riches of the City and Temple was over, the whole area looked like a great pile or heap of stones. This is exactly what the Prophets talked about when prophesying about Zion and the Temple becoming "a heap of stones." This fate of the first Temple and City was to be repeated during the destruction of the second Temple and City by the Roman legions.

Forty years before the total destruction of both the Temple and City of Jerusalem, Jesus approached the City and was greeted with great cheers by the multitudes in Jerusalem. Many of the leaders did not share the sentiments of the jubilant Jews who were on hand to welcome their King and Messiah. Then we read: **"And when He came near, he beheld the City, and wept over it, saying, if you had known, even you, at least in this your day, the things which belong unto your peace, but now they are hidden from your eyes. For the days shall come upon you, that your enemies shall cast a trench around you, and compass you around, and keep you [surrounded] on every side. And shall lay you** [or level you] **even with** [to] **the ground, and your children within you; and THEY SHALL NOT LEAVE IN YOU ONE STONE UPON ANOTHER; because you** [Jerusalem] **knew not the time of your visitation"** (Luke 19:37-44).

These were the very words God had inspired all the former Prophets of Israel to proclaim against the City and Temple in both destructions and captivities. Jerusalem and the Temple became a heap of stones and were left in utter ruins—to their very foundations. In both captivities and destructions, Jerusalem and the Temple Mount were turned into a farmland by enemy hands, according to the words of their own Prophets.

More can be added from the Biblical record, but let's now go to the pages of history and find out how did all the words of the Prophets of God come to pass. Also, did Judah really remember their Jerusalem their "chief joy"—their City of Zion, their Temples to this day? Or did they, with the passage of time, and mainly in the last millennium, forget even the true locations of their Temples and original location of the City of Zion? Strange and shocking as it may sound: Jews, Christians, and Muslims had forgotten the true location of the Temples of God and the City of Zion—at least until recent times for Zion (1875 C.E.)—because of . . . the doctrine of the **afterlife!**

Up to the years 1875-1885 C.E., when the true location of the original Mount Zion was discovered by the English Professor Birch, all believed, and dogmatically so, it was located elsewhere. Now the Jews can really "remember Zion," but what about the Temple? Prior to the Crusaders all knew that the Temple was built alongside the citadel of Mount Zion, on the Ophel Hill. Present day Jewish authorities, as well as those in the past 800 years or so, esteem very highly and venerate the enclosure of Haram—esh-Sherif, considering it to be "The Temple Mount" and previous location of all the Temples of God. Sadly, the true location still lies in waste, as prophesied by the old Prophets. It is a tragic reality that the worshipers at "The Western Wall" are directing their sincere devotions and prayers to a Roman edifice, though built by Herod the Great, but was occupied by the tenth Roman legion since 6 C.E. to the end of the third century.

The actual site of the Temple, was believed to be located—by all Jews, Christians, and Muslims—on and around the Gihon Spring, **until the end of the eleventh century**. After the war with Rome (66-70 C.E.), only few important Roman buildings were left in the area, chiefly among them was Fort Antonia—the major camp of the tenth legion. Fort Antonia was not, since 6 C.E., considered to be a part of the municipality or jurisdiction of Jerusalem. Titus had no reason to destroy it.

This is what Josephus tells us about the destruction of the City and Temple, being an eyewitness observer: "Now as soon as the army had no more to slay or to plunder . . . Caesar gave orders that they should now demolish the entire City and Temple, but should leave as many of the towers standing [which later were also demolished] . . . But for all the rest of the wall [surrounding Jerusalem] it was so thoroughly laid [waste] even with the ground [or down to its foundation] by those who **dug it up** [looking for the melted gold and other precious metals] **to the foundation, that there was left nothing to make those that came there believe [Jerusalem] had ever been inhabited.** This was the end which Jerusalem came to by the madness of those that were for innovations; a City otherwise of great magnificence, and of mighty name among all mankind" ("***War of the Jews,***" VII.1, 1, Whiston translation (emphases throughout mine).

Josephus adds: "And truly, the very view itself was a melancholy thing [just as the Prophet Jeremiah felt and recorded in his book of ***Lamentation***]; for those places which were adorned with trees and pleasant gardens, were now become desolate country every way, and its trees were all cut down. Nor could any foreigner that had formerly seen Judaea and the most beautiful suburbs of the City, and saw it as a desert, but lament and mourn sadly at so great change. For the war had laid all signs of beauty quite waste. Nor if anyone had known the place before, had he come on a sudden to it now, would he have known it again. But though he were at the City itself, yet would he have inquired for it [not able to see any sign of it]" ("***War,***" VI, 1,1.)

The eye witness accounts of Josephus and others are exactly how all the former Prophets of God had described the fate of the City and Temple after their repeated destruction. When the disciples of Jesus had asked

Him about the fate of the City and Temple in His day [Matthew 24:1-2 and Luke 19:43-44], He, in essence, was repeating the same words of the Prophets of the God of Israel. It was not a 'new' prophecy, but one that was recorded by many former Prophets, as we read earlier. Unfortunately, most uninformed and biased scholars and historians still do claim that Josephus and other eye witness observers of the total destruction of the City and Temple were exaggerating—though these men were eyewitnesses, while these modern historians and scholars were not! These short sighted and willfully blind scholars and historians—as well as most religious "spiritual leaders" of the three religions linked to Abraham—have not, obviously, read or do believe the many prophecies recorded earlier by God's Prophets. Willful ignorance is not a mark of a genuine scholar! This kind of a 'scholar' looks but cannot 'see' that his "Emperor is naked!"

Ironically, the destroyers of the City and Temple included, besides the Roman soldiers, also the Jewish defenders themselves. Once the Jews realized that Titus' army is having the upper hand, they decided to destroy as much as possible any remnant of the Temple to prevent Rome from further desecrating their Holy Temple with their abominable pagan objects of worship. In the Hebrew equivalent translation of Josephus' work, called ***"Josippon,"*** which was highly respected and trusted by many great Jewish Rabbis and scholars, we read: "'So the flames destroyed the Holy of Holies. And when the [Jewish] leaders of the rebels and their followers who were still in the City [of Jerusalem] saw that the Holy of Holies had been burned, they burned the rest of the Temple together with every mansion in Jerusalem, so that the Romans should not rule over them. And they also burned down the rest of the Temple buildings, saying: 'Now that the Holy of Holies has been burned, why go on living? Why leave any house or building?'" (***"Josippon,"*** from ***"Mimekor Israel," "Classical Jewish Folk tales,"*** collected by Micha Joseph Bin Gorion).

In an early Jewish work, called ***"Second Baruch,"*** we have further evidence that Jews did help destroy the Temple to avoid its desecration by the Romans. All scholars agree that this work was written near the end of the first century, shortly after the Temple was destroyed. In this work, the authors claim the angels on the side of the Jews commanded them to destroy the Temple to avoid desecration by the Roman soldiers. We read: "'I heard this angel saying to the angels who held the torches: 'Now destroy the walls [of the Temple] **and overthrow them to their foundations** so that the enemies [or Romans] do not boast and say, 'We have overthrown the walls of Zion and we have burned down the place of the Mighty God'" (*"Second Baruch,"* 6:3-7:1). R. Hammer, in *"The Jerusalem Anthology,"* p. 89, has more to say about this historical source.

When the Roman soldiers burned the City and Temple to the ground, all the precious metals had melted and sipped deep into the very foundational stones and bedrock. They used many Jewish captives to unearth every single stone to retrieve the great riches of the City. Knowing that the Temple served as the national treasury of the whole Jewish community in the land and the Diaspora, they did not spare any effort to exploit its riches and forced the Jewish captives to retrieve every ounce of it—including those riches which were hidden in underground caves and tunnels under the City and its Temple. Josephus tells us that the vast amount of precious metal recovered in that war, caused the price of metal to plummet by half in the Eastern part of the Empire (Josephus, *"War of the Jews,"* VI. 6, 1).

Later, Josephus says that after an absence of four months, Titus returned from Antioch to survey the destruction of Jerusalem. This is what Titus saw: "As he came to Jerusalem, in his progress [from Antioch to Egypt], and compared the melancholy he saw it then in, with the ancient glory of the City, [compared] with the present greatness of its ruins (as well as its ancient splendor). He could not but pity the destruction of the City . . . Yet there was no small quantity of the riches that had been in that City still found among the ruins, a great deal of which the Romans dug up; but **the greatest part was discovered by those** [Jews] **who were captives**, and so they [the Romans] carried it away; I mean the gold and the silver, and the rest of that most precious furniture which the Jews had, and which **the owners had treasured up underground against the uncertainties of war**" (*"War,"* VII. 5,2).

Eleazar, the Jewish commander of Masada, upon visiting the City after its destruction, wrote: "And where is now that great City [of Jerusalem], the metropolis of the Jewish nation, which was fortified by so many walls round about, which had so many fortresses and large towers to defend it, which could hardly contain the instruments prepared for the war, and which had so many ten thousands of men to fight for it? Where is this City that was believed to have God Himself inhabiting therein? **IT IS NOW DEMOLISHED TO THE VERY FOUNDATION** [as was declared long ago by all the Prophets of Israel, and lastly, by the Prophet from Nazareth], and [now] **has nothing left but THAT MONUMENT**

[Fort Antonia] **of it IS PRESERVED, I mean THE CAMP OF THOSE** [Romans] **that had destroyed it** [Jerusalem]**, WHICH** [camp] **STILL DWELLS UPON ITS RUINS;** some unfortunate old men also lie upon the ashes of the Temple, and a few women are there preserved alive by the enemy, for our bitter shame and reproach" (*"War,"*VII. 8,7).

Eleazar Added: "[God] abandoned His most Holy City to be burnt and razed to the ground" (*"War,"* VII. 8,6 Loeb). Jerusalem, Eleazar claimed, was given to a "wholesale destruction." Later, he concluded: "I cannot but wish that we had all died before we had seen that Holy City demolished by the hands of our enemies, **or the foundations of the Holy Temple dug up**, after so profane a manner" (*"War,"*VII. 8,7).

What an ironic twist of history and tragedy! While few old Jewish men were squatting on the ashes of their beloved burned Temple—which was destroyed to the ground by the Tenth Roman legion encamped at the time in Fort Antonia or **"that monument,"** as Eleazar, the Jewish commander of Masada, referred to it—some of their descendants, in complete and willful ignorance of their own history, pray, wail, shed tears, and direct their veneration (and for the last 800 years) toward the "Western wall" **OF "THAT** [Roman] **MONUMENT!"** How 'naked can their Emperor be?'

Titus had no reason to destroy Fort Antonia. Its walls remained intact, although its northern wall needed some repair. Soon after the war, it was quickly repaired. It had 37 cisterns and a special aqueduct to supply it with water. It was easily defended and perfectly suitable for his tenth legion. Before the war, it served as the camp of the tenth legion, and after the war there was no reason to abandon it. When Omar conquered Jerusalem in the early seventh century, Fort Antonia, "that monument" that became the pride of the Roman Empire, and a testimony to its crushing defeat of the Jews, was renamed "The Noble Enclosure" or Haram-esh-Sherif. More than 500 years later, the returning Jews, who previously occupied the Temple grounds and City since the days of Omar, began to regard the Haram esh-Sharif as "The Temple Mount."

Jerome, the fourth century historian, in his commentary on Isaiah 64:11, wrote: "'Our Holy and our beautiful House [quoting first from Isaiah], where our fathers praised You, is burnt up with fire; and all our pleasant things are laid waste;' and the Temple which earned reverence throughout the world **has become the refuse dump** of the new city whose founder [Hadrian] called Aelia [Capitolina]" (Prof. Moshe Gil, *"A*

History of Palestine," 634-1099, p.67, 70). Jerusalem and its Temple site remained a **refuse dump** until the day Caliph Omar began to cleanse its refuse with his own hands! He allowed the 70 Jewish families of Tiberias to settle on the Temple site on a strict condition that they keep the area clean. Ironically, while Omar the Muslim had much respect for the Temple Mount site, which moved him to begin to cleanse it with his own hands and cloak, the Jews themselves, once losing sight of the true location of their own Holy Temple and City, left it desolate to this very day! How spiritually "naked" can the people of God be? In effect, all Muslims, Christians, and Jews have lost their "sight" of the true site of the Temple of God. They all refuse to "see" that their "Emperor is naked."

Why and when did the Jews lose sight of the true location of their Temple Mount? After the three powerful earthquakes that rocked Jerusalem in 1016, 1033, and 1067, many died in the process. The pure source of water from the Gihon Spring became polluted due to rupture of the septic system of Jerusalem as a result of the devastating earthquakes. The Jews could no longer drink from it or ritualistically purify themselves in its previously sweet and pure water. They felt, as in the days of the Prophet Jeremiah, when the waters of the Gihon Spring became bitter, that God was angry with them. Shortly after the last earthquake, Jerusalem and the area was invaded in 1071 C.E. by the Seljuk Turks. To the Jews, these invaders were very strange, even in appearance. The Jewish Academy and leadership felt the end of the world was imminent. And so in 1077 C.E. they finally decided to abandon the City and Temple grounds and move the center of Jewish learning and life, first to Tyre, and then to Damascus. The reason they moved to Damascus was the belief that, according to the prophecy in Zechariah 9:1, the Messiah would come from that city. The remnant of the Jews in Jerusalem uprooted themselves from the southeastern part of the Temple area, which was now without walls due to the devastation in 1033 C.E., to an area just northeast of the Haram esh-Sharif. See Prawer, *"The History of the Jews in the Latin Kingdom of Jerusalem,"* p. 49.

Then, in 1099 C.E., when the Crusaders conquered Jerusalem, the Jews lost all their possessions in the City. The Jews were, violently, by the force of arms driven out of the City. They were forbidden for the next fifty years from entering or residing in the City. This forced abandonment of Jerusalem, after a residence of over 450 years in the Temple area, triggered a drastic change of attitude toward Jerusalem even in their theological thinking. When the 1ews came back to Jerusalem in the eleventh century, about fifty years later, after the Muslims recaptured Jerusalem from the Crusaders, they developed a different attitude to the significance of the original site of the City of Jerusalem. They decided to live just northeast of Haram-esh-Sahrif. This abandonment by the returnees to Jerusalem had baffled many Jewish scholars in later times. The returning Jews gave up their former site near the Gihon Spring, because it was polluted and unfit for their ritual bathing needs. This caused the Jews to renounce the sanctity of the Gihon Spring. Having a desire to look to a Holy Place for their religious needs, and since many began to look at the Dome of the Rock as the "new Temple of Solomon," with the passage of time even Jews began to consider this Muslim holy site as the location of the Temple of Solomon. After all, many of the "holy sites" of Jerusalem were built with many stones taken from the original sites of the Temple and City of Jerusalem. Thus, it was felt, that the transfer of these holy stones had also transferred the "Holiness" of the Holy Temple onto the new sites. As time went by, Jews, Christians, and Muslims alike, became convinced that Haram-esh-Sharif was truly the original site of the Holy Temples—and so it remained to this very day. It is most important to note that prior to the time Caliph Omar conquered Jerusalem in 638 C.E., there is no one shred of evidence among the thousands of manuscripts from Jewish, Christian, or other secular sources that dogmatically even suggests that the Temple was located on or near the Haram esh-Sharif area.

Let's recall, again, the words of the Prophets concerning the fate of Jerusalem and the Temple Mount—and seal this chapter with few last quotes, first from an eyewitness account—Eusebius. In his book, *"Proof of the Gospel,"* he wrote: "The Hill called Zion and Jerusalem, the buildings there, that is to say, the Temple, the Holy of Holies, the Altar, and whatever else was there dedicated to the glory of God, **have been utterly removed or shaken [down]**, in fulfillment of the word [of Christ, as well as the Prophets of Israel]" (*Ibid.* Sect. 405).

He added: "'Utter desolation has possessed the land. Their once famous Mount Sion [or Zion] instead as being as it once was, the center, study and education, based on the divine prophecies, which the children of the Hebrews of old, their godly Prophets, Priests and national teachers loved to interpret, **IS A ROMAN FARM LIKE THE REST OF THE COUNTRY.** Yea, with my own eyes **I HAVE SEEN BULLS PLOWING THERE, AND THE SACRED SITE SOWN WITH SEED.** And

Jerusalem itself is become but a storehouse of its fruit of old days now destroyed, or better, as the Hebrew [Prophet of old] has it, a **STONE QUARRY**. So Aquila [an early second century translator of the Hebrew Scriptures into Greek] says: 'Therefore for your sake the land of Sion shall be ploughed, and Jerusalem shall be a quarry of stone [Micha 3:12],' for being inhabited of men of foreign race it is even now like a quarry. All the inhabitants of the City choose stores [or stones] from its ruins as they will for private as well for public buildings. And it is sad for the eyes to see stones from the Temple itself, and from its ancient Sanctuary and Holy place, used for the building of idol temples [in the Roman city Aelia], and for theaters for the populace. These things are open for the eyes to see'" (*ibid.* Sect. 406).

During the days of Emperor Hadrian, the one who turned the Temple Mount and Jerusalem into a dumpsite and part of it into a Roman farm—as Micha, Isaiah, and other Prophets prophesied—some Roman coins were minted with the image and inscription of Hadrian. On one side it was inscribed, *"Imperator Caesar Trianus Hadrianus,"* and on the other side, the emperor is shown plowing on the site of the City with the pair of cattle, with the inscription in Latin, *"the colony of Aelia Capitolina has been founded."* In the background, one can see one of the standards of the tenth legion in procession. See Dan Bahat, *"The Illustrated Atlas of Jerusalem,"* p.61.

During the period of Hadrian, Fort Antonia (later to be renamed Haram—esh-Sharif and "Temple Mount" by Muslims and Jews) served as the headquarters of the tenth legion that was stationed in this Roman Camp until 289 C.E. It was responsible for securing the interests of the Roman Empire in the region until it was relocated to the southern port city of Eilat.

Let's now recap, in short, where we stand now! The Jews consider the Temple site and Jerusalem as their own Holy Place and City. History makes it very plain, including early Islamic historic accounts. They do not need to fabricate or invent stories to prove their claims. The Bible and history, including Islamic history, are on their side in this matter. They do need, however, to restudy their own early history to retrace the true location of their Temple and Holy City. Until then their "Emperor will remain naked" and in need of being dressed up with the genuine "garments of righteousness and truth." Their religious and secular leaders, being blind themselves, had led them astray. The Christian community and its leaders believe the City to be Holy, because of their claim to follow The Jewish Prophet from Nazareth, as well as His Jewish disciples and early Prophets—and that includes the Bible they were inspired to write. Yet they too, contrary to their own early historic accounts, have lost sight and ability to perceive that their "Emperor is naked."

The Muslim community has a different issue to deal with and tackle. Their Prophet Muhammad claimed he believed the words of the Prophets of Israel and had respect for them and their writings. He had respect for Jesus, the Gospel, and the Apostles. Muhammad referred to the Jewish and Christian communities as "the people of the Book." It was then natural that both Muhammad and his early followers would have great reverence and respect for Jerusalem, for Kings David and Solomon, for the prophets of Israel, and for the Holy Temple and City of Jerusalem. It would not, therefore, be strange that Muslims all over the world would consider Jerusalem and the Land of Israel as the Holy land. What is different between them and both the Jews and Christians who accept the Bible as their infallible guide for life—at least for those who do and did so for many centuries—is the nature and reasons for their claims for the Land, The Holy City, and the Temple. What is their main reason? The successor of Muhammad and first Caliph after him, Omar, conquered Jerusalem. He desired to pray at the same place Kind David, whom he had revered, built his first Altar—the place where later King Solomon had built the first Holy Temple. Omar did not, however, advance any claims over that Holy and revered site. He was benevolent toward the Jews, and unlike the "Christians" who forbade the presence of the Jews in their own city, Caliph Omar invited the Jews to live again in their own Holy City and Temple site. His two successors had done the same. So what is it that made Jerusalem a Holy City to Islam? This whole long chapter was written for this very purpose: to explain why Jerusalem is considered to be the third most Holy City to Islam—and this reason is: **THEIR FAITH IN THE DOCTRINE OF THE AFTERLIFE—IMMEDIATELY AFTER DEATH!**

You see, Omar and other faithful Muslims in his day believed that Muhammad ascended up to Heaven, at the end of his "Night Journey" which led him to Jerusalem. Omar claimed to have received a vision from Allah, through the Prophet Muhammad, showing him the approximate location of his ascension to Heaven, the place where David built his Altar, the gate through which Muhammad entered the Holy City, and from there his ascension to Heaven. Omar named that gate, *"Bab al-Nabi"* or gate of the Prophet. Originally, it was claimed, the Al Aqsa Mosque was the location from which Muhammad had ascended up to Heaven. To that end, the Al Aqsa Mosque was erected. This site became the first Holy site to Islam. Later, the place was transferred to The Dome of the Rock, and Muhammad, it was claimed, had ascended up to Heaven through the hole in the "Rock." In the days of the third Caliph, Abd al-Malik, the one who built the Dome of the Rock Mosque, it was claimed, first, that the footprint of Allah was found on the Rock, and later also the very footprint of Muhammad. Thus, the ascension of Muhammad to Heaven is, basically, the main reason why Jerusalem is the third holiest site to Islam. It is the main reason in our times why the whole world of Islam is at odds with the Jews. All the wars in the Middle East revolve, ultimately, around the Islamic doctrine of the **afterlife,** or if you please, the ascension of the Prophet Muhammad to Heaven from Jerusalem. Indeed, the very dangerous reality of a nuclear Iran, her repeated threats "to wipe out Israel," and possible clash with both the world of Islam and the Western nations, is due to the belief in Iran of the **afterlife** and the belief in the return of the twelfth Imam, The Mahdi.

This chapter, ultimately, was not written only in order to reveal the original location of the Temple Mount, the location of The City of David or Jerusalem. As important as these issues are to all concerned, there are greater issues the three religions linked to Abraham need to consider. In the previous chapters we discussed the man-made ideas of both Jews and Christians regarding the doctrine of the **afterlife**. Then, we, hopefully, illuminated the unbiased readers as to what their own "Holy Books" had to say about this universal 'belief' in the **afterlife**. In both cases, if the Holy Books are to be believed, "the Emperor was found to be naked." What about the faith of "The Believers" in Islam regarding this crucial doctrine to Muslims? Is their "Emperor also naked?" To find out, let's go in the next chapter to the very words Muhammad brought to his followers in their Holy Book, the Qur'an. What did Muhammad instruct his faithful followers concerning the doctrine of the **afterlife**? Did his followers accept his teachings concerning this important subject? Do they teach and believe the infallible words of their great Prophet on this doctrine of the **afterlife**?

CHAPTER 8

THE QUR'AN AND MUHAMMAD'S TEACHINGS
ABOUT THE AFTERLIFE

Before we read the teachings of the Prophet of Islam concerning the doctrine of the afterlife, especially those about ascending to Heaven immediately after the death of the believer, let's have some background on the origins of the revered Prophet of Islam, Muhammad. To find out this information about Muhammad, we have to delve into ancient accounts, both Biblical and historical, as preserved by Arab scholars and recorded genealogies. Some of the ancient people of Mesopotamia, the birthplace of Abraham, began migrating towards the area of the dry peninsula west and south of the River Euphrates. This area became later known as *Arabia* or *Arabu*, meaning *evening* or *west*. In later times, those people became known as Arabs, meaning, ironically, *Westerners*. This included what is called today Saudi Arabia, the Sinai Peninsula, and the arid territory east of the Jordan. The territory of Edom, which later became a sterile land by God's decree, was also called *Arabia the happy*, as one can read in the writings of the Jewish historian Josephus. Edom, also called Esau, was the twin brother of the Patriarch Jacob, grandson of the Patriarch Abraham. Esau married the daughter of his uncle Ishmael, namely, Basemath, and thus his descendants from this marriage are linked to the Arab people.

The history of all the Arab peoples began with the Biblical Joktan. He was the son of Eber, the father of the Hebrew peoples (including the Israelites), as we can read in Genesis 10:25. One of Joktan's 13 sons was Jeray. He is believed to be the first to set up the kingdom of Yemen. This country was in later times invaded by descendants of Edom from his grandson Teman. Another son of Joktan, Hadoram, is believed to be the founder of Hejaz, a kingdom along the western coast of Saudi Arabia. Some of the descendants of Edom, in later times, have also invaded the land of Hejaz. The Edomite invaders have established Medina as the capital of their Edomite Kingdom in that area. For a deeper knowledge and details about the roll and presence of Edom's descendants in the Arabian Peninsula, and their close links to the Prophet Muhammad's family, check the work, mentioned earlier in this book, about the 4,000 year history of the children of Abraham. Its title *is: "Middle East: Blueprint for the Final Solution: The Coming Fall and Rise of Western Democracy."*

After the rise of Islam, Medina and Mecca became the holiest cities in the Arab and Muslim world. According to Arab genealogists, a daughter of Hadoram, in Arabic, Jorham, married Ishmael, son of Abraham, and bore him his son Kedar. From Kedar, later on, a descendant was to be born whose name was Adnan. He became the father of all the northern Arabian tribes. From this Adnan, Arab genealogists claim, the Prophet Muhammad has descended. There is more historical documentation of Ishmael's descendants in the Middle East than that of Edom. Yet, the Biblical record has preserved the identity of Edom, though he and the world have lost the true identity of his ancestry. Ishmael, whose main stronghold became Egypt, spread also into the far flung desert lands of Arabia. While Esau's descendants, being mainly men of cattle and sword, have drifted into fertile areas. Many of them, being mixed with descendants of Ishmael and other local tribes, lived also in the arid deserts of the Middle East.

The Prophet Muhammad was born in a land inhabited both by Ishmaelites and Edomites. How much mixed blood of these two, uncle and cousin, run in his blood, only Allah knows. This mixed blood, which did run in the veins of the Prophet of Islam, is still affecting the Mideast conflict to this day. Both Ishmael and Edom, for centuries, have lost contact with the God of their fathers. His religion and Law, His Prophets and Messiah were not theirs any longer. Neither was His plan of salvation a part of their hopes and dreams. Father Abraham **"looked for a City whose maker and builder is not man, but God."** This was the heavenly Jerusalem promised to come down to earth. It was to be located at the very spot of earthly Jerusalem, the one called "God's Holy Mountain" on earth. This Jerusalem, one reads of in the Bible, is recognized by the God of Abraham as the only Holy City and location on earth. It is the City of the Great King, the City of the future reigning Messiah. Of course, Muhammad and his devout followers had and still have a different view of these matters.

For the following information about the Prophet of Islam's teachings on the **afterlife**, the author is indebted to the authoritative great translation of the Qur'an by Dawood. We shall quote, throughout, from the excellent translation of the Qur'an by the great Islamic scholar N. J. Dawood (published by the Penguin Books, 1999; printed in England by Clays Ltd., St. Ive place).

Our first quote will be Muhammad's recitation that reflects the Prophet's understanding of the fate of Jesus. Let's go now to the *Surah, Women*, and read of God's instructions to the Prophet Muhammad. On page 76, 4:153-155, we read: "The people of the Book ask you to bring down for them a book from Heaven . . . When We [God] made a covenant with them, We raised the Mount [Sinai] above them [an account not mentioned in the Book of Moses] and said: 'Enter the gate of adoration. Do not break the [seventh day] Sabbath [Notice! He didn't say Sunday or Friday, which are the first and sixth days].'" Then in pp. 76-77, 4:156-160, we read: "'They [Jews] denied the truth and uttered a monstrous falsehood against Mary. They declared: 'We have put to death the Messiah, Jesus son of Mary, the apostle of God.' **THEY DID NOT KILL HIM, NOR DID THEY CRUCIFY HIM, BUT THEY THOUGHT THEY DID . . . '"**

Muhammad believed and taught that the real Jesus was taken up to Heaven, while a body of another person was crucified. Such doctrine began to circulate among some "Christians" years after the resurrection of Christ, and Muhammad also believed it. The problem with this notion is in the teaching of Muhammad that the dead are in the dust until the last day—which is in accordance with the Bible. It is only after the first century that many Jews and Christians, and mostly in the West, have gradually began to accept the pagan teaching of the immortality of the soul, and the pagan belief that upon death all go either to Heaven or Hell. In Muhammad's days, many Jews and Christians in the East, in contrast to those in the West, still adhered to the Biblical teaching about the **afterlife**, which Muhammad himself accepted and taught. This teaching, however, presents a contradiction for Muhammad and Islam: If all go back into the dust, then how come Jesus was taken up to heaven if he is just a mortal man like any other servant of God, as Muhammad himself had taught. The Qur'an does not seem to take this point and contradiction into consideration. Why? Allah knows!

The account continues: **"THEY DID NOT SLAY HIM [CHRIST], FOR CERTAIN, GOD LIFTED HIM UP TO HIM;** God is mighty and wise. There is none among the people of the Book who will believe in him before his death [in reality, all of Jesus' followers, initially, were Jews];

and on the Day of Resurrection [all, beside Christ, who are in the dust until that day] he [Jesus] will bear witness against them."

It is important to notice that though Muhammad believed and acknowledged Jesus to be a messenger and a messiah sent from Heaven, and later went up to Heaven, he did not believe in many of His teachings or Divinity—nor did he know His true identity. Muhammad states that Jesus had ascended up to Heaven, and was not really crucified. For this very reason, when Caliph Omar conquered Jerusalem, he refused to acknowledge the sanctity of the "Rock" on which, according to Christians, the "footprints" of Christ were found. He always prayed with his back toward the "Rock."

In the following most crucial recitations of Muhammad, we shall see the real truth behind the selfishly deliberate and politically motivated great myths about the "holiness" of the "Rock" and other places, which later were invented by his followers and not by the Prophet of Islam. These myths are concerning: the supposed holiness of Jerusalem to Islam; the supposed ascension of Muhammad to the seventh Heaven from Jerusalem; the supposed supremacy of Muhammad over all of God's previously revealed Scriptures and God's Prophets—and the Religion of Israel that came before him, and the supremacy over the One who is believed to be by many, The Son of God! We shall spell it, as was done in other places, in big caps for sake of emphases.

Muhammad recited: "**NO MAN** [no human servant of God; no Prophet, except Jesus, who was Divine before and after His human experience in the flesh] **BEFORE YOU HAVE WE MADE IMMORTAL. IF YOU YOURSELF ARE DOOMED TO DIE, WILL THEY LIVE ON FOREVER? EVERY SOUL SHALL TASTE DEATH. WE WILL PROVE YOU ALL WITH EVIL AND GOOD, TO US YOU SHALL RETURN [in the last day, at the resurrection]**" (*Surah, The prophets*, p. 229, 21:34-5). No "faithful" Muslim cleric today, or for that matter, none in the world of Islam believes these words of their Prophet Muhammad, as recited in the Qur'an! They all believe, contrary to his often repeated plain statements that Muhammad ascended up to Heaven, immediately after his death—why?

In his conversations with both Jews and Christian true believers, Muhammad learned also of the true fate of the dead, immediately after their death. We can see this learning, on the part of Muhammad, in his recitations in the Qur'an concerning the correct understanding of the doctrine of Heaven and Hell. At this point, we shall bring here one example from the Hebrew Scriptures.

Speaking of the fate of the wicked, and of the afterlife, the Psalmist writes: **"None of them can by any means redeem his brother** [from death and the grave]**, nor give God a ransom for him—for the redemption of their souls is costly, and it shall cease forever—that he should continue to live eternally, and not see the pit** [or the grave]**. For he sees wise men die; likewise the fool and the senseless person perish, and leave their wealth to others** [since they can't take it with them]**. Their inner thought is that their houses will last forever . . . Nevertheless, man, though in honor, does not remain** [or live forever]**; he is like the beast that perishes. This is the way of those who are foolish, and their posterity who approve their sayings. Selah. Like sheep they are laid in the grave; death shall feed on them; the upright shall have dominion over them in the morning; and their beauty shall be consumed in the grave, for He** [God] **shall receive me** [in the resurrection, at the last day]**. Selah. Do not be afraid when one becomes rich, when the glory of his house is increased; for when he dies he shall carry nothing away; his glory shall not descend after him. Though while he lives he blesses himself** [not ever considering his mortal state and fate] **. . . he shall go to the generations of his fathers; THEY SHALL NEVER SEE LIGHT** [in a fictitious Heaven or Hell, in an after-death location—until they are resurrected in the last day of judgment]**. A man who is in honor, yet does not understand, is like the beasts that perish"** (Psalm 49:7-20). This was also the understanding of Muhammad concerning the doctrine of Heaven and Hell!

In page 241, in the *Surah, The Believers*, Sec., 23:5-20, Muhammad recited: "We created man from an essence of clay [and that man has no immortal soul that goes on living after death, as the pagans had believed, and as "spiritual" leaders of the three religions that sprang from the descendants of Abraham had later accepted and taught their followers. As for man, Muhammad was told]: then [God] placed in him a living germ, in a secure enclosure [the womb]. The germ We made a clot of blood, and the clot a lump of flesh, thus bringing forth another creation."

In the book of Genesis we read: **"And the Lord God formed man of the dust of the ground, and breathed into His nostrils the breath of life; and man became a living soul."** God did not say that man has a living immortal soul, but that he himself is a living soul with the breath of life from God. In the book of the Prophet Zechariah, Chapter 12:1, we read: **"Thus says the Lord who stretches out the heavens, lays the foundation of the earth, and forms THE SPIRIT OF MAN within him."** This spirit is a life essence, not a person that goes on living after death.

God told the prophet Ezekiel, (20:4,20): **"All souls are Mine; the soul of the father as well as the soul of the son is Mine; the soul that sins shall die** [not live on in Heaven or Hell]." And again, in verse 20, we read: **"The soul that sins shall die . . ."** This was the faith of many Jews and Christians in the East in the days of Muhammad, and he himself believed it, unlike his later followers. And so he recited again: **"YOU SHALL SURELY DIE HEREAFTER, AND BE RESTORED TO LIFE [WHEN?] ON THE DAY OF THE RESURRECTION"** (*ibid.* 23:5-20). How many Muslims believe their revered "infallible" Prophet? How many gullible "Shahids" or "Martyrs" give their lives with this knowledge in mind?

Again, Muhammad recited: "Say, 'Think! **IF GOD SHOULD ENSHROUD YOU [which He did] IN PERPETUAL NIGHT [in the grave] TILL THE DAY OF RESURRECTION**, what other god could give you light? Will you not hear?'" (*Surah, The Story*, pp. 276-277, 28:71). And again, In the *Surah, Pilgrimage*, we read: "The hour of doom is sure to come—of this there is no doubt [though all Muslims believe otherwise]. **THOSE WHO ARE IN THEIR GRAVES [not in Paradise or in Hell] GOD WILL RAISE TO LIFE"** (*ibid.* p. 235, 22:7). This is very plain! Get it strait you who call yourselves "believers!" **MUHAMMAD, LIKE ANY OTHER MORTAL, IS STILL IN HIS GRAVE! Like anyone else before and after him, he is still awaiting—in his grave—the call from above at the resurrection, in the last day!** You call yourselves "the devout" followers of your revered Prophet Muhammad, yet in this major doctrine—around which you have created many fables, like the "holiness of Jerusalem" to Islam, because, "Muhammad, according to you, had ascended from there to Heaven"—yet, in essence, you declare your Prophet to be 'a liar' for stating otherwise! What would you say and do when you face your Prophet Muhammad on the judgment day? Think about it now, before it's too late!

In the life-and-death fight today against the terror groups of bin Laden and his newly emerging theology of martyrdom and cult of death, or any other Palestinian groups of hot-headed and misguided Muslim fanatics and suicide bombers—who are willing to blow themselves up, along with their innocent victims so they can go immediately to paradise—a "lethal, theological nuclear weapon" is available! It does not cost Billions of dollars to produce! It is the 'weapon of true Islamic teachings.' It is powered by 'the twin engines' and true teachings of Muhammad and the Qur'an concerning: the Land of Israel, the City of Jerusalem, the true teachings of Muhammad and the Qur'an concerning the state of the dead immediately after death. This 'weapon' of true Islamic teachings also describes the present location of the Prophet of Islam—in the grave—awaiting, like any other mortal, the resurrection from the dead in the last day. This 'weapon' is a two-edged sword. What is applicable to Islam is also applicable to all other religions in this and other matters.

The "martyrs" and suicide bombers who are induced with deceptive promises to blow themselves up are also in the grave—not in Paradise with "thirty or seventy two bashful virgins"—and other false promises! If America or Israel, or any other nation, and any honest Muslim, want to deter, demoralize, destabilize, and ultimately destroy the misguided zeal of the suicide bombers and gullible "martyrs" from fanatic Muslim leaders and terror groups—all they have to do is call upon the 'two faithful witnesses' of Islam: the revered Prophet Muhammad, and the Qur'an's plain teachings on Heaven or Paradise. And if Muslims want to be honest all the way—they should also quote Muhammad's teachings in the Qur'an concerning the "legitimate rights" and ownership of the land of Israel—as promised by God or Allah, and repeatedly quoted by Muhammad in "the Holy Qur'an." All concerned parties can use this 'lethal weapon' and legitimate propaganda against all misguided, wasted gullible souls and lives—without ever firing one single shot! Why don't we give it a try?

And again, in Section 22:17, we read: "As for the true believers [Muslims], the Jews, the Sabaeans, the Christians, the Magians, and the pagans, **God will judge them on the day of Resurrection** [not as soon as they die]. God is the witness of all things" (*ibid.* p. 235). In contrast to Muhammad's belief and the teaching of the Qur'an, many Muslims today declare that true believers exist only in the religion of Islam—all the rest are doomed to go to Hell, but where did they get this knowledge?

In the *Surah*, *The Greeks*, Muhammad recited: "**YOU CANNOT MAKE THE DEAD HEAR YOU . . .**" *(Ibid.* p. 287, 30:50-54). Why can't they hear you? Because they are in the grave! Their spirit (not soul) went back to God who gave it, as Solomon had stated: "**Who knows** the spirit of the sons of men, which goes upward, and the spirit of the animal, which goes down to the earth?" (Ecclesiastic 3:21). A spirit without a body, the Bible makes very clear, cannot see, hear, or speak! For a person to be alive, one needs a body and a spirit! One can't exist by itself without the other! As the apostle James, half brother of Jesus, stated: **"For as the body without the spirit is dead, so faith without works is dead also"** (James 2:26).

In page 291, we read what Muhammad recited in this *Surah*: "He governs all, from Heaven to earth. **AND ALL WILL ASCEND TO HIM IN A SINGLE DAY**, a day whose space is a thousand years" (*Adoration*, Sec., 32:5). The Bible speaks of the one thousand year reign of the Messiah (Rev. 20:4-5). At the beginning of His reign, as we shall see later, the first resurrection of all those who were true believers will take place. The second resurrection of all the rest of those who ever lived will take place at the end of that millennium. Whether Muhammad was referring to this, Allah knows!

Speaking of the resurrection of the dead, Muhammad recited in the *Surah Ya Sin*: "'The Trumpet will be blown [see NT, I Cor. 15] and, behold, **THEY WILL RISE UP FROM THEIR GRAVES** [as all of God's Prophets and Apostles in the Old and New covenants' Scriptures have stated] and hasten to their Lord. 'Woe betides us!' they will say: '**Who has roused us from our resting place?** That is what the Lord of Mercy has promised: the Apostles [and Prophets] have told the truth [but few Jews, Christians, and Muslims have ever believed them, and so it is to this day]!' And with but one blast they shall be gathered all before us . . . On that day [not immediately after death, according to the pagan doctrine injected into the Truth by misguided and misinformed religious leaders] the heirs of Paradise will be busy with their joys'" (*ibid.* p. 311, 36:48-57).

In the *Surah, The Ranks*, we read: "'When they [the pagan Arabs] are shown a sign they mock at it and say: 'This is but plain sorcery. What! **WHEN WE ARE DEAD AND TURNED TO DUST AND BONES, SHALL WE BE RAISED TO LIFE** [from the grave, at the last day], we and our forefathers?' Say: 'Yes. And you shall be utterly humbled.' One blast will sound, and they shall see it all'" (*ibid.* p. 311, 36:50-51).

In the *Surah, The Throngs*, Muhammad recited: "**YOU** [Muhammad], **AS WELL AS THEY** [the unbelievers and believers], **ARE DOOMED TO DIE** [these are the words of Allah, according to the Prophet of Islam]. Then, on the day of Resurrection [at the last day], you shall dispute in your Lord's presence with one another. **Who is more wicked than the man who invents falsehood about God and denies the truth when it is declared to him?** (*ibid.* p. 324, 39:29-35). Genuine Muslim believers should properly read their own Qur'an and not let supposed and misguided religious clerics—or politicians, like the president of Iran—lead them by the nose away from the true teachings of their own Prophet and Qur'an!

In the *Surah, The believers,* Muhammad recited concerning the time of the resurrection of all the righteous servants of God: "Exalted and enthroned on high, He let the spirit descend at His behest on those of His servants whom He chooses, that He may warn them on the day **WHEN THEY SHALL RISE UP FROM THEIR GRAVES [THE PRESENT RESTING PLACE OF MUHAMMAD ALSO! HE TOO IS AWAITING THE RESURRECTION FROM THE DEAD—IN HIS GRAVE!]** with nothing hidden from God. And who shall reign supreme on that day? God, the One, the Almighty. On that day every soul shall be recompensed according to what it did. On that day none shall be wronged [as the gullible "martyrs" and suicide bombers were and still are]. Swift is God's reckoning" (*ibid.* p. 329, 40:12-17).

Again, in the *Surah, Kneeling,* Muhammad recites: "'Say: 'It is God who gives you life and then He causes you to die [not go on living in the imaginary Hell or Paradise immediately after death]. **IT IS HE WHO WILL GATHER YOU ALL [when?] ON THE DAY OF RESURRECTION.** Of this there is no doubt; yet most do not know it [and certainly the suicide bombers and misguided "martyrs" don't know it].' It is God who has sovereignty over the heavens and the earth. On the day when the hour strikes [in the last day], those who have denied His revelations will assuredly lose all. You shall see each community [of Muslims, Jews, and Christians] on its knees. Each community shall be summoned to its Book, and a voice will say: 'You shall this day be rewarded for your deeds. This Book of Ours speaks with truth against you. We have recorded all your actions'" (*ibid.* p. 352, 45:24-29). Certainly, most Muslims and fanatic suicide bombers and "martyrs," Jews and Christians, do not know it—yet! And they do not believe, because their spiritual leaders have led them astray, but not for long!

In the *Surah, Qaf,* we read: "'On that day [the Judgment at the last day], We shall ask Hell: 'Are you full?' And Hell will answer: 'Are there anymore?' And, not far thence, Paradise shall be brought close to the righteous. We shall say to them: 'Here is all that you were promised. It is for every penitent and faithful man, who fears the Merciful, though he is unseen, and comes before Him with a contrite heart. Enter it in peace. **THIS IS THE DAY OF IMMORTALITY.'"** (*ibid.* p. 366, 50:27-35).

It is very obvious what Muhammad is reciting here in plain words! His teaching to all Muslims is: Man is not to become immortal or be in Paradise, and that includes himself, immediately after death, but at the last day, after the judgment! It is at that day that immortality is achieved, not a day before! Yet now, as in the past many centuries, Muslims were led to believe otherwise, contrary to the plain teachings of their own Prophet and the "infallible" Qur'an—Why? The Bible, as we saw earlier, taught exactly the same—not the pagan or Hellenistic doctrine of the immortality of the soul, and the immediate ascension to Heaven or Hell after death—as most Jews and Christians believe it to be!

God told Adam and Eve: **"Of every tree in the garden, you may freely eat, but of the tree of the knowledge of good and evil you shall not eat, FOR IN THE DAY THAT YOU EAT OF IT YOU SHALL SURELY DIE."** (Gen. 2:16-17).

This is what God said, but what did He mean? Did He mean "you are as good as dead," or did He mean something else? Obviously he meant, as was explained later in the Bible, "you shall be as good as dead in your sins!" And this is where Satan started introducing his deception and willful lie, and the false doctrine of the immortality of the soul! In a later conversation with mother Eve, Satan, as a shrewd salesman, told her: **"YOU WILL NOT SURELY DIE"** (Gen. 3-4). Satan, in essence, was convincing gullible mother Eve, as he did later with most of her descendants, that she has an immortal soul—the real person within her—that lives forever. He convinced her that her soul would go on living, immediately after the death of the body, in a different spirit form. Since that time, this willful and clever lie and deception was passed on and believed by those who have strayed away from the path of the Truth and Light of the Maker of us all.

Again, speaking about the Resurrection, in the *Surah, Qaf,* Muhammad recited: "Listen on the day when the Crier will call from near; the day when men will hear the fateful cry. **ON THAT DAY** [not immediately after death] **THEY WILL RISE UP FROM THEIR GRAVES.** On that day [in the last day of Judgment] the earth will be rent asunder over them [those who are in the grave], **AND FROM IT** [not from Heaven or Hell] **THEY SHALL EMERGE IN HASTE.** To assemble them is easy enough for us" (*ibid.* pg. 367, 50:43-44). As we saw earlier, both the Old and New Testaments have taught exactly the same doctrine. In this area, Muhammad and the Qur'an are in perfect agreement with "the previous Scriptures" the Prophet of Islam claimed he "came to confirm and believed in."

In the *Surah, She Who Pleaded*, we read: "**ON THE DAY** [the last day] **WHEN GOD RESTORES THEM ALL TO LIFE HE WILL INFORM** [or judge] **THEM OF THEIR ACTIONS**" (*ibid.*, pg. 384, 58:6). Here it is spoken about those who opposed Muhammad, nevertheless, such is the fate of all: they must all wait in the grave until the last day.

In the *Surah, Cheating*, Muhammad recited: "'The unbelievers claim they shall not be raised to life [in the last day]. Say: 'Yes, by the Lord, **YOU SHALL BE ASSUREDLY RAISED TO LIFE** [from the dead]! Then you shall be told of all that you have done. That is easy enough for God.'" Then Muhammad added: "The day on which He will gather you, the day on which you shall be gathered—that shall be a day of cheating [of your reward, since you don't believe]. Those that believe in God and do what is right shall be forgiven their sins and admitted to gardens watered by running streams [on earth, the true Biblical teaching on Paradise], where they shall dwell forever [up to that day, they all were in the grave, as Muhammad and everyone else before and after him are, with the exception of Christ the Messiah]. That is the supreme triumph [not the fabricated one many believe in to this day]. But those that disbelieve and deny Our revelations [including: the Torah, the Prophets, the Gospel] shall be the inmates of fire . . ." (*ibid.* p. 395, 7:10).

Speaking of the fate of the unbelievers, Muhammad recited in the *Surah, The Ladders*, the following: "Are they each seeking to enter a garden of delights? Let them play until they face the day they are promised; **THE [LAST] DAY WHEN THEY SHALL RUSH FORWARD FROM THEIR GRAVES**, like men rallying to a standard, with down cast eyes and countenances distorted with shame. Such is the [last] Day they are promised" (*ibid.* p. 406, 70:36-44). The 'enlightened' president of Iran, Ahamadinejad, and all those "spiritual leaders" around him, should consider these words before it is too late!

Again, in the *Surah, Noah*, Muhammad recited: "God has brought you forth from the earth like a plant, and **to the earth He will restore you** [as he told Adam: **"For dust you are and unto dust shall return**]. **Then He will bring you back afresh** [from the grave]" [*ibid.* p. 407, 71:18-21].

Speaking of the Day of Judgment in the last day, Muhammad recited in the *Surah, The Resurrection*, these words: "'I swear by the day of Resurrection, and by the self reproaching soul! Does man think We shall never put his bones together again? Indeed, We remold his very fingers! Yet man would ever deny what is to come. 'When will this be,' he asks, 'the day of Resurrection?' . . . No, there shall be no refuge. **FOR TO YOUR LORD, ON THAT [LAST] DAY, HE SHALL RETURN.** Man shall on that day be told all his deeds, from first to last . . . On that day there shall be joyous faces, looking towards their Lord. On that day there shall be mournful faces, dreading some great affliction (*ibid.* pp. 412-413, 75:1-22).

Muhammad and the Qur'an, just like the Hebrew and New Testament Scriptures, make it very plain: at the moment of death, all go back to the dust, not Heaven or Hell! At the time of the resurrection from the dead, at the last day, all shall return to the Lord for the judgment day.

Muhammad adds, in the *Surah, Those That Are Sent Forth*, the following: "**When the stars are blotted out; when the apostles [all of God's servants and messengers] are brought together [from the grave] on the appointed [last] day—when will all this be? UPON THE DAY OF JUDGEMENT! Would that you knew what the day of judgment is! On that day woe betide the disbelievers! HAVE WE NOT MADE THE EARTH A HOME FOR THE LIVING AND FOR THE DEAD? On that day woe betide the believers! Such is the day of judgment. WE WILL ASSEMBLE YOU ALL, TOGETHER WITH** [all those who lived in the] **PAST GENERATIONS.**" (*ibid.* p. 415, 77:1-41). These very clear words! This is where all of us are placed, from Adam to the last one of us—in the grave or earth—where we shall all be awaiting the resurrection at the last day!

In the *Surah, The Tidings*, Muhammad recites words concerning the fate of the believers and the unbelievers. We read: "**FIXED IS THE DAY OF JUDGEMENT. ON THAT DAY THE TRUMPET SHALL BE SOUNDED, AND YOU SHALL COME IN MULTITUDES [OUT OF THE GRAVE].**

Compare this statement with the words of the Apostle Paul: "**Behold, I tell you a mystery: we shall not all sleep** [or die], **but we shall be changed—in a moment, in the twinkling of an eye, at the last trumpet. For the trumpet will sound, and the dead** [who are in their graves up to that moment, not in Heaven or Hell] **will be raised** [or resurrected from the dead] **incorruptible, and we shall be changed. For this corruption must put on incorruption, and this mortal must put on immortality** [since we don't have anything immortal about us now—and the contradictory pagan concept notwithstanding]. **So when this corruptible has put on incorruption, and this mortal has put on immortality, then shall be brought to pass the saying that is written: Death is swallowed up in victory"** [quoted from Isaiah 25:8] (I Cor. 15:51-54). Tragically, neither Jews nor Christians do believe these words as quoted from their own Bibles. Why? Because their "Emperor is naked" and they have no eyes to 'see.' Muslims are no different!

Muhammad continues: "The gates of Heaven shall swing open, and the mountains shall pass away and become like vapor [both the Hebrew and New Testament Scriptures described the same events in similar words] . . . As for the righteous [after describing the fate of the unbelievers], they shall surely triumph. Theirs shall be gardens and vineyards [on earth, not Heaven, as the Bible made very plain throughout, and Muhammad, unlike his 'followers,' believed it], **AND HIGH-BOSOMED MAIDENS FOR COMPANIONS: A TRULY OVERFLOWING CUP** [Ah, the martyr's dream!] . . . That day is sure to come" (*ibid.* pp. 416-417, 78:1-39).

Again, Muhammad recited concerning the trumpet at the last day, in the *Surah, The Soul Snatchers,* these words: "'On the day the trumpet sounds its first and second blast, the hearts shall be filled with terror, and all eyes shall stare with owe. **THEY SAY: 'WHEN WE ARE TURNED TO HOLLOW BONES, SHALL WE BE RESTORED TO LIFE? A FRUITLESS TRANSFORMATION!' BUT WITH ONE BLAST THEY SHALL RETURN [FROM THE GRAVES BENEATH] TO THE EARTH'S SURFACE"** (*ibid.* p. 417, 79:1-10).

Speaking of the same subject and event, the Patriarch Job asked: **"If a man dies, shall he live again? All the days of my hard service I will wait** [in the grave], **till my change comes** [as the Apostle Paul stated later, **"we shall all be changed"**]. **You shall call, and I will answer You; You shall desire the works of Your hands"** (Job, 14:14-15).

At the time Muhammad was given the Qur'an, many, in both the Jewish and Christian communities in the Middle East had still, basically, the same understanding concerning this subject. With the passage of time, the three communities, gradually and then fully, adopted the pagan teachings and understanding concerning the immortality of the soul and the doctrine of Heaven and Hell. And so it is still accepted to this very day!

In the following *Surah, He Frowned*, Muhammad recites: "From what did God [Allah] create him? From a little germ He created him and gave him due proportions. **HE MAKES HIS PATH SMOOTH, THEN CAUSES HIM TO DIE [not go to Heaven or Hell immediately after death] AND STOWS HIN IN A GRAVE. HE WILL SURELY BRING HIM BACK TO LIFE WHEN HE PLEASES** [yet, if one is alive in Heaven or Hell, what need is there to bring him back to life?]. Yet he declines to do His bidding" (*ibid.* p. 419, 80:18-22).

Again, speaking of the fate of the righteous and the unbelievers, Muhammad recites in the *Surah, The Unjust*: "**DO THEY NOT THINK THEY WILL BE RAISED TO LIFE UPON A FATEFUL DAY, THE DAY WHEN ALL MANKIND WILL STAND BEFORE THE LORD OF THE UNIVERSE? . . . On that day woe betide the disbelievers who deny the last judgment [and the fact that ALL ARE DEAD AND IN THE GRAVE UNTIL THE LAST DAY]! None denies it except the evil transgressor who, when Our revelations are recited to him, cries: 'Fables of the ancients!' No! Their own deeds have drawn a veil over their hearts. No! On that day a barrier shall be set between them and their Lord. They shall burn in Hell, and shall be told: 'This is the scourge that you denied!'**" (*ibid.* p. 421, 83:1-20). The president of Iran, who advances the lie of the Mahdi's soon return; who seeks, hatefully, to bring a total destruction on Israel, the Western nations—and all those who oppose his vision of the world, including those in the world of Islam—should consider these words of his Prophet before it is too late!

How many "devout believers" in Islam are being taught what their revered Prophet really said concerning the **afterlife**? Those who fabricated the myth that Muhammad, as well as other servants of God, went to Heaven; those who claim to this day that Jerusalem is a Holy City (al-Quds), because Muhammad has ascended up to the seventh Heaven, "riding on his beloved horse" through the hole in the Rock, over which the Dome of the Rock was later erected, are in blatant defiance of the words of their own Prophet and his "infallible" words (as they believe it to be) received from Allah through the angel Gabriel!" Of such "believers," Muhammad recited: **"They shall burn in Hell, and shall be told: 'This is the scourge that you denied!'"**

174

Of his unbelieving fellow Arabs, Muhammad recited: "Why then do they not have faith, or kneel in prayer when the Qur'an is read to them? [Many Muslims kneel in prayer but do not believe **ALL** the words in Qur'an and of their own Prophet—yet they claim to submit to Allah] The unbelievers indeed deny it [since those who deny the words of the Prophet concerning the grave, deny the Qur'an]; but God knows best the falsehood they believe in. Therefore proclaim to all a woeful doom, save those who embrace the true faith and do good works; for theirs is an unfailing recompense" (*Surah, The Rending*, p. 422, 84:16-25).

Those Muslims who believe in the myth of Muhammad's ascension to Heaven from Jerusalem, deny the "true faith" given to them, according to Muhammad! President Ahmadinejad and his fellow Iranian Shiites believe that the twelfth Imam is soon coming, from Paradise, to deliver all those who look up to him. They want to "prepare the world for his imminent coming." They want to "go nuclear" and eliminate Israel and the Western nations—and for that matter, all nations that do not believe in the Imam—the one, according to them, "who has ascended up to Paradise where Allah is hiding him until the day of his appearance to his devout believers." If Ahmadinejad is correct, then Muhammad was lying to his followers. But if Muhammad is correct, then Ahmadinejad and all Muslims who believe in the ascension to Paradise of the Imam, or any other Muslim, are lying to their followers. **YOU CAN'T HAVE IT BOTH WAYS!** If your claim is true, then the words of your Prophet, the "infallible" Qur'an, and Allah are fables. But if you hold the words of Allah, your revered Prophet, and the Qur'an to be true, then you are all in error. And if so, then all your claims concerning Muhammad, the Imam, and the Jerusalem issue are fables! Make up your mind! And the sooner, the better for you!

Speaking of life and death, Muhammad recited again in the *Surah, The Nightly Visitant*: "**SURELY HE HAS POWER TO BRING HIM BACK TO LIFE [from the grave], ON THE [LAST DAY OF JUDGMENT, THE] DAY WHEN MAN'S CONSCIENCES ARE SEARCHED**" (*ibid.* p. 423, 86:1-10). Again, concerning all that is written about the fate of the righteous and the dead, Muhammad recited in the *Surah, The Most High*: "All this is written in earlier Scriptures of Abraham and Moses [As well as in the Psalms, the Prophets, the New Testament, and the Writings of the true followers of God and Christ.]" (*ibid.* p. 424, 87:19).

In the *Surah, The War Steeds*, Muhammad recited: "He loves riches with all his heart [the wicked]. But is he not aware that **WHEN THE DEAD ARE THROWN OUT FROM THEIR GRAVES** [where all are until the Resurrection] and men's hidden thoughts are laid open, their Lord will on that day have full knowledge of them all?" (*ibid.* p. 431, 100:1-11).

How many Muslims are or were willing to believe these plain words of their "infallible Prophet of Islam?" How many Muslims are really reading and hearing the "infallible" words of their Qur'an? Well, only Allah knows! In reality, those who taught and are still teaching; those who believed and are still believing such anti-Qur'an statements, are a disgrace to the teachings of the Qur'an and of the Prophet of Islam, and above all, to Allah! Again, this is what the Prophet of Islam, who is considered to be infallible by all Muslims, had to say in the Qur'an about his own mortality, and that of all of humanity.

The question before us is very obvious: either he is right, or his followers are! **BOTH SIDES CAN'T BE CORRECT WHEN THEY CONTRADICT EACH OTHER!** Caliph Omar, the first successor of the Prophet of Islam, claimed he had a vision from Allah, which was delivered to him through the Prophet Muhammad. In this vision, he claimed, he saw Muhammad enter the Holy city of Jerusalem through the southern gate of Haram esh-Sahrif, which he named *Bab el-Nabi, or door of the Prophet*. From there, he claimed, Muhammad had ascended up to Heaven at the end of his "*Night Journey*" from the "*Great Mosque in Mecca to the Little Mosque Al Aqsa*." If Caliph Omar was speaking the truth, then Muhammad was deceiving his followers about the **afterlife** and his own mortality. But, if Muhammad was speaking the truth about the true state of the dead, then Caliph Omar was not, and for the simple reason that both can't be right. Why didn't Caliph believe the words of his own Prophet about the state of the dead, only Allah knows—and that goes for every "devout" Muslim to this day!

The naked fact is that the Haram esh-Sharif, or the "Temple Mount" to the Jews, is not and never was a "Holy Place." While the Temple and Jerusalem were still standing, all Jews regarded the Haram esh-Sharif, or its original name, **Fort Antonia**, with great contempt. They did their level best to avoid this Gentile area, unless they had to be there for official Roman affairs. Once they left this Roman property, the Jews would purify themselves before entering the Temple. Yet in the last 800 years, once they had abandoned the Temple site to the south, they began to direct their worship and faces towards the "Western Wall" of the disdained former Fort Antonia. How "naked" can their "Emperor" be—and none can "see" his nakedness! **THE SUPPOSED "HOLINESS" OF THE PRESENTLY BELIEVED "WESTERN WALL," THE "TEMPLE MOUNT," OR HARAM ESH-SHARIF, IS THE GREATEST HOAX OF THE MILLENIUM!** All this is due to the fables and superstitions about the **afterlife, coupled with the lack of the love of the Truth**! And consider this naked reality: if the "spiritual leaders" of the three religions, those who ascribe "Holiness" to the "Temple Mount" or Haram esh-Sharif, believe and teach, dogmatically, the ascension to Heaven of the "righteous" immediately after death, what else have they 'sold' their followers on?

Speaking of those who do not believe the purity of the truth, The apostle Paul stated: **"Indeed, let God be true but every man a liar"** (Rom. 3:4). In like manner, one may say: "let Muhammad be true in what he said in the Qur'an concerning the **afterlife**, or let those who distort his writings be considered liars." Muhammad never taught that Jerusalem is holy to Islam—His followers did! Muhammad never ascended up to the seventh Heaven riding on an imaginary horse, since he himself had repeatedly and consistently recited in the Qur'an the reality of his own mortality and inevitable death. Muhammad never claimed the land that was given to Israel, forever, by God or Allah, to be a sacred Arab land—His followers did so, long after his death. If Muhammad, the great Prophet of Islam is dead, awaiting the resurrection at the last day—Just like any other mortal human being—what makes the Arab or Muslim "martyrs" think that upon their death they will immediately be taken up to Paradise and be granted those "thirty (or seventy two nowadays) bashful and high bosomed virgins?" What a cruel hoax to play on ignorant, gullible, young, and misguided miserable souls! These young and ignorant "martyrs" waste their own lives, while those who dupe them to do it are reaping the "glory" of vain hopes! How "naked can your Emperor be"?

In the next *Surah, Pilgrimage,* we read of Muhammad's teaching concerning the Sacred Mosque in Mecca. He recited: "'When We prepared for Abraham the site of the Sacred Mosque, We said: 'Worship none besides Me. Keep My House clean for those who walk around it, and those who stand upright or worship.' Exhort all men to make the pilgrimage [not to Jerusalem but to Mecca]'" (*ibid.* p. 236, 22:26-28). The Qur'an was 'revealed' by Muhammad to his followers about 2500 years after Abraham had died. God gave Moses the Torah 430 years after He gave the covenant to Abraham, when he was about 85 (see NT, Galatians 3:17). In the Torah, in the book of Genesis, Moses had recorded a clear description of the life of Abraham, as dictated by God Himself. Yet nowhere in that personal and direct revelation of God to Moses do we read anything about Abraham and the Sacred Mosque! Did God 'forget' all about it then, and only in the days of Muhammad 'remembered' it again? Allah knows!

Notice again that Muhammad directed his followers to regard Mecca as the only Sacred Site, hence, the only place for the yearly pilgrimage to the only Holy Mosque! Certainly, Jerusalem, with the Holy Site or Holy Temple, which was not in existence in Muhammad's day, was never on the mind of Muhammad. It is his politically motivated followers who invented the myth about the supposed "holiness" of Jerusalem to Islam. These "believers," did not believe their own Prophet and his clear teachings in the Qur'an concerning his own death and the **afterlife**. They did not believe his words about his "resting place" in the grave until the last Day of Judgment and resurrection. That's why we have an ever-boiling Middle East conflict, which will not be resolved until the day of the resurrection. That's why we have "blind" leaders in Iran, in Gaza, in the West Bank, in Lebanon, in Pakistan, and throughout the Muslim world—who daily seek the destruction of others. Caliph Omar and later his two successors were benevolent and kind to the Jews in their days. Still, because of their belief in the fable of the **afterlife**, which was contrary to the teachings of their own Prophet in the Qur'an, they ascribed holiness to Jerusalem based on a superstitious belief in Muhammad's supposed ascension to Heaven from Jerusalem. Caliph Omar claimed he had a vision from God about a holy site in Jerusalem that was relayed to him by the Prophet Muhammad. The Prophet himself taught, in many passages which we have just read, that he was, after his death, destined to remain in the grave until his resurrection—in the last day. Who is speaking the truth? Who is responsible for the rivers of blood that were shed for Jerusalem's sake since the days of Caliph Omar in the name of Allah and Muhammad? If Muhammad did not convey the vision to Omar, since he was dead and in the grave, then who did? We shall find this out in the next chapter.

Since Muhammad made it very clear about his being dead until resurrection time at the last day, honest Muslims should ask themselves questions about the wasted lives and blood of the "Shahids" or "Martyrs," and that of their innocent victims? They all died because of the fables and lies of the Muslim clerics about the "glorious fate of the martyrs in Paradise, immediately after death. Who will avenge their blood and that of their victims? How about the lies of the Palestinian clerics about the boy, Muhammad al-Dura—who supposedly is now in Paradise flying a kite on the beach, and calling on other young children to become "martyrs" for the Holy Land, and thus follow in his footsteps! According to the Prophet Muhammad, both of them are dead and buried, and will remain in their graves until the "last day of resurrection." This is exactly where the young twelfth Imam is now—in his grave, awaiting the resurrection! What's the purpose of teaching and living a lie and wasting lives for it? What's the purpose of Iran's intense preparations for the soon appearance of the Mahdi from Heaven? Can peace in the Middle East, under this state of confusion and disinformation, ever be achieved as long as such lies are being fed, daily, to the ignorant and superstitious masses?

Regardless of the well intentioned, and not so well intentioned, efforts to resolve the age-old bloody conflict—until all the children of Abraham become genuine followers in his footsteps, and believe the truth about the **afterlife**, as Abraham and Muhammad did—rivers of blood shall continue to saturate the parched lands of that region of chronic contentions and fables. And, tragically, all that confusion is based on the false doctrine, which is religiously and fervently taught by ignorant Muslim clerics about the **afterlife**! What would it take for the "blind" to "see" that the "Emperor is naked"? The answer is very simple: an honest and passionate love of the truth. Tragically, this most precious quality is very rare and hard to find.

Still, there are some honest Muslims out there! These honest Muslims should ask themselves frank questions and consider this naked reality: A. Muhammad himself taught that no one has ascended up to Heaven with the exception of Christ, as we read previously in his own words. B. He stated, repeatedly, that he himself is appointed to die, be buried, and remain in the grave until the last Day of Judgment and resurrection. At the last day, he recited, "the trumpet shall be blown and the dead shall rise from the graves to life." C. Since he did not ascend to Heaven, but is still in his grave, dead, he certainly did not travel on his "Night Journey" to Jerusalem. He did not enter the City through the southern gate of Haram esh-Sharif, as Caliph Omar "saw in his vision," nor did he ascend to the seventh Heaven, "accompanied by the angel Gabriel, to be received by God Himself." Muhammad never proclaimed Jerusalem as a Holy City to Islam, he never mentioned it even once in the Qur'an, and he certainly did not consider the Land of Israel an Islamic "Arab Land," Holy to Islam. Instead, he taught, repeatedly, that the land was given to Isaac, to Jacob, to Israel—not to Ishmael or to Muslims! Consequently, since Jerusalem is not a Holy City to Islam, according to Muhammad and the Qur'an, there is no valid and honest reason for any Muslim to call Jerusalem or Al Quds, the third Holy City of Islam—after Mecca and Medina. And because there is no reason to do so, there is also no justifiable reason to call the returning Jews to their homeland, according to Muhammad and the Qur'an, "occupiers." And because they are not "occupiers" but "rightful inheritors," according to Muhammad and his statements in the "Infallible and Holy" Qur'an, it is most unjustifiable, by any Muslim who claims to follow Muhammad, to desire "to throw the Jews into the sea." Iran's Ahmadinejad's hateful and intense desire to destroy Israel, because of the supposed "holiness of Jerusalem" to Islam, is an affront and a slap on the face of the revered Prophet of Islam!

The whole Jew-Arab conflict over the land God gave to Isaac, Jacob, and Israel, according to Muhammad, is based on fables that contradict the very teachings of Muhammad and the Qur'an. For Muslims to claim that Jerusalem is a Holy City to Islam, because the Prophet Muhammad had ascended up to Heaven from the Haram esh-Sahrif area, and later, in specific, from the Dome of the Rock, is to declare that Muhammad is a false Prophet! Honest and genuine Muslims should give serious considerations and thoughts to this "naked" reality. They should, if they have the love of the Truth, acknowledge the fact that perhaps their own clerics and leaders been deceiving them in the past 1400 years. Those who deceived them and caused them to shed much innocent blood, for which they will have to give account in the Judgment Day, are willfully "naked." All of them read the Qur'an and should know better! They have no excuse for blaspheming and contradicting their own "infallible" Prophet and the teachings of the Qur'an for their personal selfish agenda! Devout Muslims should decide for themselves whether they want to "see" or remain, by choice, and willfully, blind. The choice is yours to make, fellow Muslims! You can be "The Believers" or the "Naked Deceivers?" Which will it be?

For Muslims to call Jerusalem Al Quds or Holy City, because they revere the Prophets of God and Israel, because they revere the Kings of Israel, like David and Solomon, because they revere the Temples of God in Jerusalem, as Caliph Omar did—and vowed that if God would give him the victory, he would rebuild the Temple of God in Jerusalem—well, that can be understood and respected. But, when they call Jerusalem "the third holiest City of Islam," because "Muhammad ascended up to Heaven through the southern gate of the City, or the "Rock," they declare themselves the enemies of Muhammad and his teachings in the Qur'an about the true state of the dead! To add insult to injury, they spill innocent blood, they declare a total war of annihilation on the very people Muhammad declared as the rightful owners of the land and the Holy City—and audaciously call them "occupiers!" How "naked" can the "believers" be? Get it straight "believers" of Muhammad before it's too late! Your revered Prophet did not ascend up to Heaven neither from Jerusalem, nor from his burial ground! There are no "Muslim rights" over the Land and Holy City given to Israel, forever, as Muhammad himself attested to in the Qur'an! Your supposed "ownership of "Arab Lands" in the land of Israel, and of Jerusalem in particular, is a product of willful and deceitful fables about the **afterlife** taught by "naked" and willful deceivers who had no regard for the words of your own revered Prophet and his teachings in the Qur'an! In the name of Allah and Muhammad, and of the Qur'an, your own clerics and leaders have lied to you! They are the ones who should be regarded by the genuine Muslims and believers as your worst enemies, not "the hated Zionists" who were highly respected by Caliph Omar and his two successors.

These noble Caliphs have invited the Jews of their days to come and reside again in their own Holy City and Land. They allowed them to settle near their Temple site, which was turned into a dumpsite by the hateful Romans and Christians of that time. Contrary to the will of the leaders of those Christians, and even though, initially, Caliph Omar had promised, in the name of Allah, not to allow the Jews into Jerusalem or the Temple area, he compassionately listened to the petition of the Jews, changed the terms of the agreement by renegotiating the agreement with the Christian leaders, and allowed the rightful owners, according to Muhammad, to come back home. Where are those noble Muslims who really believe the words of their revered Prophet Muhammad today? At the beginning of the 19th century, the noble Muslim Mufti of Jerusalem had, like noble Caliph Omar, the first successor of the Prophet Muhammad, invited the Jews of his day to come back home to their rightful lands and Holy City—according to the teachings of his Prophet Muhammad. He had respect for his revered Prophet and his teachings in the Qur'an concerning the land of Israel—unlike the hateful Mufti of Jerusalem, who, few decades later, "proposed" to Hitler the plan of "The Final Solution" for the Jews. Are the noble clerics and leaders of Islam gone forever?

In the last Day of Judgment, when you rise from the dead out of the grave, along with your own revered Prophet Muhammad, he will condemn you as "naked," miserable liars, because you teach lies in his name and despise his very teachings—which you falsely claim to follow and believe in. In short, fellow Muslims: your "Emperor is naked!" Your claims for the "Occupied Arab Lands" are based on superstitions and lies about the **afterlife—and they are contrary to the teachings of your own revered Prophet!**. You need to find an honest child among you who can 'see' and proclaim, and shout aloud in the name of Allah and Muhammad: "the Emperor is naked!" Time is short my friends! If you want to know your ultimate fate and how things will end up, read the book mentioned earlier, titled: ***"Middle East: Blueprint for the Final Solution . . ."***

CHAPTER 9

EDOM'S LINK TO ISLAM, MUHAMMAD, THE QUR'AN, AND JERUSALEM

Edom or Esau was the twin brother of the Patriarch Jacob—the father of the twelve tribes of Israel. Esau was the eldest of the two twins, yet God had decreed that Jacob should get the birthright, which included, initially, the whole land of Israel. For the full story, read Genesis, chapter 25:20-23 and chapters 27-28 for full details. Also, for more details, check this author's monumental work on the subject in the work titled: "Middle East: Blueprint for the Final Solution . . ."

The borders of this land were to stretch "From the River of Egypt to the great River, the River Euphrates . . ." (Genesis 15:18; Deuteronomy 1:24; Joshua 1:3-4. Obviously, brother Edom or Esau didn't like a bit—and still does not to this day! That's why we have an eternal boiling conflict in the Middle East between brothers of common ancestry.

The issue of Jerusalem and the land, which each side claims to have the sole ownership over, is a direct result of the ancient conflict between the twins—Edom and Jacob—and between Ishmael's descendants and those of Isaac. Had the Muslim world accepted the teachings of the "infallible" Qur'an and that of their revered prophet Muhammad, things would have been different.

With the passage of time, the descendants of the children of Abraham have been scattered in all directions. In the previously mentioned work about "The Middle East" one can find the whereabouts of all the children of Abraham in our days. Some of the descendants of Edom have migrated back to the 'old country' of father Abraham from which he was earlier told to depart and come to the land of Canaan. Since the land promise given to Abraham's descendants was to stretch all the way "to the Euphrates," it was natural for his grandson Edom to head in that direction. And so in the adjacent territory of the Euphrates we find one major center of Edom. It is no coincidence that one of the major cities of Iraq, or ancient Babylon, is named by its people Bozrah, or Basra. It is named so after the ancient capital of Edom in Mount Seir, just below the Dead Sea.

The different clans and growing nations of Esau, migrated from their original land in Seir to fertile lands along the Red Sea. Later, they migrated into present day Lebanon, Yemen, the Gulf of Aden, and into the breadbasket of the Euphrates. The blessing the Patriarch Isaac pronounced on his son Esau was to include the dew of heaven and the fatness of the land. The breadbasket between the Euphrates and Tigris Rivers became a part of the major fulfillment of that prophecy. Also, the narrow fertile strip of land stretching along the Red Sea to Yemen and up the coast to Modern Iraq became a part of his blessing. Today, we find small nations in all of those territories. Some of them constitute the descendants of the dukes of Edom who in later times mixed with other tribes of Ishmael's descendants.

In Jeremiah, Chapter 9, which records Edom's fate, the prophet speaks of Dedan, a son of Keturah the third wife of Abraham. He also speaks of Teman, a son of Esau now located in the territory of modern Yemen. We should also remember, from the Genesis 36 genealogy of Edom's descendants, that Esau did marry a daughter of Ishmael, namely, Basemath. Four Dukes, later becoming small nations, were the result of this marriage. The descendants of these four Dukes became later the inhabitants of Kedar, Dedan, Teman, and part of Saudi Arabia. Their territories are mostly a desert environment and fit the description of Ishmael who was a man of the desert. He liked the desert life, though eventually he integrated and subdued the land of Egypt, a land that is mostly a desert. Gradually, Egypt became his chief nation. This prime land of Ishmael is fertile only along the Nile Delta and River.

Esau, unlike his brother Jacob, has later rejected a relationship with the God of his fathers Abraham and Isaac. He also gradually rejected the God of Israel and his religion. He did not follow the teachings of the prophets of Israel, nor looked forward to the Messiah of Israel. In losing the birthright promises, he lost both the physical and spiritual promises. The Scepter that was to give birth to the "Star of Jacob," the Messiah, was not Esau's inheritance. These crucial elements were to play a major part in the future history of Esau, in his religious life, and in his relationship with the God of his fathers. Of course, the same became equally true with Ishmael, though for a time, Ishmael worshiped the God of his father

Abraham. Later, just like all the rest of Abraham's children, both Edom and Ishmael became idol worshipers. With the rise of the prophet Muhammad, Ishmael and part of Edom, those remaining in the area, returned to the God of their father Abraham, though with a different set of teachings.

For a brief century and a half, a part of Edom that invaded the land of promise that was denied him, found himself under the threat of the sword. He was forced to worship the God of his father Isaac, and practice the religion of his hated brother Jacob. This period was thoroughly covered in the story of the Jewish history, prior to and during Rome's merciless and cruel rule over Judea and the land of Israel. Few centuries later, Edom bounced back with a reverse reality in his relationship toward his brother Jacob. In the area of Kedar, in upper Saudi Arabia, a unique man was born. His name was Muhammad. Kedar was the son of Ishmael, but Edom's descendants have also inhabited that area. A brief history of that territory and its peoples may be most revealing to the student of history. It would shed light on the nature of the developing conflict in the Middle East after the fall of Jerusalem. Let's recall, briefly, the history of the Patriarch Abraham after his migration from Babylon into Canaan. For years, his wife Sarah could not bear the son of promise. She then took Hagar, the Egyptian maid, given to her while in Egypt by Pharoah Sesostris II, and gave her to Abram for a wife. This was the responsibility of a barren wife, according to the Babylonian custom out of which both came into Canaan. Ishmael was born from this marriage. He had twelve Dukes born to him from his Egyptian and other wives he married later. Who are those wives? This question is important to our understanding of the present widespread conflict that affects the whole Arab and Muslim world, not just Esau.

To find out this information, we have to delve into ancient accounts, both Biblical and historical, as preserved by Arab scholars and recorded genealogies. The ancient people of Mesopotamia, the birthplace of Abraham, called the area of the dry peninsula west and south of the River Euphrates, Arabia or Arabu, meaning west. In later times, those people became known as Arabs, meaning, ironically, Westerners. Thus, the arid areas west and south of Mesopotamia became known as Arabia, or the West. This included what is called today Saudi Arabia, the Sinai Peninsula, and the arid territory east of the Jordan. The territory of Edom, which became a sterile land by God's decree, was also called Arabia, as we read earlier in Josephus' writings.

The history of all the Arab peoples began with the Biblical Joktan. He was the son of Eber, the father of the Hebrew peoples (including the Israelites), as we can read in Genesis 10:25. One of Joktan's 13 sons was Jeray. He is believed to be the first to set up the kingdom of Yemen. The descendants of Edom from his grandson Teman had, in later times, invaded the land of the South or Yemen. Another son of Joktan, Hadoram, is believed to be the founder of Hejaz, a kingdom along the western coast of Saudi Arabia. Also, in later times, other descendants of Edom have invaded the western coasts of Saudi Arabia. The Edomite invaders have established Medina as the capital of their Edomite Kingdom in that area. After the rise of Islam, Medina and Mecca became the holiest cities in the Arab and Muslim world. According to Arab genealogists, a daughter of Hadoram, or in Arabic, Jorham, married Ishmael and bore him his son Kedar. From Kedar, later on, a descendant was to be born whose name was Adnan. He became the father of all the northern Arabian tribes. From this Adnan, Arab genealogist claim, the prophet Muhammad has descended. There is more historical documentation of Ishmael's descendants in the Middle East than that of Edom. Yet, the Biblical record has preserved the identity of Edom, though he and the world have lost the true identity of his ancestry. There is a Biblical reason for this puzzling reality. We shall see that later, when we discuss the identity of the descendants of the lost ten tribes of Israel and that of Edom in other lands. Their fate is closely linked with the present Mideast crisis, and its main players and allies.

Ishmael, whose main stronghold became Egypt, spread also into the far flung desert lands of Arabia. While Esau's descendants, being mainly men of cattle and sword, have drifted into fertile areas. Many of them, being mixed with descendants of Ishmael and other local tribes, lived also in the arid deserts of the Middle East.

To get back to our story, the prophet Muhammad was born in a land inhabited both by Ishmaelites and Edomites. How much mixed blood of these two, uncle and cousin, run in his blood, only Allah knows. The Jews who also lived in the same land, felt the stinging consequences on their backs from this mixture of Ishmaelite and Edomite blood. This mixed blood, which did run in the veins of the prophet of Islam, is still affecting the Mideast conflict to this day. Both Ishmael and Edom, for centuries, have lost contact with the God of their fathers. His religion and Law, His prophets and Messiah were not theirs any longer. Neither was His plan of salvation a part of their hopes and dreams. Father Abraham "looked for a city whose maker and builder is not man, but God." This was the heavenly Jerusalem promised to come down to earth. It was to be located at the very spot of earthly Jerusalem, the one called "God's Holy Mountain" on earth. The God of Abraham recognizes Jerusalem as the only holy city and location on earth. It is the City of the Great King, the city of the future reigning Messiah.

In contrast to these Biblical assertions of God (or Allah), His prophets and apostles, we find in the region of Ishmael and Edom a new foreign reality in the making. The rise of the prophet Muhammad and his newly proclaimed religion—Islam—has created a new concept of God, a new religion and prophet, a new "book" and messiah or Mahadi. This prophet and son of Abraham began to challenge much of what the God of his father has proclaimed and taught the children of Abraham. Though he led his people away from idolatry and into the belief in one God, he did not lead them to believe and obey the pure Biblical teachings of the God of Abraham, Isaac, and Jacob. He did not even teach them the original faith of Ishmael, who was taught by his father Abraham the Law of God. It was not the religion, the Law and the Prophets of the God of Israel Muhammad was to lead his people to follow. It was not about the Messiah of Israel, and his plan of salvation for Israel and all mankind, the prophet Muhammad was teaching his new converts. It was not "The Book," written by those inspired by the God of his father Abraham, the prophet was to reveal to his followers, even though he often acknowledged them and claimed that he came to confirm them, and even believed in them. No, it was simply another message and law, a different religion and prophet, another messiah and plan of salvation, a different location for worship and a holy place.

The great prophet of Islam, Muhammad, included some of the teachings of the God of his father Abraham and Israel in his own version of the original Book of The Maker. Yet, his Qur'an or Sacred Book to Muslims, could not link his followers with the original teachings and God of his fathers, no matter how sincere his efforts might have been. God gave His people one Law and one Way to worship Him—nothing else is acceptable to Him. Man's sincerity is not enough. He has to be willing to say, "Not my will, but Your will be done." Esau's descendants (and those of Ishmael) were not about to serve, with their brother Jacob, the God, Law, and religion of their fathers Abraham and Isaac. He was not interested in the will of the God of his father, but that of his own.

Instead of the God of Israel, the followers of Islam were now to follow Allah. Still, Muslims do recognize Israel's God as the God of Abraham. Instead of God's Law, as given in Sinai and amplified by the Prophets, and later by the Messiah in Jerusalem, and by His apostles, the Muslims now had a new holy Book—the Qur'an. They had a new messiah and prophet, a new doctrine for the afterlife. Instead of Jerusalem, the only Holy place and City of the Great King-God, it was now a new man-sanctified site. Instead of the Holy of Holies in Jerusalem, where God dwelt between the cherubim when on earth, it was now the Kaaba in Mecca—toward which all worshipers of Islam were now to face and pray, even though, originally, in order to gain the Jews on his side, Muhammad commanded all Muslims to pray toward Jerusalem. Yet the God of the patriarchs has declared only Jerusalem, His City, not man's, to be His only Holy Mountain and City of worship.

Instead of Isaac being almost sacrificed on Mount Moriah, as a type of the ultimate sacrifice of the coming Messiah, Islam now taught that Ishmael was actually the one—albeit in a dream, being offered to God. It was conveniently forgotten by the children of Ishmael that their father was sent away earlier by his father Abraham at the age of sixteen with his mother Hagar. By the time Isaac was to be offered, Ishmael was already married and living in the wilderness of Paran, below the Negev Desert. It was in the Negev Desert, according to God's account, that Hagar and Ishmael were lost without water. Yet, according to Islam, it happened near Mecca. All these "new" doctrines of Islam, which are still devoutly believed to this day, were introduced into the world of Islam twenty centuries after God had revealed these facts to Moses, in person, on Mount Sinai.

The God of Israel wanted His Law taught to all mankind through Israel's example and conduct, not by the edge of the sword. Later, He sent His prophets and apostles to teach the same Royal Law of love, as messengers of peace who come with good tidings to the world. Yet the followers of Islam, often, as a matter of religious doctrine, had chosen to embark on a holy crusade or Jihad against the "infidels." They, at times, forced them, by the edge of the sword, to either convert to Islam or face death, or, sometimes, only servitude. When John Hyrcanus, the Maccabean, forced the Edomites, by the edge of the sword, to convert to Judaism, he was not in accord with the Law of God and Israel. When the crusaders and the Spanish inquisition did the same to the non-believers, they were not in accord with the Royal Law of Christ. The believers in Islam have chosen to follow the wrong example of other children of Abraham. They often used the sword, as a matter of faith, to gain more believers for their prophet of the sword—Muhammad. Such was not the will of the God of Abraham—as was recorded in the Torah, the prophets, and the later teachings of Christ and his apostles.

The Patriarch Isaac proclaimed to Esau, "By your sword you shall live." Muhammad was called "the man of the sword." Is it just a coincidence? Could it be that some of Edom's blood was flowing in his veins? Was it leading his spirit to lift up his sword and conquer the lands and souls of other children of Abraham? The millennia-old struggle between Islam and the Western religion of Judeo-Christian doctrines is a direct result, as we shall see later, of the family conflict between the children of Abraham. Only the coming conquering Messiah of Israel can put it to rest.

The union between Ishmael, the man called by the God Abraham "a wild man," and Edom, who loved blood and lived by the sword, proved to be a most potent and lethal combination—and it is still so to this day. "The day of infamy" of September 11 is but one painful reminder of this tragic and bloody reality. The Jews who rejected Muhammad's attempts, though friendly at first, to convert them to his new doctrine, "received from Gabriel the Archangel," according to later Muslim scholars, were the first to feel the impact of that lethal combination of "the wild man" and "the man of the sword.". For the next 13 centuries, throughout the Middle East, Jews were to taste the wrath of both Edom and Ishmael times without number. To this day, some Jews still feel the wrath of the sword of Islam. They experience it, daily, in a few Arab countries, in some Western nations, and mostly in the land God gave to His people Israel, as Muhammad himself had often acknowledged in the Qur'an.

Still, the fact was: Jews living under the ever threatening sword of Islam, did have more peace and better treatment than those who lived in the past many centuries, at least until Nazi Germany, under the sword of Christianity. Yet, the God of Israel or Allah was not the author of either one of these two swords. Both prophets and apostles spoke of the time when this matter shall be settled once and for all by the King of Israel, and for the ultimate benefit of them all.

Quoting the Jewish prophet Jeremiah, the apostle Paul, who did not come to teach a new religion, contrary to both Christian and Jewish scholars' misinformed opinions, stated: "'Behold, the days are coming,' says the Lord, 'when I will make a new covenant with the House of Israel and the

House of Judah [not the house of Edom, Ishmael or Gentile Christianity at large], not according with the covenant that I made with their fathers [who were neither Edomites, Ishmaelites or Gentile Christians] in the day when I took them by the hand to lead them out of the land of Egypt; because they did not continue in My covenant and I disregarded them,' says the Lord, 'for this is the covenant that I will make with the House of Israel, after those days,' says the Lord, 'I will put My laws [not any man's laws] in their mind and write them in their hearts.'"

God's laws are not those taught by Islam or popular Christianity—though some of those laws have been adopted by these offshoot religions. Neither are they, in totality, the ones taught by Jewish Halachah or tradition. They are the laws He gave Israel in Sinai by His Law-Giver—Moses. These laws have been adulterated and altered by the three religions that sprang from Abraham's children.

God added: "'I will be their God [not Ishmael's, Edom's, or any other nation, unless they too become a part of the Commonwealth of Israel's Faith], and they shall be My people. None of them shall teach his neighbor and none his brother [God's laws and religion], saying, 'know the Lord,' for all shall know Me [the God and Messiah of Israel] from the least of them to the greatest of them, for I will be merciful to their unrighteousness and their sins and their lawless deeds I will remember no more'" (Hebrews 8:8-12).

Yet today, as in the past, tragically, as the prophet Isaiah has bemoaned, "Who has believed our report? And to whom has the arm of the Lord been revealed?" (Isaiah 53:1). Faith in the God of Abraham and Israel, then and now, was never a common currency among all the children of Abraham. That's why we have a chronic Middle East conflict with its worldwide ramifications and tragic consequences, as the latest one, which, like a thunderbolt in a blue sky fell on an unsuspecting America on September 11—"the day of infamy." Neither most Jews, nor Arabs (mostly children of Abraham), or most of those called Christians, do believe and obey the genuine teachings of the God of Israel—But soon they all will. He said so!

Let's now, for the sake of understanding Historic Islam's point of view, find out what is it really that the prophet of Islam, Muhammad, had to say about the land Arabs call, "Palestine" or "Arab lands," and the land the Jews call "The State of Israel." Who are the legitimate owners of the land, according to the revered prophet of Islam? What did Muhammad have to say about the Bible and the people of Israel. What did he have to say about Jerusalem and about the New Testament' teachings, as well as about its central figure—Jesus Christ. What did he have to say about his own mortality and death in contrast to what later Muslims came to believe in after the days A careful reading of the Koran should illuminate all of us as to what really the prophet of all Muslims had to say—and its relevance to the present day Jew\Arab volatile issues, as well as the Western\Islam brewing conflict. Let's find that out from the very mouth of Muhammad! Let's give him and genuine Islam an "equal time," in a thorough manner, to reveal to all of us the Koran's real teachings about the issues that concern Ishmael's brother, Isaac, and his nephew Jacob or Israel—the father of all Jews and Israelites.

According to Islamic scholars, Muhammad was influenced by both Jewish and Christian teachings. Those teachings, however, as we shall see later, have gradually been changed somewhat since that time. The Qur'an or The Recital, is regarded by all devout Muslims to be the last infallible word of God or Allah. His prophet Muhammad, who had some five or six scholars, one of them a Jew, transcribe the Koran from the writings of "the angel Gabriel," according to later Islamic commentators, is to be viewed as the greatest and most infallible prophet of Allah. Muhammad himself, however, did not reveal the name of the angel as being Gabriel—his followers claimed that later. Let's assume, for a moment, this to be true—and with this assumption in mind, let's read, methodically, the words recited by the prophet of Islam concerning the issues presented in this work, which affect Jews, Palestinians, Arabs, Muslims, as well as Christians.

We shall quote, throughout, from the excellent translation of N.J. Dawood of the Qur'an, which was published by the Penguin Books in 1999, and printed in England by Clays Ltd, St Ives plc. We shall also follow the traditional sequence of the Surahs. These Surahs are basically accounts of different revelations given to Muhammad, according to Islamic scholars, on different occasions. Sometimes, the revelations are given through the voice of Gabriel, at others, when we see the pronoun "We," it is referring to the voice of God.

In the Surah, The Cow, (p. 14, 2:39-53), we read: "Children of Israel, remember the favor I have bestowed upon you. Keep your covenant, and I will be true to mine. Dread My power. Have faith in My revelations [the Koran], which confirm your Scriptures . . . Children of Israel, remember the favor I have bestowed upon you, and that I exalted you above the nations." Then speaking about the plagues that God inflicted upon Egypt, and the Law in Sinai, we read: "We gave Moses the Scriptures and Knowledge of right and wrong, so that you may be rightly guided" Consider the implications of this passage! The Qur'an is supposed to confirm the Scriptures, as previously given to Moses and the prophets of Israel, not to alter or replace them!

Concerning himself, Muhammad wrote: "And now that an apostle has come to them (the Jews) from God confirming [never denying] their own Scriptures, some of those [not all] to whom the Scriptures were given cast off the Book of God [Old and New Testaments] over their backs as tough they know nothing and accept what the devils tell of Solomon's kingdom Not that Solomon was an unbeliever . . ."(ibid. p. 19, 2:98-2:104).

In their attempts to destroy all evidence of the first Temple of Solomon, as well as the last one, on the Temple Mount, some Palestinians today are claiming that no Temples have ever been erected there. In doing so, they contradict their own prophet and the Koran.

Speaking of the Jews, we read: "Many among the people of the Book . . ." (ibid. p. 20, 2:109). God and the angel Gabriel, in the Qur'an, refer to both Jews and Christians as "the people of the Book." Also, let's remember that throughout the Qur'an, the One who is inspiring it, according to Muhammad, is constantly attesting to the fact that the writings and revelations given to the prophet Muhammad were not to contradict, but to confirm all the Scriptures God had revealed earlier to Moses and the prophets of Israel. This also included the New Testament writings, as we shall later.

Of the people of Israel, Muhammad records Allah's words: "Children of Israel, remember the favor I have bestowed upon you, and that I exalted you [and will, again, according to the Book Muhammad came to confirm, as we shall see later] above the nations" (ibid. p. 22, 2:122).

Of the direction the believers were to face, when praying to Allah, we read: "The foolish will ask: 'What has made them turn away from their Quiblah?" In footnote, No. 1, we read: "The direction in which the Muslim faces in prayer. At first [when Muhammad was trying to win the Jews to his side, knowing that Jerusalem is the Only Holy Mount of God or Allah] the believers were ordered to turn toward Jerusalem, afterwards [when the Jews refused to follow Muhammad, he ordered them to look] to Mecca." (ibid. p. 24, 2:125).

In this Surah, The Imrans, Muhammad is recording also the story of Mary, the birth of John the Baptist, and that of his father's encounter with the angel Gabriel in the Temple. He also refers to the Shrine, The Temple of God and of Israel. He recites: "Therefore Zacharias prayed to his Lord . . . And as he stood praying in the Shrine [the Temple is called a Shrine in the Koran, while the one in Mecca is called a Temple], the angels called out to him, saying: 'God bids you rejoice in the birth of John, who shall confirm the Word of God [the Hebrew Scriptures]" (ibid. p. 46, 3:36-39).

According to the Waqf or religious leader in charge of the Temple Mount and Mosques in Jerusalem, as well as other "Muslim scholars," no Temple of Jews had ever existed in that location. In the past several years, with the tacit "approval" or blind eye of recent Israeli governments, the Waqf had undertaken massive construction works of religious sites on the premises while, on the other hand, obliterating any shred of evidence as to the existence of the former two Jewish Temples in that very area. This malicious and deliberate attempt to falsify history and Truth runs contrary to the very words of the Qur'an and Muhammad himself. In essence, it brands the revered prophet of Islam a liar—since he recorded in the Qur'an just the opposite concerning the Temple at Jerusalem—and that he did several times.

In pages 46-47, we read of the coming birth of The Messiah through Mary: "The angels said to Mary: 'God bids you rejoice in a Word from Him. His name is the messiah, Jesus son of Mary. [Muhammad does not acknowledge Jesus as The Messiah, just a messiah.] He shall be noble in this world and in the world to come, and shall be one of those who are favored . . . He [God] will instruct him [Jesus] in the [Hebrew] Scriptures and in wisdom, in the Torah and in the Gospel [the New Testament], and send him forth as an apostle to the Israelites.'" As for his understanding of "The After Life," Muhammad Quotes God: "I shall take you away from the unbelievers and exalt your followers above them till the day of Resurrection. Then to Me you shall return and I shall judge your disputes [at the Resurrection day]" (ibid).

As we shall see more clearly later, Muhammad never taught nor believed in going to Heaven or Hell immediately after death. He did neither teach nor believe in the immortality of the soul, which supposedly goes to Heaven or Hell immediately after death. But he persistently taught that upon death all go back to the dust, and there we all await the Resurrection—as was taught in the Hebrew and New Testament Scriptures, contrary to later misguided religionists and false teachings on all sides.

Later, we read God's words to Muhammad: "Say: 'People of the Book, let us come to an agreement: that we will worship none but God, that we will associate none with Him, and that none of us shall set up mortals [speaking of Jesus] as deities besides Him.'" And again: "People of the Book! Why do you deny God's revelations when you know that they are true . . . People of the book! Why do you confound the true with the false . . . Some of the people of the Book . . ."(ibid., p. 48, 3:60-66). Throughout the Qur'an, Muhammad repeatedly referred to Jews and Christians, who followed the teachings of Israel, as People of the Book—the one revealed by Allah, and confirmed by the Qur'an.

Muhammad had consistently condemned the teaching about the divinity of Jesus, in spite of the fact that it is clearly taught, for those who have eyes to see, in both the Hebrew and New Testament Scriptures, which he admits and confesses, repeatedly, to be of God. And so he does again in this section, by reciting God's words: "No mortal to whom God has given the Scriptures and to whom He has endowed with judgment and prophethood would say to men: 'Worship me (Jesus) instead of God . . . ' When God made His covenant with the prophets [of Israel], He said: 'Here are the Scriptures and the wisdom which I have given you. An apostle will come forth to confirm them. Believe in him [Muhammad] and help him" (ibid. p. 49, 3:78-81). These Scriptures in Deuteronomy, 18:15-19, are applied in the New Testament to Jesus, but according to Muhammad, this should be applied to himself.

Muhammad had, at rare times, some good words for the Jews of his day. Quoting God, he wrote or recited, since recital is the meaning of the Koran: "Had the people of the Book had accepted the faith [of Islam], it would surely had been better for them. Some are true believers, but most of them are evildoers [since they were unwilling to follow him] . . . Yet they are not all alike [contrary to many Islamic clerics' opinions today]. There are among the people of the Book some upright men who all night long recite the revelations of God and worship Him; who believe in God and the last day . . ."

During the time of Muhammad, many Jews still believed that all shall rise from the dust and stand before the judgment seat of God. No Heaven or Hell doctrine was introduced yet in that Jewish community in the days of Muhammad. Of these Jews, Muhammad added: " . . . Who enjoin justice and forbid evil and vie with each other in good works. These are righteous men [yet the Muslim cleric from Gaza would not agree with his prophet in this matter. He teaches all Jews are evil, but Muhammad said]: whatever good they do, its reward shall not be denied them. God well knows the righteous" (ibid. p. 52, 3:110-115).

In contrast to the Jews who believed only in the Hebrew Scriptures, and the Christians who believed in the Hebrew and New Testament Scriptures, Muhammad is told: "You believe in the entire Book" (ibid. p. 53, 3:119). If Muhammad believed in the whole Book, so should his followers. They should pay attention to the Will and teachings of (their own Allah and) the God of Israel; they should learn of His will concerning the land of Israel and the fate of those who dare defy His will, which they do to this day.

Let's go now to the Surah, Women, and read more of God's instructions to the prophet Muhammad. On page 76, 4:153-155, we read: "The people of the Book ask you to bring down for them a book from Heaven . . . When We [God] made a covenant with them We raised the Mount [Sinai] above them [an account not mentioned in the Book of Moses] and said: 'Enter the gate of adoration. Do not break the [seventh day] Sabbath [Notice! He didn't say Sunday or Friday, which are the first and sixth days].'" Then in pp. 76-77, 4:156-160, we read: "They [Jews] denied the truth and uttered a monstrous falsehood against Mary. They declared: 'We have put to death the Messiah, Jesus son of Mary, the apostle of God.' THEY DID NOT KILL HIM, NOR DID THEY CRUCIFY HIM, BUT THEY THOUGHT THEY DID . . ."

Muhammad believed and taught that the real Jesus was taken up to heaven, while a body of another person was crucified. Such doctrine began to circulate among some "Christians," years after the resurrection of Christ, and Muhammad also believed in it. The problem with this notion is in the teaching of Muhammad that the dead are in the dust until the last day—which is in accordance with the Bible. It is only after the first century that many Jews and Christians, and mostly in the West, have gradually begun to accept the pagan teaching of the immortality of the soul, and the pagan belief that upon death all go either to Heaven or Hell. In Muhammad's days many Jews and Christians, in the East, in contrast to those in the West, still adhered to the Biblical teaching he himself accepted and taught. This teaching, however, presents a contradiction for Muhammad and Islam: If all go back into the dust, then how come Jesus was taken up to heaven if he is just a mortal man like any other servant of God, as Muhammad himself had taught. The Koran does not seem to take this point and contradiction into consideration.

The account continues: "THEY DID NOT SLAY HIM [CHRIST], FOR CERTAIN, GOD LIFTED HIM UP TO HIM; God is mighty and wise. There is none among the people of the Book who will believe in him before his death [in reality, all of Jesus followers, initially, were Jews]; and on the Day of Resurrection [all, beside Christ, who are in the dust until that day, but] he [Jesus] will bear witness against them."

It is important to notice that though Muhammad believed and acknowledged Jesus to be a messenger and a messiah sent from heaven, and later went up to heaven, he did not believe in many of His teachings or Divinity—nor did he know His true identity.

Concerning the revelations God gave earlier to the patriarchs and Israel, We read: "We have revealed Our will to you as it was to Noah and to the prophets who came after him; as We revealed it to Abraham, Ishmael, Isaac, Jacob, and to the tribes [of Israel]; to Jesus, Job, Jonah Aaron, Solomon and David, to whom We gave the Psalms. Of some apostles We have already told you, but there are others [including the writers of the Hebrew and New Testament Scriptures] of whom We have not yet spoken, apostles who brought good news to mankind and admonished them, so that they have no plea against God [as many Muslims do, who do not bother to read the words of the prophets of Israel, men like Job, David, and the disciples of Christ] after their coming" (ibid. p. 77, 4:163-168).

In addressing the Christian community, Muhammad writes: "People of the Book, do not transgress the bounds of your religion. Speak nothing but the truth about God. The messiah, Jesus son of Mary, was no more than God's apostle and His word which He cast to Mary: a spirit from Him. So believe in God and His apostles and do not say: 'Three.' Forbear, and it shall be better for you. God is but one God. God forbid that He should have a son!" (Ibid. p. 78, 4:171-172). As in Judaism, so it is in Islam—The Son of God, Jesus, is totally rejected as a divine being. And yet, Muhammad states that Jesus had ascended up to heaven, and was not really crucified.

In the Surah, The Table, we read: "You are forbidden carrion, blood, and the flesh of swine; also any flesh dedicated to any other God." Moses had also recorded these prohibitions as instructions from God. However, as we shall see later, The Qur'an has some modifications in this matter.

Then we read of the new faith: "This day I have perfected your religion for you and completed My favor to you. I have chosen Islam to be your faith" (ibid. p. 79, 5:3). So now, according to Muhammad, the God of Abraham has three different sets of faith—and the last one, Islam, does supersede them all, being "the last revelation and true faith."

Later, we read: "Believers, fulfill your duties and bear true witness. Do not allow your hatred for other men to turn you away from justice. Deal justly; that is nearer to true piety" (ibid. p. 80, 5:7-10). In today's conflict between Arabs and Jews, how much of such piety and justice is demonstrated by those who call themselves Muslims, only Allah knows.

In section 5:15-17, we read, in an address to Christians: "People of the Book! Our apostle has come to reveal to you much of what you have hidden of the Scriptures, and to forgive you much . . . Unbelievers are those who declare: 'God is the Messiah, the son of Mary.' Say: 'Who could prevent God, if He so willed, from destroying the Messiah, the son of Mary, His mother, and all the people of the earth?'" (ibid. p. 81, 5:15-17).

Such are the feelings of many Muslims to this day about Christ and His followers. The irony of this statement is in the built-in contradiction, which it does not address. In the book of Luke, a part of the Gospel which Muhammad recorded that it was given by God to Jesus and His disciples, we read of the angel Gabriel who told Mary, concerning Jesus: "He will be great, and will be called the Son of the Highest [God]; and the Lord God will give Him the throne of His father David . . . The Holy Spirit will come upon you, and the power of the Highest will overshadow you; therefore, also, that Holy One who is to be born will be called the Son of God . . . For with God nothing will be impossible" (Luke, 1:26-37).

In the Qur'an, on the other hand, Muhammad records the words of the angel Gabriel as well. Let's remember that Muslim commentators did later claim it was Gabriel, though Muhammad himself never said that. Only in this case, Gabriel tells him just the opposite of what, six centuries earlier, he told Mary about the divine origin of Jesus. To say the least, Either Gabriel or Muhammad is correct, but not both! We would leave this contradiction, one of many, for the Muslim clerics to solve.

In page 82, Muhammad recited the words Of Allah concerning the Jews: "Bear in mind the words of Moses to his people. He said: 'Remember, my people, the favor that God has bestowed upon you. He has raised up prophets among you, made you kings, and given you that which He has given to no other nation. ENTER MY PEOPLE THE HOLY LAND [holy to God and Israel, not to Muslims or others] WHICH GOD HAS ASSIGNED FOR YOU. Do not turn back, and thus lose all'" (ibid. p. 82, 5:19-23).

According to Muhammad, the land of Israel was not assigned to the Palestinians, Arabs, or any other nation! Those who truly believe and submit to Allah, his prophet Muhammad and the Qur'an, adhere to these words—others do not—that's why the Middle East conflict! THE PROPHET OF ISLAM MADE IT VERY CLEAR: THE HOLY LAND BELONGS, BY ALLAH'S DECREE, TO THE PEOPLE OF ISRAEL. Hence Muhammad never advanced any claim to that land, to the city of Jerusalem, or any supposed "Arab lands" in Israel! Muhammad never labeled the land Allah gave ONLY to His people Israel—"Arab land!" But who among those who claim to submit to the will of Allah and his prophet Muhammad practice what they preach! Osama bin Laden and his misguided followers certainly do not believe the words of "their" prophet of Islam. It is very doubtful that Muhammad would claim such people who defy his own teachings as his own true followers.

Again, in the Surah, The Table, we read: "We have revealed the Torah [God is speaking], in which there is guidance and light. By it the prophets [of God to Israel] who submitted to God judged the Jews, and so did the rabbis and the divines, according to God's Book which had been committed to their keeping and to which they themselves are witnesses" (ibid. p. 84, 5:44).

Consider the implications of these critical words of God, as recited by Muhammad, in relationship to the present day Middle East conflict! Are the Arabs and Palestinian peoples in accord with their own prophet and Qur'an, or are they in opposition and defiance of them both? Let the words that were recited by the prophet of Islam be a witness in this matter! Isn't it high time all Arabs and Muslims begin to pay attention to their own revered and "infallible" prophet and holy Book—the Qur'an? Isn't it about time they begin to read the words Allah spoke and revealed to Moses and the prophets—the ones He sent to His people Israel? Isn't it about time they read and consider, what according to Muhammad, Allah revealed in the Gospel to Jesus and His disciples, and act accordingly? Muhammad recited in the Qur'an many times: "Those who reject the words and revelations given to him, God will judge in the last day." How many so-called Muslims are truly honest and willing to heed and consider the Recital or Qur'an of their own prophet concerning the issues at hand with their Jewish and Christian brothers? Let the honest and true Muslims stand up and be counted—for the Day of Judgment is at hand!

Muhammad recited again: "After them We sent forth Jesus son of Mary, confirming [not doing away or changing, or superseding] the Torah already revealed [to Moses and Israel], and gave him the Gospel, in which there is guidance and light, corroborating [not changing or denying] what was revealed before it in the Torah: a guide and an admonition to the righteous. Therefore let those who follow the Gospel judge according to what God revealed therein. Evil-doers are those that do not judge according to God's revelations" (ibid., p. 84, 5:46-47).

Do Arabs and Muslims study and believe these Books, transmitted by Allah, according to Muhammad, to His people, or do they, on occasion, deface, desecrate, burn or handle them with contempt? Let Allah, Muhammad, and the Koran be witnesses in this regard! Do those who call themselves "believers" ever bother to study, consider, and learn the will of Allah—from the Books He gave His servants Moses, the prophets of Israel, and later His Servant Jesus and His apostles? Why not? Why is it that fanatic and extreme fundamentalist Muslim Clerics, like the ones who have poisoned the minds of men like bin Laden and his followers, do not teach and practice the true teachings of the "holy Qur'an" and the great prophet of Islam?

In section 5:48-49, Page 85, Muhammad recited: "And to you We have revealed the Book with the truth. It confirms the Scriptures [both the Hebrew and New Testament] that came before it and stands as a guardian over them . . . We have ordained a Law [or Torah] and assigned a path for each of you [Hebrew, Christian, and Islamic communities]. Had God pleased, He could have made of you one community: but it is His wish to prove you by that which He has bestowed upon you. Vie with each other in good works [not kill, terrorize, and butcher each other, as it turned out to be], for to God shall you all return and He will resolve your differences for you" (ibid).

Here we read the reason, from Muhammad's perspective, for the existence of the three religions that "sprung from the patriarch Abraham," as some claim. The Bible, however, has a different point of view, but this is not the place to argue this critical point. In due time, God or Allah "will resolve your differences," as Muhammad recited.

Again, in the Surah, The Table, We read: "Believers, do not seek the friendship of the infidels and those who were given the Book before you, who have made of your religion a jest and a diversion . . . Say: 'Shall I tell you who will receive a worse reward from God? Those whom God has cursed [if they do not accept Muhammad and the Qur'an], and with whom He has been angry, transforming them into apes and swine, and those who serve the devil'" (p. 86, 5:55-60). This statement became a part of Islamic thinking toward the "infidels," and to this day. This later statement of Muhammad should be contrasted with the previous one we just read. (See Surah The Table, Sec. 5:48-49, P.85).

In Page 87, Sec. 5:65-73, we read: "If the people of the Book accept the true faith [of Islam] and keep from evil, We will pardon them their sins and admit them into the gardens of delight [that is, in the last day]. If they observe the Torah and the Gospel and what has been revealed to them from their Lord, they shall enjoy abundance from above and from beneath [yet this is not the way Muslims have treated both communities since the days of the prophet of Islam]. There are some among them who are righteous men [but according to the Islamic cleric, Dr. Halabaya, who disagrees with his own prophet and the "infallible" Qur'an: all are evil]; but there are many among them who do nothing but evil." And again we read; "Say: 'People of the Book, you will attain nothing until you observe the Torah and the Gospel and that which has been revealed to you [the Qur'an] from your Lord.'"

This is the kind of preaching Muslims should have been bringing to the attention of the people of the Book in the past many centuries, not the sword of Islam and the forced conversion which has no merit in the sight of God or Allah! Muhammad, the Qur'an or Allah did not enjoin Muslims to desecrate, deface, destroy or hold in contempt any religious house of either community of the people of the Book. Nowhere can Muslims find any instructions in the Koran to destroy or convert religious shrines or synagogues into mosques, which they have done many times.

Muhammad recites again: "Believers, Jews, Sabaeans and Christians—whoever believes in God [not whoever is forcibly or willingly converts to Islam, or agrees with us] and the last day and does what is right—shall have nothing to fear or to regret. We made a covenant with the Israelites [on Mount Sinai] and sent forth apostles [or prophets] among them." Again: "Unbelievers are those that say: 'God is the Messiah, the son of Mary.' For the Messiah himself said: 'Children of Israel, serve God, my Lord and your Lord.' He that worships other deities besides God, God will deny him paradise, and the fire shall be his home . . . Unbelievers are those that say: 'God is one of three.' There is but one God" (ibid. p. 87, 5:65-73).

It is important to realize that in the days of Jesus, and later, His true disciples never taught, for nearly three centuries, the doctrine of the trinity. The true followers of Christ never taught it. Not until the beginning of the fourth century, was this pagan doctrine forcibly imposed on many by the Church of Rome. This doctrine was, basically, a recycled idea and teaching from ancient Babylon, Egypt, and other pagan religions. In this area, Muhammad and the Qur'an are absolutely correct. Also, the apostles of Christ have always repeated the statement: "There is One God and One Lord" (or Master), not three Gods, or three-in-One God.

When the angel Gabriel announced to Mary that she is to conceive and bear a son whose name is to be Jesus—and that He is to be called the Son of the Highest, "Then Mary said to the angel, 'How can this be, since I do not know a man?' And the angel answered and said to her, 'The Holy Spirit will come upon you, and the power of the Highest will overshadow you; therefore also, that Holy One who is to be born will be called the Son of God [not the Son of the Holy Spirit who came upon her]" (Luke 1:26-35). Then we read in the book of Matthew 1:18-23, again, concerning the birth of Jesus and the announcement by the angel, this time, to his adopting father, Joseph, the following: "Joseph, son of David, do not be afraid to take to you Mary your wife [who was his fiancée and bound to him], for that which is conceived in her IS OF THE HOLY SPIRIT." The simple reality is this: if God is three in one, or as others say, "God the Father, God the Son, and God the Holy Spirit," then according to the Scriptures, Jesus is the Son of God the Holy Spirit, not the Son of God the Father. But since Jesus never called the Holy Spirit His father, nor ever addressed the Spirit as a person, but always referred to God, or Elohim, as His Father; since it is to this God that He admonished His disciples to direct their worship—then obviously, from the point of view of Christ and His true disciples and followers to this day, the doctrine of the trinity is not of God!

On page 88, we read moreover: "The Messiah, the son of Mary, was no more than an apostle: other apostles passed away before him. His mother was a saintly woman. They both ate earthly food" (ibid. 5:75).

If "The Messiah, the son of Mary, was no more than an apostle," according to Muhammad, how come, again, according to him, God took

Jesus up to Heaven while Muhammad was to die and remain in his grave until the last Day of Resurrection?

In another passage, we read: "Those to whom we have given the Scriptures [Jews and Christians] know Him as they know their own children . . . Who is more wicked than the man who invents falsehood about God or denies His revelations? The wrong doers shall never prosper" (Surah, Cattle, p. 94, 6:20-23). This statement is repeated several times throughout the Qur'an and is worth considering by all.

In Page 99, 6:75, we read: "Tell of Abraham, who said to Azar, his father: 'Will you worship idols as your gods?'" (ibid. p. 99, 6:74). In the book of Genesis, where this account is recorded, the name of the father of Abraham is Terah, not Azar. This statement here, as with many other accounts or statements, does raise questions concerning accuracy and validity. Yet, again, this is a matter for the Islamic clerics to ponder about and clarify.

Speaking of many of the great men and prophets of Israel, Muhammad recited: "On those men We bestowed the Scriptures, wisdom, and prophethood . . . Those were the men whom God guided. Follow then their guidance and say: 'I demand of you no recompense for this. It is but an admonition to all mankind'" (ibid. p. 100, 6:89-90).

Repeatedly, the prophet of Islam acknowledged the Scriptures given to Israel, and later to Jesus and His Jewish disciples; to the fathers and prophets of Israel, as God's own men and writings. Again, since this is the case, why is it that his followers do not bother to abide and be guided by these Scriptures? Why don't they study and honor them—and those who follow them and their words received from Allah?

In the next statement, Muhammad is defending the veracity of his revelations before the Jews by reciting the following: "They [Jews] have no true notion of God's glory, those that say: 'God has never revealed anything to a mortal.' Say: 'Who then revealed the Scriptures which Moses brought down, a light and guide for mankind? You [Jews] have transcribed them on scraps of paper, declaring some and suppressing much, though now you have been taught what neither you nor your fathers knew before'" (ibid. p. 100, 6:91). In other words: Muhammad has the last revelation, even though many of the statements he recited are, to say the least, very different and contradictory to Moses, the prophets, and those of the Gospel, which he himself repeatedly confirmed as being from God. And Again, this should be a matter for honest and objective Islamic clerics to reconcile and clarify among themselves.

At a certain point in the Qur'an, Muhammad stated that, being unlettered, he never read a book in his life—but nevertheless, the writings of the Qur'an were given to him. Other helpers, including a Jewish scholar, have assisted him in putting the revelations of the Qur'an together. They also, obviously, had to read it to him.

In regard to Jesus, Muhammad wrote: "Creator of the heavens and the earth. How should He have a son when He had no consort? . . . There is no God but Him" (ibid. p. 102, 6:103). Islam is very uncompromising and rigid about this major point, yet God is the absolute source of truth.

Concerning clean and unclean meats, we read: "Say: 'I find nothing in what has been revealed to me that forbids men to eat of any food except carrion, running blood, and the flesh of swine—for these are unclean . . . But whoever is driven by necessity, intending neither to sin nor to transgress, will find your Lord forgiving and merciful. We forbade the Jews all animals with undivided hoofs and the fat of sheep and oxen . . ." (ibid. p. 106, 6:145147).

According to Muhammad, it is allowed to eat unclean meats, if under duress—yet the Biblical teachings are very emphatically clear: unclean meats are to be considered an abomination that defiles the flesh. God forbade His people, through Moses, to eat any creature not in the category of the clean list. There were no exceptions to this law, in contrasts to Muhammad's instructions to eat it if under duress. God told His people Israel: "You are the children of the Lord your God . . . For you are a holy people to the Lord your God, and the Lord has chosen you to be a people for Himself, a special treasure above all the peoples who are on the face of the earth. You shall not eat [under any circumstance] any detestable [or abominable] thing. These are the animals which you may eat . . ." Then, He proceeded to give them a long list of those clean animals which they could eat. However, God told them also which animals they could not eat, saying: "Nevertheless, of those that chew the cud or have cloven hooves, you shall not eat [since they come under the category of the "detestable"], such as these: the camel, the hare . . . for they are unclean to you" (Deut. 14:1-7).

The only way Israel could be the chosen and holy people to the Lord their God, was if they would obey also the laws of clean and unclean animals and other creatures. Now this was the Torah of which

Muhammad was told he, and Jesus earlier, came to confirm. And yet, as we shall see later, Muhammad recited that his followers can eat the camel, and under duress may eat any other unclean creature. This presents an obvious question! Through the prophet Malachi, God declared: "For I am the Lord, I do not change . . ." (Mal. 3:6). The apostle Paul stated: "Jesus is the same yesterday, today, and forever" (Heb. 13:8). Of his people, Israel, Paul said: " . . . Our fathers were under the cloud, all passed through the sea, all were baptized into Moses in the cloud and in the sea, ALL ATE THE SAME SPIRITUAL FOOD, AND DRUNK THE SAME SPIRITUAL DRINK. FOR THEY DRUNK OF THAT SPIRITUAL ROCK THAT FOLLOWED THEM, AND THAT ROCK WAS CHRIST" (1 Cor. 10:1-4). How plain can this be? The same Law of clean and unclean creatures, as well as the whole Law or Torah, is still in force for those who follow the God of Israel (or Moses) or Christ. The God of Israel and Jesus The Christ are the same identical Personage. Jewish, "Christians," and Muslim' belief to the contrary, notwithstanding! Muhammad, obviously, never knew that—and for that matter, most Christians and Jews do not know this Biblical fact to this day! As for the false notion that Christ told Peter that it is right for His followers to eat unclean creatures, well, let's check up what Peter was really told!

In the book of Acts the true story is recorded for all to read. In short, of Peter, the account tells us that Cornelius, the Roman righteous centurion, had a vision form God. He was told to send for Peter, and so he sent two of his Gentile servants to call on Peter. While they were on their way, Peter was hungry and went on top of the roof to pray. Falling into a trance, he " . . . Saw heaven opened and an object like a great sheet bound at the four corners, descending to him and let down to the earth. In it were all kinds of four-footed animals of the earth, wild beasts, creeping things, and birds of the air. And a voice came to him, 'Rise, Peter, kill and eat.' But Peter said, 'Not so, Lord! For I have never eaten anything common or unclean.' And a voice spoke to him again the second time, 'What God has cleansed you must not call uncommon.' This was done three times. And the object was taken up to heaven again."

King Solomon said: "Those who speak before they hear the whole matter, it is a folly unto them." And so it happened to the unwise! They read this account up to this point and said: "Peter told us that now it is alright to eat every unclean thing." But let the wise hear the whole matter!

How did Peter, a Torah observer religious Jew, explained this "difficult passage" of Scripture?

We read again: "While Peter thought about the vision [it was not real, but a vision], the Spirit [an angel] said to him, 'Behold three [Gentile] men are seeking you. Arise therefore, go down and go with them.'" And so he did. When he arrived, he told Cornelius and his household: "You know how it is unlawful for a Jewish man [didn't say, a Christian] to keep company or go to one of another nation. But God has shown me that I SHOULD NOT CALL ANY MAN [IT'S ANY MAN, NOT ANY ANIMAL!] common or unclean" (Acts, 10:1-28).

No, God or Jesus had never changed the Torah, but ignorant men did! In "the sermon on the mount," Jesus declared emphatically: "Do not think that I came to destroy [or change] the Law [Torah] or the Prophets. I did not come to destroy but to [magnify, amplify, or] fulfill. For assuredly, I say to you, till heaven and earth pass away [did they?], one jot or one title will by no means pas from the Law [or Torah] till all is fulfilled [and how many so called "Christians" believe Jesus in this matter?]. Whoever therefore breaks one of the least of these commandments [not suggestions], and teaches men so, shall be called the least in the kingdom of heaven [and this is the reward of most "Christians" and Muslims, unless they repent of this lie]. For I say to you, that unless your righteousness exceeds the righteousness [not unrighteousness] of the scribes and the Pharisees, you will by no means enter the Kingdom of Heaven" (Mat. 5:17-19).

How plain can this teaching be? And since it is—how can the same God of Moses, of all Christians, of all Muslims, say the opposite to "Christians," to Muhammad—the one who claimed that he came to confirm the Torah and the Gospel? Again, let the Muslim ulama or clerics, and also the "Christian" clergy, tackle this issue!

As for those who consider themselves to be the followers of Jesus Christ, they think, in ignorance, that the Law concerning clean meats is of Moses, hence it is applicable only to the followers of Moses—the Jews. Is it really so? Was Moses the first to receive this Law of God in Sinai or was it so from the beginning? Let's find out!

The son of Adam, righteous Able, offered God of his sheep, not one of his pigs or camels! We read in Genesis, chapter 4:2-4, the following: "Now Able was a keeper of sheep (clean animals), and Cain a tiller of the ground . . . Able also brought of the firstborn [of the sheep] of his flock and of their fat. And the Lord respected Able and his offering." Had it been a pig or a camel, the Lord would not have respected Able's offering!

In the days of Noah, right before the flood that came to destroy the rebels against the Law of God, we read: "Then the Lord said to Noah, come into the ark, you and all your household [not minus the son that, according to Muhammad, refused to come and therefore drowned], because I have seen that you are righteous before Me in this generation. You shall take with you seven each of every CLEAN animal, a male and his female; [but only] two each of animals that are UNCLEAN, male and his female" (Gen. 6:1-2). How plain can it be? Whether it be Adam, Noah, Abraham, Moses, Israel, the prophets of God, Christ, or His true followers: all were obedient to the Law of the God that does not change! Yet Muhammad, claiming to be the "Seal of the prophets," tells his followers that God, in His last revelation to Muhammad, had changed his mind and now allows them to eat those previously "detestable things" that made His people unholy. But then, how could Muhammad know, being illiterate, and not able to read the genuine words of God, though he claimed, repeatedly, that he came "to confirm the Scriptures."

Of such who still think otherwise, God declared: "I have stretched out My hands all day long to a rebellious people [and are you sure you are not one of them?], who walk in a way that is not good, according to their own thoughts [yet have the audacity to claim it is from God]; a people who provoke Me to anger continually to my face; who sacrifice in gardens, and burn incense on altars of brick; who sit among the graves [as many do to this day, thinking the dead can intercede for them before God], and spend the night in the tombs [a popular thing to do even among many Jews]; WHO EAT SWINE'S FLESH [they call it ham nowadays, Easter ham, or bacon], and the broth of abominable things is in their vessels [they call it lobster, shrimp, camel, or whatever]; who say, keep to yourself [don't tell me what's right or wrong], do not come near me, for I am holier then you [Isn't it, in essence, what many "Christians" and "Muslims" have been telling those who truly obey the Law of God or Allah concerning clean and unclean meats?]!" And what does The One who does not change—God—think about such people; and what is the future reward for those who harbor such contemptible attitude toward the Law of God? God continues: "'Behold, it is written before Me: I will not keep silence, but will repay—even repay into their bosom—your iniquities and the iniquities of your fathers [who will be judged in the last day, in the Resurrection] together,' says the Lord" (Isaiah 65:2-7).

And again: "For behold, the Lord will come with fire [the lake of fire—the real "hell fire" God will kindle in the last day for the rebels against His Law] and with His chariots, like a whirlwind, to render His anger with fury, and His rebuke with flames of fire. For by fire and by His sword the Lord will judge all flesh; and the slain of the Lord shall be many. 'Those who sanctify themselves and purify themselves [though God did not do it], to go to gardens after an idol in the midst, EATING SWINE'S FLESH [pork or ham, or a camel, and the like] and the abomination and the mouse, shall be consumed together,' says the Lord" (Isaiah 66:17) God or Allah said these words, not man—and you can argue with this all you want! The verdict had been rendered long ago: those who defile themselves with unclean meats have been placed on death row—it is just a matter of time for the execution to take place!

Again, Muhammad recites: "To Moses We gave the Scriptures, a perfect code for the righteous with precepts about all things, a guide and a benison, do that they might believe on meeting their Lord. And now We have this Book [the Qur'an] truly blessed. Observe and keep from evil, so that you may find mercy and not say: 'The Scriptures were revealed only to two communities [Jews and Christians] before us; we have no knowledge of what they read'; or: 'Had the Scriptures been revealed to us we would have been better guided than they'" (ibid. p. 107, 6:154-157).

The question, again, we might ask here is: Since God revealed His Scriptures to both the Jews and later the Christians; since Muhammad had confirmed these Scriptures in his recital of the Qur'an, then why do we have contradictions, variations—and above all—lack of respect and animosity on the part of many Muslims toward Jews and Christians? Why it is the Muslim community rejects the will of God concerning the land, which the Scriptures state emphatically, belongs, by God's decree, to Israel—forever? In reality, isn't the century old Jew/ Arab conflict a result of the rejection of the Muslim community of the words of their own prophet of Islam, and the "infallible" Qur'an's teachings that the land was given by Allah's decree to Israel—not to Arabs or Muslims? Since they consider Muhammad to be a true prophet, then why do not his followers submit to his teachings concerning the true owners of the entire land of Israel, including Jerusalem?

According to Muhammad, It was God who led Satan into sin. He wrote of Satan and his conversation with God: "'Because You have led me into sin,' he declared, 'I will waylay Your servants as they walk on Your straight path . . ." (Surah, The Heights, p. 109, 7:116-117).

Of Moses, Muhammad recited: "After those [apostles], We sent Moses with our signs to Pharaoh . . . Moses said: 'Pharaoh, I am an apostle from the Lord of the universe, and may tell nothing of God but what is true. I bring you a clear sign from Your Lord. Let the children of Israel depart with me" (ibid. p. 117, 7:103-106). For those who read the words of God to Moses, they can find out where Moses was commanded to bring the children of Israel. It was to the land God promised to Abraham, Isaac, Jacob and his descendants, forever! One cannot claim to be a Muslim, who submits to God on one hand, and then deny His will and that of the prophet Muhammad on the other! Yet this is exactly what all those who pride themselves on being the "true believers" and devout Muslims have been doing to this day!

Again, we read of Moses, as he converses with God, "He replied: 'Moses, I have chosen you of all mankind to make known My messages and My commandments. Take therefore what I have given you, and be thankful.' We inscribed for him [Moses] upon the tablets all precepts [which include the seventh day Sabbath, not Friday or Sunday], and instructions concerning all things, and said to him: 'Observe these steadfastly, and enjoin your people to observe what is best for them" (ibid. p. 120, 7:143-145)

How many Muslims, in the past many centuries, showed respect to the Torah, to the scrolls of the Torah, to the synagogues where Jews read this Torah of Allah?

Speaking of himself, Muhammad recited: "To those that shall follow the apostle [Muhammad]—the unlettered prophet [by his own admission, Muhammad said the Qur'an was given to him, a man who never read a book before]—whom they shall find described in the Torah and the Gospel [in Deut. 18: 15-19. In the New Testament or the Gospel, which Muhammad claimed was given to Jesus by God, this passage was attributed to Jesus]. He will enjoin righteousness upon them and forbid them to do evil. [Since the Scriptures earlier revealed, have abundantly done that—what need was there for more?] He will make good things lawful to them and prohibit all that is foul" (ibid., p. 121, 7:157-159).

In page 122, Muhammad speaks of the children of Israel, while in the desert, and of the obedience and lack of it on the part of some. He writes: "Yet among the people of Moses there are some who preach the truth [though many Muslim clerics claim they are all evil and liars] and act justly" . . . He added: "Ask them about the town which overlooked the sea and what befell its people when they broke the Sabbath [seventh day, the only day God had instituted in Genesis for all humanity]. On their Sabbath [which God called, repeatedly, My Sabbaths] the fish appeared before them floating . . . and when they scornfully persisted in their forbidden ways, We said to them: 'Turn into detested apes'" (ibid. p. 122, 7:158-166).

Obviously, neither Moses or the prophets of Israel, nor the Gospels have ever recorded such an insulting and demeaning slander, but Muhammad did, after the Jewish community in his area refused to accept him as a 'spiritual leader sent by God.' This spirit of contempt, tragically, is still with us today! What took place on the infamous September 11, in America, is a living testimony to this attitude found among some of the Islamic fanatics.

In the Surah, Repentance, we read the following: "Fight against such of those to whom the Scriptures were given [both Jews and Christians] as believe in neither God nor the last day, who do not forbid what God and His apostle [Muhammad] have forbidden, and do not embrace the true faith until they pay tribute out of hand and are utterly subdued. [But what about the followers of the Law and Faith God gave Moses, and those who follow the Gospel, which Muhammad himself confirmed many times?]. The Jews say Ezra is the Son of God [though no Jew who follows Moses only did ever make such a statement], while the Christians say the Messiah is the Son of God. Such are their assertions, by which they imitate the infidels of old. God confound them! How perverse they are!" (ibid. p. 136, 9:27-30). Such was the attitude and teaching of the prophet of Islam and his followers toward the people of the Book—both Jews and the genuine followers of Christ. And so it is to this day

In Page 141, Sec. 9:73, of the same Surah, Muhammad recites: "Prophet, make war on the unbelievers and the hypocrites and deal rigorously with them. Hell shall be their home: an evil fate." This was the basic approach the prophet of Islam, and his followers, had taken against all their enemies: Jews, Christians, and pagans. This attitude toward the nonbelievers is still what motivates devout, orthodox Muslim fundamentalists to this day. This is the attitude of all Islamic terrorists toward Israel, America, and the western world. This is the background to the periodically inflamed desire for a holy war or Jihad among many in the world of Islam. The teaching of "Love your enemy," or "Do good to those who hate you, so that you can be like your Heavenly Father," is not a part of the nature of Islam! Yet father Abraham lived by this Godly precept, and so do his genuine followers.

In the Surah of Repentance, Muhammad recites: "God has purchased from the faithful their lives and worldly goods, and in return has promised them the Garden [of Eden]. They will fight for the cause of God, they will slay and be slain. Such is the true promise which He has made them in the Torah, the Gospel, and the Qur'an" (ibid. p. 145, 9:11-12).

In the same section, Muhammad wrote: "It is not for the prophet or the believers to beg forgiveness for the idolaters, even though they be related to them, after it has become manifest that they have earned the punishment of hell. [Isn't it up to God only to decide that in the last day?] Abraham prayed for his father only to fulfill a promise he had made him. But when he realized he was an enemy of God, he disowned him" (ibid. p. 145, 9:1314).

The truth of the matter is, contrary to rabbinic teachings of this story that Muhammad relied on, the Scripture tells a different story. Let's read it! When Stephens was brought before the chief priests and elders on charges of alleged heresy, he said: "Brethren and fathers, listen: The God of glory appeared unto our father Abraham when he was in Mesopotamia, BEFORE he dwelt in Haran [and this was Abraham's first calling], and said to him, 'Get out of your country and from your relatives, and come to a land that I will show you.' Then he came out of the land of the Chaldeans and dwelt in Haran. And from there, when his father was dead, he moved him to this land in which you dwell" (Acts, 7:2-4). Notice that in the New Testament times the Jews knew that Abraham was still in the land of the Chaldeans when God first called him.

Let's now check this account in Genesis, where we read: "This is the genealogy of Terah: Terah begot Abram [though in the Qur'an, Abraham's father is called, Azar] . . . and Terah took his son Abram and his grandson Lot . . . and they went out with them from Ur of the Chaldeans to go to the land of Canaan; and they came to Haran and dwelt there . . . and Terah died in Haran. Now the Lord had said to Abram: 'Get out of your country, and from your father's house, to a land that I will show you . . .'" (Gen. 11:3; 12:1). This was Abraham's second calling, not the first one, as many believe.

When one compares these two accounts to what the Koran says, the reality of the true story becomes clear: Abraham, certainly, did not disown his father. On the contrary, Abraham followed his father from Ur of the Chaldeans to Haran with the intention of going to the land of Canaan. In the Genesis account, it is Terah who initiates the migration from the old country, with the intent of moving into the land of promise—Canaan. The family remained intact until the death of Tarah in Haran. Obviously, Terah was responding to the first call by God to leave their native land and move into the land of Canaan, but clearly, it was not God's intent for the whole family to be a part of Abraham's future promises at this point. Those unfamiliar with the Biblical narrative, intimately, may tend to make careless assertions to the contrary—and Muhammad, by his admission, never read a book—until he received the Qur'an. This is one major reason why the Jews could not follow the prophet of Islam, since they were intimately familiar with their own Book. They could not, hence, believe in the "unlettered prophet," as he referred to himself. As a result, they had earned his wrath, and that of his followers, to this day. And so Muhammad wrote: "Believers, make war with the [mostly Arab pagans] infidels who dwell around you. Deal firmly with them. Know that God is the righteous" (ibid., p. 146, 9:123). Islamic terror groups are still guided by this teaching to this day. In the Surah, Jonah, Muhammad recited: "This Qur'an could not have been devised by any but God. It confirms what was revealed before it [in Hebrew and New Testament Scriptures] and fully explains the Scriptures. [Though a close scrutiny of the Scriptures would reveal a far different story.] It is beyond doubt from the Lord of the universe" (ibid. p. 150, 10:38)

Of Jesus, Muhammad wrote again: "They say: 'God has begotten a son.' God forbid! Self sufficient is He" (ibid. p. 153, 10:68). Again, if The Qur'an came to confirm the Scriptures or the Gospel, why does it contradict them?

Of Israel, Muhammad wrote: "WE SETTLED THE ISRAELITES IN A SECURE LAND [the land of Israel, not Arab or Palestinian land—a terminology neither the Qur'an nor Muhammad ever ascribed to], and provided them with wholesome things [of which terrorism and those who claim the land belongs to them were never any of them]" (ibid. p. 154, 10:93).

In the next Surah, namely the Hud, Muhammad appeals to the Book of Moses to gain legitimacy. He recites: "Those that desire the life of this world with all its finery shall be rewarded for their deeds in their own lifetime: they shall not be given less. They are those who in the world to come [at the last day] shall earn nothing but the fire. Fruitless are their deeds and vain are all their works. Are they to be compared to those that have received a revelation from their Lord, recited by a witness from Him [Muhammad] and heralded by the Book of Moses, a guide [which Muslims don't read or obey] and a blessing?" (ibid. p. 157, 11:15-20).

Again, as mentioned before, In the New Testament, the disciples of Christ stated that Moses spoke of the coming of The Prophet to whom all would listen. Those who would not heed the words of this Prophet, would be condemned—and this prophet, they asserted, is Jesus. Six centuries later, Muhammad claimed that this statement actually refers to himself, hence all Jews, Christians, and others must heed his words or else! The point is nevertheless the same: Since the Book of Moses is from God or Allah, then all Muslims should read, believe, and obey its teachings. They also should consider the will of Allah concerning His chosen people, Israel, and the land He gave them, as Muhammad confirmed many times. How about that fellow Muslims? Are you willing to submit to Allah, his prophet, and the words you can read in your own Qur'an?

In Pages 159-160, Muhammad recites the story of Noah's ark. In this section, Muhammad recites that one of Noah's sons refused to board the ark and consequently had drowned. According to Moses, however, all of Noah's three sons made it aboard, including their wives and mother. Why the discrepancy? Allah knows! Muhammad explained this variation by reciting: "That which We have now revealed to you is secret history: it was unknown to you and to your [Arab] people. Have patience; the righteous shall have a joyful end" (ibid. p. 160, 11:49).

Of the three angels who came to Abraham, Muhammad recited: "Our messengers came to Abraham with good news. They said: 'Peace!' 'Peace!' he answered, and hastened to bring them a roasted calf. But when he saw their hands being withheld from it, he mistrusted them and was afraid of them" (ibid. pp. 160-161, 11:70).

In the Book of Moses, which Muhammad stated he came to confirm, we read this version: "Then the Lord appeared to him by the terebinth trees of Alon Mamre, as he was sitting in the tent door in the heat of the day. So he lifted his eyes and looked, and behold, three men [one of them was The Lord Himself] were standing by him; and when he saw them, he run from the tent door to meet them, and bowed himself to the ground, and said [addressing God] 'My Lord, if I have now found favor in Your Sight, do not pass on by Your servant . . . and they [the angels replied] 'Do as you have said.'" the account adds: "And Abraham ran to the herd, took a tender and good calf, gave it to a young man, and he hastened to prepare it. So he took butter and milk and the calf which he had prepared, and set it before them; and he stood by them under the tree as they ate" (Gen. 18:1-8).

Muhammad apparently, being illiterate, did not read this account. The Jewish rabbis, on the other hand, some years before the destruction of the Temple, claimed it is not allowed for Jews to eat meat along with dairy products. This was their interpretation of the law that prohibited Israel from seething a kid in his mother's milk. In reality, God prohibited his people to follow the Pagan Gentile practice of killing an animal while it is yet nursing, and therefore still tender, hence, the statement, "in its mother's milk." When they were confronted with the account of God and His angels eating meat and dairy products together, they altered its plain meaning to suit their own prohibition. Before this rabbinic, not God or Moses' prohibition, no such practice was followed in Israel!

The prophet Isaiah, addressing the man-made teachings of the spiritual leaders of his people, stated: "For the Lord has poured on you the Spirit of deep sleep, and has closed your eyes [and made you blind spiritually], namely, the prophets [the spiritual leaders, be they Jews, Christians or others]; and He has covered your heads, namely, the seers." He added: "Inasmuch as these people draw near with their mouths and honor Me with their lips [since that's how God views most spiritual leaders of any religion], but have removed their heart far from Me, and their fear toward Me is taught by the commandments [or Halacha] of men [not God—and that's what much of religion is all about!]. Therefore, behold, I will again do a marvelous work among these people, a marvelous work and wonder; for the wisdom of their wise men shall perish [though we call them "our sages"], and the understanding of their prudent men shall be hidden" (Isaiah 29:1013). Yes, Muhammad did not read the Book he came to "confirm"; most other spiritual leaders misread it, hence the innocent sheep were trapped ever since!

In the Surah, Joseph, we read of Joseph's dreams. His father, telling him to wait on God for the proper interpretation, adds: "Even thus shall you be chosen by the Lord. He will teach you to interpret visions, and will perfect His favor to you and to the house of Jacob, as he perfected it to your forefathers Abraham and Isaac before you" (ibid. p. 166, 12:3-9). In later chapters, when the true identity of Joseph and the rest of his brothers in our day is to be revealed, this statement will become much more meaningful.

In page 174, we read: "This [Qur'an] is no invented tale, but a confirmation of previous Scriptures, an explanation of all things, a guide and a blessing to true believers" (ibid. 12:111). Notice how often Muhammad is appealing to the previous Scriptures in order to legitimize the Qur'an's veracity. Yet most Muslims have no such regard to the Scriptures that came earlier, and to those people who follow them. To this day they do not shy away from desecrating places of worship that house the very Scriptures that Muhammad repeatedly stated he came to confirm—why? Are they truly genuine Muslims; are they believers who truly submit to the will of Allah?

In the Surah, Abraham, Muhammad recites: "Abraham said: 'Lord, make this a secure land" (ibid. p. 182, 14:30). Later Muslim commentators claimed "this" refers to Mecca, yet the Genesis account, which Muhammad came to confirm, places Abraham in the land of Canaan, mostly in the South between Beth El and Beer Sheba.

Again, we read the words of Abraham: "Lord, I have settled some of my offspring in a barren valley near Your Sacred House [Mecca, and according to Muhammad, father Abraham built that house of worship together with his son Ishmael], so that they may observe true worship" (ibid., p. 182, 14:37). Again, the Genesis account traces each movement of Abraham and his son Ishmael in Canaan and elsewhere, and it is very clear: They were nowhere near Mecca, according to the account which Muhammad and the Qur'an "came to confirm."

Since Muhammad persistently claimed "to confirm the Scriptures" which came before him, Muslims should read those Scriptures to understand why non-Muslims have difficulties accepting the Qur'an which came Two Thousand years after Sinai, with additions and contradictions in later years. In doing so, they would be able to objectively compare the earlier Scriptures with those of the Qur'an, and draw the proper conclusions about the true faith of their mutual father Abraham and his other descendants, who are also their own brothers.

In another Surah, The Bee, Muhammad recited: "The apostles [or prophets] We sent before you were but men whom We inspired with revelations and with Scriptures. Ask the people of the Book [Jews and followers of Christ], if you know not" (ibid. p. 190, 16:43).

Again, Muhammad recited: "And we have revealed to you [Muhammad] Our will saying: 'follow the faith of saintly Abraham [and what faith did he practice? Only the Book of Moses can reveal that]: he was no idolater.' The Sabbath [the seventh day Sabbath which God ordained in Genesis, in the Garden of Eden, for all humanity] was ordained only for those who differed about it [?]. On the day of the Resurrection your Lord will Judge their disputes" (ibid. p. 196, 16:123-124). And for those who now deny and defile the ONLY (seventh day) Sabbath God gave humanity in the Garden of Eden, He truly will judge in the Resurrection!

Of father Abraham, who was a righteous man and obedient to the Law of God, which was passed on from the Garden of Eden through the long-living righteous men, God said to Isaac: "Dwell in this land [of Canaan], and I will be with you and bless you; for to you and your descendants [children of Israel, not Ishmael or anyone else] I will give all these lands and I will perform the oath which I swore to Abraham your father. And I will make your descendants multiply as the stars of heaven [though many Muslims now, in defiance of Allah Himself, want them all drowned and dead]; I will give to your descendants all these lands; and in your seed shall all the nations of the earth be blessed [if they accept also the will of God or Allah]; because Abraham [unlike most of his descendants] obeyed My voice and kept My charge, My commandments, My statues and My laws [which many believe they were given first in Sinai, when actually they were ordained first in the Garden of Eden]" (Gen. 26:3-5). Muhammad had no problem with this will of Allah—which he came to confirm—yet how many really know and obey the true and unadulterated faith of Abraham? If Muhammad came to confirm these Scriptures, his followers should also obey them, if they are to be blessed with the seed of Isaac! Abraham, Isaac, Jacob and their descendants, including Christ, who said He was the Lord of The Sabbath, and His true followers to this day, keep the same Sabbath God had first ordained in the Garden of Eden for all humanity—barring none! Do Muslims follow the faith of Abraham, as Muhammad was commanded to? In the day of the Resurrection they shall find out!

In the next Surah, The night Journey, Muhammad recited: "Glory be to him who made His servant to go by night from the Sacred Temple to the farther Temple whose surrounding We have blessed, that we might show him some of our signs" (ibid. p. 197, 17:1). Muslim commentators are divided in their opinions as to the true meaning of this statement. Some take it literally; some feel it is a vision. The "Sacred Temple" is regarded as the one in Mecca. The second Temple, however, or "the farther one," was interpreted years later as being in the site of Jerusalem. From there, later Muslim commentators claimed, Muhammad had ascended up to the Throne of God, accompanied by the angel Gabriel. Is it true or false? Let's find out!

Firstly, in the days of Muhammad there was no Temple in Jerusalem, instead, a Catholic church was standing there at the time of Muhammad's death. And the questions before us are many. How did Jerusalem come to be so Holy to Muslims? Why and when was the myth of al-Aqsa created? Dr. M. Kedar, Dept. Of Arabic, Bar Ilan University writes: "Muhammad the prophet, hardly made any innovations when he established Islam. He used hallowed personages, historic legends, and sacred sites of Judaism, Christianity, and even paganism, by Islamizing them. According to Islam, Abraham was the first Muslim and Jesus and St. John were prophets and Guardians of the second heaven. Many Biblical legends that were familiar to the pagan Arabs before the dawn of Islam, underwent an Islamic conversion and the Qur'an as well as the Hadith [the Islamic oral tradition], are replete with them. The practice of Islamization was performed on places as well as persons: Mecca and the stone—al-Ka'ba—were holy sites of the pre-Islamic pagan Arabs. The Umayyad' Mosque in Damascus and the great Mosque of Istanbul were built on the sites of Byzantine churches that were converted into Mosques—good examples of Islamic treatment of sanctuaries of other faiths. [Remember! Muhammad came also "to confirm the Scriptures" which came before him, not to desecrate or destroy the houses of worship of those who follow such Scriptures!]

"Jerusalem underwent the same process: at first Muhammad attempted to convince the Jews near Medina to join his young community, and in order to persuade them, he established the direction of prayer (kiblah) to be to the north, toward Jerusalem, like the Jews; but when he failed in this attempt, he fought the Jews, killed many of them, and turned the kiblah southward, to Mecca. His abandonment of Jerusalem explains the fact that this city is not mentioned in the Qur'an even once. After Palestine was occupied by the Muslims, its capital was in Ramallah, 30 miles to the west of Jerusalem, since this city meant nothing to them. Islam rediscovered Jerusalem 50 years after Muhammad's death. In 682 CE,

Abd Allah ibn al-Zubayr rebelled against the Islamic rulers of Damascus, conquered Mecca and prevented pilgrims from reaching Mecca for the Hajj. Abd al-Malik, the Umayyad Caliph, needed an alternative site for the pilgrimage and settled on Jerusalem, which was under his control. In order to justify this choice, a verse from the Koran was chosen (Surah 17:1) which states (trans. By Majid Fakhri) & quote, glory to Him who caused His servant to travel by night from the Sacred Mosque to the farthest Mosque, whose precincts we have blessed, in order to show him some of our signs, He is indeed the All Hearing, the All Seeing & quote, "The meaning ascribed to this verse is that, &quote, (al-masjid al-Aqsa) is in Jerusalem and that Muhammad was conveyed there one night (although at that time the journey took three days by camel), on the back of al-Buraq, his magical horse with the head of a woman, wings of an eagle, the tail of a peacock, and whose hoofs reach to the horizon. He entered the horse through the Western wall of the Temple Mount and from there ascended to the seventh heaven together with the angel Gabriel. On his way, he met the prophets of other religions who are the guardians of the second heaven: Adam, Jesus, St. John, Joseph, Seth, Aaron, Moses, and Abraham who accompanied him on his way to the seventh heaven, to Allah, and who accepted him as their master. (See the commentary of Al—Jalalayn on this verse.)

"Thus Islam tries to gain legitimacy over others, older religions [and it is most important to realize that Muhammad himself did not teach these man-made ideas and myths, but his followers did, after his death], by creating a scene in which the former prophets agree to Muhammad's mastery, thus making him 'Khatam al-anbiya' (The Seal of the Prophets). The strange thing here is that this fantastic story contradicts a number of the tenets of Islam: How can a man of flesh and blood ascend to heaven?"

As was stated before, from the writings of Muhammad himself, only Jesus has ascended up to heaven from Jerusalem—all other mortals, including Muhammad himself, return to the dust to await the Resurrection at the last day (p. 229, Sec. 21:34-35).

Dr. Kedar continues: "How can a mythical creature carry a mortal to a real destination? Questions such as these have caused orthodox Muslim thinkers to conclude that the whole story of the nocturnal journey was a dream of Muhammad. Thus Islam tried to 'go one better' then the Bible: Moses 'only' went up to Mount Sinai, in the middle of nowhere, and drew close to heaven, whereas Muhammad went all the way up to Allah, and from Jerusalem itself. So shouldn't we also believe that the al-Aqsa Mosque is in Jerusalem? One good reason is that the people of Mecca, who knew Muhammad well, did not believe this story. Only Abu Bakr, the first caliph, believed him [the Umayyad caliph] and thus was called 'al-sidiq' (the believer). The second reason is that Islamic tradition itself tells us that al-Aqsa Mosque is near Mecca on the Arabian Peninsula. This was unequivocally stated in 'Kitab al-maghazi,'a book by a Muslim historian and geographer al-Waiquidi (Oxford UP, 1966. Vol. 3, pp. 958-9). According to al-Waiquidi, there were two 'masjids' (places of prayers) in al-gi'ranah, a village between Mecca and Ta'if. One was 'the closer' Mosque (al-masjid al-adana) and the other was the 'further mosque' (al masjid al-aqsa), and Muhammad would pray there when he went out of town. This description by al-Waquidi was not 'convenient' for the Islamic propaganda of the 7th century. In order to establish a basis to the awareness of the 'holiness' of Jerusalem in Islam, the Caliphs of the Ummayid dynasty invented many 'traditions,' upholding the value of Jerusalem (fadha'il bayt al-Maqdis), which would justify pilgrimage to Jerusalem. It should be noted that Saladin also adopted the myth of al-Aqsa and those 'traditions' in order to recruit and inflame the Muslim warriors against the Crusaders in the 12th century.

"Another aim of the Islamization of Jerusalem was to undermine the legitimacy of the older religions [which Muhammad did not do, since "he came to confirm the Scriptures" they received earlier and claimed that he believed in them], Judaism and Christianity, which consider Jerusalem to be a holy city. Thus Islam is presented as the only legitimate religion, taking the place of the other two because they had changed and distorted the Word of God, each in its turn. (About the alleged forgeries of the Holy Scriptures, made by Jews and Christians, see the third chapter of: M.J. Kister, 'haddith U 'banl isra 'il wa-la haraja' IOS 2 (1972), pp. 215-239. Kister quotes dozens of Islamic sources)."

In our present time, the Islamization of the whole land is very much evident in the Palestinian school, home, and street. We now quote from The Jews for Truth Now (an ad in The new Republic, Jan. 22, 2001): "Palestinian maps consider all of Israel an illegal settlement. As just one of many examples, on page 64 of the official Palestinian 5th grade schoolbook entitled, "Our Arabic language" #542, the map of Palestine includes the following "settlements": Haifa, Tel Aviv, Jerusalem, Ashkelon, Safed, Beersheba, Eilat and everything in between.

"Beyond the Schools," in the words of the official preacher of Al Aqsa mosque appointed by Chairman Arafat and the Palestinian authority: "The Islamic land of Palestine is one and indivisible. There is no difference between Haifa and Nablus, between Lod and Ramallah, between Jerusalem and Nazareth, between Gaza and Ashkelon" (Palestinian Television, Sept 8, 2000). Which brings up the question: Is the real obstacle to peace the Israeli settlements, or is it the official Palestinian Authority teaching that ALL ISRAEL IS AN ILLEGAL SETTLEMENT?" After the long quotes from Dr. Kedar and the following ad, let's go back now to the writings of the Qur'an.

In page 201, we read: "We have exalted some prophets above others. To David We gave the Psalms [Actually, several Psalms were written by other men and prophets as: Moses, Asaph, Solomon, Ethan and others.]" (The Night Journey, Surah p. 201, 17:52-58). Throughout this work, we shall cover some of these Psalms and see what God had to say about Israel's enemies—known later as Palestinians, Arabs, and Muslims.

After God delivered Israel out of Egypt, and drowned the host of Pharaoh, We read: "We said to the Israelites: 'Dwell in the land [of Israel or Canaan]. When the promise of the hereafter [Resurrection at the last day] comes to be fulfilled, We shall assemble you all together'" (ibid. p. 205, 17:104). Again, we see here the Biblical teaching that all go back to the dust awaiting there the resurrection. Also, Muhammad is confirming that God or Allah, gave the land to His people Israel. In the same section, 17:111, we read: "Say: 'Praise be to God who has never begotten a son; who has no partner in His Kingdom; who needs none to defend Him from humiliation'" (ibid. p. 205).

In the Surah on Mary, we read concerning the birth of John the Baptist: "Then Zacharias came out from the Shrine [Temple] and exhorted his people to give glory morning and evening [Arafat, Islamic clerics, and many Palestinian nowadays are claiming that Israel never had a Temple standing on the Temple Mount. Muhammad and the Qur'an stated otherwise. Who is lying?] To John We said: 'Observe the [Hebrew] Scriptures with a firm resolve.'" These Hebrew Scriptures have not changed to this day, as the latest findings of the Qumran scrolls made very clear, though Muslims and Muhammad in the Qur'an have claimed the Jews have perverted them. Muhammad adds: "We bestowed on him wisdom, grace, and purity while yet a child, and he grew up a righteous man [according to the Law of Moses] . . . Blessed was he on the day he was born and the day of his death; and peace be on him when he is raised to life [in the Resurrection, at the last day]" (ibid. p. 215, 19:12-13). In later chapters, we shall make it abundantly clear, from the Bible, God's teachings concerning the afterlife. Muhammad, as well, had much to recite concerning this issue, and we shall get to it later in this Chapter.

In pages 215-216, we read of a different version concerning Mary and the manner in which her child, Jesus, was born. While she is still a virgin, the angel announces to her the birth of her son. Her people, knowing of the righteousness of her parents, say to her: "'Mary, this is indeed a strange thing! Sister of Aaron . . . '"

Moses' brother, Aaron, and their sister Miriam, seem to be confused here with Mary. Islamic commentators, trying to uphold the honor of Muhammad, claim it means: "Virtuous woman." The Qur'an continues: "'. . . Your father was never a whore-monger, nor was your mother a harlot.' She made a sign to them, pointing to the child. But they replied: 'How can we speak with a babe in the cradle?' Whereupon he [Jesus] spoke and said: 'I am the servant of God . . . blessed was I on the day I was born, and blessed I shall be on the day of my death and on the day I shall be raised to life.' Such was Jesus son of Mary. That is the whole truth, which they still doubt. God forbid that He Himself should have a son!" (ibid. 19:12-35).

What is confusing to any objective reader of the Qur'an, is the question, one of many: How can Muhammad on one hand recite that God, through His Spirit, placed a son in the womb of the still virgin Mary, and on the other, he emphatically claims that God has no son, and it is a blasphemy to say so? In different accounts, we have covered before, pp.46, 76-77, Muhammad recited that Jesus was neither crucified nor put to death by the Jews. He claimed that God took him up to heaven, and if Jesus was taken up to heaven, being just as mortal as any other of God's servants, how come all the rest of humanity, including Muhammad, go back to the dust where they await the Resurrection on the last day?

In Page 219, Sec., 19:88-97, of the same Surah, we read: "Those who say: 'The Lord of Mercy has begotten a son,' preach a monstrous falsehood, at which the very heavens might crack, the earth split asunder, and the mountains crumble to dust. That they should ascribe a son to the Merciful, when it does not become the Lord of Mercy to beget one!

There is none [no son] in the heavens or on earth but shall return to the merciful in utter submission. He has kept strict count of all His creatures, and one by one they shall approach Him [when?] on the day of Resurrection [until then, all are in the dust—dead!]." Again, we read in the Surah, The Prophets: "We inspired all the apostles [prophets] before you, saying: 'There is no god but Me. Therefore serve Me'" (ibid. p. 228, 21:25).

In the following most crucial recitations of Muhammad, which we read earlier, and now repeat, again, for sake of double emphasis, we shall see the real truth behind the selfishly deliberate and politically motivated great myths, that later were invented by his followers, not by the prophet of Islam. These myths are concerning: The supposed holiness of Jerusalem to Islam; the supposed ascending of Muhammad to the seventh heaven from Jerusalem; the supposed supremacy of Muhammad over all of God's previously revealed Scriptures, prophets and Religion that came before him—and the supremacy over the One who is believed to be by many, The Son of God! We shall spell it, as was done in other places, in big caps for sake of emphasis.

Muhammad recited: "NO MAN [no human servant of God; no prophet, except Jesus, who was divine before and after His human experience in the flesh] BEFORE YOU HAVE WE MADE IMMORTAL. IF YOU YOURSELF ARE DOOMED TO DIE, WILL THEY LIVE ON FOREVER? EVERY SOUL SHALL TASTE DEATH. WE WILL PROVE YOU ALL WITH EVIL AND GOOD, TO US YOU SHALL RETURN [IN THE LAST DAY, AT THE RESURRECTION!]" (Surah, The prophets, p. 229, 21:34-5). No "faithful" Muslim cleric today, or for that matter, none in the world of Islam believes these words of their prophet Muhammad as recited in the Koran! They all believe, contrary to his often repeated plain statements that Muhammad ascended up to Heaven, immediately after his death—why?

In his conversations with both Jews and Christian true believers, Muhammad learned also of the true fate of the dead, immediately after their death. Muhammad's relationship with his fellow merchants was influential on his recitations in the Qur'an concerning the correct understanding of the doctrine of Heaven and Hell. At this point, we shall bring only one such example from the Hebrew Scriptures, and in a later chapter, we shall discuss this subject in greater details, from both the Old and New Testaments.

Speaking of the fate of the wicked, and of the after-life, the Psalmist writes: "None of them can by any means redeem his brother [from death and the grave], nor give God a ransom for him—for the redemption of their souls is costly, and it shall cease forever—that he should continue to live eternally, and not see the pit [or the grave]. For he sees wise men die; likewise the fool and the senseless person perish, and leave their wealth to others [since they can't take it with them]. Their inner thought is that their houses will last forever . . . Nevertheless man, though in honor, does not remain [or live forever]; he is like the beast that perish.

"This is the way of those who are foolish, and their posterity who approve their sayings. Selah. Like sheep they are laid in the grave; death shall feed on them; the upright shall have dominion over them in the morning; and their beauty shall be consumed in the grave, for He [God] shall receive me [in the resurrection, at the last day]. Selah. Do not be afraid when one becomes rich, when the glory of his house is increased; for when he dies he shall carry nothing away; his glory shall not descend after him. Though while he lives he blesses himself [not ever considering his mortal state and fate] . . . he shall go to the generations of his fathers; THEY SHALL NEVER SEE LIGHT [in a fictitious heaven or hell, in an after-death location—until they are resurrected in the last day of judgment]. A man who is in honor, yet does not understand, is like the beasts that perish" (Psalm 49:7-20). This was also the understanding of Muhammad in regard to the doctrine of Heaven and Hell!

In page 241, in the Surah, The Believers, Sec., 23:5-20, Muhammad recited: "We created man from an essence of clay [and that man has no immortal soul that goes on living after death, as the pagans had believed, and as "spiritual" leaders of the three religions that sprung from the descendants of Abraham had later accepted and taught their followers. As for man, Muhammad was told]: then [God] placed in him a living germ, in a secure enclosure [the womb]. The germ We made a clot of blood, and the clot a lump of flesh, thus bringing forth another creation."

In the book of Genesis we read: "And the Lord God formed man of the dust of the ground, and breathed into His nostrils the breath of life; and man became a living soul [not that man has a living, immortal soul, but he himself is a living soul with the breath of life from God. In the book of the prophet Zechariah, Chapter 12:1, we read: "Thus says the Lord who stretches out the heavens, lays the foundation of the earth, and forms THE SPIRIT OF MAN within him." This spirit is a life essence, not a person that goes on living after death. Later, we shall have more to say about this most misunderstood subject.

God told the prophet Ezekiel, (20:4, 20): "All souls are Mine; the soul of the father as well as the soul of the son is Mine; the soul that sins shall die [not live on in Heaven or Hell]." And again, in verse 20, we read: "The soul that sins shall die . . ." This was the faith of many Jews and Christians in the East in the days of Muhammad, and he himself believed it, unlike his later followers. And so he recited again: "YOU SHALL SURELY DIE HEREAFTER, AND BE RESTORED TO LIFE [when?] ON THE DAY OF RESURRECTION" (ibid. 23:5-20).

Again, Muhammad recited: "Say: 'Think! If God should enshroud you [which He did] in perpetual night [in the grave] till the day of Resurrection, what other god could give you light? Will you not hear?'" (Surah, The Story, pp. 276-277, 28:71). And again, In the Surah, Pilgrimage, we read: "The hour of doom is sure to come—of this there is no doubt [all Muslims believe otherwise]. Those who are IN THEIR GRAVES [not in Paradise or in hell] God will raise to life" (ibid., p. 235, 22:7). This is very plain! Muhammad, like anyone else, is still in his grave! Like anyone else before and after him, he is still awaiting—in his grave—the call from above at the resurrection, in the last day!

In the life-and-death fight today against the terror groups of bin Laden, and his newly emerging theology of martyrdom and cult of death, or any other groups of hot-headed and misguided Muslim fanatics and suicide bombers—who are willing to blow themselves up, along with their innocent victims, so they can go immediately to paradise—a "lethal, theological nuclear weapon" is available! It does not cost Billions of dollars to produce! It is the "weapon of true Islamic theology." It is powered by "the twin engines" and true teachings of Muhammad and the Qur'an concerning: the land of Israel; the city of Jerusalem; the true teachings of Muhammad and the Koran concerning the state of the dead immediately after death—and finally, the present location of the prophet of Islam—in the grave—awaiting, like any other mortal, the resurrection from the dead in the last day. As we shall see later, when we discuss these same issues in another chapter, this "weapon" is a two-edged sword. What is applicable to Islam is also applicable to all other religions in this and other matters.

The "martyrs" and suicide-bombers that are induced with deceptive promises to blow themselves up are also in the grave—not in Paradise with "thirty or seventy bashful virgins" and other false promises! If

America or Israel, or any other nation, and any honest Muslim, want to deter, demoralize, destabilize, and ultimately destroy the misguided zeal of the suicide bombers and gullible "martyrs" from fanatic Muslims and terror groups—all they have to do is: call upon the "two faithful witnesses of Islam: the revered prophet Muhammad, and the Qur'an's plain teachings on heaven or Paradise. And if Muslims want to be honest all the way—they should also quote Muhammad's teachings in the Koran concerning the "legitimate rights" and ownership of the land of Israel—as promised by God or Allah and repeatedly quoted by Muhammad in "the Holy Qur'an." All concerned parties can use this "lethal weapon" and legitimate propaganda against all misguided, wasted souls and lives—without ever firing one single shot! Why don't we give it a try?

And again, in Section 22:17, we read: "As for the true believers [Muslims], the Jews, the Sabaeans, the Christians, the Magians, and the pagans, God will judge them on the day of Resurrection [not as soon as they die]. God is the witness of all things" (ibid. p. 235). In contrast to Muhammad's belief and the teaching of the Qur'an, many Muslims today declare that true believers exist only in the religion of Islam—all the rest are doomed to go to hell. Where did they get this idea from, one may ask?

In the Surah, The Greeks, Muhammad recited: "You cannot make the dead hear you . . ." (ibid. p. 287, 30:50-54). Why can't they hear? Because they are in the grave! Their spirit (not soul) went back to God who gave it, as Solomon had stated: "Who knows the spirit of the sons of men, which goes upward, and the spirit of the animal, which goes down to the earth?" (Ecclesiastes 3:21). A spirit without a body, the Bible makes very clear, cannot see, hear or speak! For a person to be, one needs a body and a spirit! One can't exist by itself without the other! As the apostle James, half brother of Jesus, stated: "For the body without the spirit is dead, so faith without works is dead also" (James 2:26).

In page 291, we read what Muhammad recited in this Surah: "He governs all, from heaven to earth. AND ALL WILL ASCEND TO HIM IN A SINGLE DAY, a day whose space is a thousand years" (Adoration, Sec., 32:5). The Bible speaks of the one thousand year reign of the Messiah (Revelation 20:4-5). At the beginning of His reign, as we shall see later in the chapter on Jerusalem, the first Resurrection of all those who were true believers will take place. The second Resurrection of all the rest of those who ever lived, will take place at the end of that millennium. Whether Muhammad was referring to this, Allah knows!

Speaking of the Resurrection of the dead, Muhammad recited in the Surah Ya Sin: "The Trumpet will be blown [see I Cor. 15] and, behold, THEY WILL RISE UP FROM THEIR GRAVES [as all of God's prophets and apostles in the Old and New covenants' Scriptures have stated] and hasten to their Lord. 'Woe betide us!' they will say: 'Who has roused us from our resting place? That is what the Lord of Mercy has promised: the apostles have told the truth [but few Jews, Christians and Muslims have ever believed them, and so it is to this day]!' And with but one blast they shall be gathered all before us . . . On that day [not immediately after death, according to the pagan doctrine injected into the Truth by misguided and misinformed religious leaders] the heirs of Paradise will be busy with their joys" (ibid. p. 311, 36:48-57).

In the Surah, The Ranks, we read: "When they [the pagan Arabs] are shown a sign they mock at it and say: 'This is but plain sorcery. What! When we are dead and turned to dust and bones, shall we be raised to life [from the grave, at the last day], we and our forefathers?' Say: 'Yes. And you shall be utterly humbled.' One blast will sound, and they shall see it all" (ibid. p. 311, 36:50-51).

In the Surah, The Throngs, Muhammad recited: "YOU [Muhammad], AS WELL AS THEY [the unbelievers and believers], ARE DOOMED TO DIE [these are the words of Allah, according to the prophet]. Then, on the day of Resurrection [at the last day], you shall dispute in your Lord's presence with one another. Who is more wicked than the man who invents falsehood about God and denies the truth when it is declared to him? (ibid. p. 324, 39:29-35). Genuine Muslim believers should properly read their own Qur'an and not let supposed and misguided religious clerics lead them by the nose away from the true teachings of their own Prophet and Qur'an!

In the Surah, The believers, Muhammad recited concerning the time of the Resurrection of all the righteous servants of God: "Exalted and throned on high, He let the spirit descend at His behest on those of His servants whom He chooses, that He may warn them on the day WHEN THEY SHALL RISE UP FROM THEIR GRAVES [THE PRESENT RESTING PLACE OF MUHAMMAD ALSO! HE TOO IS AWAITING THE RESURRECTION FROM THE DEAD—IN HIS GRAVE!] with nothing hidden from God. And who shall reign supreme on that day?

God, the One, the Almighty. On that day every soul shall be recompensed according to what it did. On that day none shall be wronged [as the gullible "martyrs" and suicide bombers were]. Swift is God's reckoning" (ibid. p. 329, 40:1217).

Again, in the Surah, Kneeling, Muhammad recites: "Say: 'It is God who gives you life and then He causes you to die [not go on living in the imaginary Hell or Paradise immediately after death]. It is He who will gather you all [when?] on the day of Resurrection. Of this there is no doubt; yet most do not know it [and certainly the suicide bombers and "martyrs" don't know it].' It is God who has sovereignty over the heavens and the earth. On the day when the hour strikes [in the last day], those who have denied His revelations will assuredly lose all. You shall see each community [Muslims, Jews, and Christians] on its knees. Each community shall be summoned to its Book, and a voice will say: 'You shall this day be rewarded for your deeds. This Book of Ours speaks with truth against you. WE have recorded all your actions'" (ibid. p. 352, 45:24-29). Certainly most Muslims and fanatic suicide bombers and "martyrs," Jews and Christians, do not know it—yet! And they do not believe, because their spiritual leaders have led them astray, but not for long!

In the Surah, Qaf, we read: "On that day [the Judgment at the last day], We shall ask Hell: 'Are you full?' And Hell will answer: 'Are there anymore?' And, not far thence, Paradise shall be brought close to the righteous. We shall say to them: 'Here is all that you were promised. It is for every penitent and faithful man, who fears the Merciful, though he is unseen, and comes before Him with a contrite heart. Enter it in peace. THIS IS THE DAY OF IMMORTALITY.'" (Ibid. p. 366, 50:27-35).

It is very obvious what Muhammad is reciting here in plain words. His teaching to all Muslims is: Man is not to become immortal or go to Paradise, and that includes himself, immediately after death, but at the last day, after the judgment! It is at that day that immortality is achieved, not a day before! Yet now, as in the past many centuries, Muslims were led to believe otherwise, contrary to the plain teachings of their own prophet and the "infallible" Qur'an—Why? The Bible, as we shall see later, taught exactly the same, not the pagan or Hellenistic doctrine of the immortality of the soul and the immediate ascension to Heaven or Hell after death, as most Jews and Christians believe it to be!

God told Adam and Eve: "Of every tree in the garden, you may freely eat, but of the tree of the knowledge of good and evil you shall not eat,

FOR IN THE DAY THAT YOU EAT OF IT YOU SHALL SURELY DIE." (Genesis 2:16-17).

This is what God said, but what did He mean? Did He mean, "You are as good as dead," or did He mean something else? Obviously he meant, as was explained later in the Bible, "you shall be as good as dead in your sins!" And this is where Satan begun introducing his deception and willful lie, and the false doctrine of the immortality of the soul! In a later conversation with mother Eve, Satan, as a shrewd salesman, told her: "YOU WILL NOT SURELY DIE" (Genesis 3-4). Satan, in essence was convincing gullible mother Eve, as he did later most of her descendants, that she has an immortal soul—the real person within her—which lives forever. He convinced her this soul would go on living, immediately after the death of the body, in a different spirit form. Since that time, this willful and lever lie and deception was passed on and believed by those who have strayed off from the path of the Truth and Light of the Maker of us all. In later chapters, we shall have more to say concerning this most confusing issue to many religions.

Again, speaking about the Resurrection, in the Surah, Qaf, Muhammad recited: "Listen on the day when the Crier will call from near; the day when men will hear the fateful cry. ON THAT DAY [not immediately after death] THEY WILL RISE UP FROM THEIR GRAVES. On that day [in the last day of Judgment] the earth will be rent asunder over them [those who are in the grave], AND FROM IT [not from Heaven or Hell] they shall emerge in haste. To assemble them is easy enough for us" (ibid. pg. 367, 50:43-44). Later, we shall see that both the Old and New covenants' Scriptures taught exactly the same doctrine. In this area, Muhammad and the Koran are in perfect agreement with "the previous Scriptures" the prophet of Islam claimed he "came to confirm and believed."

In the Surah, She Who Pleaded, we read: "On the day [the last day] when God restores them all to life He will inform [or judge] them of their actions" (ibid. pg. 384, 58:6). Here it is spoken about those who opposed Muhammad, nevertheless, such is the fate of all: they must all await in the grave until the last day.

In the Surah, Cheating, Muhammad recited: "The unbelievers claim they shall not be raised to life [in the last day]. Say: 'Yes, by the Lord, you shall assuredly be raised to life! Then you shall be told of all that you have done. That is easy enough for God.'" Then Muhammad added: "The day on which He will gather you, the day on which you shall be gathered—that shall be a day of cheating [of your reward, since you don't believe]. Those that believe in God and do what is right shall be forgiven their sins and admitted to gardens watered by running streams, where they shall dwell forever [up to that day, they all were in the grave, as Muhammad and everyone else before and after him, with the exception of Christ the Messiah]. That is the supreme triumph [not the fabricated one many believe in to this day]. But those that disbelieve and deny Our revelations [including: the Torah, the Prophets, the Gospel] shall be the inmates of fire . . ." (ibid. p. 395, 7:10).

Speaking of the fate of the unbelievers, Muhammad recited in the Surah, The Ladders, the following: "Are they each seeking to enter a garden of delights? . . . Let them play until they face the day they are promised; the [last] day when they shall rush forward from their graves, like men rallying to a standard, with down cast eyes and countenances distorted with shame. Such is the [last] day they are promised" (ibid. p. 406, 70:36-44).

Again, in the Surah, Noah, Muhammad recited: "God has brought you forth from the earth like a plant, and to the earth He will restore you [as he told Adam: "For dust you are and unto dust shall return]. Then He will bring you back afresh [from the grave]" [ibid. p. 407, 71:18-21].

Speaking of the Day of Judgment in the last day, Muhammad recited in the Surah, The Resurrection, these words: "I swear by the day of Resurrection, and by the self reproaching soul! Does man think We shall never put his bones together again? Indeed, We remold his very fingers! Yet man would ever deny what is to come. 'When will this be,' he asks, 'the day of resurrection?' . . . No, there shall be no refuge. For to your Lord, on that [last] day, he shall return. Man shall on that day be told all his deeds, from first to last . . . On that day there shall be joyous faces, looking towards their Lord. On that day there shall be mournful faces, dreading some great affliction (ibid. pp. 412-413, 75:1-22).

Muhammad and the Qur'an, just like the Hebrew and new Testament Scriptures, make it very plain: at the moment of death all go back to the dust, not Heaven or Hell! At the time of the Resurrection from the dead, at the last day, all shall return to the Lord for the judgment day.

Muhammad adds, in the Surah, Those That Are Sent Forth, the following: "When the stars are blotted out; when the apostles [all of God's servants and messengers] are brought together [from the grave] on the appointed [last] day—when will all this be? UPON THE DAY OF

JUDGEMENT! Would that you knew what the Day of Judgment is! . . . On that day woe betide the disbelievers! HAVE WE NOT MADE THE EARTH A HOME FOR THE LIVING AND FOR THE DEAD? . . . On that day woe betide the believers! Such is the Day of Judgment. WE WILL ASSEMBLE YOU ALL, TOGETHER WITH PAST GENERATIONS."(ibid. p. 415, 77:1-41). These are very plain words! This is where all of us are placed, from Adam to the last one of us—in the grave or earth—awaiting the Resurrection at the last day!

In the Surah, The Tidings, Muhammad recites words concerning the fate of the believers and the unbelievers. We read: "Fixed is the day of judgment. On that day the trumpet shall be sounded, and you shall come in multitudes."

Compare this statement with the words of the apostle Paul: "'Behold, I tell you a mystery: we shall not all sleep [or die], but we shall be changed—in a moment, in the twinkling of an eye, at the last trumpet. For the trumpet will sound, and the dead [who are in their graves up to that moment, not in Heaven or Hell] will be raised [or resurrected from the dead] incorruptible, and we shall be changed. For this corruption must put on incorruption, and this mortal must put on immortality [since we don't have anything immortal about us now—the pagan concept notwithstanding]. For this corruption must put on incorruption, and this mortal must put on immortality. So when this corruptible has put on incorruption, and this mortal has put on immortality, then shall be brought to pass the saying that is written: 'Death is swallowed up in victory'" [quoted from Isaiah 25:8] (I Corinthians 15:51-54).

Muhammad continues: "The gates of heaven shall swing open, and the mountains shall pass away and become like vapor [both the Hebrew and New Testament Scriptures described the same events in similar words] . . . As for the righteous [after describing the fate of the unbelievers], they shall surely triumph. Theirs shall be gardens and vineyards, AND HIGHBOSOMED MAIDENS FOR COMPANIONS: A TRULY OVERFLOWING CUP [the martyr's dream] . . . That day is sure to come" (ibid. pp. 416-417, 78:1-39).

Again, Muhammad recited concerning the trumpet at the last day, in the Surah, The Soul Snatchers, these words: "On the day the trumpet sounds its first and second blast, the hearts shall be filled with terror, and all eyes shall stare with owe. They say: 'When we are turned to hollow bones, shall we be restored to life? A fruitless transformation!' But with one blast they shall return [from the graves beneath] to the earth's surface" (ibid. p. 417, 79:1-10).

Speaking of the same subject and event, the Patriarch Job asked: "If a man dies, shall he live again? All the days of my hard service I will wait [in the grave], till my change comes [as the apostle Paul stated later: "we shall all be changed"]. You shall call, and I will answer You; You shall desire the works of Your hands" (Job, 14:14-15).

In a later chapter, we shall come back, again, to this subject and its relevant statements in the Hebrew and the New Testament Scriptures. At the time Muhammad was given the Qur'an, many, in both the Jewish and Christian communities in the Middle East, had still, basically, the same understanding concerning this subject. With the passage of time, the three communities, gradually and fully, adopted the pagan teachings and understanding concerning the immortality of the soul and the doctrine of Heaven and Hell. And so it is still accepted to this very day!

In the following Surah, He Frowned, Muhammad recites: "From what did God [Allah] create him? From a little germ He created him and gave him due proportions. He makes his path smooth for him, then causes him to die [not go to Heaven or Hell immediately after death] and stows him IN A GRAVE. HE WILL SURELY BRING HIM BACK TO LIFE WHEN HE PLEASES [yet if one is alive in Heaven or hell, what need is there to bring him back to life?]. Yet he declines to do His bidding" (ibid. p. 419, 80:1822).

Again, speaking of the fate of the righteous and the unbelievers, Muhammad recites in the Surah, The Unjust: "Do they not think they will be raised to life upon a fateful day, the day when all mankind will stand before the Lord of the universe? . . . On that day woe betide the disbelievers who deny the last judgment [and the fact that ALL ARE DEAD AND IN THE GRAVE UNTIL THE LAST DAY]! None denies it except the evil transgressor who, when Our revelations are recited to him, cries: 'Fables of the ancients!' No! Their own deeds have drawn a veil over their hearts. No! On that day a barrier shall be set between them and their Lord. They shall burn in Hell, and shall be told: 'This is the scourge that you denied!'" (ibid. p. 421, 83:1-20).

Those who fabricated the myth that Muhammad, as well as other servants of God, went to heaven; those who claim to this day that Jerusalem is a Holy City [al-Quds], because Muhammad has ascended up to the seventh Heaven, "riding on his beloved horse" through the hole in the Rock, over which the Mosque of Omar was erected, are in blatant defiance of the words of their own prophet and his "infallible" word (as they believe) received from Allah through the angel Gabriel! Of such "believers," Muhammad recited: "'They shall burn in hell, and shall be told: 'This is the scourge that you denied!'"

Of his unbelieving fellow Arabs, Muhammad recited: "Why then do they not have faith, or kneel in prayer when the Qur'an is read to them? [Many Muslims kneel in prayer but do not believe ALL that is written in the Qur'an and their own prophet—yet they claim to submit to Allah.] The unbelievers indeed deny it [since those who deny the words of the prophet concerning the grave, deny the Qur'an]; but God knows best the falsehood they believe in. Therefore proclaim to all a woeful doom, save those who embrace the true faith and do good works; for theirs is an unfailing recompense" (Surah, The Rending, p. 422, 84:16-25).

Those Muslims who believe in the myth of Muhammad's ascension to Heaven from Jerusalem, deny the "true faith" given to them! You can't have it both ways! Either your claim is true and the words of your prophet, the "infallible" Qur'an, and Allah are fables—or your claims concerning Muhammad and the Jerusalem issue are fables! Make up your mind!

Speaking of life and death, Muhammad recited again in the Surah, The Nightly Visitant: "Surely He has power to bring him back to life [from the grave], on the [last day of judgment] day when man's consciences are searched" (ibid. p. 423, 86:1-10). Again, concerning all that is written about the fate of the righteous and the dead, Muhammad recited in the Surah, The Most High: "All this is written in earlier Scriptures of Abraham and Moses" [As well as in the Psalms, the Prophets, the New Testament, and the Writings of the true followers of God and Christ.] (ibid. p. 424, 87:19).

In the Surah, The War Steeds, Muhammad recited: "He loves riches with all his heart [the wicked]. But is he not aware that when the dead are thrown out from their graves [where all are until the Resurrection] and men's hidden thoughts are laid open, their Lord will on that day have full knowledge of them all?" (ibid. p. 431, 100:1-11).

How many Muslims are or were willing to believe these plain words of their "infallible prophet of Islam?" How many Muslims are really reading and hearing the "infallible" words of their Qur'an? Well, only Allah knows! In reality, those who taught and are still teaching; those who believed and do still believe such anti-Qur'an statements are a disgrace to the teachings of the Qur'an, of the prophet of Islam, and above all, Allah! Again, this is what the prophet of Islam, who is considered to be infallible by all Muslims, had to say in the Qur'an about his own mortality, and that of all humanity. The question before us is very obvious: either he is right, or his followers are. Both can't be right!

Speaking of those who do not believe the truth, The Apostle Paul stated: "Indeed, let God be true but every man a liar" (Romans 3:4). In like manner, one may say: "let Muhammad be true in what he said in the Qur'an but those who distort his writings be liars." Muhammad never taught that Jerusalem is holy to Islam—His followers did! Muhammad never ascended up to the seventh heaven riding on an imaginary horse, since he himself had repeatedly and consistently recited in the Qur'an the reality of his own mortality and inevitable death. Muhammad never claimed the land given to Israel, forever, by God or Allah, to be a sacred Arab land—His followers did after his death. If Muhammad, the great prophet of Islam is dead, awaiting the Resurrection at the last day, Just like any other mortal, what makes the Arab "martyrs" think that upon their death they will immediately be taken up to Paradise and be granted those "thirty bashful and high bosomed virgins?" What a cruel hoax to play on ignorant, gullible, young, and misguided miserable souls! These young and ignorant "martyrs" waste their own lives, while those who dupe them to do it are reaping the "glory" of vain hopes!

In page 230, Sec., 21:47-54, we read: "We showed Moses and Aaron the distinction between right and wrong [yet Muslims do not read Moses to know this distinction], and gave them a light and an admonition for righteous men: those who truly fear their Lord, although unseen, and dread the terror of the final hour" (ibid.).

By Muhammad's own testimony, servants of God like Zecharias, his son John, and Jesus, were righteous men who kept the Law [or Torah] of God as transmitted to Moses. The question one might ask is: in their time, was that Law of God already "perverted" by the Jews, as was and is claimed By Muhammad and his followers? And if not, since that was the source of their righteousness, and since that very Law and the prophets are still the same today, as was confirmed by the dead sea scrolls, albeit with minor changes, then how can anyone claim that it was perverted? Let's also consider the fact that the Hebrew Scriptures were preserved by the Jews faithfully, in spite of the fact they contain, from Moses to the last prophet, most severe condemnations and diatribes against the spiritual and civil leaders, and against the common people. In fact, the Hebrew Scriptures contain very few good comments about the people of Israel—nevertheless, the Jews did preserve them diligently. What people on earth would preserve such a record of self—condemnation if they were interested in perverting it? The Qur'an, certainly, did not follow such noble example! The new Testament Scriptures are, in like manner, filled with condemnations against believers who did not live up to the Faith revealed to them. Again, we don't see such condemnations in the Qur'an against misbehaving believers. Why is it so? This is one great convincing proof that both the Old and New Covenant Scriptures are genuine, not perverted, as Muhammad and his followers have claimed. The tragic reality is that among all the children of Abraham, and the three religions that sprung from the Faith of the Patriarch, only few are genuine believers—the rest think they are genuine.

Jesus Christ declared: "Do not think that I came to destroy the Torah or the prophets. I did not come to destroy but to fulfill. Foe assuredly, I say to you, till heaven and earth pass away, one jot or one tittle will by no means pass from the Torah till all be fulfilled" (Mat. 5:17-18). Since heaven and earth are still with us—so are the same genuine Scriptures!

Speaking of Abraham's trials, we read: "We have delivered him and Lot, and brought them to the land Which We had blessed for all mankind. We gave him Isaac, and then Jacob for a grandson [notice, he does mention Ishmael in connection with the land that was finally given to Jacob and his descendants]; and We made each a righteous man. We ordained them leaders to give guidance at Our behest, and enjoined on them charity, prayer and almsgiving. They served none but Ourselves" (ibid. p. 231, 21:71-73). Again, we read: "And tell of David and Solomon . . . We bestowed on both of them wisdom and knowledge. To Solomon We subjected the raging wind: it sped at his bidding to the land [of Israel] which We had blessed" (ibid. p. 232, 21:78-81).

In pages 233-234, we read: "We wrote in the Psalms [that is still widely read to this day in the Jewish and Christian community] after the Torah was revealed: 'The righteous among My servants shall inherit the earth [not Heaven, as Jesus had confirmed in the Sermon on the Mount].' That is an admonition to those who serve us" (ibid. p. 21:105-106). God was here, through David, talking specifically about His people and land of Israel. When the Messiah returns to His people, as was stated in many prophecies, He would restore Israel to their land—the land of Israel—not to Arab lands!

In the next Surah, Pilgrimage, we read of Muhammad's teaching concerning the Sacred Mosque in Mecca. He recited: "When We prepared for Abraham the site of the Sacred Mosque We said: 'Worship none besides Me. Keep My House clean for those who walk around it, and those who stand upright or worship.' Exhort all men to make the pilgrimage [not to Jerusalem but to Mecca]" (ibid., p. 236, 22:26-28). Muhammad recited the Qur'an about 2500 years after Abraham had died. God gave Moses the Torah 430 years later. In the Torah, in the book of Genesis, God Himself gave Moses the detailed account of the life of Abraham. Yet nowhere in that personal and direct revelation of God to Moses do we read anything about Abraham and the Sacred Mosque! Did God "forget" all about it then and only in the days of Muhammad "remembered" it again? Allah knows!

Notice again that Muhammad directed his followers to regard Mecca as the only Sacred Site, hence the only place for the yearly pilgrimage to the only Holy Mosque to Islam! Certainly, Jerusalem, as a Holy Site or a Holy Temple, which was not in existence in his day, was never on the mind of Muhammad. This fabricated story of Muhammad's ascent to Heaven was invented, in later times, by the politically motivated "believers" who did not believe their own prophet and his clear teachings in the Qur'an concerning his own death, and the last Day of Judgment and Resurrection. That's why we have a Middle East conflict, which will not be resolved until the day of the resurrection. Regardless of the well intentioned and not so well intentioned efforts to resolve the age-old bloody conflict—until all the children of Abraham become genuine followers in his footsteps, rivers of blood shall continue to saturate the parched lands of that region of chronic contentions.

Speaking of eating animals, Muhammad recited: "For every community We have ordained a ritual, that they may pronounce the name of God over the cattle which He has given them for food. Your God is one God . . ." Then we read this: "We have the camels a part of God's rites. They are of much use to you. Pronounce over them the name of God as you draw them up in line and slaughter them; and when they have fallen to the ground eat of their flesh and feed the uncomplaining beggar and the demanding suppliant. We subjected them to your service, so that you may give thanks. Their flesh and blood does not reach God; it is your piety that reaches Him. [In other words: the issue of holiness does not mean anything to God anymore.] Thus has He subjected them to your service, so that you may give glory to God for guiding you."

Again, as we mentioned earlier, God's teaching concerning clean and unclean meats has been the same since the Garden of Eden. To Moses, He said that all unclean creatures, Israel is forbidden to eat, are an abomination to Him. If they are to be holy as He is Holy, they must abstain from all unclean creatures He forbade in the Book He gave to Moses (Leviticus 11 & Deuteronomy 4). Why should the God that claimed that He does not change, alter His mind and feelings toward this matter of holiness when it comes to other descendants of Abraham, namely, in this case, Muhammad and his followers?

In the same page, we also read: "Permission to take arms is hereby given to those who are attacked, because they have been wronged. God has power to grant them victory: those who have been unjustly driven from their homes, only because they said: 'Our Lord is God.' [This was said concerning Muhammad's followers in his early days.] Had not God defended [and not called for the destruction of] some men by the might of others, MONASTERIES, AND CHURCHES, SYNAGOGUES and MOSQUES, in which His praise is daily celebrated, would have been utterly destroyed." [How come most of Muhammad's followers, in the next generations, and to this day, do not adhere to this teaching of their prophet and Qur'an?] But whoever helps God [and serves Him in any religious sanctuary] shall be helped by Him" (ibid. p. 237, 22:32-40).

What a far cry these words are from the devouring sword of Islam against "the unbelievers" and their places of worship! Certainly, the Qur'an and the words recited by the prophet of Islam are not the guiding light of most Muslims—past and present! That's why many "Muslims" did not and do not to this day hesitate to destroy, desecrate, or treat with contempt holy sites of other religions—contrary to the teachings Muhammad had recited in their own Qur'an; contrary to the will of Allah, as Muhammad had recited. And who are the greatest offenders but the clerics who often incite the gullible "believers," contrary to the will and teachings of their prophet, their Qur'an, and their Allah!

In the 2000 Al-Aqsa intifada or uprising, Palestinian mobs, incited by their Muslim clerics, have desecrated and destroyed the tomb of the Patriarch Joseph and the synagogue in it. A photo that appeared in an article, titled, "Holy targets," in the Biblical Archaeology Review, dated Jan/Feb. 2001, shows a part of the mob that ransacked the tomb of Joseph, dancing over sacred religious articles, while others were smashing gleefully anything in sight. The writer of the article states: "The hate, the fierceness of the anger, the crowd's behavior was new, but unfortunately the lack of respect for ancient Jewish sites was not. Within days of the destruction of Joseph's tomb, another stone-throwing mob destroyed an ancient synagogue in Jericho with a simply lovely mosaic floor that had been pristine in condition. Dating to the Byzantine period, the mosaic featured a stylized Torah ark in the center and, just below, a circle containing a three-footed menorah, a shofar (ram's horn), a lulav (palm frond used on the festival of Sukkot) and a Hebrew inscription from Psalm 125: shalom al Yisroel, "Peace upon Israel." The article mentions many other flagrant violations against religious Jewish sites, including many on the Temple Mount. Though Islamic clerics on the Temple Mount have been indicted for many such violations, because of the politically sensitive issues, none has been punished. The followers of Islam, especially the religious leaders, obviously have very little respect for the words of their own prophet Muhammad, the "infallible" Qur'an, and above all: the one they believe had ultimately inspired it—Allah. Denials are meaningless, but actions infested with unbridled venomous hatred speak louder than words!

In page 240, we read: "Fight for the cause of God [against the pagan Arabs] with the devotion due to Him. He has chosen you, and laid on you no burdens in the observance of your faith, He has given you the name of Muslims [those who submit to the will of Allah and are true believers, not "make-believe believers"], so that the apostle may testify against you [the ones who lie in his name and invent false doctrines, such as the one about Muhammad going up to heaven from Jerusalem and the like], and that you yourself may testify against your [Arab] fellow-men" (ibid. 22:78)

In the Surah, The believers, page 242, 23:49, we read: "We gave Moses the Book, so that they [Israel] might be rightly guided." And so to this day, those who follow Moses, not Rabbinic Judaism, are rightly guided. Those who are not, follow the teachings of men! Muhammad recited again: "We have given them their Scriptures: yet to their Scriptures they pay no heed [and this is also applicable to most Muslims]" (ibid. p. 243, 23:71).

In page 244, we read: "We have revealed to them the truth; but they are surely lying. Never has God begotten a son, nor is there any other God besides Him" (ibid. 23:90-91). On one hand, Muhammad says he came to confirm the Scriptures—which include the Gospel—on the other hand, he recites otherwise! Why? Allah knows! Again, we read: "We gave the Book to Moses and assigned to him his brother Aaron as a helper" (Surah, al-Furqan, p. 255, 25:32-40).

In page 265, in the Surah The ant, Muhammad recites: "We bestowed knowledge on David and Solomon. The two said: 'Praise be to God who have exalted us above many of His believing servants.'" (ibid. 27:12-18). Notice that Muhammad, unlike many Palestinian Muslims today, acknowledges David and Solomon's kingdoms, and obviously The Great Temple they prepared and built in their day. Many Palestinians and their clerics are willfully spreading the misinformation that neither the first Temple of Solomon, nor the second Temple ever stood on The Temple Mount. At the same time, they are busily engaged in destroying any evidence to the contrary. Muhammad would have never done that! In the Surah, The Spider, he recited concerning those who pervert the truth: On the day of Resurrection they shall be questioned about the lies they told" (ibid).

Much more can be presented here about the subject, but why not, my fellow Muslims, just read carefully the direct words of your own prophet Muhammad and be illuminated by them.

In the next chapter, we shall discuss the migrations and present whereabouts of many of the descendants of brother Edom in the "New World."

CHAPTER 10

EDOM AND THE SPANISH CONNECTION

In this author's work, as previously mentioned, "Middle East," the historic struggle between the descendants of the two twins—Jacob and Esau—was thoroughly documented. We have discussed, in detail, the Biblical and historic accounts that reveal the nature of the conflict between Esau and Jacob. These accounts dealt with an ancient rivalry, from the genesis of the conflict in Rebekah's womb, to the fall of Judah in A.D. 70. Yet our story does not end with this account, which was one of the bleakest periods in Judah's tumultuous history. Destiny has decreed that much more blood, conflict, rivalry and animosity would continue to haunt the inseparable twins. The ominous words of father Isaac were to reverberate for generations to come, as rolling thunders in the fiery skies of Jacob and Esau's lands. The rivalry had to go on as long as defiance, struggle for a lost inheritance, and hatred ruled in the heart of Esau.

Recorded history has kept pace with Edom's bloody conflict, and the love-hate relationship with Judah. Yet Esau has not lost much in his struggle with Judah. Brother Judah did not inherit the birthright, Joseph his brother did. For Edom to be locked in a deadly struggle for his lost birthright, he had also to live near the birthright possessor—Joseph. He also had to be engaged in a struggling embrace with the rest of the brothers of Joseph. They too, were to inherit a good portion of the promises and blessings, which in Esau's 'humble opinion' belonged only to him. Since the prophecies and blessings given to Jacob and Esau linked their fate, the inseparable twins had to live side by side throughout their eternal struggle. Did that ever happen? Do we see Joseph and his brothers engaged in a global match for world supremacy against uncle Edom? What can the hazy and mysterious pages of history reveal to us about the twins—who were loved by their parents but hated by each other?

To find out the whereabouts of the present descendants of Joseph and his brothers, please consult the work mentioned above. For sake of space, we shall not discuss them in this work. Instead, let's find out about "lost" Esau whose identity is more relevant to the subject at hand. History may forsake her children momentarily, but the God of Israel does not forget His children. He declared long ago: "Can a woman forget her suckling child and not have compassion on the son of her womb? Surely, they may forget, yet I will not forget you." Then He added: "For a mere moment have I forsaken you; but with great mercies I will gather you" (Isaiah 49:15, 54:7).

The identity of much of Esau's modern descendants, linked to Joseph's destiny, is of utmost importance to the final resolution of the longest conflict in history. The history of the Western world and the meteoric rise to world prominence of the British and American peoples can never be properly understood without the Edomite link. In ancient times, when all of Israel's tribes were still in their lands, Esau was also in close proximity. As the tribes, after their captivities, begun to migrate into Western Europe and later the "New World," uncle Esau was already there to "greet them." When Israel left Egypt on his way toward the promise land, uncle Edom came against him with the sword. When the birthright tribes—Ephraim and Mannaseh, children of Joseph—reached their destination in Spain, before they finally settled in their lands in the British Isles, Esau was there also. He was always one step ahead of his younger brother Jacob, but was also soon supplanted by his, destined-to-be master and brother. The story in the New World was no different.

With the expansion of the birthright inheritance, we find Jacob on the march. He again became the master, while Esau became subservient to him. It is no coincidence that both Spain and Latin America do harbor similar anti-Anglo-Saxon feelings. Twenty Latin countries, comprising one sixth of all land surface of the earth, sit across the borders of Jacob. As their remaining brothers in the Middle East, they find themselves ejected from lands they once controlled and possessed. Besides the territory of the original thirteen colonies, the Spaniards once occupied the whole land now called the United States. After the discovery of the New World, at the apex of the Spanish colonial power, the world belonged to Spain and Portugal. Yet, the birthright and blessings were given to Jacob and his descendants, not to Esau. We shall have more to say about this present reality of the past few centuries later in this chapter. But how did we get from the Middle East into this strange modern reality? How do we make a connection between Edom and the Spanish world? Let's backtrack into the dark recesses of an ancient historical link between Edom and the Spanish world.

Before we begin our investigation into the past history of Edom and his migration into the Iberian or Hebrew peninsula, we must understand certain facts: a major gap in world history does exist. Today, we are left with only few fragments of the chronicles of ancient times. Around the first captivity of the nation of Judah, about 500 B.C., a major world war had incinerated many civilizations and their records of history. These were the days of king Nebuchadnezzar (Jeremiah 25). In another period of world upheaval, (300 B.C. and first century after Christ), many libraries were burned down to the ground by conquering armies. The records of history of many nations went up in smoke. Valuable accounts and historic accounts were destroyed, except in the British Isles, Scandinavia, and other remote areas.

In a later period (A.D. 500) The Emperor Justinian's warrior, Belisarius, ravaged the known world for the purpose the new empire's boundaries. Millions of people were slaughtered and more records of history were destroyed, according to the historian Precopius. At the heels of the marching armies of the Huns and Vandals, as well as the Israelite Goths, widespread plagues ravaged the Roman Empire. Three quarters of the Roman world was decimated in one generation. The world was in chaos. Records of history and books mattered little in those perilous days. Much knowledge of Western Civilization was obliterated. Then came the Dark Ages. Still, some fragments of history were left intact. The Catholic monks, shut from the world behind their thick walled monasteries, became the only preservers of history. Unfortunately, they also became the censors of knowledge. What the Catholic Church did not see fit to preserve, it destroyed. What we are left with today is, mostly, the bits and pieces of the 'labor of love' of the Catholic monks.

Without the Bible as a guiding light to ancient history, we would be lost in the dark and misty ages of bygone eras. Because of lack of biblical knowledge many historians are still in the dark concerning many events of history. The chief area of darkness is the identity of the twins of mother Rebekah, and their destiny and location throughout history. Those who reject the Bible as a historic document, still wander aimlessly in a spiritual wilderness. They are confronted with the confusion of a maze of historic documents and what they find in the corridors of archeology. For those who can submit their minds to the rays of light of the Biblical document, the journey into the pages of history is on.

Let us now check out some remnant historical documents that would help establish the link between the migrating Edomites and their new homeland—Iberia—the land of the Hebrews. Sir Isaac Newton mentions the migration of the Siculi into Sicily about the 27th year of Solomon's reign. This migration will help us date the Iberian migration of the people of Edom from their ancient homelands into the "new world." Newton wrote: "Thucydides tells us further that the Greeks began to come into Sicily almost three hundred years after the Siculi had invaded that island with an army out of Italy; suppose it 280 years after and the building of Syracuse 310 years before the end of the Peloponnesian War; and that invasion of Sicily by the Siculi will be 590 years before the end of the war that is in the 27th year of Solomon's reign or thereabout" (Newton 1728:18).

The Siculi invaded Sicily and replaced another group that had until then inhabited the island. Who were those inhabitants and how long had they been in that island? "The Sikeloi [or Siculi, Dion. 1.22] retreated into Cicily, which was then inhabited by the Sikanoi, an Iberic people, who not long before had fled into the island from the Ligues and given it the name of Sikania. Some writers fixed the migration of the Sikeloi before the Trojan War [Dion. 1.22]; but Thucydides [6.2] places it about 300 years before the Greeks began to colonize Sicily, that is, eight or nine centuries B.C., which is consistent with the fact that Sicily is called Sikania in the Odyssey." Guest (Vol. II) 1883:11.

Thus, we see a group called Siculi or Sikeloi invading Italy around the 27th year of King Solomon's reign. They proceeded to displace the native Sikanoi an Iberic people, "who not long before" had been displaced by the Ligues, also of an Iberic stock.

Helmolt says: "Ancient traditions tell us that Iberian tribes also took possession of certain portion of Italy [that includes other Israelite tribes, as mentioned in previous chapters, as well as Edomite groups—all Hebrews]. The Sicani [Sikanoi] in specific are said to have been Iberians; and, according to Thucydides . . . Philistus of Syracuse furnishes us with like information . . . they occupied Sicily, then known as Thrinacia, in consequence of having been crowded out of the peninsula by the Ligurians; and Sicily afterwards took the name Sicania from them. However, the

Iberians do not seem to have made their way to Italy directly over the sea, but appear to have journeyed by land through Gaul and upper Italy and thence to the south, where they have been mentioned by a long series of ancient writers as the inhabitants of Latium." Gelmolt 1902:304.

Though Helmult believes the Iberians as coming from the west into Sicily and Italy, in reality the Iberians were going west. They left their old homelands in Canaan and nearby places. Then, traveling through Sicily and Italy by land and sea, they continued to migrate west toward Iberia. The long series of writers, Helmolt quotes, confirm their presence in Italy. They do not say that they came from the west through Gaul. Helmolt also relates the Sicani to the Libui. "The Libui, too, who once occupied the region between Brescia and Verona, south of Lake Gurda, as well as the Sordones, who dwelt in the eastern Pyrenees of Gaul, seemed to have set out from that region to settle the island of Sardinia, were probably of Iberian stock. These tribes are, perhaps the Rebu [Libu] and Schardana mentioned in ancient Egyptian texts. From these accounts of old writers then so much, at least, can be gathered: That at one time Iberian tribes [Israelites and Edomites] occupied certain portions of Italy" (ibid.).

The Sicani or Sikanoi are thus considered to be Iberians and related to the Rebu or Libu. Let us now find out who these Rebu are and where did they come from. Guest writes: "The country between Mount Seir and Egypt was occupied for the most part by nomad tribes, but at the coast, at Rhinocorura, was a people called by the Hebrews Ereb [Arab, meaning, Westerners] and by the Egyptians Rebu, of whom we shall speak shortly. All these tribes whether settled or nomads, seem to have been allied with or subject to the men of Seir [the land of Edom or Esau] and I believe the Egyptians upon occasions called the whole district the country of Sharu or men of Sir . . . The Edomites were the only people of that period who could have acted the part assigned to Sharu" (Guest 1883, Vol. I, 1883:188). This information does link the Rebu, Libui or Sicans, all Iberians, to the country of Mount Seir, the land of Edom. Guest adds: "Pausanias tells us [10.17.2] that the Libues [Libu or Rebu] were the first settlers of Sardinia and that they came under the conduct of Sardus, son of Macer's, who among the Egyptians and Libues was called Heracles."

That Hercules or Heracles was considered to be a deity in Spain. Baldwin tells us: "Traces of the worship of Hercules, nowhere wanting, are most abundant in the western regions of the Mediterranean and beyond the straits of Gibraltar where it was established in times far more ancient than either the Tyrian or the Sidonian period" (Baldwin 1875:155). Some believe that this Hercules, worshiped later as a deity, is none other than the patriarch of the Edomites—Edom/Esau or Seir. In ancient times, it was common for peoples to deify their ancestors and worship them as gods. The Chinese custom of ancestors' worship is still alive today in some parts of China.

Now let's see if we can trace the Rebu or Libues, who are linked to Mount Seir, to the later inhabitants of Spain. Strabo makes mention of the Ligurians or Ligues, and links them to the Greeks (Strabo Geography, 4.6.3.) who lived near the Alps. He says, "They lived in parts of the Alps that joins the Apennines and they occupy a part of the Apennines also" (ibid.2.5.18). These Ligues, mentioned by name and geographical location, identify with Dausanias' Libues. (ibid.10.17.2). The Ligues are the same people designated as Libu or Rebu.

Strabo also tells us that the Ligues came into control of all the sea routes to Iberia or Spain. He says, while advancing a reason for the war between the early Romans and the Ligues: "The latter [Ligues] had barred all the passes leading to Iberia that ran through the seaboard" (ibid. 4.6.3). Of the Ligurians, Morton writes: "From their physical character and language, Strabo considers the Aquitanians as well as the Ligurians, who occupied a part of the coast of France, to be a branch of the Iberians (lib. iv. pg. 176, fr. ed.), the ancient people of Spain" (Morton 1854; Types of Mankind).

Morton adds: "In consequence of their position on the coast of the Mediterranean, the Ligurians became known to ancient Navigators before the populations of Gaul [the Israelite tribes of Reuben and other brothers]. Greek historians and geographers speak of them in very early times. They figure among the barbarian allies of the Carthaginians as far back as 480 B.C. Thierry [in History of the Gauls 1844] adopts, enforcing by many proofs, the opinion that Aquitanians and Ligurians were both of the Iberian stock and also that they were alien to the Gaulic [Israelite] family, properly speaking" (ibid. 90).

The Baron Von Humboldt, George Dottin and the French historian Camille Julian have different ideas on the origin of the Iberians. Yet, they all agree that the Iberians were among the first inhabitants of Sicily. Also, that they finally established themselves in the Iberian Peninsula. Before their final destination, they inhabited areas in Italy, Sicily, Sardinia, Corsica and Languedoc on the Mediterranean coast of France.

The migration of the Iberians into Spain was no coincidence from the Biblical point of view. Spain was the staging area and springboard for both descendants of the twins, Jacob and Esau, into the birthright lands of Northwest Europe, the British Isles, and later the Americas.

Thierry, in the introduction to his work, The History of the Gauls (Thiery 1844:23), shows that the Ligurians (Israelites and Edomites, who migrated into Greece in earlier times, and were called Greeks by historians who did not know their true identity) and the Iberians are the same people. They were linked with the Libu or Rebu who originated from Mount Seir, the land of Edom. As for the works of the Libu or Rebu, history has the Ligurians "characterized by their small stature, light complexion, black hair and a small head," according to E. Guest. He adds, "The Rebu are always represented distinctly as white men" [in Egyptian hieroglyphics].

Also, "we find the Rebu drawn with the northern flower hanging from their necks . . . Lastly, in a hieroglyphic inscription, the Rebu are described as nomads of Se [nk] ti [Arch. 38.378] and Sati or Sakiti which is generally acknowledged to be the district lying northeast of Egypt" (Guest 1883; Vol. VI: 196). When we check the map, we find that the area northeast of Egypt is the land of Canaan and Edom. It is the land of Seir—the ancient homeland of the Spanish people, as well as those people of Edom still in the Middle East today.

Were there other peoples in the ancient world who could also be linked to the people of Mount Seir and Edom? Let us find out! Jacob Bryant, in his sixth volume of An Analysis of Ancient Mythology, states: "The true Phoenicians were the sons of Esau, who was called Edom; and they settled first at Mount Seir; and upon the Red Sea which received its name from them. Both Phoinic and Edom signify red; which the Greeks changed to Erythrus a word of the same meaning. They appear to have been a very great and knowing people; and though there are no annals of their nation remaining; and their history is very obscure; yet so far we may learn in general that they were very rich and powerful [as their later descendants became during the golden age of Spain], carrying on an extensive traffic in the sea, which they lived upon and a great way further; engrossing all the trade of the east" (Bryant 1807; Vol. VI: 227-239).

Esau, we might recall, was a very rich man. Because of his great riches, he had to separate from his brother Jacob. Genesis 36:6-8 records: "Then Esau took his wives, his sons, his daughters and all the persons of his household and his cattle and all his animals and all his goods . . . For their possessions were too great for them to dwell together; and the land where they were strangers could not support them because of their livestock. So Esau dwelt in Mount Seir."

Bryant continues: "This people in process of time got possession of Tyre and Sidon ["by your sword you shall live," stated Isaac to his son Esau, and so they did capture that land], and the adjacent country; which was called from them Phoenicia [or red, the land of Edom]; but how early they settled here, is uncertain. They sent out many colonies [since all of Abraham's sons were colonialists by nature of their blessings]; and traces of them are to be found as far as Gades [in Spain] and Tartessus. "Herodotus mentions, that they came originally from the Red Sea [Herodotus lib. 7, cap. 89]. But the best account of them is in the poet Dionysius; who celebrates for their ingenuity and knowledge; mentions the chief places where they settled; and speaks of them as the first merchants upon the earth."

So far, we gather from Bryant's account that the Edomites who were pushed out of Mount Seir and the Red Sea by David, migrated into the area of present day Lebanon (many of them are still there to this day, which explains the recent Lebanese tragedy and its ramifications to the West and Israel, and the menace of Hezbollah terror). They then took the ancient Canaanites' cities of Tyre and Sidon, resettling them, and later migrated into Spain via Italy, Sicily, and southern France. When did the Edomites take Sidon and Tyre, Bryant can't be sure, but other sources reveal the answer. Bryant adds: "Those who settled at Gades [or modern Cadiz] and the remote parts of Spain carried thither many memorials of their original country; particularly the name of Edom, by translation Erythra, which they conferred on that part, where they inhabited; and especially on an island mentioned by Pliny" [Pliny. Nat. Hist. Lib. li. cap. 22]. The original Phoenicians, therefore, were the people of Edom; who lived near the Arabians and Amalekites [since Amalek was a grandson of Edom] and intermarried with their families and are often confounded with them." Bryant also makes reference to the Phoenician language being a dialect of Hebrew. This should be natural, since both Jacob and Esau were Hebrews and sons of the same parents and grandparents.

Let us inject here a side point. Sanchoniatho, the most ancient writer of the heathen world, writes, "Kronus, whom the Phoenicians call Israel . . ." The "auxiliaries" of Kronus are called "Elohim" (Sanchoniatho by Cory 1828:800, g.10). According to this Phoenician historian, Sanchoniatho,

"Kronus [Saturn] is Israel [Edom's twin brother], that is, Jacob; while Zeus [Jupiter], his Royal son, is Judah" (Milner 1976).

In the book of Joel, Chapter 3:4-8, after describing the coming captivity of Judah or the State of Israel, God warns the modern remnant of the ancient Phoenician-Edomites: "Indeed, what have you to do with Me, O Tyre and Sidon and all the coasts of Philistia? Will you retaliate against Me?" God takes the Lebanese, and particularly the Hezbollah militia's animosity toward Israel's modern nations personally. The hostage taking tragedy (of U.S. personnel) and their acts of terror against Israel do not escape His attention. "But if you retaliate against Me," continues God, "speedily I will return your retaliation upon your own head; because you have taken My silver and My gold [by ransacking the possessions of Israel in the past as well as in the future] and have carried into your temples [anciently, and in the future into your mosques and churches] My prized possessions. Also the people of Judah and the people of Jerusalem you have sold to the Greeks that you may remove them from their borders."

Let us note that even today many Greeks are pro-Arab in politics and sentiments. This is possibly because of the ancient migration of many Edomites into Greece; of ancient Greeks into Lebanon; the remnant of the ancient Philistines who came from Crete, and are still today in the Gaza strip. In the old city of Jerusalem, we can find to this day the Greek sector adjacent to the Jewish.

The Scripture continues: "Behold, I will raise them out of the place to which you have sold them and will return your retaliation upon your own head. I will sell your sons and your daughters into the hand of the people of Judah [and this is the future fate of Lebanon: captivity and slavery], and they will sell them to the Sabeans, to a people far off, for the Lord [or Allah] has spoken." For more details, see Isaiah 60:6 and Ezekiel 27:22.

Now back to Bryant, who states of the Iberians: "Possibly Spain might receive the name of Iberian from them; who, when they settled in the parts particularly so called were distinguished by their most ancient family name Ebraei. The original name of the River Iberus seems to have been the Eber, called at present Ebro. They settled in many parts of this country, but chiefly, as I have shown, near Gades; and it is observable that there was the principal seat of the Iberi, placed by Stephanus Byzantinus . . . and mentioned by Dionysius in the same situation . . ."

Brian adds: "The Iberians therefore appear to have been the same nation as the Erythreans or Edomites; who came from Tyre and were generally mentioned by the name Phoenicians; yet, lost their original Gentile [Hebrew] name from Heber; but at times were termed Eberi or Iberi, according to the Greek manner of expressing it. The chief city of this country is at this day called Ebora and is near the ancient Gades. So wide did this active people extend themselves; and they were for ages very powerful till by degrees they were weakened in every part and insensibly sunk into oblivion."

Speaking of the judgment against Edom, God proclaimed: "For indeed, I will make you small among the nations, despised among men" (Jeremiah 49:15). Certainly, this statement reflects Edom's fate and that of the people of Iberia or Spain.

We must pose here the question: Can the Iberians, Phoenicians, and Edomites be all the same people? Could the former inhabitants of Tyre and Sidon be of a different race—not Phoenicians? Of this matter Bryant says: "Bolhart tries to invalidate these accounts of the Phoenicians and will not allow that they came from Edom and the Red Sea. He quotes every author that I have mentioned above and particularly Herodotus; but sets aside their evidence, and the reason which he gives is very extraordinary . . . he says, it is manifest that the Phoenicians were Aborigines, that Canaan was the father of them, and that he came into the country which they possessed immediately upon the dispersion [of Babel]" [Georg. Sacr. Pars. Poster. Lib. 1. cap. 43]. All of which he advances upon the authority of the Scriptures. What he mentions of the Canaanites is very true. But in respect to the Phoenicians, he plainly begs the question. They are so far from being represented in Scripture as the descendants of Canaan; that the Old Testament does not once in the whole course of its history mention their name."

Bryant adds, "Bolhart mentions a particularly learned person who differed from and asserted that the Tyrians were originally from Edom, to which he answers . . . 'For this migration of the Edomites there is no good voucher.' Strange! When so many writers are quoted for it by himself; some of whom are of the very first rank. I will transcribe them in his own words, as they stand at the top of the page: Herodotus, Strabo, Dionisius, Periegetes, Festus, Priscianus, Plinius, Solinus, Stephanus, to which may be added Trogus and Diodirus Siculus, whom he quotes for it in another place. All these are set aside with Herodotus at the head, though he had been in Phoenicia and visited Tyre and must speak from knowledge obtained upon the spot. What is extraordinary to all this positive evidence on one side, Bolhart has nothing to oppose but the doubts and scruples of Strabo, who was not quite satisfied whether the ancient Tyrians were not a colony from Greece."

Let us now see what Herodotus had to say about this issue. He wrote: "These Phoenicians dwelt in old time, as they themselves say, by the Red Sea; passing over from thence they now inhabit the sea coast of Syria; that part of Syria and as much of it as reaches Egypt, is all called [later by the Romans] Palestine" (Herodotus, bk. vii. 89). Bryant adds this statement regarding the Phoenicians: "They looked up to Belus and Chronus [Kronus or Israel, according to Sanchoniathos the Phoenician historian] for their ancestors; and held Ogus [Esau] and other heroes for their founders, of a very uncertain origin; their notions not being uniform."

Historians' History of the World attest to the same, stating: "Esau is really the name of a god and we meet with it again in Phoenician mythology in its Hellenized form of Usoosi" (Historians History of the World, Vol. II; 1905:53).

Bryant poses an honest question. He states: "I may be asked in my turn if the Phoenicians were from Edom, how it comes to pass, that the sacred writers never take notice of this circumstance, nor mention them by either of those names? The answer in this place is obvious! The name Poinic from whence came the word Puniceus of the Romans . . . was not the original name of this people, but Edom; in the room of which the former was substituted being a word of the same purport. This however was not the term that the sacred writers were used to; had they called these people by their family name, it would have been Edomites. But this would have been accompanied with some ambiguity; as there would have been two nations of the same name; and with some impropriety as they were not of that country, though in great measure of the same lineage. They therefore call them always Tyrians and the Sidonians that were the strict truth and attended with no uncertainty. As to the silence of the Scriptures concerning this people coming originally from Edom; it amounts to nothing. The scriptures are never fraught with unnecessary truths; had it been a circumstance at all necessary to have been made known and of consequence in the Jewish history; it would certainly have been transmitted to us."

It is also possible that God wanted to keep the identity of Edom, which was linked to Israel's destiny, as a historic secret to be unveiled at this later "end time." God had done the same with Israel's identity. Judah, however, apart from Zerah's line in Scotland and other locations, had to remain visible for God's purpose. Judah's purpose in this last generation, as in Ezra's time, is to prepare the way for the return of Israel's Messiah to His city, land and people.

What confused historians about the Phoenicians is the simple reality of the existence of two distinct Phoenician peoples. Isaac Newton was both a famous scientist, a historian and scholar, gives us clear evidence that show the existence of two distinct Phoenician peoples.

The original Sidonians, like all former inhabitants of Canaan, were Canaanites. They were later, just like the Canaanites, replaced by the descendants of Abraham and Isaac. In the Sidonians' case, it was by Esau's descendants who had replaced them. In more recent times, in the Americas, for example, the native Indians were displaced by both sons of Isaac: Edom and Jacob.

In Newton's Chronology we read: "David in the twelfth year of his reign conquered Edom and made some of the Edomites and chiefly the merchants and seamen fly from the Red Sea to the Philistines upon the Mediterranean, where they fortified Azoth. For Stephanus tells us: One of the fugitives from the Red Sea built Azoth [Steph. in Azoth], that is, a prince of Edom, who fled from David, fortified Azoth for the Philistines against him [David].

"The Philistines were now grown very strong by the access of the Edomites and shepherds, and by their assistance invaded and took Zidon, that, being a town very convenient for the merchants who fled from the Red Sea; and then did the Zidonians [the original Canaanite Sidonians] fly by the sea to Tyre and Araidus and to other havens in Asia Minor, Greece, and Libya with which by means of their trade, they had been acquainted before. The great wars and victories of David their enemy, prompting them to fly by sea; for they went with great multitude, not to seek Europa as was pretended but to seek new seats and therefore fled from their enemies; and when some of them fled under Cadmus [not the Danite, previously mentioned] and his brother to Cilicia, Asia Minor and Greece; others fled under other commanders to seek new seats in Lybia and there built many walled towns . . ." (Newton 1728:104)

Thus we see the original Sidonians, confused by some with the later Edomite Phoenicians, fleeing from David's armies. This allowed the Edomites to take over their land and coastlines. Today, we have historical evidence that Joab's armies, David's commander, pursued the original

Sidonian Canaanites into Libya and North Africa. On page 108, Newton writes: "Edom revolted because of Jehoram's wicked reign (II Kings 8:20-22); if we place that revolt about the middle of the first six years, it will fall upon the fifth year of Pygmalion, king of Tyre, and so was about twelve years or fifteen years after the taking of Troy; and then, by reason of this revolt, the Tyrians retired from the Red Sea [referring to the new people of Tyre of Edomite stock] and began long voyages upon the Mediterranean; for in the seventh year of Pygmalion, his sister Dido sailed to the coast of Africa beyond the Syrtes and there built Carthage" (ibid. 108). In later centuries, elements of the ten tribes of Israel, according to Steve Collins, in his work: The "Lost" Ten Tribes of Israel . . . Found, have merged with Uncle Edom to build the great empire of Carthage—the dread of Rome. Edom was a man of the sword. He was good at it, as we can see in men like Herod the Great and, later, the great Spanish generals and conquistadors. The Edomites were good warriors and also explorers, builders, talented artists and merchants.

Newton continues: "This retiring of the Tyrians from the Red Sea to make long voyages on the Mediterranean, together with the flight of the Edomites from David to the Philistines, gave occasion to the [true] tradition both of the ancient Persians and of the Phoenicians themselves, that the Phoenicians came originally from the coasts of the Red Sea to the coasts of the Mediterranean and presently undertook long voyages as Herodotus restates: For Herodotus in the beginning of his first book, restates that the Phoenicians coming from the Red Sea to the Mediterranean and beginning to make long voyages with Egyptian and Assyrian wares, among other places came to Argos [a city inhabited then by Israelites from Dan] and having sold their wares, seized and carried away into Egypt some of the Grecian [or Danite Israelite] women who came to buy them; and amongst those women was Io the daughter of Inachus. The Phoenicians therefore came from the Red Sea in the days of Io and her brother Phoroneus, king of Argos, and by consequence at that time, when David conquered the Edomites and made them fly every way from the Red Sea; some fled into Egypt with their young king and others to the Philistines their next neighbors and the enemies of David." Here we see, apparently, two flights of the Edomites from the Red Sea area to the Philistine coasts—one at the time of David and another at the time of Jehoram.

Newton adds: "And this flight gave occasion to the Philistines to call many places Erythra [or Edom] in memory of their being Erythreans or Edomites and of their coming from the Erythrean Sea [Red Sea]; for Erythra was the name of a city of Ionia of another in Lybia, of another in Locris, of another in Boeuthia, of another in Cyprus, of another in Aetolia, of another in Asia near Chius; and Erthis Acra was a promontory in Lybia and Erythraem a promontory of Crete and Erythros a place near Tybur [Tiber River?] and Erythini a city or country in Paphlagonia and the name Erethea or Erythrae was given to the island Gades [Spain] peopled by Phoenicians."

Edom, like his nephew Dan, son of Jacob, left a serpent-like trail behind him for the sharp-eyed unbiased historian to notice. Of course, a bit of faith in the Scripture may help the objective mind.

Newton also tells us: "Among the Phoenicians who came with Cadmus into Greece . . ." An earlier voyager, 600 years before, Cadmos and Danaus of the tribe of Dan, fled from Egypt after Joseph's death and came into Greece settling in Argos. It also could be that we are dealing here with the same person and migration, and a bit of confusion in historians' accounts. Newton continues: " . . . there were Arabians [with Cadmus] and Erythreans, or inhabitants of the Red Sea, that is Edomites; and in Thrace there settled a people who were circumcised and called Odomantes, that is as some think, Edomites . . . the Erythreans [or Edomites] who fled from David, settled in great numbers in Phoenicia, that is, in all the sea coasts of Syria [many are still there today] from Egypt to Zidon; and by calling themselves Phoenicians in the language of Syria, instead of Erythreans, gave the name of Phoenicia to all the sea coast and to that only" (ibid. 108). It is evident from several ancient accounts that there was more than one migration of Edomites. Edom's sailors and refugees have taken more than one route on their way to their new lands.

In another source, we read: " . . . Hadad [king of Edom] made his way towards Egypt, others took different routes, some flying to the Philistines fortified Azoth or Azotus for them; and proved a considerable accession of power and of very singular benefit to that people; and others that dealt in shipping, taking a longer way to escape the rage of the conquerors [David and Joab], or went towards or into the Persian Gulf . . ."

The oil capital of Iraq in the Persian Gulf, Basra, was named after the ancient capital of Edom in Mount Seir. When the fierce armies of King Nebuchadnezzar had later invaded and destroyed Jerusalem, Edom's generals and soldiers, now a part of his allies, had their day of sweet revenge against the last king of David's dynasty, Zedekiah. This would explain, as we have covered in an earlier chapter on Edom, why the Jewish captives in Babylon did cry: "Remember, O Lord, against the sons of Edom the day of Jerusalem, who said, 'Raze it, Raze it to its foundation!'" Then added: "O daughter of Babylon, who are to be destroyed, happy shall he be who repays you as you have served us! Happy shall he be who takes and dashes your little ones against the rock" (NKJ, Psalm 137:7-9). The account continues: " . . . In a word, they were dispersed into all parts, there being no safety for them in their country" (An Universal History, Vol. II; 1747:175).

More evidence of two Phoenician races is given by John Williams who wrote in 1858. He said, "I am speaking not of the Paleoi Phoenicians, but to use the expression of Aristotle of the Pampaleoi—of those Phoenicians whom the Persian literati described as emigrants from the Erythracean Sea [or Red Sea] and as foreign settlers in Phoenicia where they established themselves as sea traversing merchants." These Edomites were the ancient 'Palestinian' immigrants of the Middle East, fleeing the 'Zionist Jews' of their day, David and his General Joab, the General Ariel Sharon of his day. Williams adds, "The learned Persians from whom Herodotus derived his information must have well known the ethnology of Central Asia, which at that period was governed by Persian satraps; and the fathers of many of them must have been present in the camp of Xerxes, where were collected according to their races, the armed warriors of all the empire" (Williams 1858:315-316).

If we recall the history of Haman the Agagite, as discussed before in an earlier chapter, we would remember that he was an Amalekite from Edom's prolific family. Haman was the highest-ranking leader under the king of Persia. The great influence of the Edomites in that part of the Empire, must have played a role in his meteoric rise to power. That's why the rise to power of Mordecai the Jew had greatly irritated Haman.

Baldwin wrote, "The doubts and perplexities that have troubled inquiry concerning the Phoenicians are due chiefly to the influence of chronological dogmatism." He added, "The great antiquity of the people called Phoenicians was acknowledged by the ancients. Josephus mentions as a fact generally understood that the antiquity of the Phoenicians was as great as that of the Chaldeans and Egyptians" (Baldwin 1875:145). After linking the religious worship of Hercules with both the Phoenicians and Iberians, Williams says of the Phoenicians: "We are told that their aim was to establish themselves in the most western region occupied by

Hercules. That is to say, they sought to regain a country which in the most ancient times, had belonged to the ancestors of their countrymen" (Williams 1958:156).

This last statement does recognize the early occupation of parts of Spain by earlier migrations of Edomite tribes. Remember! Esau's destiny was linked to the birthright tribes. Wherever Jacob went, there was Esau also—ever vying to regain his "lost birthright." Williams also states: "When Gades was built, Spain had long been an old country, full of old cities and rich in the monuments of an old civilization, then probably like the political condition of the country in a state of decline" (ibid).

Jefries writes, "Phoenicians were acquainted with the country [Spain] long before the founding of Rome and Carthage" (Jeffries 1869:128). He adds on the same page: "The Iberians were an intelligent family, acquainted with the art of writing [as all Hebrews were from Abraham's day] at a very early period. They sacrificed human victims [as most Israelites did when they became idolatrous] to their divinities, and their priests pretending to foretell future events from an inspection of the palpitating entrails."

The Phoenicians [Edomites] also sacrificed human beings to their deities: "From the classical writers we know that human sacrifices took place on human emergencies" (Anderson 1915:99). Sayce adds: "The Phoenician priests scourged themselves or gashed their arms and breasts [as did the Hebrew priests of Baal in their encounter with the prophet Elijah, I Kings 18:28] to win divine favor . . . human sacrifices were made, to Moloch or Milkom . . . The parent was required to offer his eldest or only son as a sacrifice and the victim's cries were drowned by the noise of drums and flutes" (Sayce 1901; Quoted from Archaeological and Ethnological Papers of the Peabody Museum, Vol. II, pp. 523-524, 1901).

What did the Iberians look like? Did they resemble the Edomite Phoenicians? Jeffries made these remarks: "The Spaniards derive their descent from the Iberians . . . known to the ancients as mariners, and were closely allied to the Phoenicians, whom they much resembled. They have been grouped with the Turanian type, but erroneously, as they are evidently Aryans" (Jeffries 1869:128).

Historic accounts tell us that the heartland of the Iberian civilization was Andalucía. The Iberians were well known as good seamen. Excavations undertaken in this last century uncovered Iberian arts and industries, which show a striking similarity with those of the Phoenicians and the [Israelite and Edomite] Greeks.

History may be marred by dark shadows and dusty winds, which obscure the landscape of peoples' true identities, yet the God of Israel saw to it that His people's identity would not be blown away with the wind. He made sure that sufficient footprints would be preserved in the pages of both Biblical and secular history. With the aid of these dual sources of light, the objective, honest and inquisitive researcher can know much more. If there is one thing lacking in the field of historical research, it is an honest and faithful researcher who will combine genuine and unbiased historic facts, a bit of faith, Biblical knowledge, and trust in the words of the Master—God.

Unfortunately, for most investigators of man's ancestry, little credence is given to the Book of light—the Bible—and The Source of its inspiration. The pieces of the puzzle cannot be matched together without that light and faith that is offered by man's ultimate and most reliable record—the sure Word of the Supreme Historian—God.

In his work: "Tracing the Identity of the Spanish People," Victor Gutierez made several interesting points that we shall now consider. We should know, and hopefully can recall from previous chapters, the many statements concerning Edom's blessings, character, and dealings with his brother Jacob. The Bible is a chronicle of Israel's long history and future. It mentions all those nations who had a close relationship with God's people. If we check the names: Edom, Esau, Seir or Amalek, we shall find more than 300 references and prophecies concerning these peoples. Edom certainly, by far, besides Jacob, is mentioned the most often in the Book of the Chronicles of God's people. It is no coincidence at all.

When we peer into the history of the "lost" tribes of Israel and Judah in the past three and half millenniums, we see to our amazement an interesting reality. We find the history and destiny of the Spanish and Israelite nations to be intimately interwoven. In Europe, we find the descendants of the twins, ever interlocked in a struggling embrace for supremacy. Apart from Judah, both Esau\Edom and Jacob\Israel lost their identities. The fierce conflict over the mastery of the birthright was still the motivating force that propelled each of them in opposite directions. As they both burst onto the global scene, they carried with them their eternal, tireless struggle. The new world became the arena and new frontier for the ceaseless, fierce match of the two titans. Still, in these last days, the old battleground—the Middle East—found a new revitalized interest in the lost twins.

Whether it is in the Middle East, in Spain, in Mexico or the rest of Latin America, the ancient love/hate feelings between the descendants of the twins are still boiling. The stormy winds of the old hatred, mixed with occasional gentle breezes, are still emanating from the twins. Their fascinating relationship spiced with love/hate ingredients, continue to govern their mutual destiny. True to his nature, Jacob still supplants and exploits his older twin brother with his ever shrewd and clever subtlety. Esau responds, often, with unbridled fury, hatred and animosity.

Let us now consider some points, as mentioned by Gutierez, on page 8 of his work. "The Jews," he says, "it can be proven, resided in the Iberian Peninsula as far back as the time of Solomon. History mentions them as having contributed toward the construction and upkeep of the Temple." Ancient records tell us that the northern tribes Dan, Zebulun, and Asher did join their Edomite brothers, the sea-faring merchants of Tyre, and have jointly established colonies in Spain or Tarshish. In reality, it is these elements of Israelites who have contributed to the Temple of Solomon. In addition, according to Collins, these sea-faring people of Israel, together with their Edomite kinsmen from Tyre, have also established several colonies in the New World. It was during that period of time that huge amounts of silver have vanished from the silver mines of the Northeast of America without any trace of their final destination.

"In Phoenicians' times," Gutierez adds, "trade routes existed between Spain and the British Isles. All Irish chronicles begin their histories with Spain. At one point in history, the Old Testament Canon was kept by the Jews in Spain. Spain's relations with Britain and France [as well as other European nations]—though antagonistic for the most part—have also been very pronounced in later history. This relationship was climaxed by the invasion of the Spanish Armada with [possible] intentions of genocide for the British Isles!" Judging from the nightmarish pre-Nazi atrocities committed by the Spanish Inquisition against the Jews and other millions of Protestant Israelites in Europe, the idea of an intent to commit genocide is not too farfetched.

"And Esau hated Jacob," said the Scripture (Genesis 27:41). Of "Mount Seir" or Edom, God proclaimed: "Son of man, set your face against Mount Seir and prophesy against it and say to it, Thus says the Lord; 'Behold, O Mount Seir, I am against you; I will stretch out My hand against you and make you most desolate; I shall lay your cities waste, and you shall be desolate. Then shall you know that I am the Lord. 'Because you have had an ancient [or everlasting] hatred and have shed the blood of the children of Israel by the power of the sword at the time of their calamity, when their iniquities came to an end [as they do to this day]. Therefore, as I live,' says the Lord God, 'I will prepare you for blood and blood shall pursue you; since you have not hated blood therefore, blood shall pursue you. Thus, I will make Mount Seir most desolate'" (Ezekiel 35:2-7). The reader is encouraged to reread these passages, as recorded in early chapters, for a full impact.

In Chapter 36:5 of Ezekiel, God stated: "Surely I have spoken in My burning jealousy against the rest of the nations and against all Edom, who gave My land [the State of Israel, Western Europe and North America] to themselves as a possession [for all, at times, the unbrotherly exploitation committed by Israel's tribes against brother Edom in the U.S., Europe, and the Middle East], with whole-hearted joy and spiteful minds in order to plunder its open country." Though this prophecy is concerned mainly of the land of Israel, its implications are for all the lands of modern day nations of Israel and Edom.

The God of Israel would cause the birthright lands to temporarily fall also into the hands of brother Edom for Israel's sins, and for social iniquities against Edom and others. God is no respecter of persons! Both Edom and Jacob must come to realize this hard lesson. "Israel, according to the rabbis, is in a deadly feud [with Esau], a feud which began before its ancestors even perceived that the light of the world is perpetually carried on by their descendants and will only be brought to an end with history itself. The contest over the birthright is indicative of the struggle for supremacy between Israel and Rome [which the Jews consider a prototype of Edom. Many Edomites did remain in Italy long after their brethren migrated into their final destination in Spain]. It would seem even as if Israel, [by God's decree], despairs in asserting the claims of his acquired birthright and concedes this world to Esau" (Schechter 1909:100).

Rabbi Eleazar of Modyin says, regarding Edom and Israel: "The existence of the one necessarily involves the destruction of the other [because of Esau's defiance of God's decree]." He adds: "When will the name of the Amalekites be wiped out [Remember Haman, the Agagite and Exodus 17]?" He exclaims, using Amalek as just another name for his grandfather Esau. "Not before both the idols and their worshipers cease to exist, when God will be alone in the world and His kingdom established forever" (Mechilta, 56a, 56H, CF, M.T. 97:11. Quoted in Shecheter, p. 99).

The God of Jacob commanded Ezekiel to write this concerning Esau's final fate: "Thus I will make Mount Seir most desolate . . . and I will fill its mountains [or nations] with the slain; on your hills and in your ravines . . . Those who are slain by the sword shall fall. I will make you perpetually desolate and your cities shall be uninhabited; then you shall know that I am the Lord" (Ezekiel 35:7-9). At this time, Edom's nations do not know nor obey the God of Jacob and of their mutual father Isaac, but soon, the small remnant of Edom shall know. It is unfortunate that such an acknowledgment will come a bit too late for most of Jacob and Esau, at least in this lifetime.

The Talmud, (an ancient Jewish commentary), describes a Roman game. It is a wrestling match between two men. In this game, one is wearing a hairy pelt and the other man is smooth. Remember, Esau was hairy, while Jacob was smooth. The hairy one, the Talmud says, refers to Esau and the other to Jacob. Accordingly, when one wrestler was up or had the upper hand, the other was down. The rabbis interpreted this to mean that whenever Esau was up, Israel was down and vice versa. This deadly game is still being witnessed in our day. It will culminate in its full fury at the coming final demise of all the nations of Israel, and then that of all the nations of Edom.

Gutierez writes: "Today, this animosity, this hatred and jealousy against the United States and Britain [as well as the State of Israel], is no better manifested than in Spain and the Latin American countries. The very words, 'Yankee go home,' carry a 'Made in Latin America' label. Studies into the national character of the Latins make it very easy for the student to see the countries south of the border 'rejoicing over the children of Israel and Judah'" (Obadiah, v. 12).

Another point Gutierrez brings up, concerns the character and temperament of the patriarchs and progenitors that are preserved among their children. He says: "Esau was an integrationist with full nuptial privileges! In Genesis 28:9 he marries Ishmaelites or Arabs. In Genesis 36:2-3 and Genesis 26:34, he mixes with the daughters of Canaan" (Gutierez 1965:11). It is this mixture that gives many of Edom's descendants the olive complexion and racial variety. "Today, in accordance with their father's pattern, the Spaniards have created what amounts to be the greatest conglomeration of racial mixture possible!" (ibid.11). Wherever Edom had migrated, whether it be into other Middle Eastern countries, Greece, Spain, the Americas or the Philippines, he often tended to integrate with the natives. Israel, in contrast, remained mostly racially pure. This accounts for the differences in racial and skin complexion one finds among the descendants of the twin brothers. The tribe of Judah, however, with the exception of Zerah's line in Scotland and elsewhere, being scattered throughout the world, did not retain the same measure of purity as that of the rest of the tribes. Still, by far, all of Israel's tribes are still the same as those who left their native land long ago. Not so with Edom!

Showing that the Spanish world is responsible for the racial mixing of a continent and a half, Gutierez quotes the prophet Obadiah, verse 18, where it is stated: "The house of Jacob [all of Israel] shall be a fire and the house of Joseph [Ephraim and Manasseh—U.S. and the British peoples] a flame, and the house of Esau shall be stubble and they shall kindle in them; and devour them; and no survivor shall remain of the house of Esau; for the Lord has spoken it." This will be the result of the final global struggle between the twins.

The prophet Obadiah explains the purpose for this coming near genocide of Edom's descendants by stating: "For your violence against your brother Jacob, shame shall cover you and you shall be cut off [as sovereign nations] forever" (v. 10). He adds that because Edom joined Israel's enemies, in the past, as well as in the future, as he did during the Nazi holocaust, "Your reprisal [or reward] shall return upon your own head. For the day of the Lord upon all the nations is near" (v. 15). God will intervene in human affairs!

The prophet Amos tells us that a small "remnant of Edom" shall be left (Amos 9:12). Jeremiah the prophet says this remnant is to be composed mainly of widows and fatherless children (Jeremiah 49:11). Of course, the opportunity for salvation for all those who have rejected God, in this life, will be coming at what the Bible calls "the second resurrection." It is beyond the period of a thousand years after the first resurrection of the just. See Revelation 20:5-6 in this connection. In verse 5 we read: "But the rest of the dead did not live again until the thousand years were finished. This is the first resurrection."

Gutierez mentions another point concerning Edom or the Spanish people. He states: "Esau not only married with the Arabs, but also maintained rather close relations with them . . . Interestingly enough, there also seems to exist a rather congenial relationship between the Arabs of today and Spain [though this was not always the case, as we see at times in history. Even in the Persian Gulf War, this was quite evident]. Arabs today inhabit Andalucía, or the southern part of the Iberian Peninsula. Much of what is known as Spanish culture is really Arab culture" (ibid. 13).

It is interesting to note the similarity between the Spanish/Mexican various types of breads and that of the Arab world, namely, the Pita. Among the Spanish people we find names like Medina, a city in Saudi Arabia, anciently known as the capital of Edom located by the Red Sea. Also, the name Perez, a Jewish name, was adopted by Edom because of intermarriage. Also names like Ayala, Dalia, Edmundo (world of Edom) and Isabel, after the infamous wife of King Ahab of Israel, namely, Jezebel, a daughter of the Phoenician/Edomite king of Zidon, are most common among the Spanish. "Spain controls Spanish Sahara. Her universities carry extensive courses in Arabic and the protocol of Spanish-Arab diplomacy . . . much Arabic literature dating back many centuries has been translated only into Spanish" (ibid. 13).

The Spanish king and historian, Alfonso the Tenth, wrote about the intimate involvement between the Arabs and his country in his Genealogy of The Kings of Spain. According to him, as some scholars claim, one of the royal lines in Spain was established by a man from Medina, the ancient capital of Edom now in Saudi Arabia. This Middle Eastern king, apparently of a royal line, came to Spain and married a Spanish [Edomite] princess. With this princess, he started a royal dynasty. This royal marriage had later produced, through intermarriage with the Austrian Hapsburg family, the Spanish Hapsburgs. Many wars and 'inquisitions' were later waged by this branch of the Spanish (Edomite) Hapsburgs against some of the nations of Israel in Europe.

The loss of the coveted land of promise to Jacob proved to be a great source of distress for Edom. Yet the greater prized possession, North America, "snatched" by Jacob from the "jaws" of Esau, added insult to injury. The United States specifically, is the richest blessing given to Jacob by the God of Israel. In spite of the decree by the Pope that the Americas, among other parts of the globe, should be given to Spain, God's decree took precedence over that of the Pope.

Authors William and Henry Paddock, in Hungry Nations, state: All the perfect conditions for superabundance in agriculture and industrial output are fully combined in the United States and parts of Canada. "All this is evident, but few understand how little land there is in this not very large world of ours that combines these factors correctly" (Paddock 1964:22). The authors add, "Nowhere do these factors combine themselves so favorably as in the middle western states. We who have grown up there forget the uniqueness of this area. A square mile of Iowa farmland transported to almost any spot in Latin America [the heartland of modern Edom in the new world], Africa or Asia would be so astounding that people would make pilgrimage to it as to a shrine. This I do assure you is no exaggeration."

In the same page the authors say: "The United States and Canada have 22.7 per cent of all the world's cultivated land [and the rest of the tribes of Israel in Europe, England, Australia and New Zealand have fertile lands also]. Latin America, by contrast, has only 6.5 per cent. This is no one's fault. This is merely how the Lord [of Israel] bounced the ball."

Gutierez remarks: "Because God promised all these riches to Jacob and because 'Jacob' means 'supplanter' in reflection of his character" (Genesis 27:36), he has always supplanted Esau! "Though Jacob," Gutierez says, "later received the name of Israel for prevailing as a prince with God (Genesis 32:28), his nature as supplanter never changed [among his children]! As Esau and his descendants the Edomites tried to possess the birthright—the lands and [international strategic] gates God meant for Jacob—Israel was always ready to supplant'" (Numbers 24:18).

We see this chain of supplanting first in the land of promise. Edom's land was, at times, subjugated by David and other nearby kings. The Edomite Phoenicians have first inhabited parts of Greece, North Africa, Italy, France, Spain, and the British Isles. Later, however, the people of Joseph and other Israelite tribes have supplanted Uncle Edom's lands. Few centuries later, during the age of discovery, Edom's conquistadors invaded the new world and places like the Philippines. Yet, there too, the far-reaching hands of Jacob did ultimately grasp the birthright lands firmly.

In 1783, much of what is now called the United States was still a Spanish territory. Yet the God of Jacob had decreed otherwise. He inspired Jacob to proclaim of the birthright tribe: "Joseph is a fruitful bough, a fruitful bough by the well; his branches run over the wall [or borders]. The archers have bitterly grieved him [with the Spanish Armada, the Mexican American War and Alamo, with the drug and illegal aliens' invasions—and recently, with the grand terror attack by the Edomite Bin Laden and his cohorts], shot at him and hated him. But his bow remained in strength and the arms of his hands were made strong by the hands of the Mighty God of Jacob [and so Esau had no chance]." See Genesis 49:22-28 for the rest of blessing.

Moses, in blessing the tribes of Israel, said of Joseph, among other things: "Let the blessing come on the head of Joseph and on the crown of the head of him who was separate from his brothers! His glory is like a firstborn bull, and his horns are like the horns of the wild ox; together with them he shall push the peoples [and especially the Edomites] to the end of the earth" (Deuteronomy 33:16-17). The global grip Edom had on the world was first broken by the British Empire (of Ephraim) and later by America (Manasseh). Ironically, neither Edom nor Jacob knew who was really pulling the invisible strings that determined the course and destiny of their history. The day is near when all the tribes of Israel and Edom, all children of Isaac or Saxons, will come to know and acknowledge this reality.

The prophet Daniel, desiring to know the end-time-fate of his people, asked God, through prayers and fasting, to reveal to him this matter. The archangel Gabriel was dispatched from the throne of the universe to Daniel's place in the king's palace in Babylon. He laid before Daniel the course of history of the next 2500 years, to our time. Then, he informed him: "At that time Michael [the archangel] shall stand up, the great prince who stands watch [as protector of Israel] over the sons of your people; and there shall be a time of trouble, such as never was since there was a nation, even to that time [speaking of the soon coming final mega holocaust]. And at that time, your people shall be delivered, everyone who is found written in the Book [if they heed the warnings of the prophets of Israel and drastically change their conduct in accordance with God's laws]. And many of those who sleep in the dust of the earth [the dead] shall awake . . . But you, Daniel, shut up the words, and seal the book [for the next 2500 years] until the time of the end; many shall run to and fro [in the reality of our mobile society], and knowledge [including those matters hidden from the nations of Israel and the world—chiefly that of the identity of Israel and the "Mystery of ages," the true nature of "the Kingdom of God"] shall increase."

Then Daniel wrote, being confused by this avalanche of information: "Although I heard, I did not understand. Then I said, 'My lord, what shall be the end of these things?' And he said, 'Go your way, Daniel, for the words are closed up and sealed till the time of the end. Many shall be purified, made white, and refined [by severe persecutions, for some, to test their character], but the wicked [those who despise God's laws and break them] shall do wickedly; and none of the wicked shall understand [though it is told them], but the wise [those obeying God's laws] shall understand.'"

The commission of the prophets of God was always both easy and difficult. It was difficult because hardly anybody ever believed the prophets. Most did mock and scorn them. Many wanted to kill them. Many accused them of "bad-mouthing their nation." Yet, on the other hand, their work was easy

Middle East

CENTER OF OIL RESERVES

since they were never required to convince anybody of the veracity of their message sent from God.

After the God of Israel had appeared to Ezekiel in person (Ezekiel 1), the prophet wrote: "And He said to me, 'son of man, I am sending you to the children of Israel, to a rebellious nation that has rebelled against Me; they and their fathers have transgressed against Me to this very day [since Egypt], for they are impudent and stubborn children. I am sending you to them, and you shall say to them, thus says the Lord God. As for them, whether they hear or whether they refuse—for they are a rebellious house—yet they will know that a prophet has been among them'" (Ezekiel 2:3-5). Then, in Chapter 3:4,7, He told Ezekiel: "Son of man, go to the house of Israel and speak with My words to them . . . But the house of Israel will not listen to you, because they will not listen to Me; for all the house of Israel are impudent [hard-headed] and hard-hearted." Many self appointed prophets speak their own words, not God's, therefore they too will go into captivity along with the people of Israel. After this digression, let's go back now to Edom!

According to Gutierrez, states like Texas, Florida, New Mexico, Utah, California, Oregon and many others were under the firm control of Esau before the "Gringos" of Jacob showed up and plucked the ripened fruit away from him. The Louisiana Purchase was under the Spanish crown of uncle Edom in 1762. It did not see another flag until 1802 when France [uncle Reuben, the firstborn who also lost his birthright to Joseph] secured it on the first of October. Many of the strategic sea and land gates of Israel were once in Edom's hands. The Gibraltar, Panama Canal, Falkland Islands, Windward Passage and the strategic islands of the Philippines, were taken from Esau and given to Jacob as promised long ago. When Rebekah, the mother of the twins Esau and Jacob, was handed over by her family to be a wife for Isaac, they stated: " . . . and may your descendants possess the gates of those who hate them" (Genesis 24:60). Though Esau did first possess these gates, the birthright owner did later supplant him and took them over. If Joseph is rapidly losing these gates, it is because of his rejection of the Law and covenants of the God of his fathers.

It is tragic that many of the blessings Isaac gave to his son Edom have been, in later times, supplanted by his brother Jacob. While Jacob is sitting on his fat land, he exploits the oil and agricultural resources of Esau, both in the Middle East and in Latin America. A quick look at the oil map of the Middle East will show the vast oil reserves of that area to be in those lands that belong, or did belong, to Esau.

Gutierez says: "Even the birthright [blessings] that belonged to Edom are being taken by Jacob; I'm referring to the natural resources and the agricultural products of the Latin (Banana) Republics. In spite of Latin squawking and denials from our capitol, American industry and business, such as the United Fruit Company and others, have exploited the natural resources of Latin America! And even when there isn't a Yankee hand in the pot, the gains still point their northerly direction. For example, while most Texas oil remains underground with pumps operating way below maximum capacity, the United States imports 70% of Venezuela's annual yield of petroleum. Britain, on the other hand, gets to eat most of Argentina's beef production!" (Gutierez 1965:16).

Pointing to the statement that Esau was a man of the field," Gutierez, speaking of the agrarian society of Edom, states: "Though Spain makes up part of [highly advanced industrial] Europe, and has maintained communication throughout history with France, Germany and England, it has never gone through an industrial revolution! The case is just as negative with Latin America!" (ibid. 17).

According to Genesis, Gutierez points out, "Esau was born first, and after that came his brother out and his hand took hold on Esau's heel." Then, he adds: "Today, America holds the Latin nations by the economic heel. The economy of those nations is almost completely dependent on the United States . . . America has assumed the role of 'big brother' [though Jacob is the younger] telling the Latins where to go and where not to go for over a century now. The United States has exercised such policies as the 'big stick policy' and the 'Monroe Doctrine.'" (ibid. 17).

Gutierrez adds: "England and France, on their side of the Atlantic, have also kept a check on Spain." He quotes Paddock: "Spain had to arrange $418,000.000 in loans to stabilize its economy [in the 60's]. Spain is, it is true, more prosperous today than a decade ago. It would seem this is due not to its own activities but largely to the $1,698,000.000 [up to June 1962] that the United States has introduced into the country via military assistance, economic aid and loans" (Paddock 1964:209).

Gutierez quotes Genesis 27:29, where Isaac said to Jacob, "Be Lord over your brethren, and let your mother's sons bow down to you." Then He poses the question: "Does this relationship exist between the United States and the Spanish world?" Again, we find that Isaac told Esau: "You shall serve your brother; and it shall come to pass, when you become restless [KJV, When you have the dominion]; that you shall break his yoke from of your neck" (Genesis 27:40). By God's decree, Edom's star will rise again. He will punish Jacob for his spirit of exploitation and iniquities against his brother Esau. The whole complex issue of the "illegal aliens" in the nations of Israel (America, Britain, Israel, elsewhere) that are often being exploited in the fields and sweatshops of Jacob, will be rectified by the God of Justice. No, God is not a respecter of persons!

"The Spanish world," says Gutierez, "especially the Latin American countries [to a degree the Middle East], exist as American satellites! When America and Great Britain lose their economic stronghold, Spain and Latin America will 'break the yoke' and take over the gates of Israel (This was written more than two decades ago). They will then be in a good position to 'punish the Yankees' and betray them by not allowing them to cross the Panama Canal as they flee the enemy [See Obadiah 14]. Just as ancient Israel was refused passage through the land of Edom (Numbers 20:18-21), so in this end time the descendants of Esau shall refuse passage to the United States and Britain as they face some of the most crucial battles against Germany and the beast power" (Gutierez 1965:18).

The prophet Obadiah reveals that at the final fall of Jacob, Edom will be situated at the "crossway" [plural] of the nations (Obadiah 14). The Spanish people do stand at the crossway of Gibraltar, Panama, Straits of Magellan, the Falkland Islands and Windward Passage, according to Gutierrez. Obadiah, speaking of the judgment of Edom, says: "You should not have entered the gate of My people in the day of their calamity" (v. 13). Gutierrez adds, "The gate or gates, controlled by Israel are being gradually given back to Edom. Later, the rest of the gates will be seized by Edom when his hour of victory comes. This turn of events will prevent the birthright tribes from moving their fleets through the strategic passages crucial to their fleet movements. This will prove very devastating to both close allies—America and the British people. For this unbrotherly action, God promises a swift retribution against Edom." Read the whole account in Obadiah for more details.

Another point Gutierez brings, is Edom's nature to "live by the sword," as Isaac did proclaim to Esau (Genesis 27:40). "Did the conquistadors live by the sword?" asks Gutierez. He brings a few quotes from Walter F. Lord's work, The Lost Empires of the Modern World, to answer his question. "The Spaniards fell on the new world like devastating hordes, and dashed it out of existence. If the empire of Portugal was a triumph of thought, that of Spain, an empire of plunder and slaughter." Both Judah and Israel did feel the fury of merciless Edom during the inquisition period in Europe and elsewhere. Many Jews and mainly Israelites [Protestants], have been consumed by the devouring sword of uncle Edom. The hellish nightmare experienced by Jacob in those dark hours, did rival the latter demonic holocaust of Hitler's concentration camps, ovens, and medical experiments on helpless Jews. The God of Jacob has recorded, through his prophets, Esau's tendency to cast off all pity in the day of his vengeance. God promised to respond in kind and root out this venomous spirit from Esau's heart.

The quotes continue: "This is the grand contrast between the work of England [Ephraim] and the work of Spain [Edom]. The former is creative and conservative—the latter was destructive." Remember what a modern Edomite—Saddam Hussein—has done to a helpless nation—Kuwait! Also, what his merciless acts of genocide, through poisonous gas, did to the helpless, innocent Kurdish civilians. "This is, in a few words, the net result of Spanish interference in the new world—the substitution of barbarism for civilization. These scenes of treachery and bloodshed [in Post Columbus and Spanish new world conquests] masked with a show of legality and religious principle, make the Spanish Empire one of the most nauseating studies of history. With these exceptions, and also with the partial exception of Paraguay, Spanish history is all like the story of Mexico and Peru—a monotonous record of plunder and slaughter. It is as uninteresting as Turkish history. It is even more uninteresting, for the Turks and their fellow Muslims often built cities, which were miracles of beauty, and devised systems of legislation and social life, which were a great improvement on what they supplanted. But the Spaniard's one notion was destruction, and what was Castilian in the world was good, the rest was naught. No Turk was ever more stupid or more brutal."

"In effect, Spain was an Asiatic power of the old conquering, exterminating type." The Spanish Civil War was recognized in recent years, to be one of the bloodiest wars in history. Edom's love for bloodshed determined the nature of this war, says Gutierrez. The Iberian soldier has been known since ancient times to be a fierce warrior. The Iberian soldiers were often used as mercenaries as far back as the 5th century B.C. by the Greeks.

Francisco Ugarte, in his Panorame De La Civilization Espanola, says: "The Greek and Roman writers of antiquity describe the Iberians as dark [or tanned] and men of low stature, as fierce and independent people, warriors, stoics, proud, religious, noble and lazy" (translation by Gutierez).

Nicholson B. Adams writes: "The Spaniard is above all an individualist and greatly prizes personal autonomy . . . it has been often remarked that Spanish soldiers in the days when personal valor was preeminent requisite, were the best in Europe. When armies became more like machines [due to Jacob's industrial revolution], Spaniards lost their military power" (Adam 1943). This was one way for the God of Jacob to topple Esau from his 'high horse.' He used the natural inclination of Jacob for ingenuity and creativity to bring this "mind over matter" to pass. The ingenuity of Jacob did triumph over the inventor of the spirit of Machismo.

According to Niebuhr, "The Romans greatly respected the Spaniards on account of their courage and determination" (Niebuhr 1853, Vol. II; 285).

The many bloody revolutions and violence that take place in Edom's lands, in Latin America and nations like Iraq, are common scenes on the evening news. The unbridled examples of extreme cruelty committed by the Spanish Inquisition, is a case in point. Many of the Nazi torture ideas were actually borrowed from the Spanish horror chambers. Hitler himself was a great admirer of the Spanish inquisition's methods of torture. It is no coincidence that Spain's General Franco worked closely with Hitler. Nor is it a coincidence that many Nazi mass murderers found safe refuge in the bosom of Edom—in Spain and Latin America. Many in the Arab world, like the Edomite Grand Mufti (religious leader) of Jerusalem in the 40's, an uncle of Yasser Arafat, have admired and worked closely with Hitler. One of the heroes of Saddam Hussein of Iraq was the merciless mass killer Adolph Hitler. Saddam's father had a large portrait of Hitler in the family living room; this 'butcher' of Nazi Germany was the ever—present inspiration for the growing young 'butcher' of Bagdad.

The evidence is clear—the Iberian is a man of the sword. The God of Israel has declared: "'Therefore, as I live,' says the Lord God, 'I will prepare you for blood and blood shall pursue you; since you have not hated blood [or bloodshed], therefore blood shall pursue you'" (Ezekiel 35:6). Read the whole chapter for more graphic details of Edom's attitudes and punishment. Review also the references to Edom in earlier chapters. For sake of space, we will not repeat them.

It is a twist of irony and history that Edom was intimately involved, at times, in Israel's spiritual and physical construction and leadership. He had also, on different occasions, attempted to destroy Israel's spiritual and physical entity, yet without success. The attempted genocide of all Jews in Haman's day, and the near attempted murder of the infant Jesus, are but two examples among many. In the days of David, the Edomites who lived in Phoenicia, or "red land," did live in peace with Brother Jacob. The Edomite king of Tyre, Hiram, was a close friend of David. Later, in Solomon's days, Hiram helped Israel build the magnificent Temple in Jerusalem. In her last days, before the Roman conquest, Judah was ruled by a dynasty of Edomite kings. Herod, the Edomite king, turned the second Temple into a magnificent structure and showcase for the Roman world.

Uncle Edom has often tried to regain his physical and spiritual birthright in various ways. At times, he tried to accomplish his goal by 'peaceful' means (notice today's Israeli-Palestinian 'peace' accords), but mostly by the edge of the sword. The rise of Islam and her great prophet, called "the man of the sword," from an Edomite territory along the Red Sea was no coincidence. The famous city of Medina, the ancient capital of Edom by the Red Sea, did experience intimately the wrath of the prophet against his enemies. Many Jews living in that area did experience the fullness of this wrath, yet, ironically, one of the scholars who helped the illiterate Muhammad to assemble and canonize the Qur'an text was a Jew and a devout supporter of the prophet. Also, a most beloved wife of the prophet was a Jewess whose husband was killed by Muhammad in battle.

In the early centuries, the ruthless suppression by the Universal Church, and its forced invasion of the birthright tribes, the British people, is historically documented. Her role in terrorizing the people of Judah in the past two millenniums, at times through the bloodthirsty people of Edom, is no secret either. In the Middle East and Europe, Edom had often championed the desires and aims of two religions to oppress Jacob.

Spain, the center of Edom in Europe, has tried twice to grab both spiritual and physical leadership of the world. Yet each time, by God's decree, she has been stopped by an Israelites' country, according to Gutierez. He adds, "The inquisition was launched as a drive toward spiritual leadership, but was frustrated not only by the Netherlands in their revolt against Spain [uncle Edom's ruthless sword], but also by the British. Spain tried physical leadership of the world by sending the conquistadors for the conquest of the new world, and the Armada for the conquest of the old. The Spanish Armada was destroyed, by England [actually, by God's intervention and storm, as the Queen of England, Elizabeth I, stated: "He blew his nostrils, and they drowned in the bottom of the sea," quoting the Song of Moses], and her American endeavors were frustrated by Britain and the United States, as well as France" (Herring 1964:7910. "Again, Jacob has triumphed over his brother," writes Gutierez, "in the future he will complete the triumph, this time for good."

"After giving us a number of charts showing the comparative intellectual achievements of different countries," Gutierez states, "all representing Spain and Portugal at the lower end of achievement scale, Weyl and Possony, in their book The Geography of Intellect say: 'This table is erroneously revealing in a number of ways. We note that Spain and Portugal, which were areas of great scientific importance and intellectual leadership [with the help of Jewish and Arab thinkers] during the middle ages, had ceased to play any role of major significance in the creative work of Western civilization by the end of the 17th century [the time of Jacob's rise to world prominence].'"

The authors add, "There were many reasons for the intellectual decline of Spain." The God of Israel has spoken of Edom through his prophets: "Behold I will make you small among the nations; you shall be greatly despised. The pride of your heart [which is the hallmark trait of Edom, along with arrogance] has deceived you, you who dwell in the clefts of the rock [of Spain—a high plateau, also Gibraltar and many parts of Latin America], whose habitation is high; you who say in your heart, 'Who will bring me down to the ground?' Though you exalt yourself as high as the eagle, [and much of the Latin world is high and mountainous], and though you set your nest among the stars, from there I will bring you down, says the Lord" (Obadiah 2-4).

Scholars, unfamiliar with the Scriptures, mostly because of lack of faith, can never fully understand the true meaning of historic events. They do not know nor see the invisible hands that pull the strings of world events, but soon all will see those hands and begin to report accurately all historic information.

Weyl and Possony continue: "In 1492, all Spanish Jews who adhered to their faith were expelled from the kingdom. More than 100,000 were driven out [a great number in those days' terms]; a mere 40,000 embraced, or pretended to embrace, the catholic faith [and for this compromise they had earned God's wrath, displeasure, and consequent inquisition]. This elimination of an element that had made outstanding contributions to the intellectual, commercial and political life of the Iberian Peninsula, was followed a decade later, by a similar decree, which forced the Moslems of Leon and Castile to choose between conversion and exile. This law was characterized by Cardinal Richelieu as 'the most barbarous in history.'"

The Sultan of Turkey, who had opened his doors to the Spanish Jews, remarked: "Only a stupid king will ever do such a thing, his loss is my gain." The authors add: "To make matters worse, the Spanish inquisition raged with fury and thoroughness unknown elsewhere, burning 31,000 and condemning another 290,000 to other penalties. Spanish Protestants and relapsed Maranos [or Jews] were exterminated. Under Charles V, a Spanish Hapsburg, 50,000 persons were executed in the Netherlands, and under Philip II, his son, at least half as many.

"During the 17th century, it is estimated that 300,000 [or millions in today's terms] Protestants [all Israelites] were put to death and an equal number driven to exile. Moreover, the bloody Spanish wars of the 15th and 16th century and the conquest and settlement of Hispanic America to a very large extent, drained Spain of its aristocratic warrior element. This persecution, combined with war, did bring about genetic impoverishment" (ibid. pg. 130).

Of this matter, we read: "Will I not in that day, says the Lord, even destroy the wise men from Edom and understanding from the mountains of Esau? Then your mighty men, O Teman, shall be dismayed to the end that everyone from the mountains [or nations] of Esau may be cut off by slaughter" [Obadiah 8-9]. An end-time fulfillment of this prophecy is still ahead of us.

Weyl and Possony add: "While the Jews were certainly a major creative element in the intellectual life of medieval and renaissance Spain, it would be bad history to overemphasize their role. Their expulsion in 1492 was not followed by intellectual collapse, but rather by the 'golden century' of Spanish creativity. This was perhaps brought into being by factors resulting from the unification of the nation and from overseas conquest and Christianization of the Americas [by slaughter and violence, as in the "march of the sword of Islam" in the Arab world]. Any theory that Spanish intellectual life was entirely the result of Moorish and Jewish leadership collapses against the stubborn fact that both of these groups had been ousted by the early 1500's whereas, for examples, El Greco lived until 1614 and Cerviantes until 1616" (ibid. pg. 133). In the same context, it is also worth noting that many Spanish intellectuals were actually of Jewish background—though now all were members of the catholic faith, at least outwardly.

The wisdom of the men of Edom was legendary in the ancient world. After all, Esau was also the son of Isaac and grandson of Abraham. Yet God had determined to remove Esau's wise men from him to "make him a small and despised nation."

Of all the vast territories Edom was able to acquire by his sword in the new world, only a fraction of it is cultivable. Esau's blessings was, by far, lesser than that of Jacob. In Spain, "cultivated land makes up about 40% of Spain's total area, of this, about one acre in twenty is irrigated . . . most of the non irrigated lands have poor yield" (McGraw-Hill 1960:237).

Paddock writes in Hungry Nations: "The interiors of central and south Americas are uninhabited because they are worthless." Speaking of the national character of Edom, Gutierez writes, "God says the Edomites are very proud." He quotes Obadiah 3 and Jeremiah 49:16. "Among the nations of today," he writes, "you would be very much put out to find a prouder people than the Spaniards. Just about every picture of a Spaniard catches him with his chin in the air and an aura of importance around him. Surely the very universe revolves around Spain, at least every Spaniard would think" (Gutierez 1965:33).

Scripture tells us that Esau sold his birthright for a cheap price to his brother Jacob. He showed little appreciation for the great heritage that came from God. In modern times, we have seen a similar behavior in the Middle East. Jacob exploited and developed the oil riches or fatness of the earth given to Esau. He had for years paid little for it. In the Latin nations of Esau, we see the same attitude. The labor and products of Esau's children is being developed and exploited by Jacob's descendants for a cheap price.

The words God spoke to Rebekah came to pass: "Two manner of peoples shall be separated from your body; one people shall be stronger than the other and the older [Esau] shall serve the younger" (Genesis 25:23). To this day, Esau is still serving his younger, yet stronger, brother Jacob.

Isaac told Jacob: "Let peoples serve you and nations bow down to you. Be master over your brethren, and let your mother's sons [Esau's descendants] bow down to you." And if they don't like it, "Cursed be everyone who curses you and blessed be those who bless you" (Genesis 27:29).

Many nations found themselves in this predicament—bowing to the British Lion, and others still do to the American Eagle. Colonialism was a decree from above. The tribes of Jacob need not apologize for it, but for the abuses they inflicted on those God placed under them. But what kind of servitude was he talking about? Did he mean for Jacob to exploit his brother (or others) and rob him of his wages and inheritance? Did he mean for him to deceitfully rob his brother of his rightful blessings? Did he mean for Jacob to crush the economic backbone of Edom through his "generous" bank loans, which impoverish Edom's lands, through exorbitant high interest, of his meager blessings?

In his great Law to Jacob, God warned him against taking interest from his poor brothers. Edom is Jacob's brother. For those who could not afford it, God warned His people not to impose interest on them. See for details Exodus 22:25, Leviticus 25:36,37 and Deuteronomy 23:19. "From a stranger you may lend upon usury," God told them (Deuteronomy 23:20), but not from a needy brother. The dire predicament in which many banks often find themselves is a direct result of rejecting this Law of the God of Jacob.

God gave Jacob through Moses the great moral Law of conduct. He commanded him: "You shall not abhor an Edomite, for he is your brother" (Deuteronomy 23:7). Did Jacob obey this law, fully, at all times? God warned Jacob not to take advantage of those who serve him. He spoke His Law through Moses: "You shall neither mistreat a stranger nor oppress him, for you were strangers in the land of Egypt." He added, "Also you shall not oppress a stranger, for you know the heart of a stranger" (Exodus 22:21; 23:9). Does Jacob consider and obey this law in his dealings with his brother Edom or the stranger at his lands?

A brief stroll through the farmlands or factories of America, and for that matter Israel, in the Middle East, reveals an ugly story. Aliens and so-called "illegal aliens" from Edom are being exploited to the hilt. God is not blind, nor is He a respecter of persons. Those who transgress His laws will pay for it fully. The Egyptians who robbed Israel of her wages during their hour of slavery did pay fully for it. God is a just God. He hates robbery. Many of Edom's children are being robbed of their dignity and wages in the farmlands of agribusiness-corporate America and the modern land of Israel. Many of them are consumed and poisoned by pesticides. To even the score, God will allow Edom to rise above his oppressive brother Jacob just one last time. That's how God brings back His children to His Law. They that transgress His Law, will have to taste the bitter medicine produced by the consequences.

In the sweatshops of America, the picture is even worst for many workers. Many children of Edom, in abject poverty and servitude to brother Jacob, are being used and abused. They are forced to be silent, or face the threat of a loss of a job, or worse, being exposed to the immigration authorities. Many of Edom's children experience the hard bondage of the extremely underpaid. They are ever fearful; being illegal aliens. Often stripped of their human respect and dignity, they slave long hours, at times with their children, for their meager earnings. In some cases, they are not even paid whatever little they were promised. God forbade His people to oppress the wages of the hired servants. In due time, He will allow Edom to fully collect his lost wages. This is love and justice God's style!

Though Esau did earn his servitude, just like Israel did in Egypt; Jacob was to treat him as a brother, not an enemy or a slave. Instead, often, Jacob did abhor his brother Edom. God will reward everyone according to his works. He has no favorite pets. All are His children. For humanity's sake, He gave His Son's life. The coming captivity of Jacob, and later, that of all of his enemies, is meant to teach all nations to live in peace, with the help of God's Royal Law, with each other.

Now back to Edom and Gutierez' points. Speaking of Edom, God says: "You who dwell in the clefts of the rock, whose habitation is high" (Obadiah 3). Gutierez remarks that Edom inhabits a high place. He quotes Pettison: "Aside from Switzerland, no country in Europe is as high as Spain, but unlike Switzerland, Spain rises directly out of the sea. It is a high tableland surrounded on practically all sides by a ring of mountains and crossed internally by several principal mountain ranges. The average altitude of the country is about 2500 feet" (Pattison 1963, Vol. I; 3). Obadiah's statement about the 'Rock,' according to Gutierez, could refer to the Gibraltar. Also, many of the Spaniards live in high altitude cities in Latin America.

Another point Gutierez makes concerns the name Edom: it means red. Edom lived by the Red Sea, which he named after the patriarch Edom. Later, a part of Edom migrated into present day Lebanon. He named it red, or in their language, Phoenicia. Red or burgundy is a color associated with Spain. It is the dominant color of the Spaniard, according to Gutierez.

"A rather common name among the Spanish is Edmundo," says Gutierez. He adds: "The letters E-D-M, Does signify Edom, since both Hebrew and Phoenician languages did not have vowels. The last part of the name Edmundo, mundo, means world. Thus, Edmundo or Edom-Mundo, means world of Edom!" When the Phoenicians, as mentioned before, migrated into Italy, they were called Edomantes, a name very similar to Edmundo."

Gutierez feels that the Spanish word for Mister, or Don, are related to Edom or Adon. In Hebrew, the word for Mister or Sir is Adon. The letter 'M' is at times exchanged for 'N' in Hebrew. Thus, "the Latins simply, though unknowingly, recognize each other as a descendant of Edom," according to Gutierez" (Gutierez 1965:34).

Gutierez brings another point concerning the role Spain played in the last two World Wars. It never fought on the allies' side, but was with the axis "as one of them" [according to Obadiah's prophecy, v. 11], and so was Argentina. Other Latin nations, being dependant economically on the allies, did contribute a little to the allies' cause. They had no other choice. Spain would again be "as one of them" in the coming final round. Gutierez also says: "History depicts the Edomite tribes constantly divided among themselves. The monarchs or chiefs were not hereditary dynasties. They did not last very long (see Genesis 36), and rulership usually went to the strongest." He asks, "Is this the case in Spain or in Latin America?" In the Middle East, we see a similar state of affairs in countries conquered by Edom. Iraq and Lebanon are a case in point.

Of the hairy Iberian [and Esau was very hairy], Dixon writes: "What seems to have struck most the Greeks and Romans about the appearance of the Iberian men was their hairiness, although in their own art, they are usually represented as clean shaven. Martial, who was proud of his Spanish ancestry, contrasting his appearance with that of a smooth faced Corinthian with flowing hair, speaks of himself as covered with hair on face and limbs; and the Greek comic poet, Cratinus, in allusion no doubt to one of the Iberian mercenaries who were a familiar sight in the streets of Athens from time-to-time in the 5th century B.C., speaks in one of his plays of a 'goat bearded Iberian'" (Dixon 1940:17).

Finally, Gutierez writes: "The name Iberia is said by many scholars to come from the word Hebreo or Hebrew. But, might it be that Esau in seeking to regain his birthright also called himself Hebrew, thus passing his name on to his descendants?" Then, Gutierez quotes Bryant, who stated: "The Iberians therefore appear to have been the same nation as the Erythreans or Edomites . . . yet, lost not their original Gentile name from Heber; but were at times termed Eberi, or Iberi, according to the Greek manner of expressing it" (Bryant 1807, Vol. VI; 231).

Edom, indeed, has a complex and most fascinating personality—a person of contrasts. He is a great builder, soldier, explorer, a splendid artist and man of culture and colorful flair. He is full of life and joy of living, a loving family man and a passionate lover. Yet he is also proud, arrogant and blood-thirsty. He is a man of the sword and quick to shed blood. He loves and hates with unbridled passion, yet at times, shows contempt to the genuine treasures of life. Why is Edom so enigmatic, so ruthless and haughty at times?

The God of Jacob and Edom's father, Isaac, stated His feelings about Esau's spirit: "Jacob I loved, but Esau I hated." Why is it so? From his mother's belly, Esau was destined to scorch and plunder the earth with unbridled fury and cruel, stormy passions. Wherever he went, he left behind him trails of blood—and he loved it. What spirit got hold of Esau's soul from his mother's womb?

There are two places in the Bible of Jacob that can reveal the source and nature of Edom's spirit. Let us read about it! In a previous chapter about Edom, we have covered the strong link between Edom and Babylon. The wording and punishment of both cruel enemies of Israel—Edom and Babylon—are most striking in resemblance. In this chapter, we have seen that many Phoenicians or Edomites, later named Erythreans, were settling areas around the Persian Gulf. These Edomites founded a city at the mouth of the Persian Gulf naming it Basra, after the ancient capital of their father's land—Mount Seir. The territory around Basra, they named Erythra, meaning Edom or red.

The prophet Isaiah describes in Chapter 14 of his book a type and antitype of two personalities. After all Israel is to be restored, in the near future, to his original land, which God calls "the land of the Lord" (v. 2), God then states: "It shall come to pass in the day the Lord gives you [Israel] rest from your sorrow and from your fear and the hard bondage [of a future captivity and concentration camps] in which you were made to serve [brother Edom, among others], that you will take up this proverb against the king of Babylon" (Isaiah 14:1-4). Then we read a description of the future world tyrant, whose forces would enslave Jacob and the rest of humanity, as they did anciently. His proud attitude is later compared to that of the fallen Lucifer or Satan himself (vv. 4-15). The chapter ends with the description of the ruler of Babylon who symbolizes Satan himself in his pride, madness, and destructive and ruthless spirit. Also, the utter destruction of his land is foretold.

In Isaiah 63, God describes this final battle with the king of Babylon. He depicts Himself as a warrior with bloodstained garments returning from the battleground. The prophet proclaimed: "Who is this who comes from Edom [who dwells in Babylon] with dyed garments from Bozrah" (Isaiah 63:1). Edom's ancient capital, now in Iraq or ancient Babylon, was Bozrah or Botsra.

Let us go now to Ezekiel 26. Here Ezekiel writes: "And it came to pass . . . that the word of the Lord came to me saying, 'Son of man because Tyre [the Phoenician capital of Edom] has said against Jerusalem, 'Aha', she is broken who was the gateway of the peoples [of brother Jacob]: now she is turned over to me [finally, Edom rejoices, "the land and birthright are mine!"]; I shall be filled; she is laid waste.' Therefore, thus says the Lord God: 'Behold, I am against you, O Tyre and will cause many nations to come up against you and they shall destroy the walls of Tyre'" (vv. 1-4). Anciently, Alexander the Great had finally accomplished that. He used, among others, Israelite forces that lived in his empire (the Danite Grecians) to bring about Tyre's destruction.

In verse 17, God describes the terror that Tyre had spread on all those she ruled over. She was "the great city" of those times. Then, in Chapter 27, God describes the glory and greatness of Tyre—the Edomite sea capital of the ancient world. He also describes her destruction and oblivion. Again, in Chapter 28, we meet the type and anti-type of a man who symbolizes Satan. The man here is the Edomite king of Tyre. Ezekiel writes: "The word of the Lord came to me again, saying, 'Son of man, say to the prince of Tyre [who is called prince, while Satan, the antitype, is called king, v. 11], thus says the Lord God, because your heart is lifted up [in pride] and you say, I am god, I sit in the seat of the gods [the epitome of pride, arrogance and haughtiness], in the midst of the seas: Yet you are a man and not god, though you set your heart as the heart of a god'" (Ezekiel 28:1-2).

God then describes the great wisdom and splendor of the prince of Tyre. He vows to destroy this arrogant ruler by "the most terrible of the nations" (V. 7). In verses 11-19, God describes the pride and arrogance of the fallen angel or cherub Lucifer. He was the real invisible ruler of Tyre and all nations. It was his attitude and spirit that the Edomite king of Tyre did emulate and display. It was this spirit that influenced Edom's mind from the womb of his mother. His nature and inclinations did manifest themselves before his birth. They caused him to lose his birthright, and later, his religion and relationship with the God of his father. It is no coincidence that Edom helped champion two rival religions, different from that of his father and his brother. The history of the Spanish people and their love-hate relationship with brother Jacob, with its global implications, are the tragic results of choosing to follow the wrong spirit. The final solution will bring an end to the influence of that Satanic spirit. A new chapter between the twins will be written, this time, in love and peace for ages to come. Jacob will cease to exploit and supplant his brother Edom, and Esau will learn to obtain his birthright in accordance with the divine will. The sword of Esau and the deceitful tongue of Jacob will pierce no more the heart of a twin brother.

After the soon coming greatest holocaust, which will affect every nation on earth, God writes of a happy ending between Jacob and Edom. Speaking of the return of the Israelite captives, He states: "Surely the coastlands shall wait for me [and worship Me]; and the ships of Tarshish [or Spain, Edom's new armada] shall come first, to bring your sons [of Israel] from afar, their silver and their gold with them to the name of the Lord your God and to the Holy One of Israel, because He has glorified you. The sons of foreigners [including Edom] shall build up your walls [Jerusalem] and their kings shall minister to you; for in My wrath I struck you, but in My favor I have had mercy on you. Therefore, your gates shall be open continually; they shall not be shut day nor night, that men may bring to you the wealth of the Gentiles [which they have robbed you of in the time of your calamity] and their kings in procession. For the nation and kingdom which will not serve you shall perish . . . also the sons of those who afflicted you [as Edom and others] shall come bowing to you and all those who despised you shall fall prostrate at the soles of your feet; and they shall call you the City of the Lord . . . you shall know that I the Lord [the Messiah], am your Savior [Jesus or Joshua, meaning Savior] and your Redeemer, the Mighty One of Jacob" (Isaiah 60:10-16).

In the next and final chapter, we shall delve into the story of Jerusalem—the city of peace. It is the City of The Great King of Jacob, of Edom, of Ishmael, and the children of the earth.

CHAPTER 11

JERUSALEM—THE CITY OF PEACE

The history of peace and war are intimately interwoven with the history and nature of Jerusalem. To fully understand present day events in the Middle East and the causes behind them, we must first understand the history of Jerusalem. We should consider the mysteries of the city that has known the fruit of war and peace more than any other city on the face of the earth. Only in reaching for the highest plateau of understanding, will we be able to tie all the loose ends together. In doing so, we will be able to weave all the threads, not only of the events surrounding the past 4000 years history of Israel and her relations to other descendants of Abraham, but also of those which are yet to come.

Let us begin this saga of the city of peace from the vantage point of the story of Jerusalem. In that realm, we will unearth the beginning of the stormy history of Israel and her neighbors—the children of the patriarch Abraham. After heeding the call to leave his glamorous world behind, Abraham the patriarch and later king of Damascus, according to Josephus, arrived in the land of Canaan. During his mostly peaceful journey in the land of promise, with a side trip to Egypt, Abraham had experienced only one war. In Genesis 14, we find the account of that war.

Abraham's nephew and adopted son, Lot, did settle in an area near Sodom. Later, he moved to Sodom proper. Shortly after, five Babylonian and Assyrian kings and their dukes, according to Josephus, have declared war against the kings of Sodom, Gomorrah and their allies—because they refused to pay tribute any longer to their Assyrian task masters. In that war, which the Assyrians had won, Lot was taken captive with all the civilians from the losing side. When the mighty prince, Abraham, heard of it, he immediately took to the rescue of his nephew. He pursued his nephew's captors to Damascus and defeated them. After retrieving all that was taken by the captors, he restored them back to their lands. Abraham won decisively his first and last war, while in Canaan, against the invading Assyrian and Babylonian Armies.

The result of that war should have become a lesson to Abraham's descendants, especially those of Israel. 4000 years later, the ancient prophets of Israel have warned that God's people would experience a similar event at the end of their day. This time, it would first spell a horrendous disaster for Israel and result in captivity. Then, with the help of the conquering Messiah, both modern Babylon and Assyria's forces will be completely defeated.

When Abraham returned from his victorious expedition to his land, a unique event, understood only by few, took place. In Genesis Chapter 14:18-20, we read: "Then Melchizedek, king of Salem [or Jerusalem] brought out bread and wine; he was the priest of the Most High God. And he blessed him and said, blessed be Abram of God Most High, possessor of heaven and earth; and blessed be God Most High, who has delivered your enemies into your hands, and he [Abram] gave him a tithe of all."

Earlier, we have discussed, briefly, the identity of Malchizedek. For sake of emphases, let's discuss again the identity of this Malchizedek and His link to the final solution of the Middle East conflict. Who was this mysterious King of Salem and Priest of the Most High God to whom Abram gave a tithe of all? What is the connection between this King of Salem or Jerusalem and the story of Abraham's children. Is there a link between this King of Peace and the turbulent history and future of Jerusalem?

Let us jump forward 2000 years into the time of the apostle Paul, a servant of this Melchizedek, for an answer. Speaking to his people, the Hebrews, Paul had stated: "For this Melchizedek, King of Salem, Priest of the Most High God, who met Abraham returning from the slaughter of the kings and blessed him, to whom Abraham also gave a tenth part of all, first being translated King of Righteousness [the Hebrew meaning of Melchizedek], and then also of Salem, meaning King of Peace, without father, without mother, without [human] genealogy, having neither beginning of days nor end of life, but made like the Son of God [Adam was also called the son of God, in a human form], remains a Priest continually" (Hebrews 7:1-3).

Then in verses 15-17, Paul is quoting an oath God made in Psalm 110:4 concerning the One called Melchizedek. Let us read it in the original text! "The Lord has sworn and will not repent, you are a Priest forever, according to the order [or rank] of Melchizedek." Then in verses 5-6 we read of this Melchizedek: "The Lord is at your right hand; He shall execute kings at the day of His wrath [which is soon coming]. He shall judge among the nations, He shall fill the places [first around Jerusalem, then worldwide] with dead bodies, He shall execute the heads of many countries." There is going to be a mass execution of heads of government, and all other kind of leaders, responsible for the mess on planet earth. Read also Psalm 149 for more details.

The prophet Micah, speaking of this very personage, Melchizedek, stated: "But you Bethlehem Ephrathah, though you are little among the thousands of Judah, yet out of you shall come forth to me the one to be ruler in Israel, whose going forth have been from of old, from everlasting." Micah added, "Therefore, He shall give them up [his people Israel, who will continue to suffer], until the time that she who is in labor [Jerusalem, Isaiah 61-62] has given birth; then the remnant of His brethren [the people of Judah] shall return to the children of Israel [in a final union of Judah and the ten tribes of Israel, Ezekiel 37:15-22]. And he shall stand and feed His flock in the strength of the Lord, on the majesty of the name of the Lord His God; and they shall abide [Israel and Judah], for now He shall be great to the ends of the earth; and this One shall be peace" (Micah 5:1-5).

The prophet Micah plainly speaks of the King and Messiah of Israel. This King, like Melchizedek, has no beginning, nor end of days. In other words: He is eternal and has always been. But who is this Messiah and Redeemer of Israel and future king of Jerusalem?

The prophet Daniel writes of a vision he had of this Messiah and his encounter with the Ancient of Days. This was the One who later became known as The Father—the real God-Father. Let us read it in Daniel 7:9-14! "I watched till thrones were put in place and the Ancient of Days was seated; His garment was white as snow and the hair of his head was like pure wool. His throne was a fiery flame; its wheels a burning fire; a fiery stream issued forth from before him. A thousand, thousand ministered to him; and ten thousand times ten thousands stood before him. The court [of heaven] was seated and the books were opened . . . I was watching in the night visions, and behold, one like the Son of man [the King and Messiah of Israel], coming with the clouds of heaven; He [the Messiah] came to the Ancient of Days [or The Father], and they [the angels] brought Him [the Messiah, in a coronation procession] before Him [the Ancient of Days]. Then to Him [the Messiah] was given dominion and a glory and a kingdom, that all peoples, nations and languages should serve Him. His dominion is an everlasting dominion, which shall not pass away, and His kingdom the one which shall not be destroyed."

Et Voilá, as the French say, this is the true identity of the coming Messiah. Yet, that's not all! Speaking of this Messiah's coronation, the apostle John, also in a vision, saw and recorded the following account: "After these things, I looked and behold, a door standing open in heaven, and the first voice which I heard was like a trumpet speaking with me saying, 'Come up here and I will show you things which must take place after this.' Immediately, I was in the Spirit; and behold, a throne was set in heaven [as in Daniel's vision] and one sat on the throne. And He who sat there was like a jasper and a sardius stone in appearance; and there was a rainbow around the throne, in appearance like an emerald. Around the throne were twenty-four thrones and on the thrones, I saw twenty-four elders [top advisors of God] sitting clothed in white robes; and they had crowns of gold on their heads. And from the throne proceeded lightning and thundering and voices: and there were seven lamps of fire burning before the throne, which are the seven Spirits of God. Before the throne there was a sea of glass, like crystal [see Ezekiel 1, 10]. And in the midst of the throne and around the throne, were four living creatures [the four cherubs] full of eyes in front and in back" (Revelation 4:1-6). The rest of this chapter describes the form of worship of these cherubs, the angels, and the twenty-four elders. Now let's continue with this coronation ceremony of the King and Messiah of Israel in Revelation 5:1-16.

John describes a scroll written on both sides and sealed, which none could open. At this point, John begins to weep, believing that none could open the scroll. He wrote: "But one of the elders said to me, do not weep. Behold the Lion of the tribe of Judah, the Root of David [or the Messiah, son of David], has prevailed to open the scroll and to loose its seven seals. And he came and took the scroll out of the right hand of Him that sat on the throne [the Father]."

The outcome of this coronation ceremony is described in Revelation, Chapter 19:11-16. Here we read: "Then I saw heaven opened and behold a white horse. And he who sat on him was called faithful and true and in righteousness He judges and makes war." Whenever the God of Israel and her Savior or Messiah descends to deliver His people in the day of battle, He comes riding on a horse, not on his traveling throne as Ezekiel describes in Chapters 9 and 10. "His eyes were like a flame of fire and on his head were many crowns [after He was coroneted]. He had a name written that no one knew except himself. He was clothed in a robe dipped in blood, and his name is called The Word of God. And the armies in heaven, clothed in fine linen, white and clean, followed him on white horses. Now out of his mouth goes a sharp sword, that with it, he should strike the nations. And he himself will rule them with a rod of iron [those who rebel and will not submit to His rule and Law], He himself treads the winepress of the fierceness of the wrath of Almighty God. And he has on his robe and on his thigh a name written: King of Kings and Lord of Lords.'"

At this point, let's return to Isaiah 63:2-6 and read the prophet's discourse with this King of Israel, who is now treading on the path of war. "Why is your apparel red and your garments like one who treads in the winepress?" The prophet asks the King and Messiah of Israel. His reply: "I have trodden the winepress alone and from the peoples, no one was with me [since Israel at that point is in captivity]. For I have trodden them in my anger and trampled them in my fury; their blood is sprinkled upon my garments, and I have stained all my robes. For the day of vengeance is in My heart, and the year of My redeemed [Israel] has come. I looked, but there was no one to help [since most of Israel's armies have earlier been defeated, and the world's armies are fighting against Him], and I wondered that there was no one to uphold; therefore, My arm brought salvation for Me; and My own fury, it sustained Me. I have trodden down the peoples in My anger, made them drunk in My fury and brought down their strength to the earth."

The prophet Joel, as was covered before, has also described this very "mother of all wars." It is to be waged against all nations at the end time, as the God of Israel and her Messiah had declared. Through Joel God had stated: "When I bring back the captives of Judah and Jerusalem [prior to the founding of the modern State of Israel], I will also [few decades later, gather all nations and bring them down to the Valley of Jehoshaphat [Heb. the judgment of God, or God the Judge]. And I will enter into judgment with them there on account of My people [Israel and Judah], My heritage Israel, whom they have scattered among the nations; they have also divided up My [not Arab] land. They have cast lots for My people" (Joel 3:1-3). The rest of this chapter describes the fate of the nations responsible for the coming destruction and captivity of God's people—the thirteen tribes of Israel.

Isaiah the prophet gives us more details about the identity of this Messiah of Israel. He revealed the identity of the Deliverer who created Adam and Eve, ate lunch with Abraham, wrestled with the patriarch Jacob, and spoke to Moses face to face for forty years. In Isaiah 9:6-7 he writes of him: "For unto us a child is born, unto us a son is given; and the government will be upon his shoulder and his name will be called wonderful, counselor, the mighty God, the everlasting Father, Prince of peace [or Salem]."

This personage, the second member of the God family, was the very one who created man and all the universe as we read in John 1:1-3. Here John stated: "In the beginning was the Word, and the Word was with God, and Word was [also a Deity or] God. He was in the beginning with God. All things were made through Him [being the actual creator], and without Him nothing was made that was made." Isaiah continues: " . . . Of the increase of his government and peace there will be no end, upon the throne of David and over his Kingdom, to order it and establish it with judgment and justice [the two most lacking elements in human governments at every level], from that time forward, even forever. The zeal of the Lord of Hosts will perform this."

Though now, both Israel and Judah's nations scoff at this soon coming reality, those who will be left at the end of the coming captivity of all Israel will not! There is nothing like a good healthy 'spanking' to get carnal minded people's attention. That is one reason for the coming greatest captivity and mega holocaust. Faith is not what motivates humanity today. So the God of Israel will give humanity, beginning with Israel, the most spectacular "show of blood, sweat and tears" this world has ever seen. As the prophet Jeremiah has recorded in Chapter 30:7: "Alas, for that day is great, so that none is like it; and it is the time of Jacob's trouble [or tribulation], but he [or the remnant, about 10%] shall be saved out of it."

Also in the New Testament, in Matthew 24:21-22, we read the warning given by the Messiah of Israel: "For then there will be great tribulation, such as has not been since the beginning of the world until this time, no, nor ever shall be and unless those days were shortened, no flesh would be saved [alive]; but for the elect's sake, those days will be shortened."

In Isaiah 66:15, we read: "For behold, the Lord will come in fire, and his chariots like the storm winds [the ultimate grand operation "Desert Storm"], to render his anger in fury and his rebuke with flames of fire. For by fire and by his sword the Lord will judge all flesh and the slain of the

Lord shall be many." Elsewhere, we read that only one tenth (Isa. 6:13) of humanity will survive the coming final mega holocaust. Humanity has a difficult time believing. The prophet Isaiah, speaking of all the people of Israel, exclaimed, "Who has believed our report? And to whom has the arm of the Lord been revealed?" (Isaiah 53:1). Yet the Messiah stated, through His prophet Zechariah, during the restoration of the second Temple: "It shall be in that day that I will seek to destroy all the nations that come against Jerusalem. And I will pour on the house of David and on the inhabitants of Jerusalem the Spirit of grace and supplication; then they will look on Me whom they [mainly, the politically minded religious leaders, being instrumental with Rome] have pierced [or crucified by Rome's hands]; they will mourn for Him [or their Messiah] as one mourns for his only son and grieves for him as one grieves for his firstborn. In that day, there shall be a great mourning in Jerusalem" (Zechariah 12:9-11).

The prophet Zechariah adds: "Behold the day of the Lord [the Messiah] is coming and your spoil [Jerusalem and Judah's cities] will be divided in your midst for I will gather all the nations to battle against Jerusalem; the city shall be taken, the houses rifled and the women ravished. Half of the city shall go into captivity, but the remnant of the people shall not be cut off from the city." No Israeli force or nuclear weapons can avert this God-appointed captivity for the sins of Israel. "Then the Lord [Messiah] will go forth and fight against those nations as he fights in the day of battle. And in that day His feet will stand on the Mount of Olives, which faces Jerusalem on the east" (Zechariah 14:1-4).

In verse 12, the prophet describes the method of destruction God the Messiah will use to 'zap' the nations with. He writes: "And this shall be the plague with which the Lord will strike all the people who fought against Jerusalem: Their flesh shall dissolve while they stand on their feet. Their eyes shall dissolve in their sockets and their tongues shall dissolve in their mouths." Then, in verses 16-18, the prophet continues: "And it shall come to pass that everyone who is left of all the nations which came against Jerusalem shall go up from year to year to worship the King [Messiah] the Lord of hosts and to keep the Feast of Tabernacles." Why does He mention this feast and what religion is humanity then to obey, we shall see later. We shall also find out the fate of those who despise that "Jewish religion."

Zechariah continues: "And it shall be that whichever of the families of the earth do not come up to Jerusalem to worship the King, the Lord of host, on them there will be no rain. If the family of Egypt [being Islamic] will not come up and enter in, they shall have no rain; they shall receive the plague with which the Lord strikes the nations who do not come up to keep the Feast [of Sukkot or] of Tabernacles."

There will be no more religious confusion in the family of Abraham! One nation, certainly, would be ahead of 'the game.' It will be the nation of Judah, whose religious core has never rejected that "Jewish religion." The ten tribes of Israel, those in the West, who later became mostly "Christian nations," and the Moslem world did scoff at God's "Jewish" religion and despised it for many centuries. The apostle Paul had to deal with this spirit of contempt toward the Jews in the Gentile converts to the genuine religion of Israel and her Messiah. He reminded them: "Moreover, brethren, I do not want you to be unaware [ignorant, KJV] that all our fathers were under the cloud, all passed through the sea, all were baptized into Moses in the cloud and in the sea, all ate the same spiritual food" (I Corinthians 10:1-3).

God's religion was not just a bunch of physical do's and don'ts. Yet even Israel's idolatrous ten tribes began to despise this religion, after the division of the kingdom. They scoffed at that "Jewish religion," when King Hezekiah pleaded with them to come and observe the Passover in Jerusalem, prior to their last stage captivity (II Chronicles 30).

Paul continues: "And all drank the same spiritual drink. For they drank of that Spiritual Rock that followed them AND THAT ROCK WAS CHRIST!" (I Corinthians 10:1-4). Established Christianity as a whole had rejected God's true religion. They, instead, chose a pagan form of religious error mixed with some truth, which is practiced to this day. This Rock or The Messiah and the direct Deity of Israel, Paul is declaring to those who are ignorant of the facts, is the real Jesus Christianity and Judaism are ignorant of and do not know, yet. It was His religion that all the tribes of Israel have mostly rejected for the last 2900 years—and most of Judah had despised it as well—that's why the coming captivity! Can anything be plainer? Paul said in Romans 3:4, "Yes, let God be true and every man a liar." That included, in his day and today, especially, many of the clergy of Israel who led Israel's tribes astray since the days of Jeroboam to this day.

Jeremiah, the prophet of "gloom and doom," as many labeled him, while experiencing the final stages of the fall of Jerusalem lamented: "Your prophets have seen for you false and deceptive visions [which most of the prophets of Israel and Judah were prone to do and still are at it]; they have not uncovered your iniquities [in government, religion, industry, education and in civil life] to bring back your captives [or more correctly, 'to turn away your captivity, KJV. Even translators, at times, deceive], but they have envisioned for you false prophecies and delusions [which the innocent sheep gullibly swallow without ever checking on their humanly ordained prophets]" (Jeremiah 2:14).

To these irresponsible shepherds of Israel, which include those in all fields of education, the anciently sacred responsibility given only to the Levites, God declares through the prophet Ezekiel, as well as others: "Son of man, prophecy [or give a warning] against the shepherds of Israel [by now long gone into captivity], prophesy and say to them, 'thus says the Lord God to the shepherds [or educators in religious and secular fields of humanly devised education], woe to the shepherds of Israel who feed themselves [which is the primary purpose of most educators—a job]. Should not the shepherds feed the flocks [with right education, moral values, character based on God's laws, not humanly devised philosophies and ideas]? The weak [morally] you have not strengthened nor have you healed those who were sick [in mind and spirit] nor bound up the broken nor brought back what was driven away nor sought what was lost; but with force and cruelty you have ruled them. So they were scattered because there was no shepherd; and they became food for all the [two-legged] beasts of the field when they were scattered." God pronounces a severe judgment against those shepherds or teachers who failed to provide strong moral teachings in all areas of life. Instead, they have taught error, imaginary hellfire and brimstone, harshness, and all the faulty mis-education that has produced the universal mess we have on this planet.

"My sheep," adds God, "wandered through all the mountains and on every high hill; yes, My flock was scattered over the whole face of the earth [in search of 'illumination,' meaning and purpose of life] and no one was seeking or searching for them" (Ezekiel 34:2-6). In verses 9-10 we read: "Therefore, Oh shepherds, hear the word of the Lord. Thus says the Lord God, behold, I am against the shepherds and I will require my flock at their hand; I will cause them to cease feeding the sheep [by bringing destruction on the humanly devised 'educational' system—religious and secular alike—as we know it today], and the shepherds shall feed themselves no more [in the outrageously high cost educational industry] for I will deliver My flock from their mouths, that they may no longer be food for them."

The educational industry created a system of: 2 years pre-school, 8 years public education, 4 years high school, and 4 years college. And to add insult to injury, much of the financial burden is heaped on the breaking back of parents; and then, still, no job guarantee, no profession, and often no character and moral values. What a heartless crime of insanity!!!

To rid humanity of this scourge, the God of Israel declares: "For thus says the Lord God, Indeed I Myself [since no government or industry, who are self serving in nature, and no religion will do it voluntarily, therefore I] will search for My sheep and seek them out. As a shepherd seeks out his flock on the day he is among his scattered sheep, so will I seek out My sheep and deliver them from all the places where they were scattered on a cloudy and dark day. And I will bring them out from the peoples [in every nation and city] and gather them from the countries and will bring them to their own land [Israel, a prophecy directed mainly for our time]; I will feed them on the mountains of Israel [not Palestine, as many, in willful ignorance, at times, still insist on calling the land of the God of Israel], in the valley and in all the inhabited places of the country. I will feed them in good pasture [with no more confused knowledge and mis-education], and their fold shall be on the high mountains of Israel. There, they shall lie down in a good fold and feed in rich pasture [spiritual and physical right food and education in all areas of life], on the mountains of Israel. I will seek what was lost and bring back what was driven away, bind up the broken [which government, religious, civil and secular leaders have failed to do], and strengthen what was sick; but I will destroy the fat and the strong [or high salaried executives and bureaucrats in all levels of society, who seek their own at the expense of others, and often to their own hurt] and feed them in judgment" (Ezekiel 34:11-16).

Then The Shepherd of Israel sternly warns: "As for you, Oh my flock [all of Israel], thus says the Lord God, behold, I shall judge between sheep and sheep, between rams and goats [or those who cause harm and those who are being harmed by society's religions, economic, secular and educational systems], is it too little for you to have eaten up the good pasture, that you must tread with your feet the residue of your pasture, and to have drunk of the clear water [or proper and sane knowledge] that you must foul [or contaminate right education, as taught by God's code of morality and ethics] the residue with your feet? And as for My [unsuspecting and gullible] flock, they eat what you have trampled with your feet, the [religious and secular humanly devised rubbish] and they drink what you have fouled with your feet.

"Therefore, thus says the Lord God to them: Behold, I myself will judge between the fat and the lean sheep [the prevalent reality on planet earth: the few fat sheep have much, and the lean sheep—the majority—have little]. Because you have pushed with the side and shoulder, butted all the weak ones with your horns, and scattered them abroad, therefore, I will save My flock and they shall no longer be a prey [to a self destructive, self serving system that adversely affects all spheres of life and all levels of society]; and I will judge between sheep and sheep. I will establish one shepherd over them [or one government leader who has proved himself for forty years that he is a man and a leader according to God's own heart], my servant [the resurrected] David. He shall feed them [not himself] and be their shepherd.

And I, the Lord, will be their God and My servant David a prince among them; I, the Lord, have spoken."

Dare we argue with Him? Tragically, Israel, and people in general, do like to argue with their Creator. As Isaiah the prophet declared: "Woe to him who strives [or argues] with his maker! Let the potsherd strive with the potsherds of the earth! Shall the clay say to him who formed it, 'what are you making?'" (Isa. 45:9).

Then the God of Israel describes the outcome of right leadership and education in Israel's restored nation. He declared: "I will make a covenant of peace with them and cause wild beasts to cease from the land, [including those in the form of 'two-legged animals' also]; and they will dwell safely in the wilderness and sleep in the woods." There will be no more crime—often a product of mis-education and corruption in all levels of society. This includes the 'civil' institutions of the land as: the banking, insurance, and medical industries, to name but a few.

"I will make them," says God, "and the places all around My hill [Zion] a blessing [not a curse, as it is today]; and I will cause showers to come down in their season. There shall be showers of blessings in their seasons." How many today, in our often drought-stricken world, believe that God is the one, not fictitious "mother nature," responsible for withholding or sending showers in their due season? Man is willfully ignorant! God adds: "Then the trees of the field shall yield their fruit [naturally, not artificially], and the earth shall yield her increase. They shall be safe in their land. And they shall know that I am the Lord, when I have broken the bands of their yoke [from the coming greatest and most cruel captivity Israel is ever to experience] and delivered them from the hand of those who enslaved them.

"And they shall no longer be a prey for the nations [or corrupt and deceived leaders], nor shall the beasts [as germs, bacteria, or viruses] of the land devour them. But they shall dwell safely and no one shall make them afraid. [What politician, armed forces, or police agency can make and deliver on such a promise?] I will raise up for them a garden [of super abundant crops] of renown, and they shall no longer be consumed with hunger in the land, [there shall be no more the scourge of government and industry-contrived shameful joblessness and criminal taxation], nor bear the shame of the Gentiles [who enslaved them] any more. Thus they shall know that I, the Lord their God [and Messiah] am with them [and they will never look any more to feeble attempts of human solutions to their problems], and that they, the house of Israel, are my people, says the Lord God, you are my flock, the flock of my pasture; you are men [not demi-gods, as some pretend to be], and I am your God, says the Lord God'" (Ezekiel 34:1-31).

The patriarch Abraham knew all that. What he heard was first-hand from the mouth of Melchizedek. He knew that this Melchizedek was the God of creation. Later, he was known as the God of Israel. He became her Messiah and Savior to deliver her from the results of mis-education promulgated by the "shepherds of Israel." The peace of Jerusalem, the city of the Great King of Salem, was taken away time and time again. Jerusalem robbed by the one responsible for the present day Middle East conflict, every conflict on earth, and the 4000 years old ongoing struggle between the children of Abraham. Who is he?

Now we know who Melchizedek is, the King of Jerusalem and of Righteousness, the Prince of Peace. Let us now find out who the prince of war is! Without this vital information, we cannot grasp the true causes of man's ills. Also, we cannot understand the Middle East conflict, other world conflicts, the upheavals in the former Soviet Union (or disunion), the confused religious scene, worldwide terror, and the final fate of Jerusalem and Israel.

In his letter to the Ephesian church, the apostle Paul wrote, after describing the greatness of the resurrected Messiah of Israel: "And you, He [the Messiah] made alive who were dead in trespasses and sins [since they had not been taught the laws of God], in which you once walked [as the rest of humanity does to this day] according to the course of this world [and its religions, philosophies, ideologies and mis-education], according to the prince of the power of the air, the spirit that now works in the sons of disobedience" (Ephesians 2:1-2).

Who is this prince of the power of the air whose spirit works, motivates, and leads the sons of disobedience to God's Law? We must know the true nature of this "dark force," if we are to make sense of life and, in particular, the Middle East conflict! The apostle Paul reveals, in his letter to the Corinthians, the identity of this prince of the power of the air. Let us read it in his own words! "For such are false apostles [declares the apostle Paul of the deceived spiritual and secular teachers of this world], deceitful workers [but how?], transforming themselves [not by God's power] into apostles of Christ." The messengers of Christ speak His words and teach His royal Law, which He, the God of the fathers, personally gave Israel in Sinai, not their own paganized form of religion, mixed with a few doctrines of Christ or the God of Israel. Paul continues, "And no wonder! For Satan [the prince of the power of the air] himself, transforms himself into an angel of light. Therefore, it is no great thing if his ministers also transform themselves into ministers of righteousness, whose end [as we have read in Ezekiel 34] is according to their works" (II Corinthians 11:13-15). Do we know who these ministers are? We should! They are also in every other religion on earth!

The charge and accusation the apostle of Christ, Paul, leveled at the prophets of Satan, who diverted the flocks of Israel and others away from God's Law, is very plain and clear. The Messiah of Israel warned (Mat. 5:17) His listeners: "Do not think that I came to destroy the Law [He gave in Sinai] and the Prophets, I did not come to destroy but to fulfill" [and so must you, was the implication]. Established Christianity has been teaching, since shortly after the death of the apostles, and to this day, that the Law of the Old Testament is Jewish. "It is not for us Gentiles," they claimed.

A doctor of the Law came to Christ, asking him: "Good teacher, what good things shall I do that I may have eternal life?" Christ replied: "If you want to enter into life, keep the Commandments" (Matthew 19:16-17). Many "Christian" scholars and religious teachers have taught their flocks that the Law is a curse and was done away. The apostle Paul stated: "For not the hearers of the Law [or Torah] are just in the sight of God, but the doers of the Law will be justified" (Romans 2:13). Many religious shepherds claim: "You don't need to do anything; no need for works, Christ did it all for you." The apostle Paul stated: "What shall we say then? Is the Law [of God given in Sinai] sin? Certainly not! On the contrary, I would not have known sin except through the Law . . . Therefore, the Law is holy and the Commandment is holy and just and good . . . For we know [Satan's ministers and prophets of Israel don't] that the Law is spiritual, but I am carnal and sold under sin" (Romans 7:7,12,14). Paul informed the Corinthians that Israel did eat spiritual food and drink from the spiritual Rock—Christ. Yet this is not what "Christianity" teaches; this is not what Jews are taught about the apostle Paul's genuine teachings.

In his message to the Romans, Paul stated: "Owe no one anything except to love one another, for he who loves another has fulfilled the Law [or Torah, not does away with it, or minimizes its importance]. For the commandments, 'You shall not commit adultery,' 'You shall not murder,' 'You shall not covet,' and if there is any other commandment, are all summed up in this saying, namely, 'You shall love your neighbor as yourself.' Love does no harm to a neighbor, therefore love is the fulfillment of the [Torah or the] Law" (Romans 13:8-10, NKJV). It seems that precious few of those who call themselves Christians are able to equate love with the Law of God.

The apostle James, the half brother of Christ, commanded his followers—all children of Israel (James 1:1): "Be you doers of the word [or Law of God] and not hearers only, deceiving yourselves" [as many so called "Christians" do]. Then he added: "But he who looks into the perfect Law of liberty [not bondage, as many deceive their gullible sheep to believe] and continues in it [by obeying it] and is not a forgetful hearer but a doer of the word, this one will be blessed in what he does" (James 1:22,25).

The last apostle to survive, "the apostle of love," John, wrote, "Now by this, we know that we know him, if we keep his Commandments. He who says, I know him, and does not keep [or teach] his Commandments [or Torah] is a liar and the truth is not in him" (I John 2:3-4). Later, John stated, "Whosoever commits sin, transgresses also the Law; for sin is the transgression of the Law" (KJV, I John 3:4).

The shepherds of Israel taught for ages that since "the Law is Jewish—for us it is done away." John also said, "And whatever we ask, we receive from him, because we keep His Commandments and do those things which are pleasing in His sight" (I John 3:22). The Messiah told His followers: "Therefore, whatever you want men to do to you, do also to them. For this is [the essence of] the Law and the Prophets [which were not done away]." Then He added: "Beware of false prophets, who come to you in sheep's clothing, but inwardly they are ravenous wolves [or beasts, as He called them in Ezekiel 34], you will know them by their fruits" (Matthew 7:12, 15-16). He later proceeded to warn them that not everyone who calls Him, Lord, Lord, would enter His kingdom, soon to be established on earth in Jerusalem and Israel. This kingdom is not a fictitious heaven or paradise. This doctrine was introduced in later years into the pagan "Christian religion" of Rome and later into Judaism. Few centuries later, it was also introduced into Islam, not by the prophet Muhammad, as we have amply demonstrated earlier from the Qur'an, but by "Islamic" teachers who adopted it from the pagan Egyptian and Babylonian religions, as well as later "Christianity."

The tragic reality is this: not only "Christians," but also Rabbinic Judaism did 'hijack' the Law of God and of Moses. Jewish rabbis created a new religious hybrid of some truth and much error—a mixture of which God said: "for all [spiritual teachings or] tables are full of vomit and filth; no place is clean" (Isa. 28:8). In Isaiah, chapter 29:13-14, we read: "Therefore the Lord said: 'Inasmuch as these people draw near with their mouth [in a lip-service religion] and honor Me with their lips, but have removed their heart far from Me [which no 'man of God' likes to admit to himself, to others, or to his God], and their fear toward Me is taught by the commandments [fatwas, halacha, Canon law, Catechism or edicts] of men, therefore, behold, I will do a marvelous work among this people, a marvelous work and a wonder; for the wisdom of their wise men shall perish, and the understanding of their prudent men shall be hidden." This is applicable, also, to all men of religion.

Later, "Christian teachers" have done the same to the true teachings of The Jewish Teacher from Nazareth; to the teachings of His true apostles and disciples to this day. Their hybrid man-made religion, or "vomit" from God's point of view, also led their followers or "Christians" into a religion of "vain worship." Christ warned His disciples: " . . . Take heed that no man deceive you [and very few take heed to this day]. For many [the majority] will come in My name, saying, 'I am the Christ' [calling themselves "the ministers of the Gospel"], and will deceive many" (Mat. 24:4-5).

The prophet of Islam, Muhammad, was influenced by the twin-hybrid religions, and being illiterate, by his own admission, could not check on their genuine Writings. Consequently, Islam and the Qur'an became, at least partly, a hybrid of such influence of the two religions of Rabbinic Judaism and the post-apostolic altered Christianity. To top it all, later Islamic clerics and commentators created their own hybrid of the supposed teachings of Muhammad. This is the reality we all face today, and this is exactly what the God of Abraham was talking about through His prophet Isaiah, as well as through all of His prophets.

Few days before his death, Moses wrote: "Now the Lord appeared at the tabernacle in a pillar of cloud, and the pillar of cloud stood above the door of the tabernacle. And the Lord said to Moses: 'Behold, you will rest with your fathers; and this people will rise and play the harlot with the gods of the foreigners of the land, where they go to be among them, and they will forsake Me and break My covenant which I have made with them. Then My anger shall be aroused against them in that day [therefore, what is happening today in the Middle East to tiny Israel or in the West, especially to America, is no coincidence], and I will forsake them, and I will hide My face from them [and ignore their prayers], and they shall be devoured [and perhaps consider the reasons for their calamities]. And many evils and troubles shall befall them, so they will [finally] say in that day, 'Have not these evils come upon us because our God is not among us?' And I will surely hide My face in that day because of all the evils which they have done, in that they have turned to other [religions, fables and] gods."

Then we read: " . . . Moses commanded the Levites, who bore the arc of the covenant of the Lord, saying: 'Take this book of the Law, and put it before the arc of the covenant of the Lord your God, that it may be there as a witness against you; for I know your rebellion and your stiff neck. If today, while I am yet alive with you, you have been rebellious against the Lord, then how much more after my death? Gather to me all the elders of your tribes, and your officers [or all branches of your government], that I may speak all these words in their hearing and call heaven and earth to witness against them. For I know that after my death you will become utterly corrupt, and turn aside from the way which I have commanded you [not suggested]. And evil will befall you in the later days [speaking specifically of our modern days], because you will do evil in the sight of the Lord, to provoke Him to anger through the works of your hands'" (Deut. 31:15-29). Tragically, this is something we are not yet honestly capable of admitting to ourselves or to our God. The time is near when all of the remnants of the nations of Israel will be playing a different tune.

Let us now continue with the theme of the after-life. The one who claimed to be the Author of the resurrection and life, the Messiah, stated: "Do not marvel at this [many in His day did, as many do today]; for the hour is coming in which ALL WHO ARE IN THE GRAVES [not in heaven, God's throne, where no man has ever ascended, nor in hell, where no man has ever descended according to pagan and man's fables] will hear his voice [when the Messiah will resurrect them, as He did Lazarus] and come forth, those who have done good, to the resurrection of life [and now life after death is truly to begin], and those who have done evil [which only God's Law can define, not man's fabricated teachings of do's and don'ts], to the resurrection [from a state of death to that life and] of judgment" (John 5:28-29). Do "Christian" religious leaders and their followers, today or before, ever believed The Master in this regard?

Speaking of life after death and the resurrection, the Prince of life told His people: "And this is the will of Him who sent me that I should lose nothing of all that He has given Me, but raise it [or resurrect, bring back to life from the dead] AT THE LAST DAY [not immediately after death occurs]. For this is the will of My Father, that everyone who sees the Son and believes in Him [not in fables, or man's teachings about Him] should have eternal life; and I will raise him up at the last day. No one can come to Me [as many think they can], unless the Father who sent me draws him; and I will raise him up at the last day" (John 6:39, 40, 44, RSV). We do not choose Christ—The Father has to choose us first—and if He does not, we cannot come to Christ.

The God and Messiah of Israel made it a point to repeat His statement concerning the timing of the resurrection from the dead. He stated the words "at the last day" three times. Yet who believes Him in the man-made religion called by man, "Christianity?" Ironically, Muhammad did believe it, and recorded it many times in the Koran. Many of the Jews and Christians in his path of travel and merchant routes, even in the sixth century, still did believe the true Biblical teachings concerning heaven and hell—and it is from them that Muhammad learned of this doctrine, not from paganized Rome. All Muslims today, in contradiction to their own prophet and the Koran, follow their own early pagan faith in this matter.

It is for this fable of the after-life that gullible "martyrs" among Muslims and Palestinians do readily give, or waste, their lives for. What a tragedy!

The apostle Paul also spoke of the time-element of the resurrection from the state of death (not a fictitious life in heaven or hell fabricated by man). In the so called resurrection chapter, in I Corinthians 15:51-52, he wrote: "Lo! I tell you a mystery [and it is to this day]. We shall not all sleep [or die], but we shall all be changed [some, at Christ's coming, will still be alive. Instead of dying first, they will be transformed from flesh to spirit, but exactly when?] in a moment, in the twinkling of an eye, at the last trumpet [that's when, at the last day, just moments prior to the time the Messiah's feet will touch the Mount of Olives]. For the trumpet will sound and the dead will be raised [Revelation 20:4-6] imperishable and we will be changed [or transformed, like in Star Trek]." The prophet of Islam, Muhammad, also spoke of this very "trumpet" as the sign for the resurrection, at the last day. This is the time when the dead shall rise—not a second before.

These are very simple and clear words! Even a child can understand them! What religious leaders, in any of the three religions of the children of Abraham, believe this teaching of the coming conquering Messiah and Redeemer of Israel? The time is very near, Scripture tells us, when we shall see an awful lot of red faces among the self appointed prophets of the children of Abraham. The God of Israel declared through His prophet Micah: "Thus says the Lord concerning the prophets who make My people stray [including all the children of Abraham and mankind]. Therefore you shall have night without vision [with no clear knowledge from God], and you shall have darkness [who claim to be teachers of light] without divination. The sun shall go down on the prophets and the day shall be dark for them [since all are spiritually blind]. So the seers shall be ashamed [for teaching lies and fables mixed with bits of truth] and the diviners abashed; indeed they shall all cover their lips; for there is no answer from God" (Micah 3:5-7). Do the teachers of this world's religions believe the prophets of God? Do they believe the apostles? Do they really believe God and His Messiah?

This Messiah himself said, as mentioned earlier, "No one has ascended up to heaven [and He meant no one: not Abraham, not Isaac, not David, and none of the prophets], but He who came down from heaven [since The Messiah never saw anyone up there, though deceived men do believe them to be up there], even the Son of man which is in heaven" (John

3:13). With this plain teaching, the prophet of Islam—Muhammad—did fully agree. Yet a short time after his death, some of his followers reverted back to their pagan concepts, and managed to lead back all Muslims with them. But among those in Judaism and Christianity, who believes Christ or the God of Israel? Certainly not the 'prophets' of Israel? Concerning obedience to God's Law, John said, "By this, we know that we love the children of God, when we love God, and keep His Commandments. For this is the love of God that we keep His Commandments [Torah or teachings] and his Commandments are not burdensome [though many believe they are]" (I John 5:2-3).

The self appointed prophets of Israel claim that God's Law is hard to keep. "No man can keep it," they say. True! On our own, no one can keep it perfectly, but with God's help and Spirit all things are possible, if we are willing to obey His Law. The apostle Peter had to remind the teachers of the Law of his days of this fact. He stated, "And we are his witnesses [of the Messiah] to these things [or the miracles they performed in His power and name], and so also is the Holy Spirit, whom God has given to those who obey [not disobey His Law or] Him" (Acts 5:32).

God, His prophets and apostles, constantly equated the Law with love, yet so many, who called themselves Christians, took part in crusades, religious wars, inquisitions, pogroms, witch-hunts, wars, and raw anti-Semitism, anti-Black, anti-Chicanos, and anti-everything they didn't like or approve of. The God of Israel and her Messiah to come, the One who married Israel in Sinai, and is to marry her again, declared: "Behold, the days are coming, says the Lord, when I will make a new [marriage] covenant with the house of Israel and the house of Judah [not with Gentiles—they will come later, through Israel—the teacher-race], not according to the covenant that I made with their fathers in the day that I took them by the hand to bring them out of the land of Egypt, My [marriage] covenant which they broke, though I was a husband to them, says the Lord."

It is for the sins of Israel and the whole world that Christ had to die. Read Leviticus 16 concerning the yearly ceremony enacted on the day of Atonement by the high priest. The sacrifice for the Lord, who later took upon His head all the sins of Israel, as Isaiah stated in Chapter 53, was slain, yearly, until the coming of the ultimate sacrifice—The redeemer of Israel and The anointed Savior. This anointed Savior added, 'I will put My Law [not Jewish law, not any man-made law] in their minds and write it on their hearts [because it is not now]; and I will be their God and they shall be My people [because, spiritually, they are not now]. No more shall every man teach his neighbor and every man his brother, saying, 'know the Lord,' for they shall all know Me [not man's concepts of Me] from the least of them to the greatest of them, says the Lord. For I will forgive their iniquity [by the blood I did shed for them, as typified by the "goat for the Lord" sacrificed yearly on the day of Atonement, and the Passover lamb] and their sin, I will remember no more" (Jeremiah 31:31-34).

The time is soon coming when the religious leaders of Judaism will be made to swallow the bitter pill of their rejection of their Messiah and God, when He appears to them in person. Most Jews do not ask: what does the God of Israel or Moses would say about this or that matter? Instead, they often check the writings of men for guidance and wisdom. The "Christian" clergy of Israel will also have to swallow a bitter pill. They have accepted the Person of Israel's Messiah, while rejecting His Religion and Law—the one He gave to Moses for all of Israel (Malachi 4:4-6).

The rest of the children of Abraham will be made to swallow their own bitter pill for rejecting the genuine and true religion and Messiah of their father Abraham. They have rejected the teachings of their own prophet, who told them that the land of Israel belongs to the sons of Isaac—to Israel. They have rejected the teachings of Muhammad, their revered prophet, and his plain teachings in the "infallible" Koran concerning life after death. In doing so, they have sacrificed in vain many young and misguided lives on the altar of hatred and venom. No one will be justified before the God and Allah of Abraham and Israel—for all are equally guilty before him. They all chose the paths of war and rejected the ways of peace, to their own hurt. Corruption on all levels of society is common among all the nations of the children of Abraham. Nobody can deceive the God of the patriarchs! He is no respecter of persons!

The God of the children of Abraham commanded His prophet Isaiah: "Cry aloud, spare not; lift up your voice like a trumpet; tell my people their transgression and the house of Jacob their sins. Yet they seek me daily [in Israel's religious communities, as well as the religious "faithful" among the followers of Islam, and all other religious peoples on earth], and delight to know My ways, as a nation that did righteousness and did not forsake the ordinance of their God. They ask of Me the ordinances of justice; they take delight in approaching God" (Isaiah 58:1-2). "God seeks those who worship him in truth and in spirit," Jesus stated (John

4:23-24). Such are few and far in between, since religious hypocrisy and bigotry is the most common currency among all religions.

Through the last Hebrew prophet, the God of Israel recorded this warning in the last paragraph of Malachi's prophecy. He declared: "Remember the Law of Moses, My servant, [because most in Israel, willfully, to this day forgot], which I commanded him [and he did not invent it] in Horeb for all [the tribes of] Israel [not just for some in Judah], with the statutes and judgments. [But how are they going to remember the Law that they were taught for ages to forget?] Behold I will send you Elijah [or one in his spirit, since all are dead, as Christ himself and the prophets had stated]. And he will turn the hearts of the fathers [of Israel] to the children and the hearts of the children to their fathers [the patriarchs], lest I come and strike the earth with a curse [or utter destruction]" (Malachi 4:46). This prophet, in the spirit of Elijah, is soon to come!

Since the days of Adam and Eve, man has insisted on inventing his own religions and philosophies, his own criteria of right and wrong, his own knowledge and education—and all that he did with disastrous results. Today, man is near the end of his rope. Planet earth is gasping for its last breath, yet man still insists on going his own way. His secular and religious leaders lead him from one conflict to another, one "holy war" to another—with no end in sight. Yet the way and knowledge of peace, as revealed in the great Royal Law of our Maker, not even most of the religious leaders teach their followers. It is for this reason, mainly, the nations of Israel are ridden with chronic and unsolvable problems. When the teachers and educators of Israel have rejected the Royal Law of the God of Israel, what hope do the "little ones" have?

Through the prophet Ezekiel, God declared His intentions concerning the educators of His people and those who follow their teachings. He stated: "As I live, says the Lord God, Surely with a mighty hand, with an outstretched arm, and with fury poured out, I will rule over you. I will bring you out from the peoples and gather you out of the countries where you are scattered, with a mighty hand, with an outstretched arm, and with fury poured out [this time against Israel and those who hold His people captive]. And I will bring you into the wilderness of the peoples [or the desert area between Iraq and Jordan, or perhaps, the Sinai desert], and there will I plead my case with you face to face. I will make you pass under the rod [and deal with everyone of you personally], and I will bring you into the bond of the [marriage] covenant [as He did in Sinai, only this time,

He will write His Law on their heart and mind. See Jeremiah 31:31-34]. I will purge the rebels [those who hate God's Law, de-emphasize it, and teach others to do so] from among you, and those who transgress against Me; I will bring them out of the country where they sojourn [in captivity], but they shall not enter the land of Israel. Then you will know that I am the Lord" (Ezekiel 20:3338).

Even though God will bring back the remnant of His people out of captivity, those responsible for deceiving His people and cutting them off from their God, He will prevent them from entering into His land. The indication is that the guilty ones will be executed in the desert. Quoting Moses, the apostle Paul warned the Hebrews: "For we know Him who said, 'vengeance is Mine, I will repay,' says the Lord. And again, The Lord will judge His people.'" Paul added, "It is a fearful thing to fall into the hand of the living God" (Hebrews 11:30-31, NKJV). The prophet Amos (Amos 4:12) warned his people: "Prepare to meet your God, O Israel!"

The God of Israel engaged the educators of Israel in an imaginary argument that reflects a tragic reality. He said, "I have loved you," they retorted, "in what way have You loved us?" He responded, in Malachi 1:6, "'A son honors his father and a servant his master, if I am a father, where is My honor? And if I am a master, where is My reverence?' says the Lord of Hosts, 'to you priests [religious leaders, educators] who despise My name [but give God lip service], yet, you say,' 'in what way have we despised Your name?'" God replies, "'You offer defiled food [man-made spiritual rubbish] on my altar, but you say,' 'in what way have we defiled You' [or your teachings], 'by saying, the table of the Lord [or Law] is contemptible'" (Malachi 1:6-7).

Then God declares to the shepherds of Israel: "I have no pleasure in you, says the Lord of hosts, nor will I accept an offering from your hands [since much of the religious worship taking place in the religious assemblies of Israel does not ascend above the ceiling. God is simply not listening!].

For from the rising of the sun, even to its going down, My name shall be great among the Gentiles [or nations], says the Lord of hosts. "'But you profane it, in that you say, 'the table of the Lord [his Law and Commandments] is defiled and its fruit, its food [which some call it Jewish, some call it old stuff or Old Testament], is contemptible!' You also say, 'Oh, what a weariness' [to have to obey God's Law] and you sneer at it,' says the Lord of Hosts. 'And you bring the stolen, the lame and the sick [or false teachings], thus you bring an offering! Should I accept this from your hand?' says the Lord. 'But cursed be the deceiver, for I am a great King, says the Lord of Hosts and My name is to be feared among the nations'" (Malachi 1:10-14). The apostle Paul warned the Galatian church: "But even if we, or an angel from heaven, preach any other gospel to you [and it happened] than what we have preached to you, let him be accursed. As we have said before, so now I say again, if anyone preaches any other gospel [any teachings or Torah] to you than what you have received, let him be accursed" (Gal. 1:8-9).

Addressing the spiritual leaders, God thunders His warning to the self appointed shepherds and corrupt priests of Israel: "'And now, O priests, this commandment is for you. If you will not hear, and if you will not take it to heart, to give glory to My name' [by teaching My Laws, instead of yours], says the Lord of Hosts, 'I will send a curse upon you and I will curse your blessings. Yes, I have cursed them already [though many are too blind to perceive it], because you do not take it to heart, behold, I will rebuke your descendants and spread refuse [Heb. dung] on your faces, the refuse of your [not My] solemn feasts.'"

Man's feasts, holidays, are not God's, as recorded in Leviticus 23, where God states, "These are the feasts of the Lord." God's feasts included, first, the Sabbath, not Sunday or Friday, and also the Feast of Tabernacles. All nations will be forced to keep it (see Zech. 14) at the Messiah's coming, or else!

God adds: "And one will take you away with it," then you shall know that I have sent this commandment to you, that My covenant is with Levi [or the teachers, prophets, and educators of Israel of God's laws] . . . For the lips of the priest should keep knowledge [God's knowledge, not man's] and people should seek the Law [of God, not that of man] from his mouth [but how can they, when Israel's prophets and teachers claim the Law is done away or altered?]; for he is the messenger of the Lord of Hosts."

Then God condemns the educators of Israel by charging: "'But you have departed from the way [of God's Law]; you have caused many to stumble at the Law [by showing contempt for it and perverting its intent]. You have corrupted the covenant of Levi,' says the Lord of hosts. 'Therefore, I also have made you contemptible and base before all the people [hence Israel despises the religious leaders, teachers and preachers. They despise their teachings and double standards], because you have not kept My ways, but have shown partiality in the Law'" (Malachi 2:1-9).

These words were spoken against the religious establishment of ancient Israel and Judah. It was also aimed at all the generations of Israel to this day. And how true such words are especially in our generation! When the disciples of Christ, the One who spoke through Malachi, wanted to know of the conditions that will exist at the time of His second coming, He responded to their inquisition by first warning them: "Take heed that no one deceives you [why?]. For many [not few] will come in my name [claiming that Christ sent them, or that they are His servants], saying, I am the Christ and will deceive many" (Matthew 24:4-5). How plain can one be about the true nature of most of the "prophets" or "spiritual leaders" of Israel?

In the Chronicles of Eri, vol. ii, pp. 98-103, we read of Jeremiah the prophet's discourse to an assembly of priests and religious educators. King Heremon, the former prince who married King Zedekiah's daughter—Tamar—while in Jerusalem did convene all of the assembly of priests and educators. This prophet of God, who was called in Ireland "Olam Fola," personally saw the tragic results of the false teachings of Israel's prophets, which, in his own day, resulted in a cruel captivity. He told the educators of Ireland, gathered to ratify a covenant with the God of Israel: "It is known unto you that the Criumtear [priests] have feigned nine laws from Baal. The foundation laid in deceit, the work has been raised by impostures and propped up by ignorance on this side and by fear on that. What if five of the Laws of the old time [the Ten Commandments] only be retained at the head of the laws of Eri, not deceitfully, as commands from Baal, according to the words of the priest, but openly?

'Let not man slay his fellow.
Let not man take the belongings of another privily.
Let not the lips utter what the mind knoweth to be false.
Let man be merciful.
Let man do even as he would be done by.'"

After these practical remarks, he added: "Sons of Eri, honor and respect thy father. Love, honor and respect and tenderly cherish all the days of thy life the mother who bore thee."

Prior to the end of that historic meeting, the prophet of God, Jeremiah, saw to it that the Laws of God, given to Israel at Mount Sinai, should then be promulgated and formally read over and ratified. Dr. O'Connor notes concerning this meeting: "The nine laws established at this time were with, a very few editions, the only laws of Eri while sovereignty resided in the land." "The Laws of Eri," he adds, "set in order by Olam Fola [or Jeremiah] by which [with the addition of three others] the nations of Eri were ruled for a 1000 years. Should any fancy, from their similitude to the laws of the Hebrews, called the Ten Commandments, that these are of modern date, let the fancy vanish: The Hebrews were Scythians [or wanderers] as well as Iberians" (Chronicles of Eri, ol. ii, pg. 107, 238).

After the death of the Messiah, some of his disciples and apostles have reintroduced the religion of the God of Israel to the British Isles. As we have previously mentioned, Joseph of Arimathea, uncle of Mary, was the first to teach the royal house of David at Avalon, and later the British Kingdom, God's ways and Law. The apostle Simon the zealot, Aristobulus, and finally the apostle Paul followed in the footsteps of Joseph (Morgan, St. Paul in Britain, pg. 129). Later, when the papal religion of Rome has been finally able to stamp out what Rome considered to be "the Jewish religion," gradually, all the British Isles reverted to their old Druid religion. It was later mixed with the new brand of papal Rome's form of "Christianity," and so it is to this day.

In discussing the final restoration of Judah and Israel, the prophet Zechariah quotes God: "Ask the Lord for rain [a reality many 'prophets' of Israel and Judah today do not teach God's people] in the time of the latter rain. The Lord will make flashing clouds; He will give them showers of rain [though today it's not fashionable to believe so], grass in the field for everyone [since God does not delight in sending droughts as a reminder of his displeasure of Israel's conduct], for the [false prophets of the] idols speak delusion; the diviners envision lies and tell false dreams." Because of that, God declares: "My anger is kindled against the shepherds, and I will punish the goat herds [or the top educators in religious and secular circles, who mislead His people]. For the Lord of host will visit His flock, the house of Judah and will make them as His royal horse in the battle [and that's why Judah today is like a lion again]" (Zechariah 10:1-3).

Then in Chapter 13, God speaks of those promulgating humanly devised teachings under the guise of religion and educational enlightenment, which God considers to be idolatry. In verses 1-6 He states: "In that day a fountain shall be opened for the house of David [whose royal house today heads one of man's humanly devised religions—the Church of England—which is a mixture of Israel's religion and that of papal Rome], and for the inhabitants of Jerusalem, for sin and for uncleanness [as

God regards that brand of religion, and that of the humanly contrived unbiblical aspects of Judaism]. "'It shall be in that day' [at the Messiah's coming], says the Lord of hosts, 'that I will cut off the names of the idols [or religious and secular teachers, not of God's choosing], from the land and they shall no longer be remembered. I will also cause the prophets [of man's form of religion and education] and the unclean spirit [the true source of man's teachings], to depart from the land.'"

Then God describes the fate of man's educators, which He did not choose, and who do not teach His Laws. "'It shall come to pass, that if anyone still prophesies, then his father and mother who begot him will say to him, 'you shall not live, because you have spoken lies [which they still often do today in Israel and Judah] in the name of the Lord!' And his father and mother which begot him shall thrust him through [or beat him up] when he prophesies [or teaches man's knowledge contrary to God's laws, and as God sees it, inspired by an unclean spirit]. And it shall be in that day [God declares], that every prophet [educator, teacher in Israel and Judah, who does not teach according to God's Laws and knowledge] will be ashamed of his vision [theory, philosophy and ideas, even though today, he despises and scoffs at God's knowledge] when he prophesies [or teaches]; they will not wear a robe [or religious and secular uniform] of coarse hair to deceive.'"

Then the false teacher who has been wounded by his own parents for his false teachings, will say: "'I am no prophet, I am a farmer; for a man taught me to keep cattle from my youth.' 'And someone will say to him, 'what are these wounds in your hands?' Then he will answer, 'those with which I was wounded in the house of my friends.'" This self-made prophet will recognize farming to be a more honorable profession than that of a false teacher of religious rubbish, or an atheistic Godless secular humanism, or evolution without a creator.

In verses 8-9, we read of the results of the deception perpetrated by false education: "And it shall come to pass in all the land [of Israel's nations], says the Lord, that two-thirds in it shall be cut off and die. But one-third shall be left in it; I will bring the one third through the fire [and] will refine them as silver is refined, and test them as gold is tested. They will call on My name [after the mega holocaust], and I will answer them. I will say, this is My people, and each one will say, 'the Lord is my God'" (Zechariah 13:19). In Isaiah 6:13, we read that, after the refining process, only one tenth will come back to their land. This will be the reality of the future, after Israel and Judah are brought back from the soon coming final destruction and captivity. The purpose of this coming mega holocaust is, among other reasons, to equip God's people with the attitude of "yes, my Lord." Whether today we believe that or not, is of absolutely no consequence. Israel's future history has been already recorded, and as it was written, so it shall be done—man's lack of faith notwithstanding!

But who is really responsible for such a global deception? The apostle John tells us in the book of Revelation 12:1-9: "Now a great sign appeared in heaven, a woman [Israel] clothed with the sun, with the moon under her feet, and on her head a garland of twelve stars [Remember Joseph's dream in Genesis 37]. Then being with child [the Messiah born in Judah], she cried out in labor and in pain to give birth. And another sign appeared in heaven, behold, a great fiery red dragon [or serpent] having seven [symbolic] heads and ten horns. And seven diadems on his heads. His tail drew a third of the stars [the one third of angels who rebelled with him, as we shall see later] of heaven and threw them to the earth [as demons]. And the dragon stood before the woman who was ready to give birth, to devour her child as soon as it was born [through Herod the Edomite]. And she bore a male child who was to rule all nations with a rod of iron. And her child [the only one who has ever ascended to heaven, even according to Muhammad] was caught up to God and to His throne. Then the woman fled [speaking of the Jewish followers and true Church of Christ, small and persecuted, and still small and soon to be persecuted again] into the wilderness, where she has a place prepared by God [for the true Church], that they should feed her there one thousand, two hundred and sixty days [symbolic of 1260 years, as we saw previously in regard to Joseph's birthright. It is a day for a year principle]."

Then we read: "And war broke out in heaven, Michael and his angels [the prince in charge of Israel, see Daniel 12:1] fought against the dragon [in a soon to occur heavenly war]; and the dragon and his angels [or demons] fought, but they did not prevail, nor was a place found for them in heaven any longer [since the end of Satan's rule is to occur at the Messiah's return]. So the great dragon was cast out, that serpent of old, called the Devil and Satan [the very one responsible for the Middle East conflict, the miseries of the Russians, Africans, Bosnians, Afghans, and all evil on earth], who deceives the whole world [especially those responsible for the destructive system of false education, humanism, religion, and secularism]; he was cast to the earth and his angels were cast out with him."

Then a stern warning is given to humanity: "Woe to the inhabitants of the earth and the sea! For the Devil has come down to you, having great wrath [and will cause all hell to break loose, literally], because he knows that he has a short time." What does all that have to do with the Middle East conflict, with the terror attack against America—and those yet to come—with Melchizedek, with Jerusalem? Well, practically EVERYTHING!

Before we conclude the final scenario of this age-old drama and its final solution, let's go to the beginning of the story—long before man has appeared on the scene. Let us explore briefly the story of Jerusalem, the city of peace. Let us further investigate the origin and identify of the one who robbed Jerusalem of her children and peace. Only then, can we continue our journey into the immediate, coming future of this most troubled city on earth. Only then can we gaze at the splendor of her ultimate peace that no one will ever take away from her and her children. This peace is soon coming, in spite of her present turmoil and travail.

And so goes the story! There is a city on earth called "the city of peace" or Jerusalem. Yet this city of gold and light, as she is so often described by her loving children, has known more than her faire share of pain and sorrow. She groaned too often and wrestled with the agonies of war from the day of her birth. Jerusalem, the city that has known the myrrh of feasting and peace—like no other city on earth—has also experienced the swelling tides of tears, sorrow and war cascading down through her mournful streets. The fruit of these diametrically opposite forces and concepts are still lodged in the heart of her children and soil to this very day.

The hopes and dreams, yearnings and quests for peace, have been epitomized by the great city that sits astride the crossroads of planet earth. Yet tragically, also the streams of pain, tears and sorrows of war have flowed down the streets of the golden city time and again. Why does she experience such a paradox? The ancient prophet Jeremiah, staring tearfully at the garments of sorrow and widowhood, spread hastily on his beloved city, lamented mournfully: "How does the city sit solitary that was full of people! How is she become as a widow? She that was great among the nations and princess among the provinces, how is she become tributary! She weeps sore in the night. And her tears are on her cheeks; among all her lovers [or allies] she has none to comfort her, they are become her enemies" (Lamentation 1:1-2).

Jerusalem, the city of peace and war, epitomizes the joys and sorrows of all the cities on earth. Her share in this endless cycle, however, has been double in pain and rejoicing. Jerusalem is a city, a concept, an idea that expresses the fullness of all of man's hopes and dreams—as well as aches and pains. Why is she riddled with such a contradiction? What fiendish force is responsible for the relentless torment of the womb of all mankind? Who seeks her constant hurt and tears of blood? Who desires the constant affliction of her children that have been forced to remain planted in all corners of the earth? Why can't the city of peace that should epitomize this concept, become the fountain and source of the streams of peace. When will this eternal peace flow from her womb to water the hungry souls of all of her children on earth? Why has she become instead the source for the fiery, turbulent rivers of blood and war. Why do these streams emerge from her belly to drench the whole earth with the blood and tears of her languishing offspring?

Jerusalem means, "the city of peace." Yet to many, she has become the birthplace of war since bygone times. Who has been plundering the peace of Jerusalem, the city, the concept, "the mother of us all?" Jerusalem was meant to be a city of peace, but has often experienced the frightening sounds of the alarms of war. An ancient psalmist once admonished her children, "Seek the peace of Jerusalem." But what is the peace of Jerusalem, a city that has hardly experienced the long lasting fruit of peace? What is the source of the fruit of peace so yearningly desired by all of her longing children? What is the origin of such peace that Jerusalem, the concept, was meant to daily bask her offspring in? Who robbed the incense of peace that was to be offered on the altar of Jerusalem? Will peace ever flow like a stream out of Jerusalem? The origin and nature of peace can be revealed only by Jerusalem. The causes of war and peace; the ingredients that have been offered on the altars of peace and war, can be unraveled only by delving into the womb of Jerusalem. This city has seen and witnessed the introduction of both peace and war into, yes . . . the universe.

A song made famous in our times, concerning war and peace, lamented: "The answer, my friend, is blowing in the wind." So let us ride on the wings of that wind to capture the elusive answers to the causes, origin, and way of peace and war. The final solution to the Middle East will not come until this matter is laid to rest. This whirlwind journey will take us into far away times and places that have never been visited by the eyes of mortal man, except in visions and dreams. Yet the road has been paved and charted in a book that dramatizes the history, nature, causes and way to both war and peace. Let us begin our journey.

Before time began, there was a city that later became known to man as heavenly Jerusalem. It was the city that had no beginning, nor end. The serene streams of that city traversed the endless universe, flowing with the fruit of peace. The bubbling fountain and source of that everlasting peace was the Creator God and His eternal Prince of Peace and companion—whose hands formed the whole universe. In that city resided the King and Prince of Peace in dazzling glamour, splendor and glory. They lived life in perfect and complete harmony eternally. The sounds and winds of war have never blown in the streets of the city of the great King and His Prince—nor did such violent storms of war and its sour fruit touch any corner of the majestic universe, which was created by the Prince of Peace. The King and Prince of Peace have fashioned and molded Their perfect and complete state of mind into a harmonious concept, named later by man: Shalom, Salaam, or Peace.

The word Shalom in the Hebrew language is impregnated with two major concepts. They encompass and epitomize the very nature of the great King and Prince of Peace. The concept of Shalom, which has never been experienced fully by man, reveals the state of mind and heart of the King, Prince, and city of heavenly Jerusalem. This state of mind embodies the completeness of all the ingredients and fruit of the nature of peace. It also epitomizes a perfect and flawless condition of every ingredient that, when put together, comprise the complete mind and nature of the King and Prince of Jerusalem or Malchizedek. This concept of Shalom was later described as the Royal Law of God, Wisdom, Tree of Life, and Law of Love. It encompasses the fullness of the divine attributes of the King and Prince of Peace.

The wisest king who ever lived, the only king who ever presided over a complete and perfect, humanly speaking, period of peace in human annals—King Solomon—described this divine concept of peace. He stated, "Happy is the man that finds wisdom [the divine concept of wisdom], and the man that gets understanding. For the merchandise of it is better than the merchandise of silver and the gain thereof than fine gold. She is more precious than rubies: And all the things you can desire are not to be compared unto her. Length of days is in her right hand; and in her left hand riches and honor. Her ways are the ways of pleasantness, AND ALL HER PATHS ARE PEACE. She is a TREE OF LIFE to them that lay hold upon her, and happy is everyone that retains her. The Lord by wisdom has founded the earth; by understanding He has established the heavens" (Proverbs 3:13-19, KJV translation). Yes, King Solomon was the wisest and richest king to ever rule the city of peace. His very name was, in Hebrew, peace of God. He understood the nature and origin, source and way to peace. Yet, he as well, had later rejected that way of peace, and then returned to it, stating: "Let us hear the conclusion of the whole matter: Fear God and keep His commandments, for this is the whole duty of man. For God will bring every work into judgment, including every secret thing, whether good or evil" (Eccles. 12:13-14).

King David, Solomon's father, had a better, intimate acquaintance with the Source of Peace. He stated in one of his psalms: "The LAW of the Lord is PERFECT, converting the soul [from a state of mind of war to peace]: the testimony of the Lord is sure, making wise the simple. The statutes of the Lord are right [not wrong, as man later came to think of them], rejoicing the heart: the commandment of the Lord is pure, enlightening the eyes. The fear of the Lord is clean, enduring forever: the judgments of the Lord are true and righteous altogether. More to be desired are they than gold, yea, than much fine gold: sweeter also than honey and the honeycomb. Moreover, by them your servant is warned: and in keeping of them, there is great reward" (Psalm 19:7-11 KJV).

Unlike the warring parties in the Middle East, King David knew the way to peace, the nature and source of it. His great reward will be an eternal rule over all the nations of Israel from the city of peace—Jerusalem (Jeremiah 31:4). But this is yet to be fulfilled at the return of the Prince of Peace. Let us travel back on the winds of time to a period when a Super Being, created by the Prince of Peace, had known and experienced all that Kings David and Solomon had recorded for us in The Book of peace and war—the Bible.

The King of Peace created, by the Prince of Peace, both the universe and its children—the angels (Colossians 1:16). To the spirit composed angelic beings, the King and Prince of Peace have revealed the perfect and complete nature of peace, the Royal Law, as it was later to be called. Peace did reign supreme—both in heavenly Jerusalem, the city of the great peacemaker, God—and throughout the far reaches and lighted corners of the limitless universe. For how long we do not know. But the city of Jerusalem was later to witness the cold, stormy air of the winds of war for the first time in its eternal history.

The greatest created spirit being, brought into existence by the Prince of Peace, was named Lucifer, or in Hebrew: Haylel Ben Shahar. His name meant: The praise of the morning star of the dawn or light-bringer. And so he was as long as he walked in the paths of peace. For how long this first and most trusted counselor of the rulers of Jerusalem did walk in peace is not known. Tragically, this super archangel, who occupied the highest office in the throne of the King and Prince of Peace, chose at one point to sow the wind and reap the stormy whirlwinds of war. He rejected the way of peace and induced one third of the angels under his command to do likewise.

Let us uncover this most fascinating story in the pages of The Book of war and peace of the King and Prince of Peace—the Bible. In John 1:1-7, we read of the history of the King of Peace and his Prince, who later came to planet earth to live on its war ravaged landscape for thirty-three years. His mission was, among others, to neutralize forever, the power over death, which the former Lucifer had over man through sin and disobedience to the laws of peace.

How did Lucifer come to possess such power over man? In the book of Isaiah, the Prince of Peace began revealing the history of the downfall of Lucifer. This Lucifer was given dominion over planet earth for a purpose yet to be unfolded. At first, Lucifer, who knew the delicious fruit of peace, did rejoice with his angels at the sight of the creation of the precious jewel—planet earth.

In Job 38:1,7, the Prince of Peace related such information to Job. In verse 4, Job was asked: "Where were you when I laid the foundation of the earth . . . when the morning stars [or angels] sang together and all the sons of God [or angels] shouted for joy?" Yes, Lucifer and his angels did shout for joy. Peace, in a perfect and complete state, did reign supreme on this glorious planet earth. Yet, it did not last forever. In later accounts, the Bible reveals more about the rejection of the Way of peace by Lucifer and his angels. Jude, half brother of Christ, later revealed a piece of the puzzle in the introduction of the way of war to planet earth. He wrote: "And the angels [Lucifer and his angels], which kept not their first estate, but left their own habitation, he has reserved in everlasting chains under darkness to the judgment of the great day" (Jude 6).

Why did Lucifer and his angels bolt out of their glorious earthly residence? What was their destination? The prophet Isaiah unveils more details about the first universal war to confront the great city of Jerusalem, where the King and Prince of Peace do reside. In Isaiah 14:12-15, we read of the first evidence of the winds of war that blew shadows of darkness into the heart of Lucifer and the eternal consequences. These results still haunt us and earthly Jerusalem to this day. Isaiah wrote: "How are you fallen from heaven, O Lucifer, son of the morning! How are you cut down which did weaken the nations [with the spirit of war], for you have said in your heart, I will ascend into heaven, I will exalt my throne [on earth] above the stars [or angels] of God: I will sit also upon the mount of the congregation [or throne of God], in the sides of the north [location of the heavenly city of Jerusalem]: I will ascend above the heights of the clouds: I will be like the most High [or dethrone God]. Yet, you shall be brought down to hell [a place of restraint for fallen angels, II Peter 2:4], to the sides of the pit" (Revelation 20:1-3 KJV). In II Peter 2:4, the Prince of Peace, who stated in Luke 10:18, "I beheld Satan as lightening fall from heaven," also added, through Peter, this information: "For if God spared not the angels that sinned, but cast them down to hell [place of restraint, Greek, tartaroo], and delivered them into chains of darkness, to be reserved to judgment."

Lucifer and his angels, after an unknown period of tasting the fruit of peace and drinking of the streams of peace that do flow from its source in heavenly Jerusalem, allowed the bitter winds of war and its sour fruit to contaminate and pollute their thinking and heart. The fruit of illicit lust for power, greed, selfish interests, hate, malice and disrespect for authority, gradually drowned and erased the fruit of peace, which until then dominated their minds and actions. War, and all of its foul ingredients, seeped into every cell of their polluted spirit. The prophet Ezekiel recorded more details about the new lord of darkness and king of war—at whose altar of war man has been offering the defiled and polluted incense of war from his beginning. This is also evidenced in the 4000 year struggle for power, possessions and lands in the Middle East.

Ezekiel was told by the Prince of Peace: "Son of man, take up a lamentation upon the king of Tyrus, [epitomized by fallen Lucifer], and say to him, thus says the Lord God: You seal up the sum full of wisdom and are perfect in beauty. You have been in Eden, the garden of God [both in Jerusalem above and on earth]; every precious stone was your covering, the workmanship of your tabrets and your pipes [or musical instruments] were prepared in you IN THE DAY THAT YOU WERE CREATED. "You are the anointed cherub that covers [God's throne], and

I have set you so. You were upon the holy mountain of God; you have walked up and down in the midst of the stones of fire. You were perfect [or complete, product of peace, flawless] in your ways from the day that you were created, TILL INIQUITY [or lawlessness and ways of war] WAS FOUND IN YOU" (Ezekiel 28:1215 KJV).

Yes, Lucifer was a masterpiece creation of the Author of peace. He was complete with all the components that make peace. He was flawless and perfect, as the city of peace was complete and perfect. But he had made a conscious choice to abandon the way of peace, some of whose ingredients are recorded in Galatians 5:22-23 by the apostle Paul. These are fruits of the spirit of the King and Prince of Peace. They include: love, joy, peace, long suffering [patience, tolerance], gentleness, goodness, faith, meekness, temperance and humility. Needless to say, these ingredients are not present in the Middle East conflict, much less in the "peace talks" between the warring parties. As God has declared through his prophet Isaiah, "The way of peace they know not."

Lucifer chose to become an angel of darkness now, instead of a light bringer. He chose the ways of war whose ingredients are partly stated also in Galatians 5:19-21 by Paul. They are: Adultery [spiritual and physical], fornication, uncleanness [of body and mind], lasciviousness [or license to immorality], idolatry [spiritual adultery], witchcraft, hatred, variance [divisions of mind], emulations [jealousy], wrath, strife, sedition, heresies, envying, murders, drunkenness, revelries [rioting], etc. Many of these ingredients are certainly present in the Middle East conflict, and in every nation and conflict on earth. These are the components needed to build the machines and engines of war! For this purpose, every nation on earth finds enough resources in its otherwise empty coffers, but never enough for those needs that give life to the hungry and destitute.

These are the ways of war! They became the ingredients that propelled and caused, those now called Satan and his demons, to bolt out from their earthly residence and shoot into space to hurl the winds of war at the walls of Jerusalem. This was the first universal, titanic battle ever fought. It was the beginning of the war between "the children of light and the children of darkness." The forces unleashed by the warlord Satan against the immensely greater force of his creator, could not be perceived or measured by human instruments. The mind of finite man cannot comprehend or fathom such an infinite supernatural force. As a result of this super titanic battle, the warlord was cast down as "a lightning falling from heaven" to planet earth. But the war was not over. Three more awesome wars were to follow through the span of time, now called human history.

The second war between the war-lord Satan and his Maker and Prince of Peace, took place two thousand years ago over the city of Jerusalem on earth. It is recorded in Matthew 4:1-11, where we read of the second war of the titans. In this war Satan, now the god of war and high priest of the altar of war, was attempting to destroy his very Maker by seducing him to abandon the way of peace. At one point, we read of Satan trying to seduce Christ by offering him his satanic powers over the nations here and now. He proposed to his Maker that if he will just bow down to him at the altar of war and offer the incense of war on that altar to Satan, he would offer him the glory of all the nations.

Our Creator and Savior did not give in to such temptations, but man has been doing so since the Garden of Eden where the first battle between Satan and man was won by the warlord. Yet, the last war will ultimately result in victory for man. All he has to do is choose to walk in the way of peace. But, we are ahead of ourselves in this story.

The third war of the titans is soon to occur as a last attempt by Satan to dethrone the King of Peace in heavenly Jerusalem. This titanic battle or war, will also end in defeat for the warlord Satan. The children of light shall again overcome the forces of the children of war and darkness. We read previously of this account in the last book revealed by the Prince of Peace to his servant and friend John—in the book of Revelation. As a result of this third war of the spirit world, it will spell good news and victory for man also. As we read in Revelation: "And I heard a loud voice saying in heaven, now is come salvation and strength and the Kingdom of our God, and the power of His Christ: for the accuser of our brethren [and all mankind] is cast down which accused them before our God day and night" (Rev 12:10).

Why has the warlord Satan been accusing all mankind day and night before the King of Peace in heavenly Jerusalem? What does he know that we don't? What is he trying to achieve by such accusations? What is the substance of such accusations that cause him to ascend periodically to the city of Jerusalem? We must know such answers, because our life and peace on earth are at stake. The coming captivity and world chaos are the direct result of Satan's work on humanity, and especially on Israel. Before we get to these answers, let's cover the fourth and last war. It is the most intriguing one yet to occur right here on earth around the future city of peace, Jerusalem. This war is to take place in the future, a thousand years after the return of the Messiah and the beginning of His reign on earth. Every human being who ever lived will witness the scenario of this most devastating war for the warlord and his cohorts. You will be one of them!

The Apostle John has recorded the background to the last war nineteen centuries ago. The Prince of Peace will have been reigning by then a thousand years over the whole earth, from Jerusalem. He ruled this city during the time of the patriarch Abraham. At that time Christ was called Melchizedek, King of Salem, Priest of the Most High. Melchizedek means, King of Righteousness, as was mentioned before. How long He had been ruling the city of Salem is unknown. During the time of Isaac's dwelling near the city of Salem, years later, his wife Rebekah went to consult with Melchizedek in Jerusalem about her pregnancy.

Now Melchizedek, again in the same function as He had been before, during Abraham's time (Genesis 14:18-20), would perform such functions also in His own city of Salem, or Jerusalem. At the time of that one thousand years period, peace would reign on earth. Like streams of living waters, peace would flow from Jerusalem into all the far-reaching corners of the earth. It is the peace of The City of God the ancient psalmist had admonished the children of Jerusalem to pray for. That peace was sought and would be found by many thirsty souls. War would be unknown for generations. At the end of a thousand years of reign, those who had ever lived, from the time of Adam, would be brought back to life by the Prince of Peace—the Messiah and Savior of all men. Since they had never known the way of peace, this newly resurrected massive human population would be taught the Way to live, in peace.

In Revelation 20:4-5, John wrote about the resurrected dead and those alive in the one thousand years of the Messiah's reign. "And they lived and reigned with Christ a thousand years. But the rest of the dead [or most of humanity] lived not again until the thousand years were finished. This is the first resurrection." Something else was to happen now to prove whether humanity, in its entirety, would choose the Way and altar of peace or the way of the warlord Satan.

At the beginning of the thousand year reign of the messiah, the prince of war and his fallen angels would be locked up in a spiritual prison. In Revelation 20:1-3, we read of the imprisonment of the warlord. John, seeing it in a vision, records: "And I saw an angel come down from heaven, having the key of the bottomless pit and a great chain in his hand. And he laid hold on the dragon, that old serpent, which is the Devil, and Satan, and bound him a thousand years. And cast him into the bottomless pit, and shut him up and set a seal upon him, that he should deceive the nations no more till the thousand years should be fulfilled. And after that he must be loosed a little season." Later, in verses 7-9, after a peaceful reign of a thousand years by the Prince of Peace and his saints (vv. 4-6), Satan is freed again. True to his nature, he immediately begins to sway many to his war-like thinking. A mass of deceived human beings, who should have known better, would forget the miseries he brought them in their previous life on earth, and would willfully follow him. The destination of this 'war party' is the great city of Jerusalem, the city of The Great King and her then spirit beings—former human saints.

All the powers of the warlord and that of his demons are, for the last time, unleashed in a desperate effort to dethrone the Prince of Peace. But as we read in verse 9: "And fire came down from God out of heaven [or Jerusalem above], and devoured them [the human army]. And the Devil that deceived them was cast into the lake of fire and brimstone, and shall be tormented day and night, forever and ever." This is the final fate of Satan—not sinful man. Yet, for millennia, he deceived humanity, causing it to believe that all sinners would end up with him—in eternal hell. This final chapter in the history of Satan seals his fate and that of his fallen demons, forever. From now on peace will permeate planet earth and the universe for eternity.

We have taken this brief glimpse into the future city of Jerusalem, so we can properly understand the coming final solution. We have discovered the causes for the absence of peace and how it will be restored. Let us now backtrack and get on the trail that will first lead to Israel's restored tribes (then, the rest of humanity), back to Jerusalem and her soon coming Prince of Peace. We have covered thoroughly the multifaceted and complex root causes of the 4000 year Middle East struggle in the family of the patriarch Abraham. We have identified the chief actors of this tragic drama and saga of "blood, sweat and tears." And lastly, we have uncovered the identity of the real hidden enemy of both Jews and Arabs, of Muslims, as well as of the rest of humanity. His meddling in man's affairs was the ultimate root cause that turned the twins—Jacob and Esau—into eternal mortal enemies, while still in the womb of their mother. It was the injection of Satan's spirit, the prince of the power of the air, into the innocent minds of the twins in Rebekah's womb that stirred their first struggle.

Most Arabs and Jews, the Western nations of Israel, the Muslim world—all nations for that matter—are mostly oblivious to the reality and the impact of the prince of war on their actions, thoughts and feelings toward one another. Consequently, they end up fighting the wrong enemy—their fellow man. But soon the scales of blindness that cover the eyes of all nations will be taken away. How, we may ask? Let us read what the apostle Paul and the prophets Isaiah and Zechariah have been inspired to say of this matter. They wrote of the manner in which the blinders will be removed, first from the eyes of the house of David and Judah, then from all of Israel, and finally all of mankind.

Speaking of the rejection of the Messiah by his people, the apostle Paul stated: "I tell the truth in Christ, I am not lying, my conscience also bearing me witness in the Holy Spirit that I have great sorrow and continual grief in my heart, [which the so called "Christian" world, since that time, did not have, by and large]. For I could wish that I myself were accursed from Christ for my brethren, my kinsmen according to the flesh . . ." This is how a true prophet of God feels toward God's people. The others incited their gullible "flocks of goats" to kill, plunder, murder and hate God's people, thus revealing their true nature and identity. Paul continues, " . . . who are Israelites [not children of the devil, as many claimed in unbridled hatred], to whom [still] pertain the adoption, the glory, the covenants, the giving of the Law, the service of God and the promises; of whom are the fathers and from whom, according to the flesh, Christ came [even though many in papal Rome's religion have denied this fact, and many of its followers still do to this day], who is over all, the eternally blessed God [of Israel, who came in the flesh to save humanity]" (Romans 9:1-5). How many so called Christians in the past two millenniums have actually believed the message of God's servant, the apostle Paul, concerning his kinsmen?

Then in Chapter 10:1-3, Paul adds: "Brethren, my heart's desire and prayer to God for Israel is that they may be saved [not destroyed, as a Gentile religion sought to do for centuries, and many still do today, and, tragically, still will in the future]. For I bear them witness that they have a zeal for God, but not according to knowledge [having a misguided zeal]. For they, being ignorant of God's righteousness and seeking to establish their own righteousness [through humanly contrived teachings from man's heart, not God's], have not submitted to the righteousness of God [and suffered immensely and needlessly for it]." Again, in Chapter 11, Paul asks those ignorant of God's ways of dealings with His people: "I say then, has

God cast away His people [as many false religious teachers have claimed and taught through their humanly concocted "replacement theology"]? Certainly not! For I also am an Israelite, of the seed of Abraham, of the tribe of Benjamin. God has not cast away His people whom He foreknew. What then? Israel has not obtained what it seeks, but the elect [of Judah first, beginning with Christ's disciples] have obtained it and the rest were hardened" [by God, for a purpose]. Just as it is written (by Isaiah 6:9-10; 29:9-10, and by Moses in Deuteronomy 29:4) Paul adds: "God has given them [Israel and Judah] a spirit of stupor, eyes that they should not see and ears that they should not hear, to this day" (Romans 11:1-2, 7-8).

Then, Paul warned those Christian Gentiles who began to develop an arrogant spirit against God's people Israel: "For I do not desire, my brethren, that you should be ignorant [which they were, and so did, later, 'the Church'] of this mystery, lest you should be wise in your own [conceit or] opinion [as many, who do not heed this warning, became ignorant of this reality, and to this day, not understanding] that hardening in part [or partial blindness] has happened to Israel until the fullness [of the sins] of the Gentiles has come in. And so ALL [not just some of] Israel will be saved, as it is written: 'The Deliverer [or Messiah] will come out of Zion (Isaiah 59:20,21) and He will turn away ungodliness from Jacob; for this is My covenant with them, when I [the Messiah] take away their sins'" (Romans 11:25-27).

The apostle Paul had to address the issue of a Gentile religion, in contrast to that of God and Christ, in his letter to the Ephesian church. He wrote: "Therefore, remember that you, once Gentiles in the flesh—who are called Uncircumcision by what is called the Circumcision made in the flesh by hands—that at that time you were without Christ, being aliens from the commonwealth of Israel and strangers from the covenants of promise, having no hope and without God in the world. But now in Christ Jesus you, who once were far off, have been made near by the blood of Christ." Then he added in verses 18-20, "For through him we both have access by one Spirit to the Father. Now, therefore, you are no longer strangers and foreigners, but fellow citizens with the saints [of Israel, not instead] and members of the household of God, having been built on the foundation of the apostles and prophets [of Israel], Jesus Christ Himself being the chief cornerstone."

Paul makes it very clear: There are no Gentiles in the Church of God and Christ, but former Gentiles who are now, if truly called by God, members of the commonwealth of Israel, and hence, obedient to the Law given to Israel. This was also the case in ancient Israel, where God told them, "one law shall be to you and to the stranger who is among you." Those who propose that God had given one religion to His chosen people, Israel, and another to the Gentile world, are without any foundation and truth. God is not the author of confusion (I Corinthians 14:33), but man is the one who is often confused, because he ignorantly follows the false god—Satan—the one who deceives the whole world (Rev.12:9).

Today, all of Israel's tribes are blind. The ten tribes, most of those in the West, think of themselves as Gentiles, with a Gentile religion. Yet, Paul, quoting the prophet of Judah (Jeremiah 31:31-34), told the Hebrews and all who care to read and believe of the new marriage covenant or "Testament." He stated, "Because finding faults with them [not with His laws], behold the days are coming, says the Lord, when I will make a new [marriage] covenant [or new testament] with the house of Israel [or lost ten tribes who think they are Gentiles] and with the house of Judah [who now follow a religion of Judaism—a mixture of Biblical teachings and mostly those of their self appointed teachers]. For this is the covenant that I will make with the house of Israel; after those days, I will put My Laws [or Torah, not Israel's mostly humanly devised Christianity, nor Judah's non-Mosaic form of Judaism, Halacha, or Jewish law] in their mind and write them on their hearts; and I will be their God [though now they do their own thing and follow their own concepts of who and what is God, and the nature of His religion], and they shall be My people" (Hebrews 8:8-10).

Notice! There is no mention of a Gentile religion, as some claim Christianity to be. God is One and His religion is one. First, He is going to remove the scales from the eyes of His people, Israel and Judah, so they can see His light. Then, He will do likewise for all nations. Let us read it in God's own words! After describing the impending judgment and destruction God will soon bring on planet earth [Isaiah 24], the prophet Isaiah states: "And in this mountain [of Zion] the Lord of hosts will make for all people a feast of choice pieces, a feast of wines on the lees, of fat things full of marrow, of well refined wines on the lees [all symbolic description of God's teachings and laws]. And He will destroy on this mountain [by exposing man's false religions and teachings, and its source] the surface of the covering cast over all people [or the scales and blinders] and the veil that is spread over all nations. He will swallow up death forever [and death will be abolished for those who will live God's Way and obey His laws], and the Lord God will wipe away tears from all faces [no more wars, tragedies, sickness, terror, death]; the rebuke of His people [or persecution and captivity] He will take away from all the earth; for the Lord has spoken. And it will be said in that day, behold, this is our God [our Messiah]; we have waited for Him [but did not really know Him, neither Israel nor Judah], and He will save us. This is the Lord, we have waited for Him, we will be glad and rejoice in His salvation" (Isaiah 25:6-9).

Today we have, mostly, a non religious secular world. It is deceived, spiritually empty, and turned off toward religion. Man-tampered religions bring no one, in truth and in spirit, to God and His laws. They bring no healing to the thirsty soul. Many in this world are proud, many are faithless, and many are blind and ignorant of life's purpose. Most are like "scattered sheep," as God calls them, being devoured by the two legged "beasts" in religion, government, educational system, and the artificially high paid professions. But soon, we shall see the remnant of this disillusioned and hopeless generation turn into a completely different brand of human beings. After the immeasurable pain to come, inflicted on proud humanity as the pouring of floods during a hurricane on helpless shanty towns, the refined in-the-furnace spirit of humbled Israel and Judah will emerge. It will shine as a bright light for all to see. The scorching torrents of rivers of blood, sweat and tears, the God of Israel will cause to be poured on His people will produce, at last, its desired fruit of a genuine peace that flows from the heart of man. It will drown all the fortified towers of pride, arrogance, selfishness, rebellion and defiance against the Maker of Israel and His Law of life

In discussing the restoration of Israel's tribes, Jeremiah the prophet spoke of the stiff upper lip English Ephramites and their changed state of mind toward God's Law and religion of Israel. He wrote, "'I have surely heard Ephraim bemoaning himself: 'You have chastised me, and I was chastised, like an untrained bull [or John Bull]. Restore me, and I will return, for you are the Lord my God [exclaims now repentant Ephraim]. Surely, after my turning, I repented; and after I was instructed [in God's law] I struck myself on the thigh; I was ashamed, yes, even humiliated [by his captivity and the breaking of his haughty spirit and pride], because I bore the reproach of my youth'" (Jeremiah 31:18-19).

Speaking of this new state of mind in Israel's remnant, the prophet Hosea wrote of their new attitude. "Come and let us [Israel and Judah would say after their captivity] return to the Lord; for He has torn, but He will heal us; He has stricken, but He will bind us up, that we may live in His sight. Let us know, let us pursue the knowledge of the Lord [concerning the abundant life, not our own higher form of 'education' that has brought planet earth to the brink of oblivion]. His going forth is established as the morning" (Hosea 6:1-3). This new state of mind will become a reality only after God shutters to smithereens the haughty spirit, pride, and economy of His ever rebellious people Israel. To try to convince them of this sure reality, at this point, is a n exercise in futility.

Presently, most of Israel despises the Law of their God, and their ancient heritage and people. It never dawns on them to see the link between this rejection of God's Law and their hopelessly unbearable state of affairs. The way of peace, abundant health and prosperity—revealed by the laws of the God of Israel—are considered by God's people to be foolish and non relevant to this modern age. For this reason, the God of the patriarchs of Israel had to mournfully declare: "My people are destroyed for lack of knowledge [of the Law of abundant life given in Sinai, but why?]. Because you have rejected knowledge [in your educational institutions and religious assemblies], I also will reject you from being a priest [or a teacher to the world] for Me. Because you have forgotten [willingly] the Law of your God [despising it, and claiming that it was done away and nailed to the cross, or must be modified, and not being relevant], I also will forget your children [in the day of their calamity, soon to come]" (Hosea 4:6). Through the prophet Hosea, as well as all other prophets, the God of Israel is speaking to this generation. He is describing its soon coming captivity and also the deliverance from it.

Let us concentrate now on the ultimate outcome of the present round of the "Peace process" and those to follow. (This was written during the beginning of the Oslo accords, ten years ago.) This outcome, not by man's efforts, will finally lead us to the restoration of the new State of the reconstructed Israel, its new borders, and a new lifestyle. Much has been written, in detail at times, by the prophets of Israel concerning the chain of events that will lead to the culmination of Israel's restoration. We have attempted to present a new perspective in this work for the benefit of the readers with ears to hear. Hopefully now, a simple reading of the Maker's Handbook—the Bible—will prove to be a most fascinating journey into human history and its future.

Let us now enter the theater of prophetic life and watch the final acts in the 4000 years saga of Abraham's colorful yet turbulent family history! Isaiah describes in Chapters 1-9 the causes of Israel's first and last captivities. If you watch the news, read the paper, or just look at your crime-ridden neighborhood, you'll find out quickly what Isaiah saw in his time in Israel. The same old human nature and its sour products are still with us to this day—and for the same reasons: rejection of the Royal Law.

Isaiah began describing the state of affairs of his day by quoting God's words: "Hear, O heaven and give ear, O earth! For the Lord has spoken, I have nourished and brought up children and they have rebelled against Me" (Isaiah 1:2). Then speaking of his nation, he stated God's feelings concerning His people then and now. "Alas, sinful nation, a people laden with iniquity, a brood of evildoers, children who are corrupters! They have forsaken the Lord, they have provoked to anger the Holy One of Israel, they have turned away backward" (v. 4).

What was the outcome of rejecting God's laws of life and peace? Addressing the chronic insurmountable problems of God's people in his day and now, Isaiah exclaims: "Why should you be stricken again? You will revolt [against God's laws] more and more [no matter how bad things get]? The whole head [in leadership and government] is sick [or corrupt], and the whole heart faint [since the core of the nation is morally weak and sick, and those who belittle God's laws are called idols and heroes]. From the sole of the foot even to the head [at all levels of society] there is no soundness in it, but wounds and bruises and putrefying sores; they have not been closed or bound up [since no solution seems to work] or soothed with ointment." And this is the typical scene in Israel's nations. That's how God regards His people Israel, and that's why the coming captivity of all of Israel's tribes. And therefore God decries the spiritual sores of His people.

As a result of such a morally, socially, and economically corrupt state of affairs, Isaiah declares: "Your country is [soon to be] desolate, your cities are burned with fire [as in 9\11]; strangers devour your land in your presence; and it is desolate, as overthrown by strangers [national invasion and captivity]. Unless the Lord of hosts had left to us a very small remnant [of the many like the sand of the seashore], we would have become like Sodom, we would have been made like Gomorrah" (Isaiah 1:5-9).

In Chapter 10, Isaiah describes the destroyer of Israel—then and now—Assyria and her allies. In verses 20-23, he writes, "And it shall come to pass in that day [after the captivity of Israel by Assyria and other nations], that the remnant of Israel and such as have escaped [and survived the greatest mega holocaust yet to come on the thirteen tribes] of the house of Jacob, will never again depend on him who defeated them [Assyria/Germany or other 'allies'], but will depend on the Lord, the Holy One of Israel, in truth [not just in lip-service]. The remnant will return [about 10%], the remnant of Jacob, to the mighty God. For though your people, O Israel, be as the sand of the sea [perhaps 300-400 million today], yet, a remnant of them will return; the destruction decreed [of Israel] shall overflow with righteousness. For the Lord God of hosts will make a determined end [to Israel's lifestyle and iniquities] in the midst of all the land." Then in verses 24-27, God encourages His people (who are in captivity) not to be afraid of the Assyrians (or Germans and their allies) whom He is about to destroy, as we can read in Zechariah 14.

Then, Isaiah describes, in Chapter 11:1-9, the rule of the Messiah, son of David, and the dreamed-of utopia to come at last. Now let's read the rest of the story as a prelude to the description of Israel's final resting place—the newly restored Jerusalem and the newly reconstructed Israel. Beginning with verse 10 of Chapter 11, the prophet Isaiah declares: "And in that day, there shall be a Root of Jesse, who shall stand as a banner to the people [of Israel]: For the [remnant] Gentiles [of all nations] shall seek Him [after he had destroyed their corrupt governments, armies, false religions and economies], and His resting place shall be glorious. It shall come to pass in that day that the Lord [and Messiah] shall set His hand again, the second time [since Egypt's exodus was the first time], to recover the remnant of His people who are left from Assyria."

Notice the location of ancient Assyria in relation to the recent unfinished Persian Gulf War. The ancient Assyrian Empire, as mentioned before, ruled present day Iraq, Syria, and nearby nations. Later, they had migrated into central Europe, into Germany, Austria and northern Italy. Some of them even migrated into parts of Iran, Northern India and nearby nations. This means concentration camps all over again.

Isaiah continues, " . . . and [from] Egypt [presently an ally government, but soon to be toppled by a nationalist movement that will become Israel's enemy], from Pathros and Cush [or Ethiopia, Somalia, Sudan—all nationalistic Muslim nations and haters of Israel and the West], from Elam [in eastern Iran] and Shinear [Iraq], from Hamath [northern Syria] and the islands of the sea." This is speaking of Israel's lands in Northwestern Europe, U.S., Canada, Australia, New Zealand,

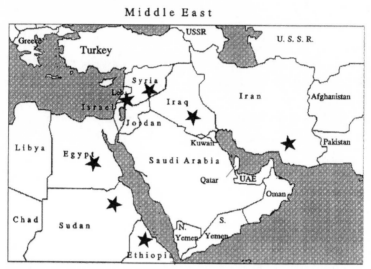

Middle East

FUTURE LOCATIONS OF ISRAEL'S CAPTIVES (Isa.11:11-12)

South Africa, etc. Aside from these territories, Isaiah states that God "will set a banner for the nations and will assemble the outcasts of [the ten tribes] Israel and gather together the dispersed of Judah from the four corners of the earth." The establishment of the State of Israel was just a prelude.

Then, Isaiah speaks concerning the deeply rooted anti-Jewish feelings among Israel's tribes since the days of Egypt. These deep feelings and animosities between Judah and Israel, mostly intensified after the division of the kingdom, and are still alive to this day in the form of anti-Semitism. Of this tragic state of mind, God declares: "Also the envy of Ephraim [toward brother Judah by the British people and fellow tribes] shall depart, and the adversaries of Judah [mainly Arab nations and, specifically, Palestinians] shall be cut off." This is a stern warning to all Arab nations from Allah. Also, to all Jew haters, this is a warning from the Messiah they claim to worship.

Scripture adds: "Ephraim [and specifically the English speaking people, the birthright tribe] shall not [anymore] envy Judah [the scepter tribe], and Judah shall not harass [antagonize, or be a thorn in the flesh of] Ephraim. But they shall fly down upon the shoulder [or the coast of the Mediterranean Sea, along Gaza and Lebanon—ancient territories of Edom and] of the Philistines toward the west [and accomplish the first stage of the final solution of the Palestinian problem]. Together [Judah and Israel], they shall plunder the people of the east [Jordan, Iraq, Iran, Arabia etc.]; they shall lay their hand on Edom and Moab; and the people of Ammon [or Jordan] shall obey them" [whether they like it or not]. And such is the will of Allah or the God of the patriarch Abraham!

Isaiah adds, "The Lord will utterly destroy the tongue of the Sea of Egypt [or Red Sea] with His mighty wind. He will shake His fist over the River [Euphrates] and strike it in seven streams and make men [the returning captives of Israel from the near east, Africa, Europe and elsewhere] cross over dry-shod." As in the days of ancient Israel, who were made to cross the Red Sea, this time, both the Red Sea and the Euphrates will be a crossing point for the two-pronged exodus from the south and northeast. Isaiah continues: "There will be a highway for the remnant of His people [Israel] who will be left [and survive the future concentration camps] from Assyria [Germany and neighboring lands], as it was for Israel in the day that he came up from the land of Egypt" (Isaiah 11:13-16).

In Chapter 14:1-3, Isaiah states: "For the Lord will have mercy on Jacob and will still choose Israel and will settle them in their own land [which some call, defiantly, "Arab lands," or "occupied territories" and Palestine], and aliens will join them and cleave to the house of Jacob. And the peoples [of Israel] will take them and bring them to their place, and the House of Israel will possess them IN THE LORD'S LAND [ultimately, not Jewish or Arab land] as male and female slaves. They will take captive those who were their captors, and rule over those who oppressed them. When the Lord has given you rest from your pain and turmoil and the hard service [in the enemy's concentration and hard labor camps] with which you were made to serve [in captivity], you will take up this taunt against the king of Babylon."

The Persian Gulf crisis is not over yet (this was written in the early stages of the first Gulf war). The second and future rounds are still ahead of us. This time it will end, initially, in a disaster for all of Israel's nations, before the conquering Messiah will reverse its tragic results. Let us read it in Jeremiah 51:1-2. "Thus says the Lord, behold I will raise against Babylon [and Assyria who anciently also ruled this area], and against them that dwell in the midst of them that rise up against Me [since when nations attack God's people, they attack God! Therefore, He will raise against them] a destroying wind [like Operation Desert Storm rounds I, II and III?], and will send into Babylon fanners that shall fan her and shall empty her land."

Then, God commands the destroyers of Babylon: "Spare you not her young men; destroy you utterly all her host [a tragic failure by the allies in Desert Storm round I. It will come back to haunt the allies]. Thus, the slain shall fall in the land of the Chaldeans, and they that are thrust through in her streets. Israel will not be forsaken, nor Judah of his God, of the Lord of hosts. Though their land was filled with sin against the Holy One of Israel," as Isaiah bemoaned. (Chapters 19)

The statements regarding Babylon are twofold. Anciently, the people God spoke of in this account lived in the area of modern Iraq and the cities of Syria and the Persian Empire. Later, many of them have migrated into central and western Europe. These people brought with them their old culture and religion, later to be "Christianized" in their new lands and "religion." The book of Revelation speaks of this revitalized ancient people and their final fate.

Through the prophet Zechariah (Ch. 10:6-10), God declared: "I will strengthen the house of Judah and I will save the house of Joseph. I will bring them back [from captivity], because I have mercy on them. They shall be as though I had not cast them aside; for I am the Lord their God, and I will hear them [and their prayers]. Those of Ephraim shall be like a mighty man and their heart shall rejoice as if with wine. Yes, their children shall see it and be glad [not scoff at it, as many do now]; their heart shall rejoice in the Lord." This is the ultimate intended purpose of the coming captivity for all Israel and the stiff upper lip Ephraim, the hardy "John Bull." "I will whistle for them and gather them, for I will redeem them; and they shall increase [as the sand of the sea shore and stars of heaven] as they once increased. I will sow them among the peoples, and they shall remember me in far countries. They shall live together with their children and they shall return [to their God and ancient land of promise]." This prophecy speaks of the time after Assyria's captivity, 2700 years ago, and the subsequent migrations into Northwest Europe and the later colonies.

God adds: "I will also bring them back [in the near future] from the land of Egypt and gather them from Assyria. I will bring them into the land of Gilead [in the East Bank of the Jordan river] and Lebanon, until no more room is found for them." These lands are now illegally occupied territories by the Palestinians, Jordan, Syria and Lebanon. These lands belong to Israel by divine decree, and will be restored to them, Arab's objections notwithstanding, and the "peace talks" are, ultimately, an exercise in futility.

Again, as in Isaiah 11:11-16, we read the same account: "He shall pass through the sea with affliction and strike the waves of the [Red] sea; all the depths of the River [Euphrates] shall dry up. Then the pride of [the land of] Assyria [or Iraq and northern Syria in this case, the ancient land of Assyria's empire] shall be brought down and the scepter of Egypt shall depart."

Iraq will again be allied with its ancient rival/ally, Assyria or modern Germany, and Asshur, a grandson of Abraham now partly in Northern Syria and mostly in Austria. As a result, God states: "'So I will strengthen them [Israel] in the Lord [with modern technology and weapons] and they shall walk up and down in His name,' says the Lord" (Zechariah 10:1-11). Other prophets describe in detail the final days and period of Israel's coming fall and rise. They also speak of her return to her ancient homeland, her God, and His pure religion—the true old religion they once followed.

Let us now explore the final scenario leading to the restoration of Israel. Let us also discuss the fate and future of New Jerusalem, the city of peace and learning for all humanity! Ezekiel has recorded this specific vision in his final eight chapters. In these chapters, God [the coming Messiah] appeared to Ezekiel, narrating to him the final events leading to the restoration of Israel. He described her new capital, constitution, religion and socio-economic life. He also mapped out the borders of the newly reconstructed land of Israel. The world and all those who meddle with Israel should pay close attention to these future plans of the God of Israel or Allah. No power on earth can alter these divinely decreed and ordained future plans. They are soon to be fulfilled before our eyes.

In Chapter 37:15-28, God spoke of the coming reunion of the kingdoms of Judah and Israel. He told Ezekiel: "And I will make them one nation in the land, on the mountains of Israel and one king [the resurrected David] shall be over them all. They shall no longer be two nations, nor shall they ever be divided into two kingdoms again. They shall not defile themselves any more with their idols [the way God regards Israel and Judah's religions and way of life now], nor with their detestable things [that led them to utter moral degradation through their "alternate lifestyles," entertainment, religious and humanistic secular life, etc.], nor with any of their transgressions [because of their unwillingness to live by God's laws]. But I will deliver them from all their [former] dwelling places in which they have sinned [though they act as if sin is done away with], and will cleanse them and they shall be My people [though presently, spiritually, they are not], and I will be their God."

As far as their new form of government is concerned, God said: "David my servant [who is soon to be resurrected] shall be king over them, and they shall all have one shepherd [not many parties and rulers]. They shall also walk in My [and not their own] judgments and observe My statutes and do them, then they shall dwell in the land that I have given to Jacob [and not to Ishmael, Edom, or the Arabs, but to Jacob] My servant, where your fathers dwelt. And they shall dwell there, they, their children and their children's children, forever; and My servant David shall be their prince forever. The twelve apostles will be under David, each ruling a tribe of Israel, as Christ promised his disciples in Matthew 19:28.

"Moreover," continues God, "I will make a covenant of peace with them, and it shall be an everlasting covenant with them. I will establish them and multiply them and I will set My sanctuary in their midst forevermore. My tabernacle also shall be with them; indeed, I will be their God and they shall be My people." As for the rest of the world, God declares: "The nations also will know that I, the Lord, sanctify Israel, when My sanctuary is in their midst forevermore."

In Chapter 36 of Ezekiel, God told Israel of his intentions to take them of all the nations where they have defiled His name, and bring them back to His land. He spoke of giving them a new heart and spirit to obey His laws. In verses 17-27, He declared: "Son of man, when the house of Israel dwelt in their own land, they defiled it by their own ways [as many say, "I did it my way," and so it was their ways] and deeds. To me, their way was like the uncleanness of a [menstruating] woman in her customary impurity." Yet Israel's nations think of themselves as highly educated, civilized, religious, and "good people."

God continues, "Therefore, I poured my fury on them for the blood they had shed [through crime and oppression] on the land. So I scattered them among the nations, and they were dispersed throughout the countries. When they came to the nations, wherever they went, they profaned My holy name." This they did with their old idolatrous religion and immorality, and also with their new adulterated religions, which they claimed to be His—the new Gentile religion called "Christianity," and

Judah's Rabbinic Judaism. God adds: "Therefore, say to the House of Israel, thus says the Lord God, I do not do this for your sake, O house of Israel, but for My holy name's sake, which you have profaned among the nations wherever you went [speaking of both Judah and Israel]. And I will sanctify My great name, for I will take you from among the nations, and bring you into your own land [since even after 2700 years, it's still Israel's land, regardless of what other nations may call it]. Then, I will sprinkle clean water on you and you shall be clean. I will give you a new heart and put a new spirit [of submission and obedience to God's Law and teachings] within you [since this is the only way to solve all of humanity's problems]. I will take the heart of stone out of your flesh [that causes you to be stubborn, corrupt, rebellious and criminal in nature] and give you a heart of flesh. I will put My spirit within you and cause you to walk in My statutes, and you will keep My judgments and do them."

After this delicate yet painful 'heart transplant' has been achieved, God promises to pour out His blessings on all Israel. But what is to happen next? Chapters 38-39 describe the last battle to take place in the Middle East. This event will take place several years after Israel is to be restored to her land. Who is this last enemy disturbing the peace of Jerusalem? In Chapter 38, Ezekiel speaks of this enemy. His armies are comprised of many nations, still in need of learning a few hard lessons. These are: Gog and Magog, the prince of Rosh [Russia], Meshech and Tubal. Also with them are: Persia [Iran], Ethiopia, Libya, Gomer [Greeks] and Togarmah.

All these invading nations, the hordes of the east as: Eastern Europe, newly rising Russian Empire, Oriental nations, and peoples of India, Pakistan, and other adjacent nations, who still have not learned who is in charge in the Middle East and on planet earth. In essence, God is the One who is bringing them into His land (vv. 3-4). He wants to teach all nations, as He did for His people and all the descendants of Abraham, that the conquering Messiah is the true God of Israel and the whole earth.

The timing of this event is recorded in verses 8-13. Here we read: "After many days you will be visited [speaking of Russia, the Eastern hordes and their allies]. In the latter years [soon to come], you will come into the land of those [just] brought back from the sword [or captivity] and gathered from many people in the mountains of Israel, which had long been desolate. They were brought out of the nations and now all of them dwell safely. You will ascend, coming like a storm, covering the land like a cloud, you and all your troops and many people with you. Thus says the Lord God, 'On that day, it shall come to pass that thoughts will arise in your mind and you will make an evil plan ["The Evil Empire," as President Reagan has labeled it, will remain evil]. You will say, I will go up against a land of unwalled villages [not big cities as today], I will go to a peaceful people, who dwell safely. All of them dwelling without walls and having neither bars nor gates [no crime], to take plunder and to take booty, to stretch out your hand against the [former] waste places [during the captivity] that are again inhabited, and against a people gathered from the nations, who have acquired livestock [being all farmers and shepherds now], and goods, to take great plunder.'"

Then in verses 17-19, we read: "Thus says the Lord God, 'Are you he, of whom I have spoken in former days [2600 years ago] by My servants the prophets of Israel, who prophesied for years in those days that I would bring you against them? And it will come to pass at the same time, when Gog comes against the land of Israel, says the Lord God, that My fury will show in my face. For in My jealousy and in the fire of My wrath, I have spoken. Surely in that day, there shall be a great earthquake [to destroy the enemies of Israel] in the land of Israel.'"

Verse 20 describes the results of the earthquake. Then comes the destruction of the invading hordes. In Chapter 39:11-16, we read of the burial of the invading armies that will take Israel seven months to accomplish. Then in verses 21-29, God declares: "I will set My glory among the nations [after the destruction of the armies of the invaders]; all the nations shall see My judgments which I have executed and My hand which I have laid on them. So the house of Israel shall know that I am the Lord their God from that day forward [since few in Israel still need some convincing]. The Gentiles shall know that the house of Israel went into captivity for their iniquity; because they were unfaithful to Me, therefore, I hid My face from them. I gave them into the hand of their enemies and they all fell by the sword [and that's why God allows wars].

"Therefore, thus says the Lord God, 'Now I will bring back the captives of Jacob and have mercy on the whole house of Israel. And I will be jealous for My holy name, after they have borne their shame, and all their unfaithfulness, when they dwelt safely in their own land [in Northwest Europe, America and elsewhere] and no one made them afraid [because God had protected them, though only the few would acknowledge it]. When I have brought them back from the peoples and gathered them from their enemies' lands, and I am hallowed in them in the sight of many nations, then they shall know that I am the Lord their God [since now most of them don't, and do not care] who sent them into [the soon coming] captivity among the nations, but also brought them back to their own lands and left none of them captive any longer. And I will not hide My face from them anymore [as he had done in the past, and during the recent holocaust and the mega holocaust soon to come], for I shall have poured out My spirit on the house of Israel,' says the Lord God" (Ezekiel 39:21-28).

Thus will end the 4000 years of turbulent history of Abraham's squabbling and rebellious family—especially that of Israel. Now we are ready for the final scene in this long chain of tragic events. For millennia, they have marred the peace of Jerusalem, of the land of Israel and her neighbors, and of the whole earth. The prophet Ezekiel recorded his last vision concerning this soon coming age of utopia. It is to spring forth from the bowels of the city of peace, Jerusalem. He wrote: "In the twenty-fifth year of our captivity [in Babylon, Iraq], in the fourteenth year after the city [Jerusalem] was captured, on the very same day, the hand of the Lord was upon me and He took me there. In the visions of God, He took me into the land of Israel and set me on a very high mountain. On it, toward the south, was something like the structure of the city" (Ezekiel 40:1-2). This is a vision of the restored city of Jerusalem—recorded more than 2500 years before it comes to pass.

From this point, God and an angel are doing the narration. They describe the newly reconstructed Jerusalem and Israel. Let us explore some of the highlights of this visionary, and soon to be a reality, journey into the city of peace. At the end of verse 4, the angel told Ezekiel: "Son of man, look with your eyes and hear with your ears and fix in your mind on everything I show you, for you were brought here so that I might show them to you. Declare to the house of Israel [in writing] everything you see." Then Ezekiel, in a vision, is given a tour of the future Temple quarters and is told, in detail, the purpose of each structure and item. In verse 39, he is told of the two sacrificial tables on which to slay the burnt offering, the sin offering, and the trespass offering. They were not done away with after all, as many "Christians" still do erroneously believe.

As for the priests, Ezekiel was told: "The chamber is for the priest, the keepers of the charge of the altars. These are the sons of Zadok [father of the Sadducee priests] from the sons of Levi" (v. 46). In 42:13, Ezekiel is told that those priests who are to eat the meat of the sin, and trespass offerings, are the only ones to approach God. In 43:7, God (The Messiah) tells Ezekiel: "Son of man, this is the place of My throne, and the place of the soles of My feet, where I will dwell in the midst of the children of Israel forever. And My holy name shall the house of Israel no more defile, neither they, nor their kings [or governments] by their harlotry." This harlotry refers to the religious and secular humanly devised teachings and philosophies contrary to God's law; to the unholy alliances they forge with other nations. Then in verse 10, he is told: "Describe the Temple to the house of Israel, that they may be ashamed of their iniquities." Then Ezekiel is given the "law of the house," its pattern and order of sacrifices, and the manner in which it is to be done.

In Chapter 44:2-3, Ezekiel is told by God: "This [Eastern] gate shall be shut. It shall not be opened, and no man shall enter by it, because the Lord God of Israel has entered by it. Therefore, it shall be shut. As for the prince [the physical ruler of Israel, under the soon to be resurrected spirit being, King David], because he is the prince, he may sit in it [in the eastern gate] to eat bread before the Lord, he shall enter by the way of the vestibule of the gateway and go out the same way." In verses 6-7, God condemns the house of Israel, because it had previously allowed strangers to enter into His Temple. Then in verse 9, He lays down the following law: "Thus says the Lord God, no foreigner, uncircumcised in heart [without God's spirit, or disobedient to His Law] or uncircumcised in flesh, shall enter My sanctuary, including any foreigner who is among the children of Israel." This statement makes very clear God's attitude toward circumcision in the nations of Israel. God's Law always forbade the introduction of uncircumcised men into His Temple. There will be no change in the future.

The rest of the chapter deals with priestly duties in the future Temple. It is soon to be rebuilt, after the return of Israel's conquering Messiah and God. In Chapter 45, Ezekiel is told of the division of the land into thirteen districts or provinces. Each tribe will have his own province. This territory would ultimately stretch from the River Euphrates to the River of Egypt. He also designates an area to be called "the province of the Lord." It is a holy territory and a square lot that measures 25,000 by 25,000 reeds. A reed equals 18 inches. Then Ezekiel was told: "Of this there shall be a square plot for the sanctuary [or Temple], five hundred by five hundred rods [or cubits], with fifty cubits around it for an open space [for lawn and trees]" (Ezekiel 45:2).

This 25,000 by 25,000 reed holy territory will be divided in three sections. The first 10,000 by 25,000 is for the priesthood. In the midst of it the Temple will be located. The second portion, of an equal size, will be for the Levites. The remaining 5,000 by 25,000 will be given to those chosen representatives of the twelve tribes of Israel to occupy. They will manage the affairs of Jerusalem, which will be located in that portion. We can read these details in two places: In Ezekiel 45, and with more details of the city, in 48:10-20. It is to this city of God and peace that representatives of all surviving humanity will come to seek instructions in God's way. Thus Israel will finally fulfill her anciently given roll to be the light of the nations. God stated through the prophet Isaiah: "For out of Zion shall go forth the Law [or Torah], and the Word of the Lord from Jerusalem" (Isa. 2:3). All the prophets of Israel, as well as the apostles of Jesus, have prophesied of this glorious mission of the people of God, though a misguided religion taught otherwise in the past 1900 years.

The size of the city of Jerusalem will be 4500 by 4500 cubits. In Chapter 45:21-25, God gives instructions for keeping the Passover and the feast of Tabernacles. This is not the Gentile feast of Easter, substituted by the Gentile religion of papal Rome instead of God's Passover. Other Holy Days of God, as recorded in Leviticus 23 are, obviously, included. This should give us a clue as to which religion the Messiah of Israel refers to.

Speaking to those who have some doubts concerning His religion, in His days in the flesh, He stated: "Think not [as most 'Christians' do] that I am come to destroy the Law or the prophets [as the teachers of Christianity did teach], but to fulfill. For assuredly, I say to you, till heaven and earth pass away [and they are still with us], one jot or one title will by no means pass from the Law [or the Torah] till all is fulfilled. Whosoever breaks one of the least of these commandments [which many "Christian" teachers have proclaimed was done away] and teaches men so [as they all did], shall be called the least in the Kingdom of Heaven [which is coming to earth, and that's why the true followers of Christ were commanded to pray "Thy kingdom come"]. But whosoever does and teaches them, he shall be called great in the Kingdom of Heaven" (Matthew 5:1719).

In Chapter 46:1-8, God is informing Ezekiel of the instructions regarding the keeping of God's Sabbath (not the Gentile Sunday worship, patterned after the pagan sun-worship, but Saturday) and new moons that are still being kept by the religious in Judah, and the true followers of Christ, to this day. Then in verse 9, God speaks of the solemn feasts, which He recorded through Moses in Leviticus 23. This list included God's seventh day Sabbath, the only Sabbath The Creator of all men ever gave to humanity since Adam. God called, in Leviticus 23:1-2, all these feasts, "The Feasts of the Lord." Yet many who claim to follow the Lord of Israel think their brand of religion is acceptable to Him. To such misguided 'would be Christians,' the Messiah declared: "Why call me Lord, Lord, and do not do the things which I say?" (Luke 6:46). Do we have a good answer? We better find one now!

In Ezekiel 45:8, we read of the territory of the prince. It is located on both sides of "the holy portion of the Lord." In verse 8, God states of the prince's territory: "The land shall be his possession in Israel, and my princes [or government leaders] shall no more oppress my people [as their manner was and still is now through their heavy taxation and unjust laws], but they shall give the rest of the land to the house of Israel [not nationalize or appropriate it as the manner of all human governments now] according to their tribes."

God forbade the leaders of His people from ever appropriating His land, or stealing it for selfish government's sake, and that of greedy captains of industry or real estate tycoons. This is applicable to the new lands He gave His people in other countries. It is an oppressive criminal action, what governments and wealthy individuals have done with God's earth, from God's point of view. Government, industry, and the business community as well, have been routinely robbing people of the land given to them by God.

In Chapter 46:18, again we read of the prince's responsibility. God declared: "Moreover, the prince shall not take any of the peoples' inheritance by evicting them from their [God given] property." This practice is common among Israel's lawless governments, legislators, leaders, lawyers, men in industry, in banking, in probate courts, in agribusiness; who by their own ungodly laws seize the properties of the people. God continues: "He shall provide an inheritance for his sons from his own property, so that none of My people may be scattered from his property." Today, because of the "legalized "practices of deceit, many are landless and even homeless. This is another reason for the coming captivity. In Chapter 45:9, God is warning the powers that be: "Thus says the Lord God, 'Enough, O princes of Israel [be it Washington D.C., London, Jerusalem, and others]. Remove violence and plundering.'" This is the way God regards the laws of iniquity by governments, their unjust and unlawful heavy taxation and artificial tax brackets, budget deficit, "revenue enhancing" laws, borrowing and inflation, zoning laws. Governments force the tax payer to pay the penalty for the willful robbery committed by many sectors of the business community as: the banking community, industry, the medical profession, the insurance industry, and that of the private sector. God warns these criminal elements in today's society: "Execute justice and righteousness [according to God's laws, not man's] and stop dispossessing My people, says the Lord God."

At the turn of the last century, over 90% of Americans lived on the land. Now, thanks to greedy bankers, lawyers, government agencies as: the IRS, corporate leaders in agribusiness, and other government agencies, only 3% of Americans still live on their land. This criminal tragedy committed by those in power is the lot of all citizens in all the countries of Israel and the world. The soon coming worldwide captivity and destruction of the present world order—beginning with the nations of Israel—the very ones who ought to know better, will eradicate these social iniquities forever. The new city of Jerusalem, and later, all the cities of this crime-ridden and ravaged world, will not any more experience the results of lawless and immoral greedy politicians and their counterparts in the private sector.

The God of Israel addressed this scourge of our nightmarish reality through the prophet Isaiah. He lamented of his beloved city: "How the faithful city has become a harlot [through political, social, religious, judicial, and moral harlotry]! It was full of justice; righteousness lodged in it [as the manner of many new cities and countries when they first receive their freedom], but now murderers. Your silver has become dross [and devalued money becoming worthless paper due to corrupt government policies, compounded by that of the private sector], your wine mixed with water [or cheap quality merchandise and false claims to the contrary]. Your princes are rebellious, and companions of thieves [through lobbyists and selfish special interest groups]. Everyone loves bribes [since this is often what runs the wheels of politics, government, and the economy], and follows after rewards [which no one can hide from the scrutinizing eyes of our Maker, and no one will get away with it in their day in court]. They do not defend the fatherless [but rob them of their inheritance by 'legal' means in probate courts, estate taxes, and through greedy lawyers], nor does the cause of the widow comes before them." How many widows and orphans have lost their homes, properties, farms, etc., through 'legal means' when they could not pay their taxes, or could not read the small print? "'Therefore,' the Lord says, the Lord of hosts [of the armies of Heaven], the Mighty One of Israel, 'Ah, I will rid myself of My adversaries, and take vengeance on My enemies.'" Those who oppress their fellow man are the personal adversaries of the God of Israel. Most of them are doing it under the guise of 'legality' through atrocious interest payments, 'legal' regulations, heartless taxation, and plain criminal petty thievery in all levels of government, the private sector of business and commerce, and the common outlaws.

"I will turn my hand against you," says God, "and thoroughly purge away your dross [or corruption] and take away all your alloy. I will restore your judges as at the first and your counselors as at the beginning." Jerusalem and all cities of the world began their history with a desire for a better and equitable way of life. Then, being corrupted by the scourge of human nature they went astray. God adds: "Afterward you shall be called the city of righteousness, the faithful city. Zion shall be redeemed with justice [after experiencing, first, captivity and destruction] and her penitents with righteousness [produced by God's laws, not man's]. The destruction of transgressors and of sinners shall be together, and those who forsake the Lord [as most of humanity had done], shall be consumed" (Isaiah 1:21-28). Only the fool and hopelessly insane in mind will disregard this sober and grave warning of the God of Israel! Are you, by choice, one of them? If you are, as the prophet had declared, long ago, "prepare to meet your God, O Israel."

When the God of Israel had brought His people out of Egypt into their land, He commissioned His government leaders on earth, in the persons of Joshua and Eliezer the high priest, to distribute the land, proportionately, according to the size of each tribe. Each single family was to receive a plot of land in accordance with its size. No one in government or the private sector, by divine law, was permitted to disinherit the family unit of its land, forever. When the wicked King Ahab of Israel, seduced by his wife Jezebel, disinherited one of his citizens of his family property, he and his wife earned the eternal wrath of the God of Israel. His whole dynasty was decimated by God's command. God is no respecter of persons! Those in government and the private sector today, who follow wicked Ahab's example, will reap the same fate in due time. Even the grave and death cannot hide them from the soon coming day of judgment and wrath of The One who sees and records all things.

The God of Israel had commanded Moses to inform the Levites of their duty to execute a divine command. They were to pronounce twelve specific curses on Israel, if they would transgress His commands for the nation as a whole. These curses are recorded in the Book of the Law in Deuteronomy, Chapter 27. The third curse, in sequence of importance, was pronounced on anyone—a government leader or a private citizen—who would disinherit a fellow Israelite from his land by any 'legal' or illegal means. Tragically, the chief transgressors of this divine Law are often the institutions of government, their powerful self-interest backers, and the religious community. After these chief culprits, next in line are many in the business community and the private sector. The direct consequences of these illegal and immoral acts have wrought havoc on the institution of the family. The economic and spiritual wellbeing of every family and individual on earth have become the primary target of such insidious transgression. All the ills and woes of humanity are directly and indirectly linked to the curse pronounced on those transgressing this divine Law of God.

Through Isaiah the prophet, God thundered: "What mean you that you beat my people to pieces and grind the faces of the poor, says the Lord God of hosts" (Isaiah 3:15). This is a common practice by all governments, insurance and banking industries, the medical profession, lawyers, high paid professionals and other individuals. This is another major reason for the coming destruction on all mankind. The lawgiver, Moses, said of his nation Israel: "For they are a nation void of counsel, nor is there any understanding in them. Oh, that they were wise that they would have understood this, that they would consider their latter end" (Deuteronomy 32:28). Tragically, Israel never did until it was too late

But why is it that Israel has no understanding? Moses gives the answer in Chapter 4:1-10 of Deuteronomy, where he stated: "Now, O Israel, listen to the statutes and the judgments which I teach you to observe that you may live, you shall not add to the word which I command you nor take anything from it that you may keep the commandments of the Lord your God, which He commands you this day" (vv. 1-2).

Both Israel and Judah, in their religious and secular teachings and laws; in their economic and moral philosophies, ideologies, culture, entertainment, humanism etc., have repeatedly transgressed this Law and stern warning of Moses—to their own hurt. Tragically, Israel never paid attention, as a whole, to this warning. Then in verses 6-9, Moses counseled

Israel: "Therefore, be careful to observe them, for this is your wisdom and your understanding in the sight of the peoples who will hear all these statutes and say, surely this great nation is a wise and understanding people. For what great nation is there that has God so near to it [not just in lip service] as the Lord our God is to us, for whatever reason we may call upon him? And what great nation is there that has such statutes and righteous judgments as are in all this Law, which I set before you this day? Only take heed to yourself, lest you forget, and lest they depart [which they often quickly did] from your heart all the days of your life. And teach them to your children and your grandchildren."

Sadly, to this day, Israel has rejected the sober admonition of her lawgiver, Moses—and to her own hurt. The educational system in the nations of Israel is void, mostly, of such sound teachings, due to willful decisions made by those in high places. The consequences can be seen even by the 'blind' who are robbed in broad daylight.

In Chapter 27, Moses commanded the Levites to pronounce twelve curses on those who would not obey certain laws. The first was idolatry, whether it be other gods or making something more important than God. The second was dishonoring parents, which today's media does a pretty good job at in its movies, entertainment, and the world of music. Thirdly, a curse was pronounced on anyone who would rob his fellow man of his land, his possessions, and his home. That's why God is warning the rulers of Israel to cease from plundering the citizenry, as we read in Ezekiel 45:9. Former President Reagan has stated often: "Government is the major problem, and through inflation [largely] government is robbing the taxpayer." The morally illegal laws government enacts, often for the benefit of selfish and greedy special interest groups, allow other industries and agencies to add insult to injury.

Through the prophet Jeremiah, God described the insidious and corrupt nature of the secular and religious leadership of His people. He stated, "For from the least of them even unto the greatest of them, everyone is given to covetousness; and from the prophet even unto the priest [as televangelists often do], everyone deals falsely" (Jeremiah 6:13). Then through the prophet Ezekiel, He stated: "In you [Jerusalem, symbolic of all Israel] they have taken gifts to shed blood [through contracts on peoples' lives, and bribes in political, military and civilian circles]. You have taken usury and increase and you have greedily gained of your neighbors by extortion and have forgotten Me, says the Lord" (Ezekiel 22:12).

Consider the outrageous credit cards interest rates—the curse of every economy and financial well-being of the business and private sector. That's why the chaos in the banking industry. No city or nation can be built, solidly, on the foundation of corruption and thievery. The future city of peace, Jerusalem, will not tolerate such rulers, as the prophet Micah spoke of in Chapters 2-3. Let us read those statements, again, before we return to the city of Jerusalem, which will be established on Godly justice and laws the world and Israel have not known for ages.

Considering the nature and actions of the government and business community of his day, the prophet Micah warned: "'Woe, to those who devise iniquity [by breaking God's Law of justice], and work out evil in their beds! At morning light they practice it [why?] because it is in the power of their hand [since all they have to do is pass a law]. They covet fields and take them by violence [through zoning manipulation and repossession through immoral laws], also houses and seize them [by unbearable property, probate, and estate taxes]. So, they oppress a man and his house, a man and his inheritance. Therefore, thus says the Lord, 'Behold, against this family [in those days and now], I am devising a disaster [through terror or captivity] from which you cannot remove your necks. Nor shall you walk haughtily, for this is an evil time'" (Micah 2:13). No power or sophisticated technology or 'security measures' on earth can prevent the national disaster God is devising against all the nations of Israel and Judah, but the power of national repentance! You may scoff at it today, but not tomorrow, when all these things shall come to pass!

Then in Chapter 3:1-4, Micah was inspired, by God, to give the following most graphic description of the "flesh eaters" in government and religious circles, and in the business community. He declared: "Hear, O heads of Jacob, and you rulers of the house of Israel, is it not for you to know justice [and how can they, when they have rejected God's Constitution and lawmaker—Moses?], you who hate good and love evil. [You] who strip the skin from my people, and the flesh from their bones." This they do through criminal taxation, inflation, price fixing, regulations and laws that allow the banking, insurance, medical, judicial institutions, the business professions and lawyers to gouge and plunder the helpless citizen of his often meager earnings? Micah adds: "[You] who also eat the flesh of My people, flay their skin from them, break their bones, and chop them in pieces like meat for the pot, like flesh in the caldron. [That's how God regards these lawless criminals.} Then they [the oppressors, in the coming captivity] will cry to the Lord, but He will not hear them. He will even hide His face from them at that time, because they have been evil in their deeds." When the coming unavoidable mega tragedy strikes, those who oppress now should remember these sober warnings of the God of Israel, though it will then be too late, for most, anyway!

Then the prophet Micah states, in contrast to the false 'spiritual leaders' of Israel: "But truly, I am full of power by the Spirit of the Lord and of justice and might, to declare [and not hide, or speak smoothly] to Jacob his transgression and to Israel his sin [unlike most of the shepherds of Israel, who speak smooth things to their congregations]. Now hear this, you [government] heads of the house of Jacob and rulers of the house of Israel [at all levels of society], who abhor justice [doing everything for politics, power, prestige, kickbacks' sake] and pervert all equity [from God's point of view], who build up Zion [then, the religious site of corruption, or any city of Israel today] with bloodshed and Jerusalem [or civil governments today as: Washington, London, Paris, and every capital of Israel's modern nations] with iniquity. Her heads judge for a bribe [of money, favors, political influence, special interests, etc.], her priests teach [their own brand of religion] for pay, and her prophets divine for money [fostering total corruption in civic and religious moral teachings, as God sees it]. Yet they lean on the Lord and say, 'Is not God among us? [God bless America, Britain, Israel etc.] No harm will come to us'" [since "we are good people."] Yet, what is God's response to all this civil and religious back stroking? Micah responds: "Therefore, because of you Zion [and all of Israel's nations], shall be plowed like a field, Jerusalem shall become heaps of ruins and the mountain of the Temple like the bare hills of the forest" (Micah 3:8-12). As it happened to God's city and people then, so shall it be, and much more so, to Israel's capitals and peoples now, for God is no respecter of persons.

Speaking of those to return from the soon coming great captivity of Israel, in Isaiah 4:3-6, God declared: "And it shall come to pass that he who is left in Zion [symbolic of all the cities and nations of Israel], and he who remains in Jerusalem will be called holy—everyone who is recorded among the living in Jerusalem [and all those of Israel who have escaped, v. 2]. When the Lord has washed away the filth [and this is His opinion of all of His people] of the daughters [or nations of Israel or] of Zion and purged the blood of Jerusalem from her midst, by the spirit of judgment and by the spirit of burning [the mega holocaust to come], then the Lord will create above every dwelling place of Mount Zion and above her assemblies [her huddled masses] a cloud and smoke by day, and the shining of a flaming fire by night [for total protection from the elements of nature until the cities of Israel are again rebuilt]. For all over the glory there will be a covering and there will be a tabernacle for shade in the day time from the heat, for a place of refuge, and for a shelter from storm and rain."

That is why the world is in such a mess! That is why a mega captivity is coming! The ultimate future and outcome of the "Peace Process" and any future Middle East war, and the coming military intervention by the rising super power in Europe, will result in the greatest nightmare the nations of Israel have ever experienced—and for that matter, the rest of humanity. All the brutality and atrocities committed by the Iraqis against helpless neighbors, and of those nations allied with the future rising new Nazi axis, will soon be unleashed on God's nations. Other nations will join in this carnage against God's nations of Israel—by God's decree.

The God of Israel, in a vision, while showing the prophet Ezekiel the future of Israel's city of peace and land of righteousness, warned the leaders of all the nations of Israel of the consequences of their policies, and the practices of those in the business community. Through the prophet David, God recorded the fate of all those peoples, nations and leaders involved in supporting a system that economically, spiritually and culturally enslaves all of humanity.

"Praise the Lord!" David admonished God's people, "Sing to the Lord a new song. Let Israel rejoice in their maker. Let the children of Zion be joyful in their king, for the Lord takes pleasure in His people. He will beautify the humble with salvation. Let the saints be joyful in glory. Let the high praises of God be in their mouth and a two-edged sword in their hand, to execute vengeance on the nations and punishments on the peoples; to bind their kings with chains and their nobles with fetters of iron; to execute on them the written judgment—this honor have all his saints" (Psalm 149:19).

All government and civil leaders of this world—those responsible for the chronic problems and sufferings of humanity, will be court martialed and executed. This history written in advance will soon become a reality. There is no escaping of this fate! The future city of justice and judgment will not tolerate corrupt leaders in government, religious, or in civil circles. All nations will have to obey the dictates of the rulers Jerusalem—or else!

Through His prophet Isaiah, God stated, of the coming absolute rule of Jerusalem, these words: "For the nation or kingdom which will not serve you shall perish, and those nations shall be utterly ruined" (Isa. 60:12). After warning government leaders of removing their violence through their unjust laws, court systems, enforcement agencies and correction institutions, which are often manipulated for their own selfish ends, God spoke to the business community. He stated: "You shall have just balance, a just ephah [or measuring unit] and a just bath" (Ezekiel 45:10). Too much cheating in every aspect of the business community is impoverishing the many for the sake of the greedy few—often with the tacit cooperation of those in high places.

Then God spoke to Ezekiel about the division of the land among the twelve tribes of Israel. He gave him the future outline of Israel's borders. Today, the knowledge of this outline would infuriate any Arab who would care to read of these borders devised by God himself, not the Jews or Israel. In Ezekiel 47:13-1, we can read of these new borders. These new borders include the old territories of the two nations of Israel and Judah that her enemies have seized illegally after

FUTURE TRIBAL TERRITORY OF ISRAEL (Ezek. 47:13, 21, 48:29)

Israel and Judah were taken into captivity. The "occupied territories," from God's point of view, are those illegally settled by the Palestinians, Jordan, Syria, Lebanon and Egypt—not the Jews.

The borders of Israel will stretch, initially, from the Sinai Desert to the River Euphrates. It would include the East and West Bank of the Jordan River, most of Syria, and all of Lebanon. A quick look at any Bible map from Solomon's kingdom would reveal the extent of such, soon to be enlarged, territory. Also, after Israel begins to multiply, God promised to enlarge the borders of her land. He is the owner of the whole universe, and who can say nay to him?

341

Yet, God cares also for the strangers in His land. In verses 22-23, he told Ezekiel: "And it shall be that you will divide it by lot as an inheritance for yourselves and for the strangers who sojourn among you [Arabs, or those living among other nations of Israel—and those who have culturally and religiously integrated with Israel], and who bear children among you. They shall be to you as native-born among the children of Israel; they shall have an inheritance with you among the tribes of Israel and it shall be that in whatever tribe the stranger sojourns, there you shall give him his inheritance, says the Lord God." God is fair to all of his children—he is a respecter of none!

In ancient Israel's maps, we notice a tribal division that was based on the size of the tribe. This time, all provinces and divisions will be of a uniform size. The reason for that is very simple: God will preserve an equal number of every tribe from the coming final captivity (see the indication in Rev. 7:4-8). Also, the configuration of the tribes and their location will be quite different for most of them. To the north of Jerusalem, seven tribes will be settled, beginning with Judah's royal tribe. Judah will be settled next to the territory of the priests in whose plot the Temple will be located. Next to Judah's province, northward in the following order, these tribes (if all our information is correct) will be located: Reuben (French), Ephraim (English), Manasseh (Anglo-Americans), Naphtali (Swedish), Asher (Swiss, some in Italy, anciently known as Etruscans), and Dan (Irish and some Danish). Also, we should remember those Israelites who had migrated eastward into territories stretching from northern China, India, and nearby Muslim nations. Many of them had retained even their tribal identity to this day. All of them are to be reunited with their modern western tribes—now grown into nations. To the south of Jerusalem, the other tribes will be located in the following order: Benjamin (Norway, Iceland), Simeon (scattered, many are in the south of the U.S.), Issachar (Finnish, Estonians, and many in Hungary), Zebulun (Dutch, some in South Africa), and Gad (Belgium). Other parts of the tribes of Israel, scattered in various locations around the world and in Europe, like Italy, Greece, Luxembourg, northern Germany etc., will join their respective tribes.

The approximate size of this territory of the new Israel is about 3.5 million square feet. As the tribes begin to multiply, their boundaries will be enlarged in all directions. The two tribes located on the farthest opposite extremities of northern and southern Israel, namely, Dan and

Gad, can expand in three directions. Later, many of the Israelites from each tribe would probably resettle their old territories in Europe, America and elsewhere.

Let us now concentrate on "the holy portion of the Lord!" In this area are located, to the north, the Temple in the priests' territory, and to the south, Jerusalem. Permanent residents of the capital of Israel, of each tribe, will inhabit the newly restored City of Peace. Their responsibility is to care for the needs of the city. These duties will include the following: The new international court; the schools of learning responsible for teaching God's Royal Law, both civil and religious, to all nations. Also, the accommodations for those pilgrims coming to Jerusalem on God's Holy Days, and other duties, would be the responsibility of the city residents. Later, we'll have more to say on this subject.

As for the first district, belonging to the priesthood, Ezekiel was informed: "It shall be for the priests of the sons of Zadok, who are sanctified, who have kept My charge, who did not go astray when the children of Israel went astray [during the division of the two kingdoms], as the Levites went astray" (Ezekiel 48:11). As for the land of the holy portion of the Lord, none will be allowed (by the Priests or Levites) to "sell or exchange any of it" (Ezekiel 48:14). The Temple itself, where the God and Messiah of Israel will inhabit the holiest portion of it, will have twelve gates. Each gate will bear one of the names of the tribes of Israel. Each tribe shall enter through his respective gate and depart in the opposite direction to prevent 'traffic jams.' Anyone wishing to visit the Temple from Jerusalem will have to cross the territory of Israel to its border. Then, he has to cross the land of the Levites. From the Levites' border, he has to cross half the territory of the priests to reach the southern gate of the Temple.

Ezekiel was shown a stream of water that sprang from under the altar. This stream would be "flowing from under the threshold of the Temple, toward the east" (47:1). He was told: "This water flows toward the eastern region, goes down into the valley, and enters the [Dead] sea. When it reaches the sea, its [salty] waters are healed" (47:8). "Along the bank of the river [that began as a stream from under the altar], were very many trees on one side and the other" (47:7). "And it shall be," he was told, "that every living thing that moves, wherever the river goes, will live. There will be a very great multitude of fish, because these waters go there . . . It shall be that fishermen will stand by it [the Dead Sea] from En-Gedi to En-Eglaim; there will be places for spreading their nets. Their fish will be of the same kind as the fish of the Great Sea [or Mediterranean], exceeding many . . . Along the bank of the river, on this side and that, will grow all kinds of trees used for food [among others, for the traveling pilgrims to Jerusalem]. Their leaves will not wither, and their fruit will not fail. They will bear fruit every month, because their water flows from the sanctuary, their fruit will be for food and their leaves for medicine" (Ezekiel 47:9-12).

Speaking of this "river of life," the prophet Zechariah stated: "And in that day [when the Messiah's feet shall stand on the Mount of Olives] it shall be that living waters shall flow from Jerusalem [after the Temple is built], half of them toward the eastern sea [or Dead Sea] and half of them [or the other branch of the river] toward the western sea [or Mediterranean]. In both summer and winter it shall occur, and the Lord shall be King over all the earth" (Zechariah 14:8-9).

Now what is the purpose of the city? Why are representatives of all the tribes of Israel to be settled in Jerusalem? Many of the prophets of Israel have written concerning this subject. Let us read the prophecy recorded by the prophet Micah regarding the role of the city of peace—Jerusalem. Micah wrote: "Now it shall come to pass in the latter days that the mountain of the Lord's House [Zion] shall be established on the top of the mountains [of Jerusalem and above the nations] and shall be exalted above the hills [of Israel and the nations]. And peoples [of all nations, beginning with Arabs, all children of Abraham], shall flow to it. Many nations shall come and say, 'Come and let us go up to the mountain of the Lord, to the house of the God of Jacob. He will teach us [through His representatives in Jerusalem] His ways and we shall walk [with no more scoffing any longer at God's religion, laws and feasts] in His paths. For out of Zion shall the Law [or Torah, given in Sinai] go forth and the word of the Lord from Jerusalem.'"

Notice the two distinct names: Zion and Jerusalem. They will be located at the two opposite extremes of "the holy portion of the Lord." Micah continues: "He shall judge between many peoples [and solve the national disputes and conflicts of those who come to Jerusalem for a just arbitration] and rebuke strong nations afar off [which behave like Iraq or North Korea]. They shall beat their swords into plowshares, and their spears into pruning hooks. Nation shall not lift a sword against nation, neither shall they learn war anymore, but everyone shall sit under his vine and his fig tree and no one shall make them afraid. For the Lord of Hosts has spoken" (Micah 4:1-4).

Private ownership of land is a divine right. In the future there will be no more government, selfish 'insiders' interests and industry land-grabbing; no more the indignities of the landless, the homeless and jobless. Today, many are in constant fear for their lives; in fear of losing their properties when they can't pay criminally oppressive taxes imposed on them; in fear of losing their jobs.

Speaking of the restoration of Israel and the coming rule of Jerusalem over all nations, the prophet Jeremiah stated: "The Gentiles [or nations] shall come to You [in Jerusalem] from the ends of the earth and say, 'Surely our fathers have inherited lies [false religious and secular teachings, ideologies, philosophies and] worthlessness and unprofitable things'" (Jeremiah 16:19). It is to Jerusalem that the nations shall come to be de-programmed of their false religions and reprogrammed in the God of Jacob's religion. In Zechariah 8:20-23, The God of Israel stated through the prophet Zechariah: "Thus says the Lord of Hosts, 'People shall yet come, inhabitants of many cities, the inhabitants of one city shall go to another, saying, let us continue to go and pray [not to the "gods" of Paganism, Atheism, Humanism, and Secularism, but] before the Lord and seek the Lord of Hosts. I myself will go also! Yes, many peoples and strong nations shall come to seek the Lord of Hosts in Jerusalem [since only those circumcised in heart and flesh are allowed into the Temple, where the God of Israel and her Messiah dwells in the midst of the "holy portion" of the priests], and [they will come] to pray before the Lord.'" Then He added: "Thus says the Lord of hosts, 'In those days, ten men from every language of the nations [including Arabs and Muslims] shall grasp the sleeve of a Jewish man [and other Israelites], saying, let us go with you, for we have heard that God [or Allah] is with you" (Zechariah 8:20-23)

As a result of all the nations who would flock to Jerusalem for knowledge and light, "The earth shall be full of the knowledge of the Lord as the waters cover the sea" (Isaiah 11:9). At this point, all religions, ideologies, philosophies, and ways of life not based on God's Laws, will be abolished. These few statements, among many, reveal the purpose of Jerusalem, the new site of the world court of justice, education and peace. The city will have absolute power to justly and fairly enforce decisions made in Zion, and transmitted through the leadership of Jerusalem to all nations. Elements of the twelve nations of Israel located in Jerusalem, will now teach humanity God's Laws of life and peace in every area of life. Ironically, the age-old false accusations against "the Zionists plot" for global domination" is actually a "plot" by the Rulers of Heavenly Jerusalem or Zion. Ultimately, it will be welcomed by all nations.

Of this city of Jerusalem, specifically, as well as of all Israel, God stated: "And it shall come to pass that just as you were a curse among the nations, O house of Judah and Israel, so I will save you and you shall be a blessing" (Zechariah 8:13). The nations of Israel were a mixture of blessings and curses to all the world through their warped and harmful religions, secular and selfish economic teachings, destructive technology, form of entertainment, corrupt forms of music and lifestyles.

Ancient Israel was called by God to fulfill her role as the teacher and light of humanity, but has rejected this divine calling. Instead, she often became the source of darkness and a corruptive agent of planet earth. Of His people, God said: "'Because the children of Israel and the children of Judah have done only evil before Me from their youth [in Egypt]. For the children of Israel have provoked Me only to anger with the work of their hands,' says the Lord. 'For this city [Jerusalem, and all the cities of Israel] has been to Me a provocation of My anger and my fury from the day that they built it, even to this day; so I will remove it from before My face [one last time]. Because of all the evil of the children of Israel and the children of Judah [in those days as well as today] which they have done to provoke Me to anger—they, their kings, their princes, their priests, their prophets, [with total failure in every area of leadership of] the men of Judah [as well as Israel], and the inhabitants of Jerusalem. And they have turned to Me the back, and not the face; though I taught them [through His few true servants, then and now], rising up early and teaching them, yet they have not listened [to this day] to receive instruction'" (Jeremiah 32:30-33, NKJV). This charge by the God of Israel and His true servants against His people would not be accepted, but mocked at by many until all things come to pass.

Ezekiel was informed concerning Jerusalem: "The five thousand [reeds by 25,000 in length] in width . . . shall be for general use by the city, for dwelling and common land. And the city shall be in the center. And these shall be the measurements: The size of the city will be 4500 square reeds." The city will be surrounded by 250 reeds-wide all around it, or 375 foot-wide strip around the city for the surrounding park (Ezekiel 48:15-17). Then Ezekiel was told: "The rest of the length alongside the district of the holy portion, shall be ten thousand [reeds] to the east and ten thousand to the west. It shall be adjacent to the district of the holy portion and its produce shall be food for the workers of the city."

Much of Jerusalem's suburbs shall be used for farming purposes for each family living in the city. The "workers of the city," from all the tribes of Israel, shall cultivate it. The rest of that land shall belong to the prince and his household. This is apart from the possession of the Levites and the possession of the city, which are in the midst of what belongs to the prince. The area between the border of Judah (north of the holy portion) and the border of Benjamin (south of the holy portion) "shall belong to the prince" (Ezekiel 48:18, 22)

The city will have twelve gates—each to be named after one of the tribes of Israel. Each side of the city will have three gates (Ezekiel 48:3034). This configuration of the tribal gates was first reflected in the position of Israel's tribes around the tabernacle in Sinai. Then in verse 35, the last verse of Ezekiel 48, we read: "And the name of the city from that day shall be, THE LORD IS THERE." The King of Jerusalem—the city of peace—the city of Melchizedek, priest of the most High God, who met the patriarch Abraham after he defeated the Assyrian kings and their Babylonian allies, is finally returning, 4000 years later, to His city of peace and righteousness. The descendants of Abraham, Isaac and Israel will again have to defeat the rulers of modern Assyria and her Babylonish allies, before they return to meet the ancient King of Jerusalem—Melchizedek—The Messiah and King of Israel.

This city of peace will finally fulfill her intended purpose. Israel will become the light of the world—a role Israel has rejected for most of her history. When Israel is brought back to her land as a small remnant, cleansed and purged from all her sins—which she has sinned against her God and all nations—she will become the joy of all the earth. The God of Israel has stated concerning His people Israel: "But now, I will not treat the remnant of this people as in the former days, says the Lord of hosts [no more terror and punishment, captivity and death]. For the seed [or remnant] shall be prosperous [and so shall they teach all the earth to be, by their personal obedience and example], the vine shall give its fruit, the ground shall give her increase and the heavens shall give their dew. I will cause the remnant of this people to possess all these things. And it shall come to pass that just as you were a curse O house of Judah and house of Israel, so I shall save you and you shall be blessing. Do not fear, let your hands be strong."

Israel's nations, from God's point of view, were a curse to the world through false values, destructive institutions, corrupt morality, deceitful economic practices, misguided and destructive technology, immoral entertainment. They polluted the whole earth, armed nations to their own hurt, impoverished them in the process, and brought many more curses on them and their cultures.

God continues: "For thus says the Lord of hosts, just as I determined to punish you when your fathers provoked me to wrath, says the Lord of hosts, and I would not relent, so again in these days, I am determined to do good to Jerusalem and to the house of Judah, do not fear. These are the things you shall do: Speak each man the truth to his neighbor, give judgment in your gates [or courts of injustice] for truth, justice and peace. Let none of you think evil in your heart against your neighbor, and do not love a false oath [since with few exceptions, such is now the moral fabric of all of Israel's nations]. For all these are things that I hate, says the Lord" (Zachariah 8:11-17)

The apostle Paul reminded the disciples of The King Of Israel, "It is a fearful thing to fall into the hand of the Eternal." He added, "Our God is a consuming fire." When Israel shall be restored to health and prosperity in her land, so shall all the children of Abraham be. Peace will finally come to the Middle East. It will not come by war or conquest, nor by a coercive "peace process." Before there can be peace on earth or in the Middle East, there must first be peace between man and his Maker, between man and his neighbor. Such peace will come! "Not by power or might [of man], but by My Holy Spirit, says the Lord of hosts" (Zechariah 4:6).

God promised to make the Middle Eastern deserts (Isaiah 35) bloom like a rose, and fountains of water to spring everywhere. No Arab or Palestinian family will ever have to live in shame and poverty, devoid of the respect and dignity of life all deserve to have—by Allah or God's decree. No Jew or Israelite will be forced any longer to live in fear and terror, sickness, pollution or crime-ridden corrupt society. No more will anyone fear his neighbors or his own people in any land—whether it be Jewish, Arab, Israelite, or any other poor country. All shall experience the dreamed-of reality of utopia when "the wolf also shall dwell with the lamb. The leopard shall lie down with the young goat, the calf and the young lion [since God will change human and animal nature], and the fatling together. And a little child shall lead them. They shall not hurt nor destroy in all My holy mountain, for the earth shall be full of the knowledge of the Lord as the waters cover the sea. And in that day there shall be a Root of Jesse, who shall stand as a banner to the people. For the Gentiles [many of whom were mislead to believe that they have been following the King of Israel all along, truly now] shall seek Him [both Israel, Arabs, and all mankind], and His resting place shall be glorious" (Isaiah 11:6-10).

This is "THE ULTIMATE FINAL SOLUTION" to the Middle East conflict. But even this glorious future shall only be the beginning of the story. In Revelation 20-22, we read of the rest of the story. The City that father Abraham was looking for; the City of God and Heavenly Jerusalem, where the throne of God dwells, will descend from heaven to earth and be placed in the exact location of earthly Jerusalem. It shall then be "Heaven on earth," literally. All those whose lives have been wasted and destroyed so needlessly and cruelly, will be brought back to life, again, to inhabit the City of peace and the utopian earth. From this City, the whole universe will be colonized, not by men of star-war mentality, but by men of peace—children of Jerusalem—the City of peace!

The family of Abraham will soon learn to live in peace. They will no longer produce the Osama bin Ladens and Arafats or Saddams of this hate-filled world; no longer the terror groups of the hopeless and the downtrodden. They will sit around the table of their resurrected father Abraham, as is becoming of the children of the great patriarch to whom God has declared: "And in your seed all the families of the earth shall be blessed." No man, demonic power, or any weapon on earth, can prevent the realization of this promised dream which will soon come to pass. After the violent stormy winds and gloomy dark clouds, soon to engulf this whole planet, ravaging it to its foundation, a new world order shall become a dazzling reality throughout the whole earth. No man shall lay claim or take credit for this coming bright future, but every man shall bask in its glory.

This will be the glorious Final Solution, not only for the children of Abraham, but also for all of humanity. This soon coming new world order, sought and fought for since time immemorial, will become a reality. And as all the prophets of Israel have declared concerning this world order, it shall surely become a reality, because God said so! The choice for taking this final short journey into the coming utopia is ours. Shall it be through fire and the crucible of war, or in the simple act of kneeling before the Messiah and God of Israel who swore by His throne, stating: "I have sworn by Myself; the word has gone out of My mouth in righteousness and shall not return, that to Me every knee shall bow [to the God and Messiah of Israel], every tongue shall take an oath" (Isaiah 45:23).

So it was written! So it shall! The answer, after all, is not blowing in the wind, as hopeless, faithless and helpless humanity had mournfully sung for millennia. The answer is loud and clear, it is bright and glorious, and it is coming soon, "For the mouth of the Lord had spoken!"

EPILOGUE

God's Throne has dual locations! God dwells in the Heaven or Paradise above—in the "Third Heaven," as the Apostle Paul referred to it. He wrote: **"It is not expedient for me doubtless to glory. I will come to** [or speak of] **revelations of the Lord. I knew a man in Christ above fourteen years ago, (whether in the body, I cannot tell; or whether out of the body, I cannot tell;) such an one** [or person, speaking of himself] **was caught up to the third Heaven. And I knew such a man . . . how that he was caught up into Paradise . . ."** (II Corinthians 12:1-4). This reality is very clear and is described in many accounts by God's servants. The Word of God also tells us about another location, on earth, of The Throne of God or His Paradise and dwelling place. Indicating, often, in His Word of His future plans for dwelling on earth along with His children, God had commanded Moses to make a replica of His dwelling place on earth. God had created the first dwelling place by His own hands—the Garden of Eden. In the next pages we shall delve into the history of the "Garden of the Lord" and its link to the future of man on earth.

In Genesis 2:7-10 we read and: **"And the Lord God formed man of the dust of the ground, and breathed into his nostrils the breath of life; and man became a living soul. And the Lord God planted a garden eastward in Eden; and there he put the man whom He had formed. And out of the ground made the Lord God to grow every tree that is pleasant to the sight, and good for food; the tree of life also in the midst of the garden; and the tree of knowledge of good and evil. And a river went out of Eden to water the garden; and from there it was parted, and became into four heads"** (Genesis 2:7-10).

Man began his journey in the Garden of Eden—on earth! The restoration of man, according to all the Prophets of God, will bring man back to the Garden of Eden—on earth! This time, it shall begin from Jerusalem and spread, gradually, to the whole earth. At no time did God or any of His servants speak of any other future location as being the Garden of Eden—the ultimate destination of man. Prior to the fall of the second

351

Temple, all who knew the words of the Prophets believed, based on the plain words of the servants of God, that The Garden of Eden or Paradise were to be restored to earth—not Heaven. In the first few centuries of the genuine Christian Faith, all still believed the same. When Muhammad collected the "fragments" of the Qur'an and had them assembled together, he too believed the in same Biblical description of the Paradise to come on earth—not in Heaven.

Next mention of the Biblical concept of the "Garden of Eden" is recorded in Genesis 13. When the shepherds of Abraham and Lot could not settle their water disputes in peace, Abraham gave his nephew Lot the first choice for the land. And so we read: **"And Lot lifted up his eyes, and beheld all the plain of the Jordan, that it was well watered everywhere, before the Lord destroyed Sodom and Gomorrah,** [and it resembled] **even the Garden of the Lord** [of which man was ejected] **. . ."** (Genesis 13:10). This description of the Jordan valley, as "the Garden of the Lord," was about 2,000 years after Adam and Eve were thrust out of the Garden that "the Lord has planted" with His own hands. Still, God had preserved "Paradise" conditions, long after, in His land and the areas around it. In so doing, God was indicating the future destiny of man—The Garden of Eden on earth.

When God summoned Moses to the top of Mount Sinai, he was commanded to 'create' a replica of "Heaven"—the dwelling place of God—and place it in the midst of the camp of Israel. We read: **"And the Lord spoke unto Moses, saying, speak unto the children of Israel, that they bring Me an offering; of every man that gives it willingly with his heart you shall take My offering . . . And let them** [not you] **make Me a Sanctuary** [Mikdash or Holy Place]**; that I may dwell among them, according to all I show you** [not of your own making]**, after the pattern** [of the Heavenly] **Tabernacle, and the** [Heavenly] **pattern of the instruments thereof, even so shall you make it"** (Exodus 25:1-9).

God had planted the first "Garden of Eden" with His own hands. In it God placed the first parents of all humanity—Adam and Eve. In that first "Garden of Eden" God planted the "Tree of Life"—a replica of the "Tree of Life" found in Heaven. In that Garden God walked and talked with the first parents—until they rebelled against His commands. In like manner, God walked and talked with Moses and others from His Sanctuary in the midst of the camp of Israel. When the Sanctuary and Tabernacle around it were finished, we read, **"And it came to pass in** the first month in the second year [after Israel came out of Egypt], **on the first day of the month, that the Tabernacle was reared up . . . And he** [Moses] **reared up the court round about the Tabernacle and the altar. And set up the hanging of the court gate. So Moses finished the work** [of God's Heavenly dwelling on earth]. **Then a cloud covered the Tent of the congregation** [of Israel], **and the glory of the Lord filled the Tabernacle. And Moses was not able to enter into the Tent of the congregation, because the cloud** [which contained the Throne of God and His very presence] **abode thereon, and the Glory of the Lord filled the Tabernacle. And when the cloud was taken up from over the Tabernacle, the children of Israel went onward in all their journeys; but if the cloud was not taken up, then they journeyed not till the day that it was taken up. For the cloud of the Lord was upon the Tabernacle by day, and fire was on it by night, in the sight of all the house of Israel, throughout all their** [forty years] **journeys"** (Exodus 40:17, 33-38).

For forty years "Paradise" was on earth—in the midst of the camp of Israel. This was an indication of things to come for both Israel and later all the nations on earth. After a period of forty years of wanderings, the tribes of Israel had finally received their inheritance in the conquered land of Promise. This land was a type of the "Garden of Eden" or "Paradise." Moses admonished the people of Israel: **"Therefore you shall keep the commandments of the Lord your God, to walk in His ways** [not yours] **and fear Him. For the Lord your God brings you into a good land, a land of brooks of water, of fountains and depth** [of water] **that spring out of valleys and hills** [as the Gihon Spring in the City of David over which the Temple was built]; **a land of wheat and barley, and vines, and fig trees, and pomegranates; a land of olive oil and honey; a land wherein you shall eat bread without scarceness, you shall not lack anything in it; a land whose stones are iron, and out of whose hills you may dig brass"** (Deuteronomy 8:6-9).

Moses added: **"Therefore shall you keep all the commandments** [which will insure a "Garden of Eden" life, or if disobeyed, "Hell on earth"] **which I command you this day** [in God's name]**, that you may be strong, and go in and possess the land, where you are going to possess it. And that you may prolong your days in the land** [if you obey]**, which the Lord swore unto your fathers** [Abraham, Isaac, and Jacob] **to give unto them and to their seed, A LAND THAT FLOWS**

WITH MILK AND HONEY . . . the land, where you are going to possess it, is a land of hills and valleys, and drinks water of the rain of Heaven; A LAND WHICH THE LORD YOUR GOD CARES FOR; THE EYES OF THE LORD YOUR GOD ARE ALWAYS UPON IT, FROM THE BEGINNING OF THE YEAR EVEN UNTO THE END OF THE YEAR" (Deuteronomy (8-12). This was Israel's "Garden of Eden" on earth—but they 'blew it,' at least for the time being!

In that "Garden of Eden," Israel had finally settled—and in Shiloh they placed, for the next few centuries, the Earthly "Throne and Dwelling Place of the God of Israel. Later, in the days of David's reign, he moved the Sanctuary of God to what became the City of David. Why did he choose that particular place for God's "Throne" in Israel's "Garden of Eden?" In the book of II Samuel, Chapter 24, we read: **"And again** [one among many] **the anger of the Lord was kindled against Israel, and He moved David against them to say, go number Israel and Judah"** (Verse 1). God's own Law had forbidden the leaders of Israel to number the people. In Exodus 30:12 we read: **"When you take the sum** [or census] **of the children of Israel after their number, then shall they give every man a ransom for his soul unto the Lord** [in a census where only men were counted for military reasons], **when you number them; that there be no plague among them, when you number them."** David, obviously, did not follow this clear instruction by God, since He wanted to punish Israel for unspecified sins that were not recorded. Sure enough, after David numbered Israel, God smote Israel with a three days pestilence. He first gave David three choices, and David chose that of the God-ordained three days pestilence. We read: **"So the Lord sent a pestilence upon Israel from the morning even to the time appointed; and there died of the people from Dan even to Beer-Sheba SEVENTY THOUSAND MEN** [of war]. **And when the** [death] **angel stretched out his hand upon Jerusalem to destroy it, the Lord repented Him of the evil, and said to the** [death] **angel that destroyed the people, it is enough; stay now your hand. And the** [death] **angel of the Lord was** [standing] **by the threshing place** [or farm land] **of** [King] **Arunah the Jebusite. And David spoke unto the Lord when he saw the** [death] **angel that smote the people, and said, Lo, I have sinned** [which he did], **and I have done wickedly** [which he did, and few are those who think like David]; **but these sheep, what have they done? Let Your hand, I pray You, be against me, and against my father's house."** Few are those who are willing to take the guilt on their head. As a consequence of David's willingness to offer himself as the 'sacrificial atoning lamb,' we read: **"And Gad** [the Prophet] **came that day to David, and said unto him, go up, rear an altar unto the Lord** [which David did] **in the threshing floor of Arunah the Jebusite"** (II Samuel 24:1-25).

In the very place where "Hell" was stopped, God decided to place His "Garden of Eden" or "Paradise" forever. Later, when Caliph Omar conquered Jerusalem, he wanted to know where was the exact place King David had erected his altar. He knew that the very Temple of God was built around that very spot. Where was the altar of David located? King David placed in its vicinity the Tabernacle after bringing it to Jerusalem. In II Samuel 6:16-17, we read: **"And the Ark of the Lord came into the City of David . . . and they brought in the Ark of the Lord, and set it in its place, in the midst of the Tabernacle that David had pitched for it . . ."**

After God caused David's child from his illicit affair with Bat-Sheba to die, we read, **"David therefore besought the Lord for the child; and David fasted, and went in** [into the Tabernacle's courtyard], **and lay all night upon the earth.** [Then, when he found out that the child died, he] **. . . arose from the earth, and washed** [or purified himself in the sanctifying waters of the Gihon Spring, which were inside the Tabernacle's courtyard], **and anointed himself, and changed his apparel, and came into the house of the Lord, and worshiped; then he came to his own house** [after the whole ordeal was over] **. . ."** (II Samuel 12:16-20).

Before his death, King David commanded the High Priest to anoint his son Solomon as the next king of Israel. Where did the coronation take place? We read: **"And King David said, call me Zadok the** [High] **Priest, and Nathan the Prophet . . . and they came before the king. The king also said unto them, take with you the servants of your lord, and cause my son Solomon to ride upon my own mule, and BRING HIM DOWN TO THE GIHON** [Spring] **. . . So Zadok the** [High] **Priest, and Nathan the Prophet . . . went down** [to the Spring Gihon, which was inside the Tabernacle, to ceremonially sanctify King Solomon in its water], **and caused Solomon to ride upon King David's mule, and brought him to Gihon** [which was located inside the Tabernacle]. **And Zadok the** [High] **Priest took a horn of oil out of the Tabernacle, and anointed Solomon. And they blew the trumpet** [inside the Tabernacle, where all future kings were to be coroneted—as well as all High Priests];

and all the people said [or rather shouted], **God save King Solomon"** (I kings 1:33-39).

In the very spot where King Solomon was coroneted by the Gihon Spring, he later, in his fourth year (see I Kings 6:1), built the first Temple of God, which God honored with His very Presence. We read: **"And it came to pass, when the priests came out of the Holy Place, that the cloud** [which was earlier ever present in the Tabernacle in the wilderness] **filled the House of the Lord, so that the priests could not stand to minister because of the cloud; for the Glory of the Lord had filled the House of the Lord"** (I kings 8:10-11). Now the Temple was to serve as the earthly "Garden of Eden" or "Paradise" for all of Israel and the strangers that came to honor the God of Israel. Tragically, because of the grievous sins of Israel, the Temple site was destroyed and became, again, a threshing floor and farmland for the Gentiles. The same fate happened after the destruction of the second Temple. But the story is not over yet!

God gave the Prophet Ezekiel a vision, " **. . . In the fourteenth year after the City** [of Jerusalem] **was smitten . . ."** (Ezekiel 40:1). In this long and detailed vision (chapters 40-48), God showed Ezekiel the end-time most glorious City and Temple of God, which is yet to be built. This City and Temple would by far eclipse the glory of the former City and Temple of King Solomon. Of this yet to be built Millennial City and Temple, God told Ezekiel: " **. . . Son of man, the place of My Throne, and this place of the soles of My feet, where I will dwell in the midst of the children of Israel FOREVER . . ."** (Ezekiel 43: 7). The God of Israel gave the prophet Ezekiel, over 2500 years ago, this vision of the future Temple, while he was in Babylon among the first exiles of Jerusalem. At that time, God had already determined to bring back all the captives of Israel to the land He swore to give them forever. He made it very plain through all of His Prophets that His Temple shall be built at the end time, and that He will personally dwell **"in the Midst of the children of Israel forever."** No power on earth can alter this Divine decree and future reality!

As was mentioned earlier, Ezekiel was shown in his vision " **. . . Waters** [that] **issued out from under the threshold of the House** [or Temple] **eastward; for the threshold of the House stood toward the east** [facing the Dead Sea], **and the waters came down from under** [or below the Temple] **from the right side of the House, at the south side of the altar"** (Ezekiel 47:1).

When David brought back the Ark of the Covenant to Jerusalem, he pitched the Tabernacle by the Gihon Spring—about a third of a mile southeast of the present location of Haram esh-Sharif or the alleged "Temple Mount." The "living waters" of the Gihon Spring were indispensable necessity for the Tabernacle and the later Temples. It was needful for purification and washing away the blood of the sacrifices. Without this source of "living waters" the Temple could not function. The Psalmists of the Temple (sons of Korah) sung: **"His foundation is in the Holy Mountains** [of Jerusalem]. **The Lord loves the gates of Zion** [a name modern Muslims abhor] **more than all the dwellings of Jacob. Glorious things are spoken of you, O City of God . . . As well the singers as the players on instruments** [in the Temple] **shall be there; All My** [Gihon] **springs are in you** [Jerusalem]" (Psalm 87:1-7). It was by the Gihon springs, within the Tabernacle, that David commanded the High Priest Zadok to anoint Solomon as the future king of Israel. It was over the Gihon Spring that Solomon built The Temple of God. The Temple of Zerubabel, and later the enlarged "Temple of Herod," was also built over the Gihon Spring. In like manner, the future "Temple of Ezekiel" will be built over the Gihon Spring. This Gihon Spring of "living waters" is described by the Prophet Ezekiel as coming from **"under the threshold of the House."** This **"healing waters"** will flow east and west, from **"under the threshold of the House"** and would bring **"healing"** to the land—to the Dead Sea. This is just one description of many of the coming "Garden of Eden" to the land of Israel—which would later spread to the whole earth as the nations gradually submit to the rule of the God of Israel.

As was mentioned earlier, Ezekiel recorded the words of the angel concerning the 'River of Life' that issues from beneath the Temple: **"And he** [the angel] **said unto me, son of man, have you not seen this? Then he brought me and caused me to return to the brink of the river. Now when I had returned, behold, at the bank of the river were very many trees on the one side and on the other. Then he said unto me, these waters issue out toward the east country** [of Jerusalem], **and go down into the** [Judean] **desert, and go into the** [Dead] **Sea; which being brought forth into the** [Dead] **Sea, the** [extremely salty] **waters shall be healed. And it shall come to pass, that everything that lives, which moves, wherever the river shall come, shall live; and there shall be very great multitude of fish** [in the previously totally Dead Sea], **because these waters shall come there; for they shall be healed; and everything** shall live wherever the river comes. **And it shall come to pass, that the fishers shall stand upon it** [the Dead Sea] **from En-Gedi even unto En-Eglaim; they shall be a place to spread forth nets; their fish shall be according to their kinds, as the fish of the great sea** [the Mediterranean], **exceeding many"** (Ezekiel 47:6-10).

In the above account we read of a classic example, one among many, of the future "Garden of Eden" and "Paradise" conditions that will soon prevail on earth. The Dead Sea, the deserts, the desolate places, and other such 'cursed' areas shall be 'resurrected' from death to life. And this is the sure future of the whole planet! Yes, that's how "Heaven" shall engulf the earth!

In the last part of Chapter 47, Ezekiel unveils the details about the future "City of God"—Jerusalem. The City shall be located about 15,000 Cubits (60 cm per Cubit) south of the Temple. The City will be surrounded by gardens and trees, and will have farmlands for growing produce for the "City workers." The City workers will include members of each tribe of Israel. The City will have twelve gates "after the names of the twelve tribes of Israel" (47:31). **"'The name of the City from that day shall be, 'The Lord is there'"** (47:35). This is the City of God, the "Garden of Eden, the "Paradise" all the Prophets spoke of in many accounts—but there is yet another Final City of God to come. We shall come to it at the end of this Book.

In the book of the Prophet Zechariah, we read the following about the City of God: **"Again the word of the Lord of Hosts came unto me, saying, thus says the Lord of Hosts; I was jealous for Zion with great jealousy, and I was jealous for her with great fury. Thus says the Lord; I am returning unto Zion, and I WILL DWELL IN THE MIDST OF JERUSALEM** [and no other city]**; and Jerusalem shall be called the City of Truth; and the Mountain of the Lord of Hosts** [shall be called] **the Holy Mountain. Thus says the Lord of Hosts; there shall yet [be] old men and old women** [of the people of Israel] **dwell in the streets of Jerusalem, and every man with his staff in his hand because of very ripe old age. And the streets of the City shall be full of boys and girls playing** [without fear of Arab terror] **in the streets thereof . . . Thus says the Lord of Hosts; behold I will save My people** [Israel out of their places of captivity] **from the East country, and from the West country; and I will bring them, and they** [and no other nation] **shall dwell in the midst of Jerusalem; and they** [and no others] **shall be My people, and I** will be their God, in truth and in righteousness . . . For the seed shall be prosperous, the vine shall give her fruit, and the ground shall give her increase, and the heavens shall give their dew; and I will cause the remnant of the people [of Israel] to possess all these things. And it shall come to pass, that as you were a curse among the nations, O house of Judah and House of Israel; so will I save you, and you shall be a blessing; fear not, but let your hand be strong. For thus says the Lord of Hosts; as I thought to punish you, when your fathers provoked Me to wrath, says the Lord of Hosts, and I repented not [or changed My mind]; so again have I thought in these days to do well unto Jerusalem and to the house of Judah; fear you not. These are the things that you shall do: Speak you every man the truth to his neighbor: execute the judgment of truth and peace in your gates; and let none of you imagine evil in your hearts against his neighbor; and love no false oath; for all these are things that I hate [and God's people, sadly, have not behaved themselves in these areas—and that was a part of the reason they were "a curse unto the nations"], says the Lord. [And when the people of Israel shall return to their God] . . . Many people and strong nations shall come to seek the Lord of Hosts in Jerusalem, and pray before the Lord [in His new Temple]. Thus says the Lord of Hosts; in those days it shall come to pass, that ten men shall take hold out of all the languages of the nations [including Arabs and Muslims], even shall take hold of the skirt of him THAT IS A JEW, saying, we will go with you; for we have heard that God is with you [not with us]" (Zechariah 8).

These are the words of the God of Israel, not of man—and you can argue with it all you want! God said, "it shall come to pass," but what about those who would resist this sure coming reality? To them, God has declared, "For the nation and kingdom that will not serve you [Jerusalem] shall perish: yes, those nations shall be utterly wasted [and that goes also for "the mighty empires" of China, Iran and Russia]" (Isaiah 60:12).

God is not impressed with the 'clowns' that occupy the high seats of power! Of all the nations of the earth put together, the King of Israel said, "Behold, the nations are as a drop in a bucket, and are counted as a small dust on the scales . . ." (Isaiah 40:15).

The City of God, the future central location of the "Garden of Eden" or Paradise" on earth, has been in the planning stages in the 'corridors of the Courts of Heaven' for a very long time. In the Mind of God it is already a reality. Many of the details have been recorded by all the Prophets of the God of Israel, as well as the Apostles of Christ, throughout the pages of the Bible for all to read. When we reach the end of the story in the book of Revelation, we shall read similar details about the City of God as those recorded by the Prophets of old.

The Prophet Isaiah described the Paradise conditions that will prevail in the land of Israel and throughout the world at the beginning of the reign of the Messiah, and throughout His reign on earth. This age of utopia will not, tragically, be ushered in before "all Hell breaks loose," first. He wrote: **"And it shall come to pass in the last days, that the Mountain** [or Kingdom] **of the Lord's House** [or Temple] **shall be established at the top of the Mountains** [or nations], **and shall be exalted above the hills** [or small nations]; **and all nations shall flow unto it. And many people shall go and say, come you and let go to the Mountain of the Lord, to the House of the God of Jacob; and He will teach us of His Ways** [in contrast to our destructive ways], **and we will walk in His paths** [and no more in our paths]; **for out of Zion** [a name most Muslims speak ill of] **shall go forth The Law** [or Torah, which now is disdained by most people], **and the Word of the Lord from Jerusalem. And He will judge among the nations, and shall rebuke many** [rebellious Torah hating] **people; and they shall beat their swords** [or modern weapons] **into plowshares, and their spears into pruning hooks; nation shall not lift up sword against nation, neither shall they learn war anymore"** **(Isaiah 2:2-4).** In Chapter 11:6-8, Isaiah added: **"The wolf also shall dwell with the lamb, and the leopard shall lie down with the kid** [or young goat]; **and the calf and the young lion and the fatling together; and a little child shall lead them. And the cow and the bear shall feed** [together]; **their young ones shall lie together; and THE LION SHALL EAT STRAW LIKE THE OX. And the suckling child shall play on the hole of the asp, and the weaned child shall put his hand on the adder's den."**

This is not a fairy-tale story—it shall come to pass in spite of us! And though about 90% of rebellious humanity shall be decimated—according to Biblical prophecies, in the coming super mega-holocaust—immediately afterward utopia shall come to pass! The Prophet Micah recorded the same prophecy and added, **"But they shall sit every man under his vine and under his fig tree; and none shall make them afraid; for the mouth of the Lord** [not man] **has spoken it"** (Micah 4:1-4).

Isaiah the Prophet adds: **"For the Lord shall comfort Zion** [which many Muslims curse day and night]. **He will comfort all her waste places** [which Muslim armies and their allies would be allowed to destroy, temporarily, because of Israel's sins against her God]; **AND HE WILL MAKE HER WILDERNESS LIKE EDEN, AND HER DESERT LIKE THE GARDEN OF THE LORD; joy and gladness shall be found therein, thanksgiving, and the voice of melody** [and no more grief and mourning]" (Isaiah 51:3).

The Prophet Ezekiel recorded these words of the God of Israel: **"Thus says the Lord God; in the day that I shall have cleansed you from all your iniquities I will also cause you to dwell in the cities, and the wastes** [or desolate places] **shall be built. And the desolate land shall be tilled, whereas it lay desolate in the sight of all that passed by. And they shall say, this land that was desolate HAS BECOME LIKE THE GARDEN OF EDEN . . ."** (Ezekiel 36:33-35).

This is the true "Garden of Eden" and "Paradise" all the genuine servants of God have often spoken of and described in their writings! Despite the Muslim nations' desire to turn the land God gave Israel, even according to Muhammad, into a hellfire zone, the God of Jacob had declared long ago His intentions to make the land the ultimate "Garden of Eden" and "Paradise" all dream about.

Of His people Israel God said, **"And I have put My words in your mouth, and I have covered you in the shadow of My hand, that I may plant the** [new] **Heavens, and lay the foundations of the** [coming new] **earth, and say unto Zion, you are My people** [and no Zionist hater Muslim is going to change this sure reality]" (Isaiah 51:16). Before God would turn the land of His people Israel into the promised "Garden of Eden," some hard lessons would first have to be learned by them for forsaking His Law and Ways. God declared: **"Awake, awake, stand up, O Jerusalem, which had drunk of the hand of the Lord the cup of His fury; you have dunk the dregs of the cup of trembling, and wrung them out. There is none to guide her among all her sons whom she has brought forth** [having no competent leaders at the helm]; **neither is there any that takes her by the hand** [to lead her in the right path] **of all the sons that she has brought up. These two things shall come unto you; who shall be sorry for you** [since most nations hate you]? **Desolation and destruction, and the famine and the sword; by whom shall I comfort you? Your sons have fainted, they lie at the head of all** the streets, as a wild bull in a net; they are full of the fury of the Lord, the rebuke of your God" (Isaiah 51:17-20).

Israel and the world must realize that God is the ultimate One responsible for punishing them through human instruments and natural disasters, yet this is not the end of the story. To Israel, God said through Moses, **"See now that I, even I, am He, and there is no god with me: I kill, and I make alive** [through the resurrection at the end time], **I wound, and I heal; neither is there any that can deliver out of My hand"** (Deuteronomy 32:39).

Isaiah continues: **"Therefore hear now this, you afflicted** [Israel], **and drunken, but not with wine; thus says your Lord, and your God that pleads the cause of His people, behold, I have taken out of your hand the cup of trembling, even the dregs of the cup of My fury** [because of your sins]**; you shall no more drink it again; but I will put it into the hand of them that have afflicted you** [and this is a warning to all of Israel's enemies]**; which have said to your soul, bow down, that we may go over** [or walk all over you]**; and you have laid your body as the ground, and as the street to them that went** [all] **over** [you]**"** (Isaiah 52:21-23).

This is the "Hell" God's people will first have to endure because of their chosen ways. Yet, soon after, for those who remain and turn away from their ungodly conduct, the "Garden of Eden" shall engulf their land. And so the Prophet now describes this coming age of "Paradise" on earth. He writes: **"Awake, awake, and put on your strength, O Zion; put on your beautiful garments, O Jerusalem, the Holy City; for henceforth THERE SHALL NO MORE COME UNTO YOU THE UNCIRCUMCISED AND THE UNCLEAN** [and all foreigners shall no more occupy your City]**. Shake yourself from the dust** [that your enemies cast you into]**, arise, and sit down, O Jerusalem; loose yourself from the bands of your neck** [that your enemies placed on it]**, O captive daughter of Zion. For thus says the Lord, you have sold yourselves for nothing** [worthy of]**; and you shall be redeemed without money** [or ransom, since your God will deliver you from your soon coming captivity]**. For thus says the Lord God, My people went down in old times into Egypt to sojourn there; and the Assyrians oppressed them without cause** [when the 10 tribes of the Northern Kingdom of Israel were taken into captivity, as well as in the future]**. Now therefore, what have I here, says the Lord, that My people is taken away for nothing? For they**

that rule over them [or subjugate them] **make them to howl, says the Lord; and My name continually is blasphemed** [because of His people's calamity]. **Therefore My people shall know My name** [which now they don't, though they think otherwise]; **therefore they shall know in that day that I am He that does speak; behold,** [He declares to His now 'blind' people] **it is I** [the Savior and Redeemer of Israel—Your Messiah]" (Isaiah 52:1-6).

Through His Prophet Zechariah, the Savior and Messiah of Israel declared over 2,500 years ago: "**The burden** [or oracle] **of the Lord for Israel, says the Lord . . . Behold, I will make Jerusalem a cup of trembling unto all the people round about** [and certainly it came to pass], **when they shall be in the siege both against Judah and against Jerusalem. And in that day** [our day] **I will make Jerusalem a burdensome stone for all people** [including those in the world of religion and politics]; **ALL THAT BURDEN THEMSELVES WITH IT** [in an attempt to divide it] **SHALL BE CUT IN PIECES, THOUGH ALL THE PEOPLE OF THE EARTH BE GATHERED AGAINST IT** [since they are not a match for God]. **In that day, says the Lord, I will smite every horse** [symbolic of modern weapons] **with astonishment** [or confusion], **and his rider with madness, AND I WILL OPEN MY EYES UPON THE HOUSE OF JUDAH, AND WILL SMITE EVERY HORSE WITH BLINDNESS . . . And the Lord** [and Messiah of Israel] **also SHALL SAVE THE TENTS OF JUDAH FIRST** [since He is coming to His own first, as He did in the past], **that the glory of the** [royal] **House of David** [as you can read in the book on "*The Middle East*"] **and the glory of the inhabitants of Jerusalem do not magnify themselves against Judah . . . And it shall come to pass in that day, that I** [the Messiah and Savior of Israel] **shall seek to destroy ALL the nations that come against Jerusalem. And I will pour upon the House of David, and upon the inhabitants of Jerusalem the spirit of grace and of supplications; AND THEY SHALL LOOK UPON ME WHOM THEY** [2,000 years ago] **HAVE PIERCED** [since God places a collective guilt on all, though only few were personally responsible], **and they shall mourn for Him** [their Messiah whom they now still reject in ignorance, being 'blinded' by their "blind spiritual leaders"], **as one mourns for his only son, and shall be in bitterness for him** [when their eyes would finally be opened to "see" how "naked their Emperor was"], **as one that is in bitterness for his firstborn** [which their Redeemer was]" (Zechariah 12:1-10).

This would be a part of the "Hell on earth" God's people would have to go through, before they are ushered in into their promised "Paradise" on earth. Only God can bring about this turn of events! No man has the capacity to open anyone's eyes until God Himself chooses to do so! And God is the One who declared long ago: "**I** [and not man] **will pour upon the House of David and upon the inhabitants of Jerusalem, the spirit of grace and supplications; and** [only then] **they SHALL look upon Me whom they have pierced." God stated through the Psalmist, "Unless the Lord** [and not man] **shall build the house, the weary builders toil in vain.**" There are many sincere "weary builders" out there, and they still don't get it: if God does not do it, don't waste your time!

Let's go now to the final scenario that describes the ultimate City of God and its long ago planned location. About 4,000 years ago, we are told, the patriarch Abraham was looking forward to and embraced the City many have dreamt about—though only the few knew of its true future location. Writing to his fellow kinsmen, the Hebrews, the Apostle Paul stated: "**BY FAITH Abraham, when he was called to go out into a place which he should after receive for an inheritance,** [at the resurrection, 4,000 years later], **OBEYED** [since faith without obedience or "works" is dead according to James 2:17] . . . **BY FAITH he sojourned in the land of promise, as in a strange country** [since he was not given a possession of it in his life time], **dwelling in tents with Isaac and Jacob** [and notice that Ishmael and Esau are not mentioned], **the heirs with him of the same promise** [which none received in their lifetime]; **FOR HE LOOKED FOR A CITY** [the City of God] **WHICH HAS FOUNDATIONS, WHOSE BUILDER AND MAKER IS GOD . . . THESE ALL DIED IN FAITH** [and are still dead], **NOT HAVING RECEIVED THE PROMISES** [even in Paul's days], **BUT HAVING SEEN THEM AFAR OFF** [into the future], **AND WERE PERSUADED OF THEM, AND EMBRACED THEM** [by faith], **AND CONFESSED THAT THEY WERE STRANGERS AND PILGRIMS ON EARTH**" (Hebrews 11:8-13).

Let's now fast-forward 5,000 years from the days of father Abraham to the future manifestation of the City of God, which all the true servants of God were looking forward to the day they would be in it. In the final vision God gave to His servants—at the end of the first century of this era—we are finally introduced to "Heavenly Jerusalem" and City of God. This City will come down to earth at the end of the 1,000 years reign of the Messiah over all the earth from His Throne in Jerusalem. Many Prophets and Psalmists wrote about the City of God, but none gave us the detailed descriptions and location of that "Majestic City of God" of which many "glorious things" have been spoken of old. The Apostle John or Yohanan, meaning, "the Grace of God," was honored by God with the vision of the coming "Heavenly Jerusalem," the City of God. This was the City father Abraham saw in his day. He wrote: **"And I saw a new Heaven and a new earth** [of which Isaiah the Prophet spoke at the end of his book]; **for the first Heaven and the first earth were passed away; and there was no more sea** [upon the earth]. **And I John saw the Holy City, New Jerusalem, COMING DOWN** [to earth] **FROM GOD OUT OF HEAVEN, PREPARED AS A BRIDE ADORNED FOR HER HUSBAND. And I heard a great voice out of Heaven saying, behold, THE TABERNACLE** [or Mishkan in Hebrew, which means a dwelling place] **OF GOD IS** [finally] **WITH MEN** [and no more in Heaven], **AND HE WILL DWELL WITH THEM, AND THEY SHALL BE HIS PEOPLE, AND GOD HIMSELF SHALL BE WITH THEM, AND BE THEIR GOD. And God shall wipe away all tears from their eyes; AND THERE SHALL BE NO MORE DEATH, neither sorrow, nor crying, neither shall there be any more pain; for the former things** [like mortality, sickness, pain, and death] **are passed away. And He that sat upon the Throne** [God] **said, behold, I MAKE ALL THINGS NEW. And He said unto me, write; for all these things are true and faithful. And He** [God] **said unto me, it is done. I am Alpha and Omega** [and so is **His** Messiah], **the beginning and the end. I will give unto him that is thirsty OF THE FOUNTAIN OF THE WATER OF LIFE** [or eternal life] **FREELY** [as was originally offered to Adam and Eve in the Garden of Eden on earth]. **HE THAT OVERCOMES** [Satan, self, and society's perverse ways] **SHALL INHERIT ALL THINGS** [as eternal life, divinity, and the universe]; **AND I WILL BE HIS GOD, AND HE SHALL BE MY SON** [just like the "firstborn Son of God"].

"... **And he** [the angel] **carried me away in the spirit to a great and high Mountain, and showed me that Great City, the HOLY JERUSALEM, DESCENDING OUT OF HEAVEN** [to earth] **FROM GOD, having the glory of God; and her light was like unto a stone most precious, even like a jasper stone, clear as crystal; and had a wall great and high, and had TWELVE gates, and at the gates TWELVE angels, and names were written thereon, WHICH ARE THE NAMES**

OF THE TWELVE TRIBES OF THE CHILDREN OF ISRAEL [The True Church and Bride of The Lamb. Listen to the full details in our free website: www.teachingthelaw.org] . . . **And the wall of the City had TWELVE foundations, and IN THEM** [written] **THE NAMES OF THE TWELVE APOSTLES OF THE LAMB** [all Jews] . . . **And the City lies foursquare, and the length is as large as the breadth; and he measured the City with the reed, TWELVE thousand furlongs. The length and the breadth and the height of it are equal. And he measured the wall thereof, an hundred and forty and four cubits, according to the measure of a man, that is, of the angel. And the building of the wall of it was of jasper; and the City was pure gold, like unto clear glass. And the foundations of the wall of the City were garnished with all manner of precious stones . . ."**

Speaking of the soon coming redemption of Jerusalem and her children, the people of Israel, the King of Israel stated: **"O you afflicted, tossed with tempest, and not comforted, behold, I will lay your stones with fair colors, and lay your foundations with sapphires, and I will make your windows of agates** [precious stones], **and your gates of carbuncles, and all your borders of pleasant stones"** (Isaiah 54:11-12). This was the time and City the Apostles of Christ were looking for when they asked Him, prior to His ascent to Heaven, **" . . . Lord, will You at this time RESTORE AGAIN THE KINGDOM TO ISRAEL** [not to the Gentile Church]" (Acts 1:6). The **TWELVE** Apostles were promised, **" . . . You who have followed me, in the regeneration when the Son of man shall sit in His Throne of His glory** [in Jerusalem], **YOU ALSO SHALL SIT UPON TWELVE THRONES, JUDGING THE TWELVE TRIBES OF ISRAEL** [not the Gentile Church]" (Matthew 19:28). In His commission to the **TWELVE** disciples, and those to follow them until His second coming, Jesus told them, **" . . . Go not into the way** [or world] **of the Gentiles, and into any city of the Samaritans enter you not; but GO RATHER TO THE LOST SHEEP OF THE HOUSE OF ISRAEL. And as you go preach, saying, THE KINGDOM OF HEAVEN IS AT HAND** [not Gentile Church substituted message of "Jesus loves you," though He certainly does] . . . **And you shall be hated of all men for My name's sake** [because they will hate your message and teachings]; **BUT HE THAT ENDURES TO THE END** [when I return] **SHALL BE SAVED** [not when one is baptized or "goes to Heaven"] . . . **for verily I say unto you, YOU SHALL NOT HAVE GONE OVER**

THE CITIES OF [the twelve tribes of] **ISRAEL** [not the Gentiles], **TILL THE SON OF MAN COMES BACK** [to Israel]" (Matthew 10:5-7, 22-23). And lastly, the Apostles of Christ—being all Jews who were raised on the Scriptures—knew very well what the King of Israel said about His rebellious people's future and destiny. He declared through His prophet Hosea: **"Yet the numbers of the children of** [of the twelve tribes of] **Israel shall be as the sand of the sea, which cannot be measured nor numbered** [and to fully understand this statement and the whereabouts of the whole house of Israel throughout history, check the monumental work, over 700 pages, mentioned earlier, titled, "*Middle East . . .*"]; **And it shall come to pass where it was said unto them, you are not My people, there it shall be said unto them, you are the sons of the living God. Then shall the children of Judah and the children of Israel** [the ten northern tribes who now think they are Gentiles, and most of them are members of the "Christian World"] **be gathered together, and appoint themselves one head** [since they live side by side along the children of Judah, yet still are unaware of each other], **and they shall come out of the land; for great shall be the day of Jezreel"** (Hosea 1:10-11).

Speaking again about His people Israel—the whole house of Israel—at the end time, God declared: **"Therefore, behold, I will allure her, and bring her into the wilderness, and speak comfortably unto her . . . And it shall be at that day, says the Lord, you** [Israel] **shall call Me Ishi** [or my husband]; **and shall call Me no more Baali** [or my Baal]. **And in that day will I make a covenant for them . . . and I will break the bow and the sword and the battle out of the earth, and will make them to lie down safely** [in their "Garden of Eden" on earth]. **AND I WILL BETROTH YOU UNTO ME FOREVER** [and this is the true marriage of The Lamb all the Apostles were talking about]; **YES, I WILL BETROTH YOU UNTO ME IN RIGHTEOUSNESS, AND IN JUDGMENT, AND IN LOVING KINDNESS, AND IN MERCIES. I WILL EVEN BETROTH YOU UNTO ME IN FAITHFULNESS; AND YOU SHALL KNOW THE LORD** [as Adam knew his wife Eve]" (Hosea 2:14-20). Notice that God repeated the word **"BETROTH"** three times, and as it was stated, **"by the mouth of two or three witnesses shall the matter stand."**

Who is this God who has declared His intentions, 2800 years ago, to **BETROTH** or marry repentant Israel at the end time? The Gentile Church had claimed for the last almost 2,000 years: "You Jews have your God—the God of the Old Testament—and we Christians have our Christian God, namely, Jesus—the Christian God. What did the Apostle Paul, the Apostle to the Gentiles, have to say about this matter? We read his words to the Corinthian church: "**Moreover, brethren, I would not that you should be ignorant** [since, obviously, they were, as many "Christians" are to this day], **how that all OUR fathers were under the cloud** [where God was], **and all passed through the sea; and were all baptized unto Moses in the cloud and in the sea; and did all eat the same SPIRITUAL MEAT; and did all drink the same SPIRITUAL DRINK; for they all drank of that SPIRITUAL ROCK that followed them; AND THAT ROCK WAS CHRIST [!!!]**" (I Corinthian 10:1-4). Did you know that the people of Israel were the first "Christians" to follow Christ? This was not the teaching of the Gentile Church for the last two thousand years! This Gentile Church, on one hand, had 'embraced' the Person of Jesus Christ, while on the other, rejected the **SPIRITUAL FOOD AND DRINK** He gave to His people and "wife" Israel at Mount Sinai, and for the next forty years.

There is here a great twist of irony: Christ, first, "came to His own, and His own [as a nation] had rejected Him," yet kept His Law or Torah despite all persecutions from the "Christian Church." The Gentile Church, on the other hand, had accepted the Person of Jesus, The Messiah of Israel, yet rejected His Torah. For the next two millenniums it had made great attempts—by 'friendly' persuasions, at times, and mostly by violence—to force the Jews to 'accept' Jesus and reject His Torah. Of His end time coming, Jesus declared: "**Not everyone that says unto Me, Lord, Lord, shall enter into the Kingdom of Heaven** [which will be on earth, in the midst of the land of Israel and its center—Jerusalem]; **BUT HE THAT DOES THE WILL** [or Torah] **OF MY FATHER** [Who is also the God of Israel]. **Many will say to Me in that day, Lord, Lord, have we not prophesied in Your name? And in Your name have cast out demons? And in Your name done many wonderful works? And then will I profess to them, I NEVER KNEW YOU; DEPART FROM ME, YOU THAT WORK INIQUITY** [and that transgress Mine and My Father's Torah]" (Matthew 7:21-23).

We all know that no Jewish Rabbi or a devout Jew would ever approach Christ at His second coming and make statements about "**preaching, teaching, healing, doing wonderful works, or casting demons in Jesus' name.**" But those claiming to be "Christians" certainly would! Those who profess to be "followers of Christ, "Vicars of Christ on earth," or "ministers of the Gospel," or missionaries "in Christ's service," they certainly would make these statements upon seeing the door being shut in their face.

To the last generation, prior to His return to earth **as King of Kings**, the Redeemer of Israel had His Prophet Malachi record this stern warning: "**REMEMBER THE LAW** [Heb., Torah] **OF MY SERVANT MOSES, WHICH I [JESUS, THE SPIRITUAL ROCK OF ISRAEL] COMMANDED UNTO HIM IN HOREB** [or Sinai] **FOR ALL ISRAEL** [all Jews and the ten tribes of Israel, who are now mostly members of the Gentile Church, though ignorant of it. See our book on "*The Middle East* . . ." for details]**, with the statutes and judgments** [all five books of Moses]**. Behold, I will send you Elijah the Prophet** [or rather one who would come in his spirit—one of "the two witnesses" mentioned earlier] **BEFORE** [the resurrection and] **the coming of the great and dreadful day of the Lord; and he SHALL turn the heart of the fathers to the children, and the heart of the children to their fathers, LEST I COME AND SMITE THE EARTH WITH A CURSE [OR UTTER DESTRUCTION]**" (Malachi 4:3-6).

Besides the healing of the broken family and marriages, God is mainly speaking about the "breach" that now exists, **because of transgression against the Torah in both Judah and Israel,** between the Fathers of the nation (Abraham, Isaac, and Jacob) and their rebellious children. The purpose of the coming "Two Witnesses" would be, among other tasks, to restore the hearts of all of the **"lost sheep of the House of Israel"** to their God and His Torah or teachings—from Genesis to Revelation. As a consequence, many would repent and come back to their God and His Torah, but, as God made very plain long ago: "**AND THE LORD SHALL SAVE THE TENTS OF JUDAH FIRST . . . And it shall come to pass in that day, that I** [Jesus and Redeemer of Israel] **shall seek to destroy all the nations that come against Jerusalem. AND I WILL POUR UPON THE HOUSE OF DAVID, AND UPON THE INHABITANTS OF JERUSALEM** [the Jews]**, THE SPIRIT OF GRACE AND OF SUPPLICATIONS; AND THEY SHALL LOOK UPON ME WHOM THEY** [or their leaders, in specific, along with the Romans] **HAVE PIERCED, AND THEY SHALL MOURN FOR HIM** [with no more denials]**, AS ONE MOURNS FOR HIS ONLY SON, AND SHALL BE IN BITTERNESS FOR HIM, AS ONE THAT IS IN BITTERNESS FOR** [the loss of] **HIS FIRSTBORN**" (Zechariah 12:7-10).

The Prophet Jeremiah quoted God's intentions for His people at the end time. He wrote: **"Behold the days come, says the Lord, that I will make a NEW [MARRIAGE] COVENANT with the house of Israel and with the house of Judah** [not with The Gentile Church]; **not according to the [marriage] covenant which I made with their fathers in the day that I took them by the hand to bring them out of the land of Egypt; which My [marriage] covenant they broke; ALTHOUGH I WAS A HUSBAND UNTO THEM, says the Lord.** But this shall be the [marriage] covenant that I shall make with the house of Israel [again, not with the Gentile Church]; **after those days, says the Lord, I WILL PUT MY LAW** [or Torah, which the Gentile Church despises] **in their inward parts, and write it in their hearts; and will be their God [and Husband], and they shall be My people [and wife]"** (Jeremiah 31:31-33).

Later, the Apostle Paul, a Jew, quoted this very statement in his letter to the Hebrews, Chapter 8. Of this matter, Paul declared to the Ephesian church: **"Wherefore remember** [and many since have forgotten], **that you being in time past** [or 'you used to be'] **Gentiles in the flesh, who are called Uncircumcision by that which is called the Circumcision in the flesh made by hands; that at that time YOU WERE WITHOUT CHRIST [AS ALL GENTILES ARE UNTIL GRAFTED INTO THE "NATURAL TREE OF ISRAEL"], BEING ALIENS FROM THE COMMONWEALTH OF ISRAEL, AND STRANGERS FROM THE COVENANTS OF PROMISE, HAVING NO HOPE, AND WITHOUT GOD IN THE WORLD [AND THIS IS THE SPIRITUAL STATE OF ALL GENTILES TO THIS DAY—THOUGH MOST HAVE CONVENIENTLY FORGOTTEN THIS BIBLICAL FACT]; but now in Christ Jesus you who in the past were far off are made near by the blood of Christ"** (Ephesians 2:11-13).

Paul, the Apostle to the Gentiles, made it very clear to the Gentile brethren: there are no Gentiles in the Church or Body of Christ, but 'former Gentiles.' In other words: there is no such thing as a "Gentile Church." Once God grafts a Gentile into the Church, that person becomes an Israelite—a member of the commonwealth of Israel. To the 'Gentile' church in Thessalonica, Paul wrote: **"For you brethren, became followers of the** [religion of the] **churches of God which in Judea are in Christ Jesus . . ."** (I Thessalonians 2:14). Why did they follow them? Because, as Jesus stated, **"You [Gentiles] do not know what you worship; we** know what we worship; FOR SALVATION IS OF THE JEWS" (John 4:22). Of these Jews, Paul stated: "**What advantage then has the Jew? Or what profit is there in circumcision?** MUCH IN EVERY WAY [was his response]; **chiefly, because unto them** [not to the Gentile Church] **were committed the Oracles of God**" (Romans 3:1-2). Paul added: "**I say the truth in Christ, I lie not, my conscience also bearing me witness in the Holy Spirit that I have great heaviness and continual sorrow in my heart** [which the Gentile Church did not]. **For I could wish that myself were accursed from Christ for my brethren, my kinsmen according to the flesh** [which, certainly, neither the leadership, nor the members of the Gentile Church had ever felt likewise, but preferred to curse the Jews]; **who are Israelites; TO WHOM PERTAINS THE ADOPTION** [or sonship], **AND THE GLORY, AND THE COVENANTS, AND THE GIVING OF THE LAW [OR TORAH], AND THE [DIVINE] SERVICE OF GOD, AND THE PROMISES; WHOSE ARE THE FATHERS, AND OF WHOM AS CONCERNING THE FLESH CHRIST CAME, WHO IS OVER ALL, GOD BLESSED FOREVER. AMEN**" (Romans 9:1-5).

Let's face these unchangeable facts and reality: All the Apostles are Jews; all the Prophets are of Israel. God has inspired His prophets and apostles, who were of the stock of Israel, to record the Bible. The Apostle peter wrote: "Of this salvation the prophets [of Israel] have enquired and searched carefully, who prophesied of the Grace that would come to you, searching what, or what m manner of time, THE SPIRIT OF CHRIST WHO WAS IN THEM was indicating when He testified beforehand of the sufferings of Christ and the glories that would follow" (I Peter 1:11).

Also, the pure religion of God was given to Israel. It was their responsibility to disseminate this unadulterated Way of God and Christ to the whole world. All promises, covenants, teachings, and manner of worship were entrusted into the hands of Israel, not the Gentile Church! In the old Temples and in the new Temples to come—including the one in Heavenly Jerusalem—everyone wishing to approach God, must enter through a gate bearing the name of one of the twelve tribes of Israel—and there is no other way! The Gates of Heavenly Jerusalem bear the names of the twelve tribes of Israel. The twelve foundations of Heavenly Jerusalem bear the names of the twelve Jewish Apostles of Christ. The mother of Jesus is a Jewish woman of the House of David—of the tribe of Judah. Christ came "to His own." The Messiah will come back to His own, and the "tents of Judah shall be saved first." The King of Israel will make a new marriage covenant "with the house of Israel and with the house of Judah." His Sanctuary will be in "their midst forever." He "will dwell in their midst forever." Need we go on?

This is why only few Jews, and mostly because of constant and severe persecutions by the Gentile Church, have ever caved in and gave up their faith for the cheap substitute that was offered to them by the Gentile Church. Most of them, despite of some blind spots, or as Paul called it, "blindness in part," knew better. They looked at the 'Emperor' and declared: "The Emperor is naked!"

The Apostles of Christ, the Messiah and Redeemer of Israel, knew all these statements and were looking forward to the "restoration of that kingdom to Israel," not to the Gentile Church! It is for this reason that the Gentile Church had attempted, in the "dark centuries" of the not too far away past, to stump out the Bible, to burn it when it could, and to burn at the stake those who translated it—who were mostly children of Israel, but unaware of it—yet not for long. Reading the Bible in that Gentile Church, for many centuries, was considered to be sin. Those who insisted on discussing the Bible were often excommunicated. Why? Because it exposed the "nakedness" of the Gentile Church! Yet any "child" in that "naked church," and among her "daughters," can still declare—if he has eyes to see—like the one little child in the Emperor's court, "The Emperor is naked!" This is exactly what many "little children" had done in the past many centuries, though many of them were burned as heretics at the stake. These faithful "children of the Kingdom" shall be in the coming new glorious Jerusalem of the King of Israel! The Jerusalem of the soon coming reigning Messiah of Israel, despite all of her fabulous glory and splendor, as the Prophets described her, will be but a shadow in comparison to the ultimate Heavenly Jerusalem that will descend from Heaven to earth and occupy The general location of the soon to be built Jerusalem.

John's account in Revelation continues: "And the TWELVE gates were TWELVE pearls . . . and the street of the City was pure gold, as it were transparent glass. AND I SAW NO TEMPLE THEREIN; FOR THE LORD GOD ALMIGHTY [the Father] AND THE LAMB [no "Third Person"] ARE THE TEMPLE OF IT. And the City had no need of the sun, neither of the moon to shine in it; for the glory of God did lighten it, and the Lamb is the light thereof [and again, no "Third

Person" is mentioned]. **And the nations of them that have been saved** [from the final death] **shall walk in the light of it; and the kings of the earth do bring their glory and honor into it. And the gates of it shall not be shut at all by day; for there shall be no night there . . . and there shall enter in no wise into it anything that defiles** [which only the Law or Torah of God can define], **neither whatsoever works abomination, or makes a lie** [like the one on the **afterlife**]; **but they which are written in the Lamb's book of life**" (Revelation, Chapter 21).

In the last chapter of the book (22), John continues to describe the final scenario of **Heavenly Jerusalem**, which is at that point on earth. He writes: "**And he** [the angel] **showed me a pure river of water of life, clear as crystal, proceeding out of the Throne of God and of the Lamb** [and still no "Third Person" is in sight]. **In the midst of the street of it, and on either side of the river, was there the tree of life which bare TWELVE manner of fruits, and yielded her fruit every month** [or **TWELVE** months], **and the leaves of the tree are for the healing of the nations** [the meaning of which we'll find out when we have arrived]" Revelation 22:1-2).

Let's remember the description that the Prophet Ezekiel gave us of the Temple of the God of Israel, **which will be built a thousand years before Heavenly Jerusalem descends to earth.** In that "Ezekiel Temple," as some call it, a "**river**" with "healing waters" would also come forth from beneath the Temple "**and bring healing everywhere it flows into.**" The feature of the "River" did not originate in the earthly "Paradise" where Adam and Eve were placed, but in "Heavenly Jerusalem" or "Mount Zion" above. King David stated: "**You will show me the Path of Life; in Your presence** [in Heaven] **is fullness of joy; at Your right hand there are pleasures for evermore . . . They** [who serve You] **shall be abundantly satisfied with the fatness** [or blessings] **of Your House** [in Heaven]; **and You shall make them drink of THE RIVER of Your pleasures**" (Psalms 16:11 and 36:8). Speaking of "Heavenly Jerusalem" or the "City of God," the Psalmist stated: "**THERE IS A RIVER, the streams whereof shall make glad THE CITY OF GOD, the Holy Place of the Tabernacle of the Most High. God is in the midst of her** [both above and when He comes down to earth to dwell with His people]; **she shall not be moved** [ever elsewhere]; **God shall help her . . .**" (Psalm 46:4-5). David declared: "**You visit the earth, and water it; You greatly enrich it WITH THE RIVER OF GOD . . .**" (Psalm 65:9).

John continues with his description of Heavenly Jerusalem: "**And there shall be no more curse; but the Throne of God and of the Lamb shall be in it** [and, again, no "Third Person" is mentioned, and "he that has an ear, let him hear"]; **and His servants** [not those who think they are] **shall serve Him; and they shall see His face; and His name shall be in their foreheads. And there shall be no night there; and they need no candle, neither light of the sun; for the Lord God shall give them light** [since His face shines as the sun]; **AND THEY SHALL REIGN FOREVER AND EVER** [AS DIVINE BEINGS, AS GOD DECLARED FROM THE BEGINNING: "LET US MAKE MAN IN OUR IMAGE, AND OUR LIKENESS," and few are those who believe Him—but not for long]. **And he said unto me, these things are faithful and true** [despite man's lack of faith in it]; **and the Lord God of the Holy Prophets** [not the false ones] **sent His angel to show unto His servants the things that must shortly be done. Behold, I [The Messiah] will come quickly; blessed is he that keeps** [or believes] **the sayings of the prophecy of this book** [which most people of 'religion' obviously do not] . . . **And he said unto me, SEAL NOT the sayings of the prophecy of this book; for the time is at hand. He that is unjust, let him be unjust still; and he which is filthy** [with stained "cloths of unrighteousness"], **let him be filthy still; and he that is righteous** [and clothed with "garments of righteousness"], **let him be righteous still; and he that is holy** [which only the Law or Torah of God can define], **let him be holy still. And, behold, I come quickly; and My reward is with Me, to give every man according as his work shall be** [when I come at the end time, not, according to the fable of the 'afterlife,' immediately after death] . . . **Blessed are they THAT DO HIS COMMANDMENTS [OR TORAH AND INSTRUCTIONS, not those who claim, falsely, they were done away], that they** [not those who despise them] **may have the right to the tree of life, and may enter in through the gates into the City** [or in other words, as Christ declared: **"If you will enter into life, keep the Commandments"**]. **For without** [or outside of the city] **are dogs** [who do not belong in the House], **and sorcerers, and whoremongers** [be it physical or spiritual], **and murderers, and idolaters** [who bow down and pray to dead people], **and whosoever loves and makes a lie** [which most "spiritual leaders" in every religion on earth are guilty of]. **I Jesus** [the Savior of Israel] **have sent My angel to testify unto you these** things in the churches [or houses of prayers]. **I am the root and the offspring of David, and the bright and MORNING STAR."**

The prophet Balaam, under inspiration from God, declared: **"I shall see Him, but not now; I shall behold Him, but not near; THERE SHALL COME A STAR OUT OF JACOB, AND A SCEPTER SHALL RISE OUT OF ISRAEL . . . OUT OF JACOB SHALL COME HE THAT SHALL HAVE DOMINION . . ."** (Numbers 24:17-18).

John continues: **"And the Spirit and the Bride say, Come. And let him that hears, say, come. And let him that is thirsty come. And whosoever will, let him take the water of life freely"** (Revelation 22:17).

Though our main subject in this work is the **"Temple Mount,"** let us pose the question and answer it briefly: who or what is the "Spirit"? As we saw and noticed several times, no "Third Person" is mentioned or is present in the Temple of God and Heavenly Jerusalem. **Why?** According to the doctrine of "Christianity" **God is a "Trinity."** If He is, how come the "Third Person" in this "Trinity" is not present in the Temple of God. We saw, repeatedly, that only God and the Lamb are mentioned and present in their Temple. What happened to the "Third Person" in this equation? Why is "He" missing? We'll now have a brief discussion of this most important issue, but if you desire to have the full explanation, as recorded in the Bible, you are welcome to check it on our free to download website: www.teachingthelaw.org in the section, *"The nature of God."* But let's now have a brief clarification on this matter.

In his final address to the **leaders of the Jewish community in Rome,** the Apostle Paul stated to them, since most of them did not believe his message: **" . . . WELL SPOKE THE HOLY SPIRIT by Isaiah the Prophet unto our fathers, saying, go unto this people and say, hearing you shall hear and shall not understand; and seeing you shall see, and not perceive; for the heart of this people is waxed gross [or fat] and their ears are dull of hearing, and their eyes they have closed; lest they should see with their eyes, and hear with their ears, and understand with their heart, and should be converted, and I should heal them"** (Acts 28:25-27). To find out the identity of the **"HOLY SPIRIT"** Paul was referring to let's go to the original message by Isaiah the Prophet. **In doing so, we shall finally understand what was on the mind of Paul, or any other writer, when they so often spoke about the "Holy Spirit."**

In Chapter 6 of Isaiah the Prophet, from which the Apostle Paul quoted the words of **"THE HOLY SPIRIT,"** we read: **"In the year that**

King Uzziah died, I saw also the Lord [YHVH] sitting upon a Throne, high and lifted up, and His train [or garment of light] filled the Temple. Above stood the Seraphim [or angels] . . . And one cried unto another, and said, Holy, Holy, Holy, is the Lord [YHVH] of Hosts; the whole earth is full of His glory. Then I said, woe is me! For I am . . . a man of unclean lips; for my eyes have seen THE KING, THE LORD OF HOSTS . . . And I heard the VOICE OF THE LORD, saying, whom shall I send, and who will go for us? Then said I, here am I, send me. AND HE [THE KING AND LORD OF HOSTS] SAID, GO, AND TELL THIS PEOPLE, hear you indeed, but understand not; and see you, but perceive not. Make the heart of this people fat, and make their eyes heavy, and shut their eyes; lest they see with their eyes, and hear with their ears, and understand with their heart, and convert, and be healed. Then said I, LORD, HOW LONG? And He answered . . ." (Isaiah 6:1-11).

The Apostle Paul knew full well who was speaking to Isaiah. He knew it was **THE KING, THE LORD OF HOSTS,** yet he referred to Him as **THE HOLY SPIRIT.** Why? Let's continue with another passage before we answer this question. Regarding the circumstances around the birth of Christ, this is what the Scriptures reveal to us: "**Now the birth of Jesus Christ was on this wise: When as his mother Mary** [or Miriam] **was engaged to Joseph, before they came together, she was found with child OF THE HOLY SPIRIT [and notice that he DID NOT SAY, "OF GOD THE FATHER"]. Then Joseph, her husband** [though still just engaged], **being a just man, and not willing to make a public example** [in which case she would have been put to death for adultery], **was minded to put her away privately. But as he thought on these things, behold, the angel of the Lord [God] appeared unto him in a dream, saying, Joseph, you son of David, fear not to take unto you Mary** [or Miriam] **your wife; for that which is conceived in her IS OF THE HOLY SPIRIT [AGAIN, HE DID NOT SAY, "OF GOD THE FATHER"]**" (Matthew 1:18-20). Then we read in verses 24-25 these words: "Then Joseph being raised from sleep did as the angel of the Lord [God the Father] had told him, and took unto him his wife; **and knew her not** [sexually] **TILL SHE HAD BROUGHT FORTH HER FIRSTBORN SON . . .**" After the birth of Jesus, Mary and Joseph had sons and daughters, as the Scriptures make very clear—and the Catholic Church's contention to the contrary will not change this historic reality!

Mary was not a "virgin maiden" after Joseph and her came "together" and had several children besides Jesus.

Let's go now to the account in the book of Luke for more details of the birth of Christ. Here we read: **"And in the sixth month the angel Gabriel was sent from God** [The Father] **unto a city in Galilee, named Nazareth, to a virgin engaged to a man whose name was Joseph, of the House of David; and the virgin's name was Mary. And the angel came unto her, and said, hail, you that are highly favored, the Lord** [God The Father] **is with you; blessed are you among women . . . And the angel said unto her, fear not, Mary; for you have found favor with God** [The Father]. **And, behold, you shall conceive in your womb, and bring forth a son, and shall call His name Jesus** [or Yehoshuah]. **He shall be great AND SHALL BE CALLED THE SON OF THE HIGHEST** [NOT THE SON OF THE "HOLY SPIRIT"]; **AND THE LORD GOD** [HIS FATHER] **SHALL GIVE UNTO HIM THE THRONE OF HIS FATHER DAVID. And He shall reign over the House of Jacob** [His true "Church" and "Bride"] **forever; and of His Kingdom there shall be no end. Then said Mary unto the angel, how shall this be, seeing I know not a man? And the angel answered and said unto her, THE HOLY SPIRIT SHALL COME UPON YOU** [?], **AND THE POWER OF THE HIGHEST** [GOD THE FATHER] **SHALL OVERSHADOW YOU; THEREFORE ALSO THAT HOLY THING** [OR CHILD] **WHICH SHALL BE BORN OF YOU SHALL BE CALLED THE SON OF GOD** [NOT THE SON OF THE "HOLY SPIRIT"]**"** (Luke 1:26-35). Confused enough? No need to be! The answer is very simple to those who have "eyes to see, ears to hear, and a heart to understand!" God is Spirit! He is Holy! **GOD IS THE HOLY SPIRIT! That's one of His names—as the Prophets and the Apostles made very plain time and time again for those who are not spiritually blind!** The real purpose for the introduction of the doctrine of the "Trinity" by later 'theologians' was to camouflage the true destiny of man—divinity. By creating a close circle of the supposed "three beings" **in the Godhood,** Satan was attempting to hide the real purpose of God for man: **creating man in His own image and in His own likeness — literally!**

How about Christ? Let's read the plain words of the Apostle Paul concerning this matter! He wrote to the Corinthian church concerning his people and Christ: **"But their minds were blinded** [just like those "spiritual leaders" in the world of Christianity who think they know better]; **for until this day remain the same veil not removed when they read the Old Covenant** [or Hebrew writings]; **which veil is done away** [or removed] **in Christ. But even unto this day, when** [the Torah given by] **Moses is read, the veil is upon their heart. Nevertheless, when it** [the heart] **shall turn to the Lord, the veil shall be taken away. NOW THE LORD IS THAT [Holy] SPIRIT** [that all the Prophets and Apostles referred to as "The Spirit," or "the Holy Spirit"]; **and where the Spirit of the Lord is** [which is Him], **there is liberty** [not lies and darkness, or deceptions]. **But we all, with open face beholding as in a glass the glory of the Lord, are changed into the same image [of God] from glory to glory, even as by the SPIRIT OF THE LORD** [which is the Lord]" (II Corinthians 3:14-18).

Those who have eyes to "see," will understand why there are only two Divine beings mentioned as residing in Heavenly Jerusalem—God and the Lamb! There is no "Third Person" in that Temple for obvious reasons: there is no "Third Person" in the Divine realm! No Apostle ever taught that doctrine of confusion! As was mentioned earlier, those interested in knowing the full Biblical teaching **about the "Trinity,"** check our website: www.teachingthelaw.org, section: "*The nature of God.*" In this section you'll learn what the Bible teaches about this important issue, not what "The Church" teaches.

Again, writing to the Corinthian church—this time about a matter discipline—he stated: "**For I verily, as absent in the body, but present in spirit** [through his teachings], **have judged already, as though I were present, concerning him that has done this deed. In the name of our Lord Jesus Christ [who is also called "The Spirit" or "The Holy Spirit"], when you are gathered together, AND MY SPIRIT, with the power of our Lord Jesus Christ, to deliver that person unto Satan** [by removal of the protection of God over him] **for the destruction of the flesh, THAT THE SPIRIT [of that person] may be saved in the day of the** [judgment, at the end time, of the] **Lord Jesus**" (I Corinthians 5:3-5). God "formed the spirit of man within him" (Zechariah 12:1), and that spirit **is man, not somebody inside him!** This is what the Apostle Paul was talking about!

Let's now return to the last words recorded by the Apostle John in Revelation, chapter 22:17. He stated: "**And the SPIRIT [OR JESUS, THE HUSBAND] and the Bride [Israel—the true Church] say, come, and let him that hears** [or has ears to hear] **say, come, and let**

him that is thirsty come. And whoever wills [since the "door" is now open for all], **let him take the water of life freely. For I [Jesus] testify unto every man that hears the words of the prophecy of this book** [or for that matter, every word of God], **IF ANY MAN SHALL ADD UNTO THESE THINGS** [which many did], **GOD [THE FATHER] SHALL ADD UNTO HIM THE PLAGUES THAT ARE WRITTEN IN THIS BOOK; AND IF ANY MAN SHALL TAKE AWAY FROM THE WORDS OF THE BOOK OF THIS PROPHECY** [which many have defiantly done], **GOD SHALL TAKE AWAY HIS PART OUT OF THE BOOK OF LIFE, AND OUT OF THE HOLY CITY** [at that time on earth], **AND FROM THE** [promised] **THINGS THAT ARE WRITTEN IN THIS BOOK . . . The grace of our Lord Jesus Christ be with you all. Amen"** (Revelation 22:17-21).

These words about the coming of "Heavenly Jerusalem" or "The City of God" to earth have been recorded about 19 centuries ago. All the religious leaders of "Christianity" had access to them. There was no reason for anyone of them to be misled—yet they chose to blind their eyes and were unwilling to declare: "The Emperor is naked!" Why? The Leaders of the Catholic Church, which call themselves, "The Holy Mother Church," have had an access to the words of God—form Genesis to Revelation—about the "**afterlife**" and other matters, yet they chose to create a "Mary Religion" of worship and adoration to "The Queen of Heaven." The Bible, even the Catholic version, tells them plainly and clearly that, like all the true saints of God, Mary is still dead and buried—and is waiting, like all of God's true servants, for the resurrection from the dead at the end time. Yet they all chose to blind their eyes and refuse to declare: "The Emperor is naked!" Why? All the words of the Prophets of God have been there for ages for all to read—yet many have chosen, in both the Jewish and Christian communities to blind their eyes. They refuse to this day to declare: "The Emperor is naked!" Why? The Leaders of the Mormon Church had access to the words of the Prophets and the Apostles concerning the "**afterlife**" and other matters—yet they too chose to blind their eyes. They refuse to declare: "The Emperor is naked!" Why?

What about the believers in Islam, in the Qur'an, in Muhammad? All Muslims claim to be devout believers of the Qur'an and Muhammad the Prophet. Before Muhammad came on the scene, all Arabs were idol worshipers. They believed, like many other pagans, in the immortality of the soul and the **afterlife**. Muhammad the Prophet taught them, as we read in many verses in the Qur'an, that no man has an immortal soul. He taught them that every person, just like him, must remain in the grave until "the last Trumpet would sound" at the last day—and only then the true believers will be ushered into Paradise. Muhammad taught that he himself also, according to the will and word of God, must remain in the grave until the resurrection at the last day. Shortly after the death of the Prophet of Islam, it was made very evident that hardly any of his followers have believed his teachings about the **afterlife**. To this very day, many fanatic Muslim clerics teach and believe that for a Muslim to enter immediately after death into Paradise, he or she must become a martyr for Allah. Many gullible fools—who are either too illiterate to read the true teachings of the Qur'an concerning the **afterlife**, or just don't bother to do so—readily offer their lives for the "noble cause of Martyrdom and Allah." They all believe, sincerely, that as soon as they blow themselves up to shreds—along with their enemies—they will all be ushered into Paradise and there they will be offered their promised and most coveted "rewards." Shiite Iran and her Hell-bound President and religious leaders are devoting and wasting enormous resources to "go nuclear" and arm themselves to the teeth—while many Iranians are in poverty, unemployed, or getting poorer — and for what? They believe, contrary to the teachings of their own Prophet and the clear teachings of the Qur'an, that their "Mahdi, who is now supposedly in Heaven," will soon be revealed by God—and will soon be sent back to earth "to bring world peace" to all Muslims.

Many of the teachings of this world's 'religions' should be featured prominently, daily, in the "comedy hour." They are all a "black eye" to the God of Heaven! Whether we like to hear it or not, much of what is considered to be 'religion' constitutes "Public Enemy Number One!" No wonder why most of the wars throughout history were fought "in the name of God." The question is: who is this god? The Apostle Paul spoke of him when he stated: "But if our good tidings are hid, they are hid to them that are lost [in the mist of darkness and confusion]; in whom **THE GOD OF THIS WORLD [OR SATAN] HAS BLINDED THE MINDS OF THEM WHICH BELIEVE NOT, LEST THE LIGHT OF THE GLORIOUS TIDINGS OF CHRIST, WHO IS THE IMAGE OF GOD [as all repentant men and women would finally be], SHOULD SHINE UNTO THEM**" (II Corinthians 4:3-4).

The truth of the matter is very simple to comprehend for the unbiased in heart and spirit: the one responsible for deceiving humanity, "The Prince of the power of the air," Satan, is, ultimately, behind the "HOAX OF THE MILLENNIUM." Much has been said, and more can be said, but the bottom line is this: if there is any child out there in any walk of life and religious persuasion who can "see," let him or her shout aloud, "The Emperor is naked!"

CPSIA information can be obtained at www.ICGtesting.com
Printed in the USA
LVOW12s1343040515

437154LV00001B/258/P

9 781467 028400